GW01465766

Rethinking Early Greek Philosophy

Rethinking Early Greek Philosophy

Hippolytus of Rome and the Presocratics

Catherine Osborne

Cornell University Press

ITHACA, NEW YORK

First published 1987 by Cornell University Press

Library of Congress Cataloging-in-Publication Data

Osborne, Catherine.
    Rethinking early Greek philosophy.

    Bibliography: p.
    Includes index.
    1. Philosophy, Ancient.   2. Hippolytus, Antipope, ca.
170-235 or 6.   3. Philosophy and religion.   I. Title.
B188.083   1987   182   87-47719
ISBN 0-814-2103-9

Photoset in North Wales by
Derek Doyle & Associates, Mold, Clwyd
Printed in Great Britain by
Redwood Burn Limited, Trowbridge

Contents

Preface

This book is intended to be the starting-point from which new work on the Presocratics will derive impetus and inspiration, and not just the end-product of work already done. Although it represents the results of my doctoral research and although it offers positive suggestions and conclusions, nevertheless its statements should not be read as final or complete; the point of the exercise is to advocate a new approach which will prove itself more fully in future work. Hippolytus' evidence is a small part of the wide scope offered by Presocratic philosophy, and serves here as a testing ground for the method. It is my hope that the suggestions put forward here will stimulate further ideas in this and other related areas.

The book is addressed primarily to readers with a particular interest in Presocratic philosophy and secondly to a wider readership of those historians and historians of ideas who employ evidence culled as fragments from literary sources, and to whom the methodological issues discussed here must be of interest. By the use of translation and some transliteration I have attempted to make my arguments comprehensible to the reader with little or no Greek. The result is cumbersome but I hope worthwhile. The peculiarity of some of the Greek may render the translations helpful even to those who know a little Greek.

The text of the main passages of Hippolytus relevent to this discussion is included at the end of the book, in a photographic reproduction of Wendland's text which is now unobtainable except in libraries. The working translation which faces it is a translation of Wendland's text; the few points at which I have argued for an alternative reading in the main part of the book are marked with notes to the translation. Book One of Hippolytus' *Refutatio* is not included here since it is not central to this work and is readily available in Diels' *Doxographi Graeci*.

Appendix D contains other passages of Greek that are translated and discussed in the book.

The texts from the Presocratics are cited throughout by their number in Diels-Kranz (1951); the letter B indicates that the text was classified by them as a fragment. References to Hippolytus' *Refutatio* are to book, chapter and section of Wendland's edition. Irenaeus' *Adversus Haereses* is cited by Massuet's numbering, and Hippolytus' *Contra Noetum* is quoted from the edition of Butterworth (London 1977).

My work on this subject has benefited from criticism and discussion with many scholars. In particular I should mention Christopher Stead, Geoffrey Lloyd, Malcolm Schofield, and my Ph.D examiners Richard Sorabji and Henry Chadwick. Others, and not least Gwil Owen, have formed and influenced my ideas in the course of the many meetings and seminars characteristic of Cambridge ancient philosophy in the early 1980s.

New Hall, Cambridge   C.J.O.

Introduction

A. The methodological question

This book starts from a question: how can we study the works of the Presocratic philosophers when none of them are preserved? The question has never been fully explored. Traditionally it has been assumed that we possess fragments; words and phrases are quoted by later writers and these can be assembled to form an independent text. The question of *how* we can use that text, and whether further methodological problems arise beyond its lamentable state of incompleteness, is not asked.

My present task is to raise these further questions, to point out the weaknesses of the traditional approach to the Presocratics and to offer a new methodology which takes account of the objections. The primary concern is with the study of ancient philosophers and attention is here restricted to the specific problems of the Presocratic philosophers, but many of the methodological issues arise in connection with later Greek philosophy and indeed in any field in which we rely on texts embedded as 'fragments' in the works of later writers.

(i) The traditional approach

A large proportion of the works of the Presocratic philosophers is lost. We are left with a rag-bag. To fill this rag-bag scholars have proceeded to extract 'fragments' from the quotations of later writers; once extracted and reassembled these are taken to constitute an adequate basis for study: further information is to be dismissed where possible as a likely source of distortion. Secondary reports are treated with suspicion. Thus G.S. Kirk, in Kirk, Raven, Schofield (1983), p.6:

It is legitimate to feel complete confidence in our understanding of a Presocratic thinker only when the Aristotelian or Theophrastean interpretation, even if it can be accurately reconstructed, is confirmed by relevant and well authenticated extracts from the philosopher himself.

Whatever we take to be the meaning of 'complete confidence' it is clear that Kirk advocates that such confidence should be placed only in the authority of 'genuine fragments'.[1] The same approach is adopted by Jonathan Barnes:[2]

The doxography is unreliable. Our knowledge of the Presocratics must rest upon their ipsissima verba. Few verba survive. Hence our knowledge of the Presocratics is exiguous.

Barnes is here being deliberately provocative, and both he and Kirk do advocate judicious use of doxographical material where necessary. However, as soon as the doxography can be shown to have interests of its own it is worse than useless and is best set aside and ignored. Thus Kirk:

In view of these defects in the authors of the ancient assessment it is safer to attempt the reconstitution of Heraclitus' thought, in the first instance, on the basis of the extant genuine fragments.[3]

and Barnes:

We have enough of Heraclitus' own words to reconstruct his thought without continual reliance on the doxography.[4]

C.H. Kahn takes this a stage further. He prints Heraclitus' 'fragments' without their context in the writers who quote them, and he argues that because the ancient interpreters read the text within their own interpretative framework they were therefore mistaken and must be dismissed; we, on the other

[1] Kirk and Raven (1957) p. 187. Cf. Kirk, Raven, Schofield (1983) p. 186.
[2] Barnes (1979) vol. 1, p. 14.
[3] Kirk and Raven (1957) p. 187. Cf. Kirk, Raven, Schofield (1983) p. 186.
[4] Barnes (1979) vol.1, p. 58.

hand, in every respect superior to our ancient predecessors, are able to select an interpretative framework free from the assumptions of our own time – a framework of our own choice within which to read the supposedly objective text which Kahn presents.[5]

Examples of the use of fragments without context in scholarly discussions of the Presocratics are manifold. Edward Hussey, for example, quotes without reference to the context throughout his paper on epistemology and meaning in Heraclitus (1982); again the authority of the 'fragments' is supreme:

> Ultimately it is the fragments which must be the ground of any decision to take Heraclitus seriously as a thinker or a sage, or not to do so. (p.35)

(ii) What is a fragment?

All these statements of approach depend upon the assumption that while the ancient interpretations represent an interested or biased reading, the 'fragments' do not. How can this assumption be justified? A consideration of the status of these supposed fragments soon demonstrates that such a division between 'text' and 'interpretation' cannot be maintained: the material we possess represents a small sample of a much more extensive text, but that sample is not a random one. It is a selection based on the interests of those who quote, the ancient interpreters themselves. It represents the same interested and biased readings as the notorious doxography. If we were to use the fragments as fragments we should need to assess the relationship of the sample we have to the text from which it was selected, but this is necessarily impossible. Even to examine the interests of those who quote them and their reasons for quoting them, which is possible, is hardly worthwhile; such an approach yields little fruit for the study of Presocratic philosophy, and its conclusions are almost entirely negative.

There are, of course, questions which may legitimately be asked about the sample of quotations which are preserved and

---

[5] Kahn (1979) pp. 87-95. See below pp. 23-4.

the extent of our knowledge, or lack of it, and the answers will have some bearing on what we can do with such texts as we have. Thus we may ask whether the doxographer had reasons for promoting a particular theme; or did his interests prevent him from quoting texts on a particular subject? In some cases a doctrine is mentioned by the doxography but no writer quotes a text in support of it. An example of such a case is the view attributed to Empedocles on the subject of sexual relations, on which Hippolytus' evidence is examined below.[6] While it would not have caused surprise if Hippolytus had quoted a text in support of this doctrine if there was one available, the fact that he does not need not imply that Empedocles wrote nothing on the subject; nor is it evident that any other writer would have had a particular reason to quote on this subject. It is possible that the doctrine was not explicit and that Hippolytus' evidence is based on inference and interpretation, but this does not mean that his inference had no justification. On the traditional view such evidence without supporting quotations would be considered inadequate, but it is worth considering whether there is reason to suspect that it is misleading. In such cases the evidence comes in the form of explicit interpretation, the basis of which can often be determined; in cases where quotation is included the interpretation may be less obvious but it is there all the same.

We already read the text within a restrictive framework provided by the writers who preserve our present text. But what of the words granted the status of 'genuine fragments', 'ipsissima verba', the philosopher's 'own words'? In the modern editions these are placed within inverted commas, or in bold type, but such devices were not available to the writers who actually quoted them, even supposing that they were concerned to quote with the accuracy expected today. Such standards of quotation were not normal in the ancient world where the difficulty of locating a reference in a book meant that short passages would often be cited from memory or from notes, and it is unlikely that the reader was expected to be critical of the detailed accuracy of the quotations. Where more than one writer quotes what appears to originate from the

[6] See below, Chapter 4.

same text it is rarely the case that the words are the same; these texts are often classified as the same 'fragment', but which version is actually a fragment of the philosopher's 'own words'?

Consider the following example. Diels-Kranz give three texts for Heraclitus fragment B76:

Maximus of Tyre 41.4 (p.481):
Fire lives the death of earth and air the death of fire; Water lives the death of air, earth that of water.'

Plutarch *De E* 18. 392C:
'The death of fire is birth for air, and the death of air is birth for water.'

Marcus Aurelius 4.46:
'That the death of earth is to be born as water and the death of water is to be born as air, and that of air to be born fire, and vice versa.'

In addition Diels-Kranz include, as a different fragment B36, this text cited by Clement: *Stromateis* 6.17.2 (II.435.25):[7]

'Death for souls is to be born as water, death for water is to be born as earth, but from earth water is born and from water soul.'

Are these one fragment, two fragments, or four fragments? Is Maximus right in using 'lives' (*zei*) or is the 'birth' (*genesis*) and 'to be born' (*genesthai*) of the other three texts more correct? Which is the correct sequence: earth, fire, air, water, earth, or earth, water, air, fire? The latter is the reverse of the former, but is it true that it can be reversed as Marcus Aurelius suggests? Is it correct to find a reference to air or to souls? If we wanted to use the text as a reliable fragment, free of its later context, these questions would have to be answered and we should need to decide which were the right words. It is more valuable, however, to look at the context in which each

---

[7] Other authorities could also be cited, including Hippolytus *Refutatio* 5.16.4 and Philo *De Aet. Mundi* 109 (VI p. 106 Cohn), and compare also Diels-Kranz B77.

version is cited: this gives the key to understanding the four
texts and renders the unanswerable questions of detailed
accuracy irrelevant.

Clement cites his text in a passage purporting to show that
the Greeks borrowed ideas from each other. He likens
Heraclitus' saying to some verses which he attributes to
Orpheus (fr 226K, *Strom.* 6.17.1):

> From soul there is water – death is an exchange into waters,
> but from water there is earth, from earth there is water again;
> from which water there is indeed soul, changing the whole
> aether.

His citation of Heraclitus may be from memory since he
introduces it vaguely ('something like this' – *hôde pôs*). All the
terms he attributes to Heraclitus (soul, water, earth, death)
also appear in the Orpheus text, and it is possible either that
Clement misremembers Heraclitus' 'air' as 'soul' by analogy
with the Orpheus text, or that he remembers Heraclitus' text
precisely because it did use 'soul' like the Orpheus text. The
two texts which he cites after Heraclitus both list the four
Empedoclean elements earth, air, fire, water, so that Clement
could have used the text in the form found in B76 had he
known it. The significant point is surely the fact that Clement
understood the Heraclitean text in such a way that it was
proper to read 'soul'.

The three writers listed under B76 also use the text in
connection with the changes and chances of human life, either
within the life of a man as he changes from babyhood to
boyhood and manhood, and from the man of yesterday to the
man of today (Plutarch), or in history as one power succeeds
another as a sort of reincarnation process (Maximus of Tyre),
or as the events which a man encounters in his life, being not
random but a rational sequence (Marcus Aurelius). Maximus
of Tyre links the saying with part of B67, also known from
Hippolytus, which seems to employ a notion of immortality in
the process of living and dying. None of these writers sees a
cosmic sequence of elements in B76. We are misguided if we
start by asking about the details of 'cosmological processes';
we should begin by questioning whether the text concerns

cosmic change at all, and explore the implications of understanding it with reference to human life and immortality, as the ancient interpreters do.

In cases such as this we simply do not have the philosopher's 'own words'. We do not know whether Heraclitus wrote 'soul', whether he had a sequence that included 'air' or not. We do not even know whether these texts derive from the same original or not, and it is unrealistic to classify them as one or more 'fragments'.

The 'fragments' are often paraphrases quoted from memory, and may be adapted to the context in which they are used; they may be given in reported speech, the terms are sometimes glossed or changed to a more familiar wording.[8] In all these cases we read the text in the form in which it is presented by the ancient interpreter, and his presentation is governed by what he thought the text ought to say.

The traditional approach which places its emphasis on 'genuine fragments' does so on the basis of an optimistic assumption which is spelled out by Barnes:

> It is often plausible to believe that these fragments preserve the most important and most interesting of their philosophical doctrines.[9]

Such optimism, however, is unfounded: it is more often the case that the selection of fragments is governed by curious and perverse personal preoccupations on the part of the doxographers; thus much of Sextus Empiricus' material on Heraclitus, Protagoras, Democritus and Xenophanes derives from the sceptic's concern with identifying scepticism in the Presocratics; Clement of Alexandria selects on the basis of Christian doctrines, while Plato and Plutarch often quote simply for fun. Even when the criteria of selection are serious they are not insignificant: Simplicius records extensive sections of Parmenides' poem explicitly for the sake of preserving it,[10] but we cannot be sure that the sections he

[8] Paraphrase: e.g. Anaximenes 13B2. Glossing of terms: e.g. Heraclitus 22B2. Change of term: perhaps Heraclitus 22B118.
[9] Barnes (1979) vol. 1, p. 14.
[10] Simplicius *In Phys.* 144.25.

chooses as most important are the same ones that we should
have chosen. Even in the course of this century there has been
a marked change in what is considered of interest in ancient
philosophy, and it is clear that the selection of texts presented
by an ancient writer will depend upon his philosophical
preconceptions and the interests current at the time.

(iii) What use is a biased reading?

Given the influence of the ancient interpreters on the selection
of material preserved, there is no case in which we can afford
to ignore or discount the nature and interests of the sources we
are using. There is, however, more of value in the ancient
readings than simply the selection of literal quotations. There
is little use in the knowledge that we have an authentic word
quoted, with its 'author' identified, if we have no means of
reading it in a meaningful context. A word is not a window to
anyone's mind; it may be the starting point for an inquiry into
possible readings of the text but it will not in itself prove
sufficient. Each quotation once came from some context in the
philosopher's work which would have had a bearing on the
reader's interpretation of the words. That context is lost, and
we find the text embedded in a new context provided by the
ancient interpreter. Very rarely can we hope to reconstruct the
original context, but in most cases the ancient writer was
selecting from a much more extensive body of material than he
presents to us, and his reading is likely to have been influenced
by the context in which the text he quotes occurred. We are
not in a better but a worse position to pass judgment on his
reading, and before dismissing it as worthless we should take
note of what it has to offer as a possible interpretation of the
text.

The 'context-free fragments' approach extracts the 'fragments' even from the context in which they are preserved, but
without some context they resist interpretation. Thus it is the
collection of 'fragments' in groups by modern editors, working
on the basis of their own preconceptions, which provides the
context in which they are currently read.[11] This approach

[11] See below.

introduces a new element of arbitrary interpretation to the fragmented text.

The reason for rejecting the ancient interpretations without trial was the notion that they were biased or defective. This suggests too simple an attitude to the evidence, since biased material is only misleading if it is treated as if it were not biased; if its interests are recognised and accounted for the problem is defused. Since the 'fragments' themselves represent the reading of those who preserved them, the use of such material as if it was unbiased cannot be sound. It is thus the traditional use of the 'fragments' without their accompanying context which represents an uncritical approach based on potentially misleading evidence. Rather than setting aside the large body of material provided by the ancient interpretations, we should aim to make full and critical use of all the evidence that is available.

(iv) The advantages of studying the embedded text

What we are trying to do in studying the Presocratic philosophers? The question is important and basic to the methodological issues considered here. In studying their works as philosophy we are working on the assumption that the complete text, more extensive than anything we possess now, was once the expression of a wealth of ideas; it will have supplied a range of meanings for those who read it. Most of the original text, in terms of the actual words, is lost and we cannot hope to reconstruct it precisely. What we have are some odd bits, disconnected words and phrases. If we collect only these, the 'genuine fragments', we have a small heap of bolts and screws and no structure in which to make them work; a text of this form will offer nothing of the range of meanings that the complete text once offered.

The point of the exercise is clearly to make the texts we now have mean something. The fuller and richer the range of meanings, and the more interesting the philosophical ideas to be found in the material, the better is our appreciation of that material. Since the ancient interpreters knew more material than they cite and make their versions of it mean a range of different things, theirs are the interpretations which press us to overcome the limitations of the fragmented text, and it is these interpretations which, I suggest, should be the jumping-off point for our own explorations of possible readings of the Presocratics.

While it is true that the ancient interpreters make the text perform, in some cases it is clear that they make it perform in a way which its original construction would not have allowed. Such is perhaps the case with Hippolytus' use of Heraclitus B63 as a quotation about resurrection, a passage which is discussed below in Chapter 5; how can Hippolytus treat Heraclitus' text as if it mentioned a concept that belongs to the Christian era? In such a case it is not until we can appreciate *how* the interpreter could have read it in the way he did that we can start to question the value of his reading: the way he read it may be the clue that enables us to appreciate the productive nature of the text and the possible ways in which it might have functioned in another context.

Reading an embedded instead of a fragmented text we read it as a functioning and meaningful system, governed by the preoccupation of an interpreter whose interests we can assess, rather than a set of disjointed parts, detached from the context in which they might mean something. Each interpretation will start from a biased approach, but once this factor is recognised we are in a better position to proceed. The aim is not a single conclusive reading but an exploration of the range of meaning brought out by the creative use of the text.

This approach is most necessary where the preservation of the philosopher's work is extremely fragmented, but it may none the less be both relevant and fertile even where substantial portions of the work are preserved. In cases where we have long unbroken quotations we are not entirely dependent on the interpreter's context for our own reading of the text, nor do we lack the means to reconstruct some portions of a coherent text in its own right. However, even then we cannot afford to ignore the fact that what we read is an embedded text: Parmenides' *Way of Truth* for example, preserved as extensive quotations in Simplicius' commentary on the *Physics*, is the best-known portion of Parmenides' work, while the details of the *Way of Seeming* are mainly lost. The reason for this is that Simplicius, and Plato and Aristotle before him, were most interested in the *Way of Truth* as the expression of Parmenides' most important doctrines. It is possible that our interpretation of Parmenides is relatively impoverished as a result, just as our view of Empedocles would be if we understood him only through the eyes of the Aristotelian tradition which stresses the physical doctrines. We need to take account of the interests which have governed the selection of the texts we possess, and recognise that these govern our overall interpretation even of Parmenides' thought. The same is true of the longer passages of Empedocles, also quoted by Simplicius, which by reason of their length and coherence occupy a more important place in our texts of Empedocles than would necessarily be justified in their original context. Again our reading is influenced by Simplicius' judgment of which sections are interesting, a judgment governed by the fact that he is commenting on Aristotle, as well as his arrangement of the lines and reconstruction of the text.[12]

There is thus no case in which it is irrelevant to consider the text in the context of the interpretation which governs its preservation, and while we are less dependent in detail upon this context where the quotations are long and coherent, it is often with this material that the effects of selection have actually had a more powerful influence on the proportions of the text we read, and hence on our interpretation.

(v) A heretical approach

The aim of this study is to justify a new approach to the Presocratics, one which centres on interpretations. The justification lies in the results, presented here in the form of readings of Heraclitus and Empedocles achieved through a study of one ancient interpretation, that of Hippolytus in the *Refutation of All Heresies*. These readings are not intended to be conclusive; they are provocative in that they offset the readings of earlier scholars, but they represent only one view. Every different interpretative standpoint will produce different insights, and this justifies the exploration of each ancient

[12] See, for example, Empedocles B17 where a comparison with the other sources suggests that Simplicius has strung his lines together freely.

interpretation as a legitimate reading of the text.

Hippolytus' work is also used as an example to demonstrate the inadequacy of the traditional approach to fragments and the value of reading the embedded text. Thus the first part of the book presents some test-cases which argue for the need for a new method, demonstrating the weaknesses of the traditional approach, as well as illustrating Hippolytus' own techniques which are the basis for assessing his interpretation; the second part illustrates the method in action.

In so far as this study starts from a recognition of certain problems in the doxography and in the status of fragments it follows in the wake of classic studies such as that of Cherniss, whose work on Aristotle's doxography of the Presocratics[13] explores the questions concerning the interests of the doxographer and the extent of his distortion of the material which are fundamental to any study based on the 'fragments'.[14] Thus Cherniss sets out the problem of the influence of the doxographers on our understanding of early Greek philosophy:

> With the exception of the works of Plato the original pre-Aristotelian philosophical writings exist only in meagre fragments, and we are constantly forced to resort to the reports of later writers in our attempt to gain some adequate notion of the development of the philosophical and scientific thought ...[15]

His own concern is with problems of distortion by Aristotle:

> At the same time it has long been vaguely recognised that Aristotle was capable of setting down something other than the objective truth when he had occasion to write about his predecessors.[16]

Cherniss' task is thus to establish an account which constitutes 'objective truth' by rejecting those parts of the

---

[13] *Aristotle's Criticism of Presocratic Philosophy* (Cherniss 1935).
[14] See above p. 3.
[15] Cherniss (1935) p. ix.
[16] Ibid.

doxography which are not reliable, or by attempting to deduce
the truth from them:

> ... and once the reason is so established there is a good chance
> with the aid of our other criteria of stripping off the Aristotelian
> form or at least of establishing in what direction the statement
> is likely to have deviated from the original meaning of the
> theory reported.[17]

The basis of such an account will clearly be the fragments,
and Cherniss does not consider the question of bias in the
selection of fragments.[18]

Thus Cherniss works within the framework of the
traditional approach, although recognising problems in that
approach. His conclusions are therefore essentially negative,[19]
and it is these negative conclusions which provide the
instigation for the present search for a more positive approach
to the ancient interpretations. Recognising that history is
interpretation we need not agree with the statement that 'in
their new form [the doctrines] can be of use to the historian of
philosophy only if Aristotle's process of interpretation can be
reversed so as to regenerate them in the form they had before
Aristotle employed them as his material.'[20] The present study
is not part of the programme of critical examination of our
sources suggested by Cherniss;[21] rather it stands itself as the
beginning of a new programme of reading and interpretation of
the Presocratics embedded in those later texts. The aim is not
to discard these texts as dross but rather to discover when and
how they bear fruit.

(vi) Hippolytus' Refutation of All Heresies

Among the sources of information on Presocratic philosophy
Hippolytus' *Refutatio* is a classic example of the sort of work
which incurs suspicion from those who seek reliable objective

[17] Cherniss (1935) p. xiii.
[18] See above p. 7.
[19] Cherniss (1935) p. 347.   [20] Ibid.
[21] Cherniss (1935) p. xiii; cf. for example McDiarmid (1953) on
Theophrastus.

evidence. It dates from the late second or early third century A.D.; it is the work of a Christian, probably a bishop or clergyman of the church of Rome in the time of Pope Callistus.[22] The purpose of the work is the refutation of heresies by means of a comparison with Greek philosophy. All of this suggests an attitude governed by prejudice and a tendency to fit the material to bizarre preoccupations. In the eyes of scholars of the Presocratics Hippolytus' only virtue has been his mindless copying of sources.[23]

A close examination of Hippolytus' work, however, reveals that his procedure is not one of mindless copying, and the studies presented here aim to demonstrate the extent to which the work is constructed and adapted to the purpose in hand; it is clear that not only the argument but also the selection of quotations with which it is illustrated is carefully fitted to the task of refutation. Hippolytus' handling of the material is sensitive rather than mindless and original rather than second-hand.[24]

Hippolytus is primarily concerned with religious ideas and it is in this field that we should expect to find his interpretation most interesting. Aristotle's approach to Presocratic philosophy, by contrast, tends to concentrate on those aspects that fit his classification of natural philosophy. It is the Aristotelian preoccupation that has tended to carry most weight in modern discussions of the Presocratics, whose views on the 'material principle' are their best-known doctrines.

Hippolytus provides a valuable alternative source of information. Although the material he includes is not restricted to theology, it concentrates on those questions of conventional values, morality and beliefs which are largely

[22] On the question of the identity of the author see the collection of essays by Loi et al. (1977). The use of the name Hippolytus in this book does not imply commitment to more than is directly evident from the text itself.
[23] This verdict is spelled out by, among others, Marcovich (1966) p. 263. See below.
[24] There are some passages which are simply taken over from an earlier writer (e.g. the passages paralleled in Sextus Empiricus in books 4 and 10). These occur in parts of the book where Hippolytus is not presenting a case of his own and it is important to note the distinction from the main parts of his work in which he is constructing parallels between philosophers and heretics.

ignored by the Aristotelian tradition. That the Presocratics' attitude towards matters of conventional belief is important in the development of philosophy and science needs no argument, and we may thus benefit in our understanding of that process by exploring Hippolytus' interpretation of Presocratic thought as a means to offset the Aristotelian preoccupation with natural philosophy.

(vii) Hippolytus' strategy

Hippolytus' work is a 'refutation of all heresies'. The scheme is to demonstrate that the ideas of the heretics are comparable with those of pagan philosophers and scientists by juxtaposing each heretic with an appropriate philosopher. The first four books, of which books 2, 3 and part of 4 appear to be lost, contained a preliminary survey of pagan thought; books 5 to 9 constitute the detailed work on the heresies and the demonstration of their affinities with certain selected pagan thinkers; book 10 gives a brief and inadequate summary of the doctrines of both the philosophers and the heretics and concludes with a statement on true Christian doctrine.

Hippolytus implies that the strength of his refutation lies in the demonstration that the doctrines of the heretics include ideas that are related to those of the philosophers. An over-hasty reading of the argument might assume that he reasoned thus:

1. Greek philosophy is untrue
2. Heretics repeat the ideas of Greek philosophy
3. Therefore the heretics' doctrines are untrue.[25]

Yet Hippolytus nowhere demonstrates that pagan philosophy is untrue per se, and without it the argument would clearly be unpersuasive. Indeed although he does suggest that some pagan ideas are false,[26] in other cases he mentions the Greeks

[25] Cf. Stead (1976) on an argument which he calls '*reductio ad haeresim*', but note that this requires that the earlier doctrine has been already condemned by the church.

[26] E.g. the doctrines attributed to the Chaldaeans, astronomers and Magi, all in *Refutatio* 4.

with approval both in terms of their attitude towards the divine[27] and in their science.[28] In these matters the Greeks are said to be better than the heretics who give a poor imitation of the wisdom they have copied.[29] Hence we must reject the idea that Hippolytus is using pagan philosophy as a sort of canon of falsehood, as Irenaeus and Tertullian before him had attempted to use a canon of truth in the form of scripture and tradition.

The main task which faces Hippolytus, as well as his immediate predecessors, is the refutation of gnostic heresies.[30] These pose a particular problem as a result of their claim to secret divine revelation and their rejection of certain scriptural texts. Hence there is no agreed canon of scripture or tradition, and refutations on the lines adopted by Irenaeus and Tertullian are powerless against the gnostic claims. Hippolytus' strategy takes a different line by attacking them on their strongest point, the claim to new divine revelations. If these can be shown to be identical with human wisdom of centuries earlier the basis of their claims is undermined. Thus Hippolytus presents a strong argument of the following form:

1. The heretics claim new divine wisdom
2. What they teach is the same as Greek philosophy
3. Greek philosophy is old-fashioned human wisdom
4. Therefore the heretics' doctrines are neither new nor divine and their claims are bogus.

Hippolytus does not spell out his argument clearly.[31] The majority of his work is simply concerned with the attempt at identifying the doctrines of Greeks and heretics, without indicating how this constitutes a refutation. But Hippolytus is consistent in his statements that the heretics are theory-

[27] *Ref.* 1 *praef.* 8; 7.36.2.
[28] *Ref.* 8.15.3.
[29] *Ref.* 1 *praef.* 9.
[30] Noetus' (book 9) is the only heresy which fails outside this category; it is plausible that the strategy is geared primarily to the gnostics.
[31] Explicit indications that his strategy is as I have suggested are found at *Ref.* 5.6.2; 5.7.1; 6.21.3; 7.29.2; 8.17.1-2; 9.8.

stealers, *klepsilogoi*.[32] It is not that the theories they steal are inherently false, for they may be either true or false, but they are not the new secrets they are claimed to be, nor are they the exclusive property of the gnostics; rather they are the common knowledge of Greek philosophy.

(viii) The use of 'he says' in the Refutatio

A prominent feature of certain passages of the *Refutatio* is the frequent insertion of 'he says' (*phêsin*) in the reports of the views of other thinkers. The significance of this usage is important for those whose interest is in the views reported: does it introduce quotation or interpretation?

This question has occasioned particular discussion in connection with the material on the *Apophasis Megalê* in the section on Simon Magus in book 6. 9-18. This passage has a high incidence of *phêsin* and has been the subject of debate concerning the accuracy of its account of the *Apophasis*. The feature was studied by Frickel (1968) who argued that Hippolytus was copying from a paraphrase of the *Apophasis*; for this reason he asserted that the insertion of *phêsin* was no indication of whether Hippolytus was following his model closely or not. Frickel wished to suggest that Hippolytus was following his immediate model exactly throughout.

Frickel started from the assumption that it is natural to understand *phêsin* as indicating paraphrase or summary rather than verbatim citation. There are, however, two constructions used with *phêsin*, direct speech and oratio obliqua: the distinction is clearly important and it is only in the latter construction that it is natural to read the passage as paraphrase, whereas the direct construction clearly suggests quotation.[33] In the *Apophasis* passage Frickel counts 43 occurrences of *phêsin* and makes no distinction between the two usages. 39 of Frickel's occurrences are of the direct quotation type, and in addition there is one in the plural[34]

---

[32] *Ref.* 1 *praef.* 11; 4.51.14 and passim.

[33] On these meanings of *phêsin* see Marcovich (1966) p. 263 and Marcovich (1959) p.1ff.

[34] *Ref.* 6.15.3. The plural may be an error.

which he does not count.

On a priori grounds it is promising to suggest that *phêsin* with the direct speech construction serves a function similar to inverted commas. In the case of the *Apophasis* we do not possess the original text to check the quotations: two other passages should be compared.

(a) The account of Aristotle

Phêsin is rare in any construction in the account of Aristotle, *Ref.* 7.15-19. The major part of the account is not quoted directly from Aristotle's own works though there is some loose paraphrase. There are three quotations, all introduced by 'he says' with direct speech. At *Refutatio* 7.18.5 the definition of what is in a substrate (*en hupokeimenôi*) is accurately quoted from *Categories* 1a24-5: Hippolytus writes

> in the substrate, he says, is 'that which subsists in something not as a part, and which is incapable of being separate from that in which it is'.

which corresponds with this sentence from the *Categories*:

> By in the substrate I mean that which subsists in something not as a part, and which is incapable of being separate from that in which it is.

The other two quotations are clearly made from memory. At *Ref.* 7.19.6 Hippolytus quotes a definition of soul which corresponds roughly to *De Anima* 2, 412b4-5 although it does not specify that the actuality of the soul is a 'first actuality'. At *Ref.* 7.19.7 he cites 'thought of thought' as a definition of Aristotle's god. Aristotle says (*Metaphysics* Λ 1074b33-4):

> He thinks of himself indeed, if he is the best, and his thought is thought of thought.

If this is the basis of Hippolytus' information he has cited a definition not strictly of god but of the thinking that is his activity. Nevertheless since the Aristotelian god is literally his characteristic activity Hippolytus' definition is correct, though his correctness depends upon an understanding of a much more extensive passage of *Metaphysics* Λ. In both cases the terminology is correct, the interpretation is reasonable, but the word order differs from Aristotle's. Although these definitions would not count as 'fragments' of Aristotle's text, they are informative quotations.

(b) The account of the Peratae, Ref. 5.12-18

This is another passage with a high incidence of *phêsin*. The Peratae are always referred to in the plural and Hippolytus names no leader for them; yet throughout the account the words for 'he says', *phêsin* and *legei*, occur in the singular, particularly in the section 5.12.5-7 (where *phêsin* occurs in every sentence) and 5.16.1-16 (where *phêsin* occurs 39 times). Between these sections are passages of continuous quotation (chapter 14) and summaries in which the verbs are in the plural (chapters 13 and 15).

No singular subject is named for the singular verbs, but the first sentence of 15.14.1 suggests that *legei* must be taken to mean 'it says' referring to the book from which Hippolytus is copying. During the continuous extract in 5.14 *legei* or *phêsin* is not repeated, but in chapters 12 and 16 we may have short extracts each introduced by a new insertion of *phêsin*. Thus *legei* or *phêsin* would be used to mark the start of a new quotation from the book in question: 'the text says ...'.

B. Preparing the way

The aim of the studies in Part One of this book is twofold: on the one hand to show that there is a problem which has to be faced before we can say anything about the Presocratics, and on the other to discover what is the nature of the problem in the particular case of Hippolytus and how it should be faced in order to make use of his work.

The clearest evidence that there is a problem which cannot be avoided by the traditional approach to fragments emerges from the account of Aristotle. This is because it is only in this case that we can make use of a known quantity, our own interpretation of Aristotle's text as opposed to another untried reading, as a comparison for the reading derived from Hippolytus. This comparison undermines the assumptions behind the attempt to glean 'fragments' of an earlier writer from the text of a later writer: the idea that these will be accurate 'quotations' in the modern sense is anachronistic and the belief that they will be informative when abstracted from their context proves to be unfounded. Few of Hippolytus' words can be identified as 'fragments' of Aristotle, and though the words he does quote are indeed words that can be located in Aristotle's text yet they cannot be said to be reliable indicators of what Aristotle meant when he wrote them. Without some context they are meaningless; Hippolytus' comments on them can tell us what they might have meant if read in their original context.

Hippolytus' comments tell us what the original text might have meant only in the sense that they represent what he saw in the text, or perhaps read into it: what it meant for him. The idea that his influence can be ignored on the grounds that he was an uninspired and ignorant compiler who copied mechanically whatever was to hand must clearly be rejected. It is evident that Hippolytus was no fool. In terms of his argument the scheme he adopts for refuting the heretics is not only original but also an improvement over attempts made by his predecessors in the same field. It shows an appreciation of the problems of refutation and of the strengths of the heretics' case.

The studies in Part One show that the choice of material presented by Hippolytus is not simply a matter of chance but of careful selection by a writer who knows what he is looking for and has a considerable wealth of material from which to choose. In book 6 he is able to select material from the text of Simon Magus which itself incorporates the references to Greek philosophy which he requires. In book 7 he chooses to offer a curious sceptical account of Aristotle, not because this is the only account of Aristotle available nor because he knows nothing else,[35] but because this is the slant on Aristotle that

[35] Hippolytus shows knowledge of Aristotle's own treatises (see below Chapter 1) and also offers a different account of Aristotle in book 1.20.

he wants in order to bring out the pattern he wishes to illustrate. The term 'source-dependent' must be used with caution of Hippolytus, for he is independent in many ways: he is not dependent upon the first source that comes to hand but selects one which suits his purpose; thus he does not use the over-simple doxography that he used for book 1 when it comes to the later accounts of the philosophers but adopts a new source in each case, sometimes making use of more than one source for the same subject. It is also clear that he is prepared to rearrange the material as he does in re-using Irenaeus' account of the life of Simon Magus, and he is regularly strictly selective concerning what is relevant to the case he has to make.

This aspect of Hippolytus' independence is also confirmed by his use of sources in book 1;[36] here we cannot conclude, with Diels (1879), that Hippolytus is dependent on a meagre and confused source book and fails even to recognise its inadequacies on the subjects which are his primary concern. On the contrary the idiosyncrasies of his accounts of the Presocratics stem from the need to condense material from a richer source to fit the scope of his preliminary survey in book 1.

On the other hand, while Hippolytus is no fool he is not an expert on every subject. His determination to be sure that he has omitted nothing, which he mentions at *Refutatio* 5.6.1 and 7.27.7, naturally leads him to attempt to give an account of subjects for which he is not equipped. This is surely the case with some of the subjects in book 4 of the *Refutatio*, and here we are more entitled to speak of source-dependence. In his account of Chaldaean astrology he is relatively fortunate in having chosen Sextus Empiricus (or the source used also by Sextus Empiricus) and thus provided himself with a relatively well-informed account together with a refutation of the doctrines. In dealing with the astronomical doctrines reported in *Refutatio* 4.8-11, however, he is less fortunate. It is clear that he did not understand the contents of the account, nor trouble to check the mathematics involved; had he done so he could have discovered that the sets of figures did not tally with each

[36] On this see Appendix A.

other. In this case he has taken over material uncritically from a source which includes both error and weak argument.[37] Here we are dealing with a quite different situation where Hippolytus has not the ability to use his source critically or selectively but simply copies. The primary influence on the text as we read it in these passages is not that of Hippolytus but that of his source, in which case we must size up the situation in order to pick through the layers of adaptation and reinterpretation which have created the text which we read. When Hippolytus simply copies, it does not indicate that the text is likely to be a more reliable witness of the original theories; it simply means that we have to look further for the influences involved, and that the unpredictable effects of ignorance are likely to have had a much greater part to play.

Hippolytus carries out his purpose by selecting evidence which he thinks fits his scheme rather than twisting it to make it fit, but he sees a 'fit' where others might not have seen it, thus throwing an idiosyncratic emphasis on to patterns of thought which might otherwise have gone unnoticed. It is not words which are of interest but interpretations; the words which Hippolytus records are merely an illustration of his interpretation, and will remain such even when abstracted from their context.

This factor cannot be avoided; it can only be recognised. There is no way that one can cut through the layers to some 'objective truth' about the meaning of the 'fragments'. In Hippolytus' work we read the text of the Presocratics through several interpretations, both his own and those of his sources, and it is important to be aware of the interests which govern those interpretations. When it comes to the Presocratics scholars have no justification for asserting that what Hippolytus saw in the text was not there or was incorrect as a reading of that text: many of the ancient interpreters, including those used by Hippolytus as well as Hippolytus himself, had more of the text before them than we have, and they produce the evidence to support their readings; but it does

<hr/>

[37] For a detailed analysis of this section of the text and the theory which it reports see my article 'Archimedes on the dimensions of the cosmos', *Isis* 74 (1983) pp. 234-42.

matter whose that reading was and why he read it in that way. No subsequent reading based on the words they quote can have greater validity than their own readings. We can proceed to use Hippolytus' material on Heraclitus and Empedocles only when we are already familiar with the way in which he selects and interprets his texts and when we are in a position to appreciate the interest and value of his reading. The preliminary studies in Part One aim to put us in that position of familiarity.

C. Empedocles and Heraclitus: problems of the fragmented text

It has long been observed that the arrangement in which 'fragments' of Heraclitus are presented profoundly affects the interpretation of the reader: the editor chooses to present them in a certain order on the basis of his notion of what is important, and that is what emerges most prominently as a result. Recognising this factor, Diels chose to avoid imposing any interpretation of his own, and listed his fragments in groups from the same author in alphabetical order of the author quoting them. Most recent editors have preferred to present their own re-ordering, criticising Diels' arrangement on the grounds that it fragments Heraclitus' thought.[38]

In a sense, however, it is the recent editors who fragment Heraclitus by reshuffling the evidence. Diels' arrangement appeared confused because it showed up clearly that each group of fragments belonged to a different interpretation and made sense in that context. In Diels we read a series of individual versions of Heraclitus in succession. In shuffling these interpretations the more recent editors have concealed them by fragmenting them, but those ancient interpretations remain the contexts in which the fragments once made sense. The Heraclitus of the context-free 'fragments' appears deceptively objective, but it represents the unacknowledged reading not only of the modern editor who selects and rearranges but also of the ancient writers who originally selected and used the words they quoted.

[38] E.g. Kahn (1979) p.6; Marcovich (1967) p.xvi.

Kahn, in his excursus 'on reading Heraclitus'[39] professes to take account of the hermeneutical aspect of any reading of Heraclitus. He observes that we must be aware that we read Heraclitus within a conceptual framework provided by our own time, but in assuming that we can 'deliberately construct or select our own interpretative framework'[40] he fails to observe that we already read the text within an interpretative framework imposed long ago by those writers who preserved our present text: what did not fall within their own framework could not be preserved, and what we read has been adapted by successive interpretation. This framework we cannot select, for it inheres in the very text we read, and every modern reading is a reading of those earlier readings.

Thus it is Kahn who is an 'unconscious and hence uncritical prisoner' not of 'whatever hermeneutical assumptions happen to be in the air'[41] but of the hermeneutical assumptions which governed the selection and transmission of our text, and of his own assumption that we can ignore those interpretations and select a reading that is entirely our own. Kahn, more than most, chooses to disregard the context in which the words he selects as 'fragments' are preserved, and fails to discuss the interpretation which secured their preservation.

The handling of the fragmentary evidence for Empedocles poses similar problems. Just as the juxtaposition of 'fragments' of Heraclitus has tended to expose one theme more prominently at the expense of others, so it has been the assignment of verses of Empedocles to one or other of the two poems usually attributed to him that has governed the interpretation of his thought in modern times and has originated major issues of interpretation. Recent editions and discussions of Empedocles, almost without exception, have been based upon the assumption that two works of Empedocles can be identified and that they were distinct in subject

---

[39] Kahn (1979) pp. 87-95.
[40] Kahn (1979) p. 88.
[41] Ibid.

matter:[42] '*On Nature*' (*Peri Physeos*) concerned the 'physical universe' and the '*Katharmoi*' was a 'religious poem'.[43]

The ancient evidence for these assumptions is scanty in the extreme. No ancient author specifies that Empedocles wrote two major poems and none mentions any distinction of subject matter in what he wrote.[44] Rarely does any author identify the work from which he is quoting, and this fact suggests either that there was only one work from which they quoted or that they recognised no distinction of any importance between the two works if there were two.

The hypothesis that there might have been only one work might seem at first sight to be ruled out by the fact that we have ancient testimony for two titles. On examination, however, this objection proves to be insubstantial; there is no conclusive evidence that these were not alternative titles for the same work. Most authors give only one title if they give one at all, and Diogenes Laertius is the only single author to use both *Peri Physeos* and *Katharmoi* as titles for Empedocles; but Diogenes Laertius admits that he has composed his account of Empedocles from numerous different sources,[45] and it is highly probable that the titles he gives at various points reflect the terminology of his sources. It is not clear whether Diogenes had direct knowledge of Empedocles' own

[42] This observation was made by H.S. Long (1949) p. 144. Sturz (1805) p. 71ff. suggested that *Katharmoi* refers to certain books of *On Nature*, but still assumes that these books can be distinguished in terms of subject matter from the physical poem proper. Even Van der Ben (1975), who transfers most of Diels' *Katharmoi* fragments to a supposed 'proem' to the *Peri Physeos*, nevertheless assumes that there was *another* work called *Katharmoi* (pp. 7-16 and passim).

[43] Cf. the widespread use of such labels without question: e.g. O'Brien (1981) pp. 14-15 'poème religieux', 'poème cosmique'; Kahn (1960) pp. 22-3 and passim 'the religious poem', 'the physical poem'.

[44] This is leaving aside the question of his supposed medical works and tragedies. Diogenes Laertius discusses the authenticity of some of these in book 8.58.

[45] Among the sources he names in his Life of Empedocles are Hippobotus, Timaeus, Hermippus, Heraclides, Eratosthenes, Apollodorus, Satyrus, Favorinus, Neanthes, Theophrastus, Alcidamas, Aristotle, Hieronymus, Xanthos, Timon, Diodorus of Ephesus, Demetrius of Troezen and Diogenes' own epigrams.

work; he may have had access to extracts and anthologies but
it is unlikely that he had a complete text.

It is widely recognised that *Peri Physeos* is unlikely to have
been a title used by Empedocles himself; it is a title which is
often used by later writers to describe the contents of the
works of the Presocratics, following the Peripatetic classification of these thinkers as *physikoi*.[46] On the other hand
Katharmoi has a much better claim to be Empedocles' own title,
in as much as there are no strong reasons to doubt its
authenticity.[47] It is therefore quite plausible to suggest that
Empedocles wrote one poem on nature, called *Katharmoi*.

There are two other issues which have been thought to
support the idea that there were two separate poems; one
concerns the subject matter and the addressees of the poem,
the other the information concerning the length of
Empedocles' work. In both cases the hypothesis that two
separate works are involved entails as many problems as it
solves, while the suggestion that there is only one work
resolves many difficulties. The argument from subject matter
is largely circular, given that there is no ancient evidence for a
distinction in content between *On Nature* and the *Katharmoi*.
The distinction is therefore made on the basis that the
Katharmoi must have been a religious poem and *On Nature* a
scientific one. On the basis of a good nineteenth-century gulf
between religion and science the fragments are then divided in
such a way as to exclude all 'religion' from *On Nature*, with the
result that the two groups of fragments look to be different in

---

[46] See the discussion in Wright (1981) pp. 85-6; but note that the
Hippocratic treatise *On Ancient Medicine* 20 does suggest that *peri physeos* was a
traditional way of describing the contents of the work of Empedocles among
others.

[47] In particular Wright's arguments (1981) p. 86, against this being
Empedocles' title carry no weight for the following reasons: (1) Aristotle
uses the phrase about the prohibition on killing anything animate (*peri ton mê
kteinein to empsuchon*) not as a title for Empedocles' poem but to refer to the
subject matter of the couplet which he quotes at *Rhetoric* 1373b14; (2)
Neither Plato *Republic* 364c nor the scholiast on Aristophanes *Frogs* 1033
(who may well derive his information from Plato) implies that there were
books attributed to Musaeus or Orpheus under the title *Katharmoi*. (3)
Neither of these points would preclude *Katharmoi* being Empedocles' title.

subject matter. It is a problem for this approach that only three fragments are explicitly assigned to the *Katharmoi* in the ancient sources and, out of these, two would be assigned to *On Nature* on the grounds of subject matter were it not for their testimonia.[48]

H.S. Long suggests that 24 out of 153 fragments can be assigned to the separate poems with something approaching certainty.[49] About half of these are explicitly cited in the sources as coming from *On Nature* or *Katharmoi*; the certainty of the other twelve depends upon whether they include second person singular or plural forms, since the two poems are supposed to be distinguished by their addressees. However this criterion for dividing Empedocles' work is not so secure as has been supposed.

The idea that the poems were addressed to different persons is based upon information given by Diogenes Laertius, but Diogenes is not explicit on the subject. At 8.60-61, on the authority of Aristippus and Satyrus, Diogenes mentions that a certain Pausanias was Empedocles' beloved, and that it was to him that Empedocles addressed the *Peri Physeos*; Diogenes quotes fragment B1, 'But you listen to me, Pausanias son of the wise Anchitus', but he does not suggest that this was the beginning of the work.[50] On the other hand at 8.54 Diogenes notes that Empedocles came from Acragas and quotes fragment 112 lines 1-2a as evidence, which he says Empedocles spoke at the beginning of the *Katharmoi*,[51] and which addresses some or all of the citizens of Acragas. He does not say that the whole poem was addressed to this audience. Thus Diogenes' evidence is consistent with the possibility that Empedocles wrote only one poem whose opening lines addressed a wide audience of Acragantines before turning to detailed teaching for Pausanias, the main addressee of the poem.

In any case it is certainly not possible to claim that the

[48] Fragment 153(a) and Hunger's new fragment (Wright fr. 152). See Zuntz (1971) p.235n.1, Bollack (1965-9) vol. 3 p.539 and n.7; Wright (1981) p. 298; Van der Ben (1975) p. 15 n. 11.

[49] H.S. Long (1949) p. 144.

[50] The *de* (but) possibly suggests that it was not the first line; cf. Wright (1981).

[51] *autos enarchomenos tôn katharmôn phêsin.*

addressees were consistent throughout each of two poems, since many verses are explicitly addressed to other persons: the Muse in B131 and B3, the gods in B3 and mankind in general in B124 and perhaps B136 and B141. Thus on any account a division of fragments on the basis of singular or plural addressees is certainly insecure. It is highly probable that the poem, in addition to calling upon the Muse, made some contrast between the majority of mankind, among whom the citizens of Acragas may be included, who fail to understand and accept Empedocles' doctrine[52] and Pausanias who, by contrast, will listen and learn.[53] Among the fragments which include plural forms only B112 is certainly addressed to a specific audience of Acragantines, with B114 a probable second.

Thus far the evidence for two poems is at best inconclusive; when it comes to the testimonia concerning the length of Empedocles' work the difficulties for the traditional view are severe and have led scholars to attempt considerable 'emendations' of the texts concerned. These testimonia are provided by Diogenes Laertius 8.77, at the end of his life of Empedocles, who states that 'Empedocles' *Peri Physeos* and the *Katharmoi* extend to five thousand verses, and his medical treatise to six hundred ...' and the *Suda* which claims that 'he wrote in verse on the nature of things two books (and they are about two thousand verses), and Medical works in prose and many other things'.[54] The lack of correspondence between these two reports is curious since they are almost certainly based on the same source.[55] Whether the numerals have been transmitted correctly is unclear: it has been suggested that Diogenes' five thousand verses is somewhat large even if he thought that there were five books[56] and there is some evidence, of dubious quality, for an alternative reading, 'three books, two thousand verses' in the *Suda*.[57] Thus arguments

[52] B2, 11, 114, 136.
[53] B1, 2, 3, 4, 111.
[54] DK 31 A 2.
[55] Lobon fr. 19 Crönert.
[56] Guthrie vol. 2 p. 135; Wright (1981) p. 21 and n. 107.
[57] This reading was employed by the first editors of the *Suda* on the basis of unknown manuscript support: 'surely with some MSS support' Wright (1981) p. 20 n. 104. cf. O'Brien (1981) pp. 8-9.

cannot be hung on the number of verses and books alone; indeed it is possible that both texts should read two thousand verses.

The main problem for the traditional view of Empedocles is the apparent failure of the *Suda* to mention the *Katharmoi*. Since Diogenes mentions it surely it must have appeared in Lobon; why then should it be absent from the *Suda*? The question has caused much discussion and alterations to the text.[58] But the *Suda* fails to mention the *Katharmoi* only if its reference to *peri physeos* is intended to be the title of a poem, and if the capital letter supplied by modern editions is omitted it looks unlikely that this is the case. Whereas Diogenes writes, 'The (poem) "*On Nature*" ...' (*ta men oun peri phuseôs autôi*), the *Suda* says, 'He wrote about the nature of things in verse ...' (*kai egrapse di' epôn peri phuseôs tôn ontôn*). This gives no title for Empedocles' work, neither *Katharmoi* nor *On Nature*, and there is no reason why it should not refer to the whole of Empedocles' work.

Which of these two testimonia, if either, preserves the phraseology of Lobon? Although the *Suda* is late and perhaps indirect evidence it is quite possible that it reflects Lobon fairly closely here. If so the origin of Diogenes' variant is easily explained: Diogenes, and Diogenes alone, knows two titles for Empedocles' work; faced with Lobon's unspecific reference to Empedocles' writing, Diogenes prefers to mention the titles that he knows and has used in his chapter; he alters the phrase 'He wrote about the nature of things ...' to what he considers to be equivalent: 'His poem *On Nature* and the *Katharmoi* ...' On this reconstruction it is entirely unclear whether Diogenes thought that these titles referred to the same poem or different poems. In any case what Diogenes thought was the case is no guarantee of the truth, and if there was only one poem this might explain why Lobon, an earlier if somewhat untrustworthy source, did not differentiate between two titles.

The hypothesis that Empedocles wrote only one poem enables us to accommodate all the other ancient evidence on the number of Empedocles' books. In the context of Diels' fragments two books of *physica* are attested.[59] However

---

[58] E.g. Zuntz (1965) pp. 236-9; Van der Ben (1975) pp. 11-16; O'Brien (1981) pp. 4-13; Wright (1981) pp. 20-1.
[59] 'Book 1': B6, 8, 17, 96. 'book 2': B62.

Hunger's new fragment[60] suggests that there were two books of *Katharmoi*. Tzetzes' evidence for a third book of *Physics*,[61] if it is accepted, makes the conventional total of *Physics* plus *Katharmoi* five books; but if *Physics* and *Katharmoi* are alternative titles for the same work we have a maximum of two or at most three books and this result coincides precisely with the two possible readings of the *Suda*. These are all the books that we need to attribute to Empedocles.

One further point should make the arguments in favour of one poem compelling. Fragment B115 has long been a problem on account of Plutarch's introductory words to a group of lines at *De exilio* 607c: 'Empedocles proclaims at the beginning of his philosophy "There is an oracle of necessity ..." ' What is 'the beginning of his philosophy'? On the traditional two-poem view this is strange and problematic; Plutarch should have specified natural philosophy or religious philosophy. His vagueness is particularly frustrating to the majority of editors who would assign the verses to the *Katharmoi*: surely, it is felt, Plutarch could not have referred to the religious poem, which must have been the less well known of the two, as simply 'his philosophy';[62] furthermore many prefer to think that in terms of chronology the *Physics* would come before the *Katharmoi*.[63] There are also problems concerning the content of B115 since lines 1-2 are twice quoted in the context of the cosmic cycle,[64] usually considered the subject of the *Physics*; the remaining lines (3-14 on Diels' reconstruction) are felt to belong to the theme of the 'religious poem'. If they really belong together they threaten the barrier between 'scientific' and 'religious' subject matter, whichever poem they are finally allotted to.

If, however, there was but one philosophical work of Empedocles, Plutarch's introduction is perfectly natural and

---

[60] Published by H. Hunger (1967) p.5. Fragment 152 in Wright (1981).

[61] Tzetzes *Chiliades* 7.522.

[62] Van der Ben (1975) pp. 16-20 and n. 17, referring to earlier editors. Arguments against the conclusion that *philosophia* must mean physics are given by Kingsley (1979) p. 60 n. 1 and O'Brien (1981) pp. 14-15. Cf. also Wright (1981) pp. 81-2.

[63] Guthrie vol. 2 pp. 124-5 and p. 125n. 1; Wright (1981) p. 81 n. 23.

[64] Hippolytus 7.29.23; Simplicius *In Phys.* 1184.6; both associate the 'necessity' with the necessity of alternating effects of Love and Strife.

no barrier between the scientific and the religious is to be expected. Empedocles' philosophy is Empedocles' philosophy and there is no need to specify a title or division of philosophy. Simplicius' quotation of lines 1-2 in connection with B30 and B26 is no problem, nor is Hippolytus' use of the lines in association with other 'physical' passages; and similarly we need not worry that Stobaeus connects the necessity with ethical necessity and that it is related to the exile of the *daimones* in B115.3-14. The connection between the necessity of the cosmic cycle and the necessity of the fall of the *daimones* may have been explicit in Empedocles.[65] When Plutarch says that Empedocles introduced B115 at the beginning of his philosophy he means that it occurred fairly early in Empedocles' one poem.[66] This seems plausible since the notion of a decree of necessity is fundamental to both cycles of change.

In interpreting Empedocles we may gain much by freeing ourselves from the idea that he wrote an objective, secular, scientific work on the one hand and a personal, mystical, religious work on the other. Current trends have sought to interpret his thought as a unity, but it is doubtful whether there were ever two stories to be related. Freed from the assumption of a gulf to be overcome we may approach the text as it stands in a new light. The ancient interpreters know of no division in Empedocles' thought, and they treat it as a straightforward unity. An approach which starts from an appreciation of the ancient interpreters gives us an opportunity to do likewise.

---

[65] Kingsley (1979) p. 51 n. 3 offers an argument against placing B115 in particular among the '*Physics*' fragments; his point is based upon a subjective impression of the style of teaching offered in the two poems – impersonal in the *Physics* and personal/autobiographical in the *Katharmoi*. I doubt that this contrast would be so clear if one had not begun by reading the fragments in two groups; the argument runs the risk of circularity since it is this sort of criterion that was used to divide the fragments in the first place. It is unlikely that Empedocles would have regarded personal involvement as proper only to religion and not to natural science.

[66] It is clearly possible that some lines occurred more than once and it does not necessarily follow that the whole of B115 occurred early in the poem. Plutarch quotes lines 1, 3, 5, 6 and 13 at this point.

Part Two of this book is based on a reading of an embedded text. It explores Hippolytus' interpretation of Heraclitus and Empedocles and the use he makes of their texts, and it experiments with the possibilities of pushing his interpretation beyond what is explicit in his own work. In this way we can pursue a new reading of the philosophers by taking Hippolytus' text as a jumping-off point, and by this means we are able to solve some of the hermeneutical difficulties of the context-free fragments and the traditional approach.

Part One: The Test Cases

Two sections of Hippolytus' *Refutatio* are used here as test cases to illustrate his method of work, his handling of sources and the way in which his interests govern his selection and use of material. The section on Aristotle provides evidence of the extent of Hippolytus' knowledge and his interpretation of philosophical texts, as well as demonstrating the inadequacy of using the *Refutatio* simply as a quarry for fragments. Part of Hippolytus' account of Simon Magus illustrates how extensively he adapts and rearranges material even when he is largely copying from an earlier text. Both passages clearly show Hippolytus as an independent interpreter of the material he presents.

A thorough examination of Hippolytus' approach in cases where we have some means of control is a necessary preparation for the use of his work in other contexts. It is on the basis of the results of these studies, which indicate that his methods are neither mechanical nor stupid, that it is possible to justify the use made of his interpretations of Heraclitus and Empedocles in Part Two. The studies in Part Two start from the assumption that the ideas put forward in the *Refutatio* are worthy of attention.

1. Aristotle

A. Where did Hippolytus derive his information from?

Two accounts of Aristotle's thought occur in Hippolytus' *Refutatio*: (i) a brief outline in the preliminary survey of philosophy in book 1.20; (ii) a more detailed account geared to the task of refuting the heretic Basileides in book 7.15ff.

(i) The account in book 1 is not of great significance. Like the account of Plato which precedes it it probably derives from some handbook, and it reflects a tendency to assimilate the doctrines of Plato and Aristotle. It shows no extensive knowledge of the school works of Aristotle beyond a summary of the ten categories. The remaining doctrines listed include a claim that the soul survives death and is absorbed into the fifth element, and an account of the three sorts of good required for happiness. Both of these may reflect a knowledge of exoteric works rather than works which are now extant.[1] Finally it comments on the names of the Stoic and Peripatetic schools and the reasons for them. It is unlikely that this summary includes much that is specifically Hippolytus' work; rather it reflects the contents of some popular manual.

(ii) The account in book 7 is quite different and of greater interest. The main passage is 7.15-19, but further items occur in the course of the account of Basileides, 7.20-7. Hippolytus is here employing the material for a specific task and is not simply reproducing the summary from a handbook.

Is this account of Aristotle the work of Hippolytus himself or has he merely derived it from some other source?

---

[1] The claim that there was mention of a link between soul and the fifth element in *De Philosophia* has been challenged by D.E. Hahm (1982). The mention of the requirements for happiness might be based, at some remove, on the *Protrepticus*. Cf. Düring *Protrepticus* A1.

(i) Adaptation of the account to its present context

One indication that the account of Aristotle has not simply been taken over unchanged from another context is the degree to which it fits into the scheme of the present work. The main account (7.15-19) is introduced as a general summary of Aristotle's doctrines, but nevertheless there is very little material in it that does not bear some direct relation to the comparison with Basileides for which it is to serve. The information included and the way in which it is presented are closely geared to the context in which it appears in Hippolytus. This is true a fortiori for the items which occur in the course of the account of Basileides, prompted by some immediate parallel. There is thus no reason to suggest that the account of Aristotle is simply an extract taken from a handbook and inserted without regard to its detailed relevance to the matter in hand.

(ii) Characteristics of the account

The most striking feature of the account of Aristotle in book 7 is its critical attitude. Whereas the summary in book 1 simply presents an outline of the doctrines and makes no comment except to observe their similarity to Platonic views, the account in book 7 is largely discursive and analyses in some detail the implications of the doctrines it reports. The passage depends upon these critical analyses in order to establish a parallel between Aristotle and Basileides; it is thus central to Hippolytus' purpose that he present this hostile view of Aristotle.

Are there any indications in the text as to the influences which contribute to this reading of Aristotle? The most likely quarter from which Hippolytus might have learnt this attitude to Aristotle seems to be the Sceptics. There is very limited evidence for criticism of Aristotle by the other major schools during the hellenistic period.[2] The fact that, unlike the

_____

[2] Very few explicit references to Aristotle's works can be found before the first century B.C. and even on the most optimistic view of the availability of texts of the school works it cannot be claimed that they were well known even to philosophers.

summary in book 1, the account in book 7 is based entirely on the school works of Aristotle suggests that it belongs in the period of renewed discovery of Aristotle after the first century B.C., but even when the school works were more widely read there is little evidence that the Stoics or Epicureans devoted much attention to detailed refutation of them. Hippolytus' criticisms are unlikely to be of Stoic origin since the non-existence of *genos* (genus) and *eidos* (species) which they find objectionable in Aristotle, is a doctrine held by the Stoics. The Sceptics, on the other hand, certainly argued against the Stoic *genos* and *eidos* on these grounds, and it seems likely that they would have done the same for Aristotle.

Hippolytus certainly knew the work of the Sceptics, and quotes passages from them at some length.[3] However, we know no direct parallel for this passage, and some of the argument is certainly fairly crude. It is possible that the ideas derive from Hippolytus' familiarity with scepticism, such that he adopted methods of argument commonly used by the Sceptics, while the account of Aristotle presented here is actually his own construction.

Many features of the arguments offered against Aristotelian doctrines in the main passage, *Ref.* 7.15-19, can be paralleled in material found in Sextus Empiricus. In the first part of the passage two arguments are offered against Aristotelian *ousia* (substance). The first argues that *ousia* comes to be from what is not (namely *genos* and *eidos*). The absurdity of coming to be from what is not is often used in Sextus' refutations of other thinkers,[4] but in addition we find the use of puzzles concerning the relationship between universals and particulars similar to those used to criticise the relation of *genos*, *eidos* and individuals by Hippolytus. In *Adv. Math.* 1.74, in an argument to prove that *grammatikê* does not exist, Sextus uses the point that the universal exists only in so far as it is instantiated – a point closely related to Hippolytus' observation that the *genos* is not any single one of its species, and one that can be used in

---

[3] On the parallel passages in Hippolytus and Sextus Empiricus see Janáček (1959). It is also possible that Hippolytus used a sceptical interpretation of Heraclitus; see below pp. 132-4.

[4] Cf. e.g. *Adv. Math.* 10.342.

support of the same conclusion about the non-existence of the *genos*. Sextus also observes that none of the individuals is the genus,[5] which involves the corollary that the genus is none of the individuals;[6] this latter is the one employed by Hippolytus.

Sextus includes one argument specifically designed to refute *genos* and *eidê* ('species', plural) at *PH* 2.219-27, but at the start he says that he will deal with the subject more fully elsewhere, this being only a brief summary. No further passage on the subject occurs in his extant works, but we may assume that he would have had further arguments on the same lines. Here the criticisms are not specifically against Aristotelian doctrines of *genos* and *eidê* but also Platonic and Stoic theories; the argument is a general one, and like Hippolytus' argument it centres on puzzles about the existence of *genos* and *eidos* and their relationship with particulars.

The second argument against *ousia* in Hippolytus, 7.18, seeks to demonstrate that *ousia* is composed of non-existents. This type of refutation is also common in Sextus who argues against time (*Adv.Math.*6.63), number (4.34), music (6.52,61) and rhetoric (2.106) on the grounds that they are made up of things which do not exist. Hippolytus argues similarly that primary substance is composed of *genos* and *sumbebēkota*, neither of which can exist in its own right (7.18.6).

Hippolytus mentions a third alternative account of *ousia* as matter, form and privation at the beginning of chapter 19. The expectation is that a further refutation will be supplied for this alternative, but instead Hippolytus simply claims that it is no different, giving no justification for the claim. Hippolytus' purpose in the present context does not require that he give a complete refutation of Aristotle, and for the parallel with Basileides the important point is the demonstration that *genos* and *eidos* are non-existent, and apparently the origin of existent things. Hippolytus implies that he knows of an argument against the third division of *ousia* but that it is superfluous to his present purpose, and he merely states that the conclusion amounts to the same as that of the previous arguments.

---

[5] E.g. *Adv. Math.* 10.288. Cf. also *Adv. Math.* 4.17ff.
[6] *Adv. Math.* 10.289.

The remainder of chapter 19 shows similar evidence of abbreviation of arguments, particularly in the dismissive references to the soul (7.19.5-6) and god (7.19.6-7). In the first of these Hippolytus states that Aristotle's doctrine of soul is unclear: 'for in three whole books it is impossible to say clearly what Aristotle thinks about the soul'; he goes on to state the definition given for soul, asserting that the meaning of it is a subject of much enquiry and debate. This refusal to explore the issue in detail while acknowledging that it is a subject of dispute is worth noting: it suggests that Hippolytus is not simply copying from a basic handbook of the sort which gives a brief but over-simple account of the doctrines with no indication of any complexities.[7] On the other hand Hippolytus does not give us the detailed scholarly debate which lies behind his brief comment. It appears that he knows of a much more extensive discussion ('a matter requiring much argument') of the issues on which he does not intend to go into detail in this context. Precisely the same is true of the comment on god, where again the Aristotelian definition is given and Hippolytus comments that it is even more difficult to grasp than that of soul, and requires a much longer discussion. In this case he concludes that god, on this definition, is non-existent and this may suggest that the discussions of these issues, which Hippolytus knew and here refers to, were further refutations of a sceptical nature such as he gives in full on the subject of *ousia*. It is certainly common procedure in the sceptical arguments in Sextus Empiricus to start by quoting a definition, build up a dilemma concerning alternative interpretations of what this might mean and conclude that all of them are unacceptable, often on the grounds that they imply that the subject is non-existent.[8]

Many features of Hippolytus' account of Aristotle suggest

[7] Cf. e.g. Diogenes Laertius *Life of Aristotle* 32-4.

[8] For the argument starting from a quoted definition, cf. e.g. the discussion of *topos* and *chôra* at the beginning of *Adv. Math.* 10.1-36, among many other examples. On the impossibility of 'thought of thought' compare *Adv. Math.* 7.310 and 348. Sextus mentions Aristotle's god at *Adv. Math.* 10.33 but under a different definition, *peras tou ouranou*, in connection with arguments against *topos*.

that it is based on a hostile reading of Aristotle and that the arguments he summarises or alludes to resemble those of the Sceptics of his day in style and attitude. These arguments may be Hippolytus' own, devised under the influence of his knowledge of Scepticism, or may be more or less closely based on arguments he had read or heard elsewhere. In either case he has been selective in what details he chooses to include as relevant to his present purpose, and has given a hostile reading of Aristotle that suits his comparison with Basileides.

B. How extensive a knowledge of Aristotle does Hippolytus display?

The style of argument and the polemical approach of the passage may be influenced by Sceptical procedures, but the details of the argument and the basis on which Aristotle is attacked come directly from the works of Aristotle. How much of Aristotle's work is used in this passage?

The main section of Hippolytus' account is concerned with the Aristotelian doctrine of substance. Hippolytus quotes some material from the *Categories*, and the longest discussions given by Hippolytus appear to be commenting on and criticising the doctrine of substance in the *Categories*. However, the discussion raises issues which are prominent in other Aristotelian passages, and particularly *Metaphysics* Z.

(i) Substance in the Categories and Metaphysics Z

The simple scheme of primary substance (the individual),[9] and secondary substances, *eidos* and *genos*, which is outlined in the *Categories* raises a number of problems. Aristotle aims to allow some substantial status to *genos* and *eidos* despite the fact that they do not satisfy the criteria of being the subject of predication, rather than themselves predicated,[10] and being a 'this': secondary substances fail in this respect since they seem to signify a 'this' but in fact indicate a 'such' concerning

---

[9] *Categories* 2a13-14. *ho tis anthrôpos, ho tis hippos.*
[10] Cf. 2a34. In this respect *genos* is at a further remove than *eidos* from being properly substance.

substance, 3b20. In *Metaphysics* Z the requirements for being substance are investigated in more detail: in this case the problems of denying substantial status to universals, with the consequence that the objects of definition and knowledge are not substance, are broached and discussed at length.

In *Metaphysics* Z the question 'What part of each thing is its substance?'[11] replaces the simple question 'What is a substance?' of the *Categories*, which is taken up in the first chapter of Z.[12] The move from considering that the individual thing is itself most properly substance to the suggestion that there is something which is its substance requires explanation. Why does Aristotle find it necessary to ask about the substance *of* a thing? Two reasons may be suggested: (1) the requirements of priority in definition, knowledge and time, listed at Z1, 1028a32-3, as criteria for substance, imply a superior claim on the part of candidates such as the universal to be properly substance than the compound individual; (2) the Platonists ascribe substantial status to Forms rather than particulars, and this claim must be adequately rejected by Aristotle.

Aristotle is thus obliged to consider the possibility that the substance of a thing is its form, matter, essence or some other feature, but this does not mean that he actually subscribes to any of these views. He certainly resists the Platonists' claim that Forms are substances: the form fails to meet the criterion of separate existence on Aristotle's view,[13] and the fact that no universal exists separately or signifies a 'this' is fundamental to Aristotle's rejection of the Platonists' account of substance.[14]

[11] The substance *of* a thing is the subject of discussion from chapter 2 of Z (1028b8). It recurs explicitly in ch. 6 and throughout ch. 13 (1038b10, b12; also 1040b16, b24, 1041b27-8).

[12] E.g. 1028a17-18, 26-7.

[13] The Platonists do of course assert the separation of Forms, and Aristotle recognises that this is necessary if they are to be substance, 1040b27.

[14] Once a form is made separable and a 'this' it becomes indefinable and no longer the object of knowledge, 1040a11. Thus the substantial Forms of the Platonists do not have the advantages which might be claimed for universals which are prior in definition and knowledge.

Aristotle is aware of the problems of denying that the universal can itself be substance. If no substance is made out of universals due to the fact that they indicate a 'such' and not a 'this' (1039a14-16), and a substance cannot be a composite made up of substances (a16-17), then all substances must be simple and indefinable (a17-19). This is a heavy price to pay, since substance is thought to be most of all what is defined (a19-20). Yet Aristotle does not evade the problem, since to allow that the universal is substance or signifies something separate and a 'this' makes it like a Platonic Form and opens it to problems of the 'third man' (1038b34-39a3). It cannot, therefore, be right to interpret *Metaphysics* Z as allowing that forms or universals are properly substance;[15] rather it seems plain that the tendency throughout Z is to cast doubt on the claims of each proposed candidate in turn, while recognising that there are some remaining arguments in their favour. Since none of these candidates satisfies in its own right the criteria of being separate, prior and a 'this', it is impossible to accept any one of them as in itself the substance of a thing.[16] None the less their claims within the context of the individual composite whole are restored in Z17 and H1, since it is not true to say of the composite individual that its form or its matter or any other feature of it is *not* part of its substance. The composite whole (*sunolon*) is a 'this' and a substance precisely because it has both matter and form.

On this view of the strategy of *Metaphysics* Z the search for something separate which constitutes the substance of *x* and is itself more substantial than *x* proves to be misguided. The verdict resembles that of the *Categories*: primarily substance is the individual, *x*, and its *genos* or *eidos* are not more properly substance but less so, despite their apparent claims to priority and knowability.

This verdict leaves Aristotle with major problems, many of which he spells out in the course of *Metaphysics* Z. Among these the most serious is perhaps the fact that substance appears to be indefinable and unknowable; but this failure is bound up with

[15] As for example many recent discussions have attempted to do, e.g. Woods (1967), Albritton (1957), Hughes (1979).

[16] On this strategy in Z see G.E.L. Owen (1978/9).

the general difficulties concerning the priority of substance.
The criteria for substance listed at 1028a31ff. asserted that it
must be prior in time, definition and knowledge, and all these
claims appear to be problematic for the theory that substance is
the composite individual.[17]

The problem of substance which is taken up by Hippolytus is
that of composition, and, following from that, one concerning
becoming. Substance appears to be composite, since the *sunolon*
is made up of parts. As Aristotle observes, 1029a30-2, the
compound is posterior to its parts, and the parts of things which
are definable are, at least sometimes, prior to the whole,
1035b3, 1036a16. The problem becomes explicit at 1038b23: if
a substance is composed of things it must be composed of
substances – a substance cannot be composed out of
non-substances, since that would imply that qualities and the
like were prior to substance. On the other hand there is no
doubt that a single substance cannot be composed of more
than one actual substance, 1039a14-15, 1041a4-5. What is
more properly substance is the compound of matter and form;
yet the elements of which it is composed have no substantial
existence in their own right.

Hippolytus takes up two criticisms of Aristotelian substance
along these lines. The second attack he brings to bear on the
subject concerns composition out of non-substantial parts, as
in the problems raised here by Aristotle. Hippolytus attacks
substance as being a composite of *genos* and *sumbebêkota*
(accidents), by which he means the non-substantial categories
and particularly quality (*poiotês*), neither of which can exist in
its own right.[18] Hence the individuals are made up of

---

[17] The individual is capable of separate existence but this does not
necessarily ensure priority in time (cf. Hughes (1979) p. 126); the individuals
are prior in perception, but it is the universal that is prior in *logos*, 1018b32-4;
knowledge is of the definition, although we may recognise the individual
before recognising the universal it instantiates (cf. Lesher (1972) p. 172).
Definition ought to be of the universal, but at 1028a34 definition of a thing
requires definition of the substances and the discussion in Z 10-11 suggests
that definition of a substance involves more than just the form and may
include matter, 1036a26ff. Nevertheless the individual cannot be defined,
1036a2.

[18] 7.18.6.

non-existents. The first attack on *ousia* concerns genesis of the individuals, which Hippolytus suggests come into being from the *genos* and *eidos*, neither of which exist in their own right. Hence the individuals come to be from non-existents.

How much of these arguments derives directly from Aristotle's own discussion of the difficulties concerning substance? It is apparent that the details can be located in the discussions in the *Categories* and *Metaphysics*, although the style of attack is not Aristotelian.

(a) The first argument against ousia, Refutatio 7.15-18.1

The attack on genesis of the individual substances, like that on their composition, is comparable with problems raised explicitly in *Metaphysics* Z. The coming-to-be of the individual is discussed in detail in Z8 in which the example used is the bronze sphere: here there is a particular problem due to the sphere being manufactured from pre-existing matter. Neither the matter, bronze, nor the form, sphere, itself comes into existence when a particular bronze sphere is made. Rather it is the composite individual which is made out of form and matter. On the other hand Aristotle cannot allow that either the form or the matter existed apart as a 'this' before the individual sphere was made: sphere is 'such and such' (*toionde*); the only substance that exists apart is the individual bronze sphere that comes to be.[19]

Hippolytus approaches the problem of the genesis of the individual, attacking a similar problem, namely whether the individual substance comes to be from things which themselves have no substantial existence. His example is not the manufactured object, the bronze sphere, but the individual man, Socrates or Diogenes,[20] and he does not consider the non-substantial status of the matter as Aristotle does in the case of the bronze sphere. However, Hippolytus' example is not unconnected with the discussion in Z8 where Aristotle explicitly extends the implications of the account of the bronze sphere to deal with examples such as that used by Hippolytus:

[19] *Metaph* Z 8, 1033a24-b24.
[20] *Ref.* 7.18.1.

every individual, such as Callias or Socrates, is like this individual bronze sphere, and man and animal are like bronze spheres in general, 1033b24-6. Thus Hippolytus, who considers first the relationship of species such as man, horse, dog to the genus animal (*Ref.* 7.16.2-17.1) and then the relationship of individual men, Socrates and Diogenes, to the species man and the genus animal (*Ref.*7.18.1), is following a line suggested by Aristotle's own analysis of the genesis of the individual.

Hippolytus argues that the *genos*, and hence also the *eidos*, does not exist on the grounds that it is *oude hen*, not a single thing: the *genos* animal is neither ox, nor horse, nor man, nor god, nor any specific thing at all, 7.16.1. If then that animal is not any one of these things, the things that come to be derive their subsistence from non-existents (*ouk onta* 7.17.1).

The reasoning behind Hippolytus' move from the fact that the *genos* is *oude hen*, not a single thing, to the verdict that it is *ouk on*, non-existent, may be simply that *oude hen* suggests a connection with *ouden*, nothing, in which case his argument is a poor one. But there is much to be gained from suggesting that the point is in fact picking up Aristotle's assertions that substance must be a *tode ti*, a separate 'this';[21] the *genos* on Aristotle's own admission cannot exist separately,[22] and what is common to many things cannot be *ousia*. Hippolytus' assertion that the *genos* is not a single thing may be a reference to the fact that it cannot qualify as a 'this', or one thing,[23] on Aristotle's terms.

In support of this interpretation it is worth examining Hippolytus' claim that the *genos* is a 'heap', *sôros*. This claim is central to his argument in that he claims that species and individuals are derived from the *genos* as if from a 'heap'. Aristotle himself never describes the *genos* as a heap, nor does he imply that species derive from it in this way; but *sôros* is an important term in Aristotle, used to refer to a random accumulation without organic unity. Aristotle uses it to

---

[21] This requirement is found in the *Categories* 3b10 and reiterated frequently in the *Metaphysics*, e.g. B6,1003a9, Z3, 1029a28.

[22] *Metaph*, I 2, 1053b21.

[23] For the suggestion that substance must be one, cf. *Metaph.* Z12, 1037b24ff.

ridicule false ideas of substances in *Metaphysics* Z16, and this passage is surely the origin of Hippolytus' claim that the Aristotelian *genos* is a heap. As part of a dialectical attack on Aristotle's position, Hippolytus points out that the *genos* must also be denied the status of substance on the grounds that it too is a heap.

A comparison of the two passages makes the connection clear:

> *Metaphysics* Z16, 1040b5:
> But it is clear that also the majority of those things which seem to be substances are in fact potentialities: in the parts of animals (none of these is separated, for when they are separated then they are stuff like matter in general) and earth and fire and air; for none of these things is a single thing, but like a heap, before they are concocted and something comes to be a single thing from them.

> Hippolytus *Refutatio* 7.15.2:
> But the genus is as it were a heap mixed up of many different seeds, and from this genus all the species of things that come to be are separated off as if from a heap.

The heap of 'seeds' in Hippolytus' passage might correspond to the potentialities which are like a heap in Aristotle. Like Aristotle Hippolytus goes on to argue that because it is a heap and not one thing[24] it cannot be *ousia*. The Aristotelian *genos* is itself merely a heap, it has no unity nor does it exist in actuality but only as a potentiality, as do the heaps condemned by Aristotle as false claimants to the status of substance in Z16.

This argument has more than one advantage for Hippolytus' purpose. In addition to suggesting that the Aristotelian *genos* cannot be *ousia*, for which better material is available later in Z16, it also enables Hippolytus to argue that if the *genos* is a heap of potentialities, then its relationship with its species and its individual members must be that they are derived from it to become separately existing actualities as if taken from a heap. But if that is the case, and the heap itself is not substance nor

---

[24] *oude hen: Ref* 7.16.2, 7.17.1; cf. Aristotle's *ouden gar autôn hen estin*.

actually existent, then the individual substances come to be from what is not. Thus Hippolytus can argue not just against *genos* but against primary substance as well.

(b) The second argument against ousia, Refutatio 7.18.2-6

This argument seeks to demonstrate that *ousia* is composed of non-existents. Although the problem is clearly related to Aristotle's discussion of the composite nature of the *sunolon*[25] the material explicitly used by Hippolytus for his argument is mainly taken from the *Categories*. The passage begins with a quotation from *Categories* 2a11, stating that it is the individual which is primarily termed substance:

> 7.18.2. Aristotle calls this primarily, most of all and most properly substance, that which is neither said of a substrate (*kath' hupokeimenou*) nor in a substrate (*en hupokeimenôi*).

Hippolytus then explains, with further extensive quotation from the *Categories*, what the terms 'of a substrate' and 'in a substrate' mean, and tells us that the *genos* is said of a substrate and *sumbebêkota*, such as qualities, are in a substrate. Neither of these can exist in its own right (7.18.5-6):[26] what exists in its own right is primary substance, the individual.

Hippolytus completes the move from the non-existence of *genos* and *sumbebêkota* to the non-existence of primary substance by assuming that primary substance is composed of these non-substances:

> 7.18.6. The individuals are made up of these things.

This does not appear to come directly from Aristotle, for whom the individual is the substrate of which universals are predicated and in which qualities occur,[27] but is not apparently made up of these things. Is Hippolytus unjustified in his assumption? He is certainly entitled to ask what is left to be

---

[25] *Metaph.* Z13, 1038b23ff. See above p.43.

[26] This is not supported by any quotation from the *Categories*. It is implied by *Cat.* 2b3-6 and explicit in *Metaph.* Z1, 1028a13-25.

[27] *Cat.* 2a19-35, etc.

the individual substrate if we remove the *genos* and all the incidental qualities. The answer begins to look very much like that explored by Aristotle in *Metaphysics* Z3, where the substrate is in question and the result of the exercise is to identify something indeterminate which cannot qualify as substance.

In *Metaphysics* Z3 the chief candidates to be identified as the substrate are form and matter, although neither of them proves sufficiently individuated to count as substance. It is therefore surprising that Hippolytus does not mention matter, and makes little reference to form, in the second argument against *ousia*. The deficiency appears to be about to be remedied when Hippolytus proceeds at the start of chapter 19:

> 7.19.1. About substance enough has been said. However substance is not only said to be genus, species and the individual, but also matter and form and privation.

He is apparently aware that he has not dealt with these candidates for substance, but his present purpose does not justify including a further argument against substance: what he has said on the subject will suffice, so far as his purpose of providing a parallel with Basileides goes.

The group matter (*hulê*), form (*eidos*), privation (*sterêsis*) occurs as a list of principles several times in Aristotle's works, but is not a feature of *Metaphysics* Z, where the opposition matter/form is prominent. It belongs rather to the *Physics* and *Metaphysics* Λ,[28] but since Hippolytus gives no further details concerning the three principles, and does not provide any argument against them, it is impossible to tell which text he knows. Both passages have some affinities with the discussion of substance in *Metaphysics* Z; in *Physics* A7 Aristotle mentions in passing that it is not yet clear whether form or *substratum* is substance.[29] *Metaphysics* Λ3 also considers three types of substance: matter, the nature (*phusis*) or final state (*hexis eis hên*), and the compound of the two, the individuals (*kath'*

---

[28] See *Physics* A7, 190b17-191a22; *Metaph.* Λ 1069b32; 1070b19.
[29] 191a19-20.

hekasta) such as Socrates or Callias,[30] a passage which recapitulates some of the material in Z. Either context provides good reason for associating this list of principles with questions of substance as Hippolytus does, and it is possible that both texts are involved.

The arguments against substance in *Refutatio* 7.15-19.1 imply a detailed knowledge of material from Aristotle's *Categories, Metaphysics* Z and one or both of *Physics* A and *Metaphysics* Λ. The remainder of the account of Aristotle in *Refutatio* 7.19 does not include such detail, and does not necessarily imply more than a superficial knowledge of the contents of the works mentioned. Following the mention of the three principles matter, form, privation, Hippolytus claims that Aristotle had a threefold division of the world: sub-lunary region, superlunary region and *epiphaneia*. His concern appears to be with the need to identify parallels for Basileides' threefold 'sonship'.[31] Corresponding with the divisions of the world is a threefold division of Aristotle's works into *Physics, Metaphysics* and theology. This observation is not, apparently, intended as an exhaustive division of Aristotle's works, which are later said to include psychology and ethics, but rather identifies a connection between the structure of the Aristotelian cosmos and the structure of one group of Aristotelian treatises. The observation implies some acquaintance with the content of the same group of works as the discussion of substance, namely sections of the *Metaphysics* and *Physics* and *Metaphysics* Λ.

Some knowledge of *Metaphysics* Λ is also behind the section on the Aristotelian god, 7.19.6-7. Hippolytus quotes the definition *noêsis noêseôs* (thought of thought) which is based on *Metaphysics* Λ 1074b33-4. The argument against the doctrine of god is clearly abbreviated as Hippolytus presents it, but may have depended upon a much more detailed knowledge of Λ than the one phrase quoted here. The same is clearly true of the passage concerning the *De Anima*,[32] where a definition of soul is quoted from *De Anima* 2, 412b4-5, but Hippolytus

---

[30] 1070a9-13.
[31] *Ref.* 7.22.7f.
[32] *Ref.* 7.19.5-6.

implies that he knows much more detail concerning the theory and debates about its meaning than he is prepared to include in the present context.

Hippolytus completes his summary of Aristotle with two brief comments; first that the kosmos is eternal and imperishable. This appears to be a reference to the *De Caelo*[33] but is too vague to be clear. Finally he mentions the *Ethics*, which he claims aimed to make the student's character good. Neither of these last comments imply much familiarity with the works in question, and there is no indication that Hippolytus had more to say on these subjects than he offers here.

(ii) References to Aristotle in the section on Basileides

Aristotle is mentioned explicitly five times in the course of the account of Basileides, *Refutatio* 7.20-7. Of these one is unimportant, occurring as a passing reference to the fact that Plato was Aristotle's teacher in a passage concerned with Plato's *Phaedrus*.[34] Two others refer back to items mentioned in the main account of Aristotle and add nothing to what has been said there: at 7.21.1 Hippolytus links Basileides' non-existent god with Aristotle's god and repeats the definition 'thought of thought' for Aristotle's god; at 7.22.5 he links the 'seed' of Basileides with the Aristotelian *genos* and refers back to his description of the *genos* as something which is cut up into an indefinite number of species but is itself non-existent.

The remaining two points are of greater interest since they add new material beyond that found in the main account of Aristotle. The first concerns homonymy: Hippolytus comments on the fact that Basileides said that there were not enough names to go round the number of different things in the world, and explains that the disciples of Basileides had appropriated this key doctrine from the Peripatos and tried to propound it as his own new doctrine:

---

[33] Particularly 279b4-283b22 and 296a33, but cf. also *Phys.* 250b11-252b5.

[34] *Refutatio* 7.22.10. The reference to Aristotle seems to be an attempt to make the mention of Plato's *Phaedrus* relevant to the comparison in hand.

7.20.4 For Aristotle, who lived many generations before Basileides, laid down the doctrine concerning homonyms in the Categories.

Hippolytus does not go into detail on the doctrine of homonymy, which he treats as fairly well known, but his mention of the *Categories* suggests that he may know the text itself as opposed to merely second-hand accounts.

Secondly, at 7.24.1-2 Hippolytus mentions the Aristotelian account of the soul again, giving more details than he had included at 7.19.5-6. He quotes twice the same definition as he had given before, but he also specifies that the soul acts in the body, cannot function without the body, is superior to the body in various ways and is the work (*ergon*) and finished product (*apotelesma*) of the body. Whereas in the earlier account Hippolytus had dismissed the doctrine of soul as unclear, here he mentions a number of precise features of it, a fact which supports the suggestion that the earlier dismissal was not based on ignorance of the details of the doctrine but a refusal to enter into a complicated discussion.

These references to Aristotle in the course of the account of Basileides are much more closely linked to the detailed comparison which Hippolytus is concerned to draw than is the general account of Aristotle. There is no doubt in any of these five allusions that the reference to Aristotle has been inserted by Hippolytus in constructing his refutation, and is not derived from any reference in Basileides' own work. It is thus reasonable to suggest that Hippolytus shows some immediate knowledge of Aristotelian works, and that he is not confined to copying an earlier handbook.

Again the works with which Hippolytus shows familiarity are among those given prominence in the general summary: the *Categories, Metaphysics* Λ, and *De Anima.* Thus the list of treatises which figure clearly in this part of book 7 of the *Refutatio* as a whole includes the *Categories, Physics* Α, *Metaphysics* Λ, other parts of the *Metaphysics,* particularly Z, and the *De Anima.* Less use is made of the *De Caelo* and *Ethics.* This is an impressive list of the school works of Aristotle, and the account is, as we have seen, closely based on central issues raised in these texts. How should one set about handling this material?

C. The implications of the account of Aristotle: a test case

The account of Aristotle's philosophy is the only major example of Hippolytus' work in which we have first-hand access to the texts to which it refers. As such it constitutes an important test case in relation to the sections concerning the Presocratic philosophers, where Hippolytus' work is a significant contribution to our own knowledge. A number of questions are worth asking: (1) How does the concern with providing a parallel for the related heresy affect the presentation of Aristotle? (2) Can the traditional approach to fragmented texts be justified? (3) What is interesting or of value in this interpretation of Aristotle?

(i) The parallel with Basileides

Hippolytus' account of Basileides is not the only account that we possess, since there is also evidence given by Eusebius (from Agrippa Castor), Clement of Alexandria and a group including Irenaeus and writers who derive, probably, from Hippolytus' own earlier *Syntagma* (including Epiphanius, Ps. Tertullian and Philaster). Although some features of Hippolytus' account here in the *Refutatio* can be identified in Clement of Alexandria, the remaining authorities clearly represent a quite different tradition and no serious attempt can be made to reconcile the two.[35] It is now generally agreed that Hippolytus' account in the *Refutatio* represents the authentic Basileides.[36]

This means, however, that the other supposed authorities for Basileides cannot have any bearing on our assessment of Hippolytus' account as regards its detailed accuracy and how fully it describes the system. Clement's material is principally on ethical subjects, which do not figure significantly in Hippolytus' account; this fact in itself suggests that Hippolytus does not offer a summary of the entire Basileidean system. In other respects we have only internal evidence to suggest

[35] See Hort's discussion of the problem in the *Dictionary of Christian Biography* vol. 1. pp. 268-81.
[36] See Grant (1959).

whether the summary omits points necessary to our
understanding of the system or not. The account gives a
general impression of coherence, and in order of exposition
follows a chronological system starting from before creation
and recounting events up to the final restoration (*apokatastasis*)
which leaves the world in a state of eternal bliss. At the end of
the account is an item added as an afterthought, 7.27.7, which
explains the nature of the 'gospel' and the life of Jesus; this
alone is out of the chronological sequence. Hippolytus
introduces it with a claim that he aims to leave nothing out;
while it is clear that it cannot be literally true that nothing of
Basileides' doctrine is left out, the aim seems to be that
everything that is fundamental to a basic understanding of his
tenets is included, and for this his position on the life of Christ
and what was meant by gospel, both of which play an
important rôle in the soteriology outlined in the preceding
account, are relevant. How closely Hippolytus adheres to a
Basileidean text in constructing this summary is not clear.

There is no systematic correspondence between the
accounts of Aristotle and Basileides, such that they could be
put in parallel while maintaining the order in the text. There is
thus no reason to suggest that Hippolytus constructed the
account of Aristotle by systematically going through his
account of Basileides and seeking a parallel for each point in
turn, or vice versa. The relations between the two accounts are
complex and do not simply involve one-to-one correspondence.

(a) Genesis from the non-existent

This is clearly a theme of central importance. A large
proportion of the account of Aristotle is concerned with the
derivation of *ousia* from non-existents. Corresponding with this
are two themes in Basileides: the non-existence of the god who
makes the world seed, and the non-existence of the world seed
from which the world comes to be.

A number of verbal parallels link Basileides' non-existent
god with Aristotle's non-existent *genos*. Both are defined in
apophatic terms:

7.16.1 This animal is not ox, not horse, not man, not god, not any other of those which it is possible to identify in any way whatsoever, but simply animal ...

7.21.1. When therefore there was nothing, not matter, not substance, not insubstantial, not simple, not composite, not beyond mind, not beyond sense, not man, not angel, not god, not any of the things which are named or grasped by sense or thought of ...

Similarly both are described as *oude hen* (not a single thing):

7.16.2. Each of the other animals takes its origin from the simple animal which itself is not a single one of these. (17) But if that animal is not a single one of these, then the subsistence of the things which come to be comes from non-existents, according to Aristotle.

7.20.2. There once was when there was nothing, he says, but even the nothing was not any of the things that are, but plainly and ingenuously without any sophism there was absolutely not a single thing.

The parallel between the Aristotelian *genos* and Basileides' world-seed, on the other hand, is explicitly pointed out by Hippolytus at 7.22.5:

7.22.5. This is the seed, which has within itself all the all-seed, which Aristotle says is the genus cut up into unlimited species, as we cut off from animal the ox, horse, man, while animal itself is non-existent.

Furthermore the all-seed (*panspermia*) is referred to as a heap, as had the *genos* been;[37] both constitute a heap of potentialities. This parallel is also supported by the last sentence of chapter 17, which reads:

But who it is who lays down the substance as the origin of the things which come to be later, we shall say when we come to the proper account of these things.

[37] *Ref.* 7.15.1; 22.5; 22.6; 25.6; 27.5.

Hippolytus appears to suggest that there is some agent who 'lays down' or 'deposits'[38] the *genos* as the origin of things. The most satisfactory explanation of this comment is that it is a reference to the parallel situation in Basileides where it is the non-existent god who 'deposits' the world-seed; in order to complete the parallel, Aristotle too should have an agent responsible for the deposition of the *genos*, and this should be Aristotle's god, a subject which Hippolytus will mention at a later stage.[39] Basileides' god and Aristotle's god are explicitly identified by Hippolytus at *Ref.* 7.21.1. The basis seems to lie in the fact that Aristotle's god was considered non-existent, *Ref.* 7.19.7.

(b) Tripartite divisions

Here again the parallels are complex. The Aristotle account includes a series of tripartite divisions: substance is divided into genus, species and individual (*atomon*) (7.15.1) and then into matter, form, privation (7.19.1); three divisions of the world are listed at 7.19.2 and three divisions of philosophy at 7.19.3. In the Basileides account the divisions are more complicated. At 7.22.7 the threefold 'sonship' is introduced. This does not precisely correspond with a threefold division of the world since none of the sonships is identified with the world but all three eventually rise to the place of the non-existent god. No explicit parallel is made between the three sonships and any of the tripartite divisions in Aristotle.

In terms of cosmic divisions the correspondence is clearer. Basileides' system begins with a basic polarity between the region of the non-existent above and the cosmic seed below. When the second sonship ascends (7.22.10) the Holy Spirit which it used as a 'wing' is left to form the firmament, a barrier between the cosmos and the region of the non-existent

---

[38] *katabeblêtai* is used of Aristotle 'issuing doctrines' at 7.19.8, but this meaning does not make good sense of the context. The term is also used for the depositing of the world-seed by Basileides' non-existent god at 7.21.4 and 7.21.5.

[39] There are a number of problems with this sentence; it is possible that the word order has become confused and should have read: τίς δὲ ὁ ταύτην καταβεβλημένος τὴν ἀρχὴν τῶν γεγονότων, ὕστερον ἐπὶ τὸν οἰκεῖον ἐρχόμενοι τούτων λόγον ἐροῦμεν.

(7.22.14; 7.23.1).[40] The lower region is then divided into two, the ogdoad and the hebdomad, (7.23.3-24.4). Thus we have three divisions, the *huperkosmia* (supramundane) being the region of the non-existent, and the *kosmos* (7.23.1) divided into ogdoad and hebdomad. These three divisions correspond in some respects with those in Aristotle at *Refutatio* 7.19.2. In Basileides the ogdoad is the region above the moon and as in Aristotle is governed by providence (*pronoia*).[41] The hebdomad is the region below the moon which operates by nature (*phusis*).[42] The region of the non-existent is related to Aristotle's outermost section in that the word *huperkosmios* is used for both.[43]

(c) Other parallels

There are two other points on which Basileides is explicitly linked with Aristotle: (1) his use of homonymy, and (2) the analogy between the Aristotelian doctrine of soul and the relation of the archon and his son.

(1). It is not clear from the text how explicit was the reference to homonymy in Hippolytus' source of information on Basileides, and how much is Hippolytus' own inference. The first reference to homonymy at 7.20.4 occurs in what appears to be a comment from Hippolytus:[44]

> For the homonymy of things had caused difficulty and error to the disciples.

However, it is not certain that Basileides' concern was with homonymy as such, since he begins with a point concerning the non-existent which is beyond any name (7.20.3) and goes on to say:

[40] This scheme forms a tripartite structure of *huperkosmia*, firmament and *kosmos*. Cf. 7.23.2.

[41] *Ref.* 7.24.3.

[42] *Ref.* 7.24.5.

[43] *Ref.* 7.19.3; 7.23.1.

[44] *phêsin* does not occur in this sentence although it occurs in each of the preceding seven sentences; that is every sentence from the beginning of the account of Basileides. On the significance of this usage see above pp. 17-19.

nor indeed are there even enough names for the *kosmos*, because it is divided into such a multitude of parts, but they fall short.

Since this follows a reference to something with no name it is possible to interpret it as suggesting that some things lack a name, rather than sharing a name. The following sentence ought to decide the issue but the text is corrupt. The main part of it reads thus: 'and I cannot, he says, find proper names for all things, but it is necessary to understand with the intellect ... unspeakably the characteristics of the things named.'[45] What is clear is that Basileides specified that he could not find proper names, rather than that he could not find names at all, which might favour the conclusion that homonymy was involved.

(2). The analogy between Aristotle's account of soul and body and Basileides' account of archon and son appears to be entirely Hippolytus' own inference and to be based on no explicit suggestion in Basileides. The comparison depends on a structural similarity: relations of priority and posteriority, superiority in wisdom, one thing being in control of another, one the product of another. There is no superficial resemblance between archon and son and soul and body, as there is, for instance, between Basileides' god and Aristotle's god. Indeed the sense in which the soul is the finished product (*apotelesma*) of the body is very different from the sense in which the son is the product, the offspring, of the archon. In this case we have evidence that Hippolytus is concerned not simply with facile superficial comparisons, but also with the implications of the underlying structure of the Aristotelian soul/body relationship.

The parallel with Basileides governs the presentation of Aristotle to the extent that the main account of Aristotle is selective and includes only points that have some relevance to

---

[45] The words in the gap appear in the manuscript as αὐτοῖς ὀνόματα, and suggestions have been made such as τῇ διανοίᾳ αὐτῇ ἄνευ ὀνομάτων, or οὐ τοῖς ὀνόμασι or ἐκ τῶν αὐτῶν ὀνομάτων; some of these imply a reference to homonymy, some to the namelessness of some things.

the comparison which is to be drawn. The main features are clear: genesis from non-existence, tripartite structures, the doctrine of god and the soul/body relationship; in addition the final comment on the aim of Aristotle's ethics to improve his students may mark a parallel with Basileides' optimistic view of nature.[46] Some of Hippolytus' arguments are severely abbreviated in accordance with what is strictly necessary for the parallel with Basileides.

It appears that Hippolytus is not concerned to force the doctrines into one-to-one correspondence, but rather to indicate more general similarities, concentrating on features which show some important structural pattern. The prevalent attitude of hostility in the account of Aristotle is a feature of this approach, since it enables Hippolytus to interpret Aristotle's system as structurally equivalent to Basileides' system. The fact that the comparison is based, not on identity of doctrines nor on identity of terminology, but on analogous relations between concepts, implies that Hippolytus has not been led to extensive adaptation, or alteration of terminology, in order to make the doctrines correspond. Nevertheless the summary of Aristotle's doctrines is peculiar to his own interests and can only be appreciated in the light of them.

(ii) The implications of this evidence for the traditional approach to fragmented texts

It is the study of a case such as this where we have independent access to the complete texts to which Hippolytus refers which can convey the strongest demonstration that it is methodologically unsound to suppose either that the greatest value of Hippolytus' text lies in the quotations he includes, or that the chief value of examining his context is with regard to occasions when he has deliberately substituted a word of his own in such a quotation, to enable us to restore the original

---

[46] Aristotle, we are told, 'changed his pupils' character from bad to good', *Ref.* 7.19.8. In Basileides everything tends upwards: 'for everything strives upwards from below, from the worse to the better', *Ref.* 7.22.6. The whole world is destined for some degree of eternal bliss (*Ref.* 7.27). It is possible that Hippolytus knew of Basileides' ethics which are correspondingly optimistic; cf. Clement *Strom.* 4.12.599-603P.

quotation to its unadulterated form.

The use of quotations in the account of Aristotle has been briefly examined above (pp. 18-19). While there are grounds for believing that Hippolytus uses *phêsin* with a direct speech construction when he is using words taken from the original text, we cannot simply refer to quotation in the strictest sense. Although the quotation from the *Categories* is given verbatim, in many cases the words are merely cited from memory of a general context. This means that we can gather a good deal of information about Aristotle's work, and even his precise vocabulary, without being able to reconstruct accurate 'fragments' from his writings. It is clear that the general context of the quotations and Hippolytus' interpretation of them can tell us far more about what Aristotle meant than any genuine 'fragments' of Aristotle abstracted from their context.

A similar conclusion emerges from the other points on which Hippolytus refers to Aristotle's own words. The information given at 7.18.2 amounts to a close paraphrase of a sentence from the *Categories*, although not given as direct speech; the word used to introduce it is missing in the manuscript. Hippolytus' text reads:

7.18.2. Aristotle (calls) this primarily, most of all and most properly (substance), that which is neither said of a substrate nor in a substrate.

Categories 2a11 reads:

Substance most properly and primarily and most of all so called is that which is neither said of a substrate nor in any substrate.

Again both the sense and the terminology are entirely accurate although the word order has been slightly altered and 'any' (*tini*) omitted in Hippolytus' text. In the absence of the text of the *Categories*, however, it would be impossible to tell how much of the sentence was quotation.

The following sentence is also instructive in this respect. It includes the word *legei*, referring to Aristotle, but it becomes clear that this signifies 'he means' rather than 'he says', and that the sentence is Hippolytus' exposition of what Aristotle means by the term 'of a substrate'. The words 'as I said' refer back to a piece of Hippolytus' own exegesis, rather than anything paraphrased from Aristotle, namely the first part of chapter 16.[47] With regard to the identification of 'genuine fragments' of an author both these features are warnings to avoid. However, in this particular case it would be a mistake to dismiss the sentence as uninformative since the account of Aristotle is faultless. Where Hippolytus illustrates 'of a substrate' with the example of the *genos* Aristotle illustrates it with the example of the *eidos*,[48] but Hippolytus is, of course, right that the *genos* is an equally good example which Aristotle could have used in this context,[49] and we are by no means misled by the substitution of this example, nor is there anything in Hippolytus' explanation of the sense in which the *genos* is 'said of a substrate' of its species which could be criticised as seriously misrepresenting Aristotle.

The insistence on the fact that the *genos*, animal, applies to all the species similarly (*Ref.* 7.18.3) is curious. This point is not made as such in Aristotle; Aristotle does point out that each species is equally much substance,[50] and it may be from this that Hippolytus has reached the unconnected but undoubtedly correct conclusion that 'animal' applies equally to all its species.[51] On the other hand Hippolytus proceeds to the important point, which figures prominently in Aristotle, that the definition of what is said of a substrate applies to its substrates. This is what characterises the *kath'hupokeimenou* and what distinguishes it from the *en hupokeimenôi* in which the definition is never predicated of the subject.[52] It does indeed

---

[47] In general it appears that verbs in the first person refer to passages that are Hippolytus' own work as opposed to quotation or paraphrase from Aristotle. Thus at 7.15.2 'I shall show' refers forward to the beginning of ch. 16 and at 7.18.1 'as I said' refers back to the beginning of ch. 15, and 'we posited' refers again to the beginning of ch. 16. At 7.18.6 'I say' refers back to 7.18.3.

[48] *Categories* 1a20.

[49] See, for example, *Cat.* 3a10ff where both examples are mentioned together; also 2a17ff.

[50] *Cat.* 2b22; cf. also *Cat.* 3a 33-9.

[51] This view is implied by Wendland's reference, p. 193 of his edition. He also cites Seneca *Ep.* 58.9, which does not seem to provide a close parallel.

[52] *Cat.* 2a19-34.

follow from this that each of the species is equally entitled to be called 'animal'. That this is what characterises the *kath' hupokeimenou* justifies Hippolytus in his statement that this is precisely what the *kath' hupokeimenou* is:

> This is what is the *kath' hupokeimenou*, what is one thing but able
> to be said similarly of many things differing in their species.

At 7.19.1 Hippolytus refers to Aristotle's own words by 'is called', indicating that the terminology *genos*, *eidos*, *atomon* and *hylê*, *eidos*, *sterêsis* is Aristotle's own. However, no further information is given about the Aristotelian theories behind the terminology. A similar reference simply to the accuracy of the terminology is implied by 'as he says', at 7.15.1: again it covers the terms *genos*, *eidos* and *atomon* (or arguably only *eidos*) and is uninformative about the reliability of the exegesis in the rest of the passage.

From this examination of the occasions on which Hippolytus quotes Aristotle we may conclude that he is reliable, at least in these cases, in indicating when he is quoting directly and when referring to precise Aristotelian terminology, although it is not always entirely clear what is the exact extent of the quotation nor how precisely it is quoted. However, the amount of information conveyed by these reliable quotations is minimal compared with that conveyed by the extensive paraphrasing and exegesis contained in the rest of Hippolytus' account, and the technical terms would be meaningless apart from the explanation provided for them. Hence it becomes clear that the significant question is not whether a particular word or phrase is a genuine quotation from Aristotle, but whether the overall purport of a passage is a fair representation of the section of Aristotle it portrays. It is true to say that we could not reconstruct the smallest part of Aristotle's *Categories* from the quotations in Hippolytus, but we could reconstruct some of the implications of the first five chapters from Hippolytus' own account of the theory. The main sections in which Hippolytus explains the Aristotelian doctrine, although not simply paraphrase, are faithful to the general substance of Aristotle's own work.

There are, however, problems. While it is true that some

sections of Hippolytus' account give a straightforward and faithful interpretation of the Aristotelian material on which they are based, nevertheless some of his comments appear surprising, and indeed the final picture which he succeeds in conveying is highly tendentious and unorthodox as an interpretation of Aristotle.

On the first score consider, for example, his comment that Aristotle's god is 'the cause of all these good things', *Ref.* 7.19.6. It might appear at first sight that Hippolytus means to imply that Aristotle's god was a creator, which would be significantly misleading. But this is surely not what Hippolytus is saying, as is clear from a simple observation of the parallel which is being drawn with Basileides' god. Basileides' god is precisely not the creator, since creation is the work of the first and second archons (*Ref.* 7.23.7 and 7.24.5), but he is in a sense the first cause of the world in that it is he who deposits a 'seed' (7.21.2-5). Hippolytus does not say that Aristotle's god is a creator or demiurge, but specifically that he is a cause, *aitios*. As first mover Aristotle's god clearly is some sort of cause of things, and Hippolytus' claim may be more precisely that he is a cause of their goodness. In this he is quite correct, since Aristotle's god is the final cause and responsible for the teleological nature of the world.

A second example might be the statement that the soul, in Aristotle's view, is the *apotelesma* of the body, *Ref.* 7.24.2. The extent to which this might be potentially misleading depends on how we understand *apotelesma*, which admittedly is not an Aristotelian term. To suggest that the soul is a separate product, a created object produced by the body, would certainly be unhelpful as an account of the Aristotelian doctrine, and the comparison with the son produced by the archon might be taken to imply that this was the intention. On the other hand there are ways of understanding Hippolytus' phrase *ergon kai apotelesma* which would be faithful to Aristotle's notion of actuality, *entelecheia*. *Ergon* may be the work or function and *apotelesma* the completion or fulfilment or perfect activity. These would be justifiable terms to describe the actuality of the body.

The second example is perhaps more problematic than the first owing to the ambiguity of the terms, but in both a careful analysis of the correspondence required by the parallel with Basileides defuses some of the problems. Only if it is assumed that the relationship between soul and body is supposed to be identical to that between Basileides' archon and his son are we led to read the statement about the Aristotelian doctrine in a misleading way. Once it is recognised that the parallel lies in the structure of the relationship, that the soul is in some sense posterior to the body as actuality to potentiality, and is also superior in that respect, as the son is posterior and superior to the archon in a different sense, the temptation to understand *apotelesma* as a separate product vanishes, although it is clear that Hippolytus himself is making use of the ambiguity.

In all these cases we have indeed an interpretation of Aristotle, and it may often be an interpretation which does not precisely correspond with our own understanding of Aristotle's text, but none the less it is usually a justifiable reading of the text. While we cannot expect to find an uncontroversial account of Aristotle's views, we do find a strongly coloured but productive interpretation.

This is likewise the case on the second score in which the unorthodoxy of the overall account arises from the fact that much of it is taken up with argument to demonstrate that Aristotle's theory leads to certain absurd conclusions. Again, however, it seems clear that a careful reading of Hippolytus' text would recognise the features characteristic of argument rather than paraphrase or report. There could be little doubt that the passage at ch. 17 is urging an interpretation of Aristotle that is not the normal one; the structure becomes that of logical argument, based on a condition: if the 'animal' is not any one of these things, we are told (and Hippolytus has just implied that Aristotle intends precisely this), then it is the case that things come to be from what is not according to Aristotle. This is clearly an argument from something that Aristotle says to something that he ought logically to admit as a result, and the implication is naturally that Aristotle did not himself make any statement of the conclusion, and probably would have been unwilling to do so. Exactly the same structure appears again at 18.6: if neither the 'animal' (the genus), nor the differentiae can come to be in its own right, and the individuals are made up of these two (and Aristotle says both these, as Hippolytus has explained), then substance is made up of things that are not, and not by composition of other existent things. But indeed if what is primarily and most of all substance consists of these things (as we have been told that Aristotle says), then it is made of things that are not, according to Aristotle.

In these two cases a careful examination of Hippolytus' argument could leave little doubt that we are dealing with interpretation in respect of what the author believes to be the logical implications of Aristotle's doctrines, and moreover that the interpretation is hostile to Aristotle since it results in a conclusion that is clearly supposed to be absurd in itself and probably also unacceptable to Aristotle. The situation is similarly clear in the case of the criticisms of the definitions of soul and god, 19.5-7. It is readily apparent that Hippolytus offers first an interpreter's judgment on the difficulty of understanding Aristotle's meaning (19.5):

> His work *De Anima* is obscure – in three whole volumes it is impossible to say clearly what Aristotle thinks about the soul. It is easy to repeat what the definition that he gives of the soul is, but what is signified by the definition it is impossible to find out.

We are then clearly given Aristotle's own formula (19.6):

> For the soul is, he says, the 'actuality of a natural organic body'.

Given the context, it is unlikely that there would be much doubt that we then return to the comments of the interpreter:

> and what that is demands much discussion and great scholarly inquiry.

A very similar pattern appears in the account of the definition of god, which follows immediately:

> but god, the cause of all these good things, is even more difficult to understand than the soul, even by studying a much longer treatise.

This is the interpreter's judgment and the comment continues almost exactly as in the case of the soul (19.7):

> The definition which Aristotle gives for god is not difficult to discover, but it is impossible to think of.

We are then explicitly given Aristotle's formula:

> For it is thought, he says, of thought ...

and then we return to the interpreter's judgment on the doctrine:

> ... which is altogether non-existent.

There is nothing specific in this last phrase to indicate that it is not a continuation of the quotation or at least a paraphrase of something said by Aristotle. It is only in virtue of our understanding of the attitude of the whole account and familiarity with the style of argument used to draw absurd implications from Aristotle's doctrines, as well as by direct comparison with the parallel passage concerning the soul, that we can conclude with some confidence, on the basis of Hippolytus' text alone, that this is the commentator's criticism and not Aristotle's own doctrine.

The implications of this section on Aristotle are fundamental:

1. There is no justification in this material for the assumption that the quotations included by the doxographer can form an adequate basis from which to reconstruct the original text.

2. The claim that Hippolytus' chief value as a doxographer lies in the words he quotes from the philosophers is unfounded.

3. When Hippolytus indicates that he is quoting the words used by the philosopher he gives the accurate terminology and he does not substitute his own terms to suit his purpose.

4. The vast majority of the secondary material included by Hippolytus is based on a close and intelligent reading of Aristotle's text and represents a well-supported interpretation

of it.

5. Such passages as are less orthodox inferences concerning the consequences of Aristotle's theories are readily apparent from the style of argument used by Hippolytus.

It is clear that this account of Aristotle requires careful handling; but what is required is not that we concentrate on making sense of the quotations, with as little reference to the interpretation offered by Hippolytus as possible, nor that we concentrate on attempting to 'emend' the quotations fearing the dishonesty of the doxographer. Rather we are required to understand the nature and value of the interpretation, of which the quotations are a relatively insignificant part, learning from it how closely it adheres to a faithful reading of the text and how far it diverges into argument.

(iii) Conclusion

The section on Aristotle, in so far as it is typical of Hippolytus' work in general, suggests that the least fruitful approach to the text is that which seeks to extract fragments and discard the interpretation. Hippolytus' account of Aristotle is not rich in 'fragments', nor are those which it does include informative or easily detached from the context. On the other hand Hippolytus' interpretation is rich, both in terms of the extent to which it paraphrases and reports much more extensive passages of Aristotle's text, and also in its exegesis. This exegesis is indeed hostile, unorthodox and perhaps even biased. It certainly represents an interest of its own, but this must be true of any interpretation; this does not prevent the interpretation being valuable or interesting.

In the case of Hippolytus' interpretation of Aristotle there can be little doubt that it merits attention. He offers a relatively extended discussion of the doctrine of substance, which appears to be based on reflection on the problems raised by Aristotle in the *Categories* and *Metaphysics*, as we have seen. The way in which a thinker of the second century approaches these texts, and the points on which he takes issue with Aristotle, is itself of interest; his discussion touches on the same points as modern discussions of the same issues. It is clear that his text would be valuable as a discussion of these issues if we were unable to consult the original texts. The quotations themselves would not be sufficient to indicate the importance or interest of these topics in the Aristotelian corpus, since Hippolytus quotes few texts by comparison with the range of which he shows knowledge. It is his commentary and his criticisms, based on a wider knowledge of Aristotle's works, which would provide some indication of the major issues raised in *Metaphysics* Z and Λ and in the *Physics*, and the central place which they occupied in Aristotelian doctrine.

Naturally we are aware, in dealing with Hippolytus' reading of Aristotle, that it is a reading peculiar to him and governed by his concern with the refutation of Basileides. This does not, however, automatically vitiate his interpretation nor make it uninteresting or unimportant. In particular it does not make Hippolytus' reading irrelevant in those cases where we depend upon him for our knowledge of a text of which he knew more than he quotes.

2. Simon Magus

At the beginning of book 6 of the *Refutatio* Hippolytus gives an account of the life and doctrines of Simon Magus, who became identified as the founder of gnosticism and the arch-enemy of the early church. As a result of this he became a figure of legend and the subject of a grandiose mythology, such as the elaborate tales found in the Clementine *Homilies* and *Recognitions*. Hippolytus' report includes some biographical material which belongs in the same tradition as Justin Martyr, Irenaeus and the Clementine works, but it also claims to have access to the contents of a work written by Simon, called the *Apophasis Megalê* (probably meaning 'Great Revelation'), which is not quoted by any other surviving source.

Controversy has raged over the accuracy of Hippolytus' account of the *Apophasis Megalê*. This issue is only of minor relevance to us here: it bears upon the question of the meaning of *phêsin* (he says);[1] but a study of this usage elsewhere is more likely to influence our conclusions about the accuracy of the report on the *Apophasis Megalê* than vice versa; it includes a few references to Greek philosophy and the question of the source of these is of some interest, but they are of minor importance by comparison with Hippolytus' material elsewhere; the main issue concerns Hippolytus' handling of the text he quotes and the extent of his adaptation and interpretation of the material, but again it is a comparison with other passages that will yield conclusions about this section of the work and not vice versa. For these reasons some suggestions about the handling of the *Apophasis Megalê* are set out in Appendix B.

As a test case from which we may derive conclusive evidence

---

[1] See above pp. 17-19.

about Hippolytus' handling of material, the section on the Life of Simon Magus is more productive. These biographical sections which come immediately before and after the report on the *Apophasis Megalê* suggest the extent to which the material in that report is likely to have been reworked, and give us an insight valuable for its bearing on other sections of the *Refutatio*.

At the start of book 6 of the *Refutatio* Hippolytus introduces Simon Magus (*Ref.* 6.7). The reference to Simon's village of origin in Samaria is also found in Justin Martyr (*Apol.* 1.26.2), probably our earliest source, but is not found in Irenaeus' account. Justin knows of Simon as someone who tried to make himself a god, the feature which is clearly foremost in Hippolytus' mind when he introduces as parallel the story of Apsethos, *Ref.* 6.7-8. However, Justin is preoccupied with Simon's success in convincing the people of the city of Rome that he was a god, so much so that (as Justin seems to have believed) they set up a statue to him there. Hippolytus does not succumb to this apparent error (he was perhaps more familiar with Rome) despite the fact that it also appears in Irenaeus.[2] Hippolytus has only a passing reference to Simon's visit to Rome, right at the end of his account, 6.20.2.

So much is material common to the biographical tradition concerning Simon. On the other hand Hippolytus includes a considerable quantity of material in his first chapter (*Ref.* 6.7) which is not common knowledge. He claims that he will demonstrate that the later heretics said the same thing as Simon, a promise which he ultimately carries out at 6.20.4 by suggesting an equation between Simon's six 'roots' and Valentinus' six aeons. Although Simon was regularly said to be the originator of all heresy (a point made three times by Irenaeus, for example) no extant writer other than Hippolytus tries to demonstrate any detailed affinity with later heresy beyond the fact that Simon's creator was inferior to his supreme deity. Hippolytus' demonstration of the relationship between Valentinus and Simon is original to him and depends

[2] *Haer.* 1.23.1 (Text 5, below p.77).

upon material from the *Apophasis Megalê*, since Simon's six 'roots' are known only from there.

Chapter 7 continues with a reference to Simon's magical practices. This time Hippolytus refers us back to his own account of magic, presumably in the section on magic in book 4, but the precise reference to Thrasymedes must be lost in the lacuna before chapter 28. Again we have an example of Hippolytus using his own inference to connect what information he has on Simon's magical practices with information he had gathered elsewhere.

These examples demonstrate that Hippolytus has not just strung together excerpts from the work of others, but is concerned with structural continuity within his own work: he takes the familiar topoi from the biographical tradition concerning Simon, his status as the originator of heresy and his magic, and he employs them in the context of his own work, relating them to material he has included earlier and will include in due course.

A similar procedure can be identified in the use of the story of Apsethos, introduced at the end of chapter 7. Here the theme taken from the traditional life of Simon is his claim to be a god, but Hippolytus has developed this extensively on lines of his own. The story of Apsethos is nowhere else found associated with Simon Magus, and Hippolytus' use of it serves not merely as illustration but fits in with his scheme in the *Refutatio*: every idea thought of by a heretic has been thought of, and thought much better, by a pagan thinker before him; Simon tried to make himself a god, but Apsethos had already made a much more tasteful attempt before him, *Ref.* 6.7.2. It transpires, however, that this is not the only feature of the story that forms a parallel with that of Simon, and a commentary on it.

In chapter 8 Hippolytus gives the whole story of Apsethos. Like Simon, Apsethos deceived many into thinking he was a god, but they were 'foolish Libyans', and Apsethos was unable to deceive the Greeks. So too it can only be the foolish who are taken in by Simon's claims (6.18.1), and anyone with any sense sees through it. Indeed it is the Greeks, that is the knowledge of Greek philosophy, who provide the clue to the demonstration of Simon's deceit, on Hippolytus' scheme.

Simon's disciples are mere parrots taught to chant empty phrases in honour of Simon, as indeed they do at 6.20.1. Simon regards the palinode of Stesichorus as being a recognition of the truth of Simon's claims and of the divinity of his companion called Helen: Stesichorus becomes a disciple of Simon (6.19.3). The true palinode (6.8.4), however, will come when Simon's disciples, his parrots, are taught to recant and reveal the falsity of Simon's claims: it is Simon who is dishonouring the memory of Helen of Troy.

The story of Apsethos fits neatly into the context for which Hippolytus selects it, but his originality is perhaps not only in the selection of the right story; we possess three other versions of approximately this story:

Text 1. Maximus of Tyre, 29.4:

And in Libya a Libyan man, Psapho by name, a lover of happiness not, by Zeus, happiness of the mean sort or this mundane sort – but he wished to be thought to be a god. Therefore taking a great number of singing birds, he taught the birds to chant 'Great god Psapho'; and he released the birds again to the mountains. And they themselves sang, and the other birds also when they had become accustomed to the sound. And the Libyans, thinking that the utterance was divine, offered sacrifice to Psapho, and for them he was a god appointed by the birds.

Text 2. Aelian *Var. Hist.* 14.30:

Hanno the Carthaginian, on account of his fastidiousness, was not content to remain within the bounds of mortal men, but thought he would spread abroad reports about himself better than the nature which he had received as his lot. Purchasing a great many birds of the singing variety he reared them in darkness, teaching them one lesson – to say 'Hanno is god'. When they had heard this one phrase and mastered it, he let them go to different places, supposing that the song about himself would pour forth through the birds. But the birds, once allowed to take wing and gaining their freedom and coming to their natural habits, sang their own songs and made bird noises, saying good bye and good riddance to Hanno and the lessons learnt in their bondage.

Text 3. Schol. to Dio Chrysostom, *Orat.* 1.14.

Such a thing is recorded to have been engineered by means of parrots also in the case of Apsephas king of the Libyans, the parrots flying and crying 'Apsephas is god'.

These differ considerably in details and vocabulary from the version found in Hippolytus,[3] but much more significant is the fact that none of these versions has the same pattern to the story as does Hippolytus. (1) and (3) both suggest that the villain was ultimately successful in establishing himself as a god and suffered no subsequent downfall; (2) on the other hand is a more sophisticated version, undercut by the final anticlimax: instead of turning out successful the trick fell flat because the birds never uttered a word after they were set free. None of these versions has Hippolytus' cunning Greek who turned the trick back on itself and caused the villain's downfall after an initial success with the gullible Libyans. It is possible that Hippolytus found the tale in the form in which he tells it, but it is just as likely that he has added the sophistication himself to fit the moral which he wants to draw for Simon Magus.[4]

[3] The name of the villain is Psaphon in (1) and Apsephas in (3). In (2) he has become Hanno the Carthaginian. In (1) and (2) the birds he uses are singing birds instead of the parrots of (3) and Hippolytus. Of the three, the brief scholion (3) seems to be the only one that could be immediately related to Hippolytus: Apsephas is closer to Apsethos than either of the other two names, and the phrase taught to the birds, *Apsephas theos estin*, corresponds with *Apsethos theos estin* in Hippolytus, as opposed to *megas theos Psaphôn* in (1) and *theos estin Annôn* in (2). In (3) Apsephas has become king of the Libyans, doubtless because the scholiast is commenting (with a certain lack of understanding, one feels) on a passage of Dio on true kingship, though the presence of Hanno the Carthaginian in (2) may represent a similar trend. (3) may have been quoted from memory, and indeed the scholiast could have encountered the story directly or indirectly from Hippolytus. One sentence of (1), 'And the Libyans, thinking that the utterance was divine, offered sacrifice to Psapho', echoes one in Hippolytus, 'For the foolish Libyans offered sacrifice to him, in the belief that they were placing their trust in a voice from heaven above.'

[4] The hand of a Christian in the transmission of Hippolytus' story can be detected in the sentence which reads 'As the birds flew off their voice went out into all Libya and their words reached the land of Greece'. This is reminiscent of the Septuagint version of Psalm 18.5, 'Their voice is gone out

These introductory chapters have certainly not been constructed mechanically from unaltered excerpts from a source work; the indications are that the composition as it stands represents Hippolytus' own creation: he has studied the material on Simon Magus and drawn his own conclusions, and is hence able to enlarge upon it as required.

A similar conclusion emerges from a study of his work on the story of Simon and Helen which he includes after the *Apophasis* report, 6.19-20. This story is another theme from the tradition concerning Simon Magus, and most of the material in this section is taken over from Irenaeus;[5] the adherence is so close that Hippolytus is used to provide the otherwise lost Greek text of Irenaeus. However the relationship between Irenaeus and Hippolytus is by no means simple.

Text 4. Hippolytus *Ref.* 6.19-20.

19. ταῦτα μὲν οὖν ὁ Σιμων ἐφευρῶν οὐ μόνον τὰ Μωσέως κακοτεχν-
ήσας εἰς ὃ ἐβούλετο μεθηρμήνευσεν, ἀλλὰ καὶ τὰ των ποιητῶν.
καὶ γὰρ τὸν δούρειον ἵππον ἀλληγορεῖ καὶ τὴν Ἑλένην ἅμα τῃ
λαμπάδι καὶ ἄλλα πλεῖστα ὅσα μετάγ(ων τά) τε αὐτοῦ καὶ τῆς
ἐπινοίας πλαστολογεῖ. εἰπέ τε (12) **ταύτην τὸ πρόβατον τὸ πεπλανημένον,** ἥτις (7)**ἀεὶ καταγινομένη ἐν γυναιξὶν** ἐτάρασσε τὰς
ἐν κόσμῳ δυνάμεις διὰ τὸ ἀνυπέρβλητον αὐτῆς κάλλος· (9) **ὅθεν
καὶ ὁ Τρωϊκὸς πόλεμος δι' αὐτὴν γεγένηται.** (8) ἐν γὰρ τῇ κατ'
ἐκεῖνον καιρὸν γενομένῃ Ἑλένῃ ἐνῴκησεν [ἐν αὐτῇ] ἡ ἐπίνοια,
καὶ οὕτως πασῶν ἐπιδικαζομένων αὐτῆς τῶν ἐξουσιῶν, στάσις καὶ
πόλεμος ἐπανέστη ἐν οἷς ἐφάνη ἔθνεσιν. (10) **οὕτως γοῦν τὸν
Στησίχορον διὰ τῶν ἐπῶν λοιδορήσαντα αὐτὴν τὰς ὄψεις τυφλωθῆναι·
αὖθις δὲ μεταμεληθέντος αὐτοῦ καὶ γράψαντος τὰς παλινῳδίας ἐν
αἷς ὕμνησεν αὐτήν, ἀναβλέψαι·** μετενσωματουμένην δὲ ὑπὸ (6)

---

into all the earth and their words to the ends of the world'. The hand is most likely that of Hippolytus, of whose liking for puns and play on words this is typical, but it is possible that he has simply derived the whole story from another anti-heretical context now lost.

[5] At the beginning of chapter 19 Hippolytus refers to the two incidents in the Trojan war used by Simon as examples of Helen's previous incarnation. These two incidents are also mentioned by Epiphanius 21.3. For the use of episodes from the Trojan war to prove previous incarnations compare Pythagoras' previous incarnation as Euphorbus (DK 14.8).

τῶν ἀγγέλων καὶ τῶν κάτω ἐξουσιῶν, οἳ καὶ τὸν κόσμον, φησίν,
ἐποίησαν, (4) ὕστερον ἐπὶ τέγους (16) ἐν Τύρῳ τῆς Φοινίκης
πόλει στῆναι, ᾗ κατελθὼν εὗρεν. (13) ἐπὶ γὰρ τὴν ταύτης πρώτην
ζήτησιν ἔφη παραγεγονέναι, ὅπως ῥύσηται αὐτὴν τῶν δεσμῶν· ἣν
λυτρωσάμενος (5) ἅμα ἑαυτῷ περιῆγε, φάσκων (12) τοῦτο εἶναι τὸ
ἀπολωλὸς πρόβατον, (2) ἑαυτὸν δὲ λέγων τὴν ὑπὲρ πάντα δύναμιν
εἶναι. ὁ δὲ ψυχρὸς ἐρασθεὶς τοῦ γυναίου τούτου, ῾Ελένης καλουμένης, ὠνησάμενος εἶχε, καὶ τοὺς μαθητὰς αἰδούμενος τοῦτον τὸν
μῦθον ἔπλασεν. οἱ δὲ αὖθις μιμηταὶ τοῦ πλάνου καὶ Σίμωνος μάγου
γινόμενοι τὰ ὅμοια δρῶσιν, ἀλογίστως φάσκοντες δεῖν μίγνυσθαι,
λέγοντες· πᾶσα γῆ γῆ, καὶ οὐ διαφέρει ποῦ τις σπείρει, πλὴν ἵνα
σπείρῃ, ἀλλὰ καὶ μακαρίζουσιν ἑαυτοὺς ἐπὶ τῇ (ξένῃ) μίξει,
ταύτην εἶναι λέγοντες τὴν τελείαν ἀγάπην, καὶ τὸ ἅγιος ἁγίων...
.λλη..ος ἁγιασθήσεται· οὐ γὰρ μὴ κρατεῖσθαι αὐτοὺς ἔτι τινὶ
νομιζομένῳ κακῷ, λελύτρωνται γάρ. τὴν δὲ ῾Ελένην λυτρωσάμενος
(14) οὕτως τοῖς ἀνθρώποις σωτηρίαν παρέσχε διὰ τῆς ἰδίας ἐπιγνώσεως. κακῶς γὰρ διοικούντων τῶν ἀγγέλων τὸν κόσμον διὰ τὸ φιλαρχεῖν αὐτούς, εἰς ἐπανόρθωσιν ἐληλυθέναι αὐτὸν ἔφη μεταμορφούμενον
καὶ ἐξομοιούμενον ταῖς ἀρχαῖς καὶ ταῖς ἐξουσίαις καὶ τοῖς ἀγγελ-
οις, ὡς καὶ ἄνθρωπον φαίνεσθαι αὐτὸν μὴ ὄντα ἄνθρωπον, καὶ παθεῖν
δὲ ἐν τῇ ᾿Ιουδαίᾳ [καὶ] δεδοκηκέναι μὴ πεπονθότα, ἀλλὰ (1)
φανέντα ᾿Ιουδαίοις μὲν ὡς υἱόν, ἐν δὲ τῇ Σαμαρείᾳ ὡς πατέρα, ἐν
δὲ τοῖς λοιποῖς ἔθνεσιν ὡς πνεῦμα ἅγιον, (3) ὑπομένειν δὲ αὐτὸν
καλεῖσθαι οἵῳ ἂν ὀνόματι καλεῖν βούλωνται οἱ ἄνθρωποι. (15) τοὺς
δὲ προφήτας ἀπὸ τῶν κοσμοποιῶν ἀγγέλων ἐμπνευσθέντας εἰρηκέναι
τὰς προφητείας· διὸ μὴ φροντίζειν αὐτῶν τοὺς εἰς τὸν Σίμωνα καὶ
τὴν ῾Ελένην πεπιστευκότας ἕως νῦν, πράσσειν τε ὅσα βούλονται ὡς
ἐλευθέρους· κατὰ γὰρ τὴν αὐτοῦ χάριν σῴζεσθαι αὐτοὺς φάσκουσι.
(16) μηδένα γὰρ εἶναι αἴτιον δίκης εἰ πράξει τις κακῶς· οὐ γὰρ
ἐστι φύσει κακὸν ἀλλὰ θέσει, ἔθεντο γάρ, φησίν, οἱ ἄγγελοι οἱ
τὸν κόσμον ποιήσαντες ὅσα ἐβούλοντο, διὰ τῶν τοιούτων λόγων
δουλοῦν νομίζοντες τοὺς αὐτῶν ἀκούοντας. φθίσειν δὲ αὖθις λέγουσι τὸν κόσμον ἐπὶ λυτρώσει τῶν ἰδίων ἀνθρώπων.

20. (17) οἱ οὖν τούτου μαθηταὶ μαγείας ἐπιτελοῦσι καὶ ἐπαοιδὰς
φίλτρα τε καὶ ἀγώγιμα καὶ τοὺς λεγομένους ὀνειροπόμπους δαίμονας
ἐπιπέμπουσι πρὸς τὸ ταράσσειν οὓς βούλονται· ἀλλὰ καὶ παρέδρους
τοὺς λεγομένους ἀσκοῦσιν, εἰκόνα τε τοῦ Σίμωνος ἔχουσιν εἰς Διὸς
μορφήν, καὶ τῆς ῾Ελένης ἐν μορφῇ ᾿Αθηνᾶς, καὶ ταύτας προσκυνοῦσι,

τὸν μὲν καλοῦντες κύριον, τὴν δὲ κυρίαν. εἰ δέ τις ὀνόματι καλέσει παρ᾽ αὐτοῖς ἰδὼν τὰς εἰκόνας ἢ Σίμωνος ἢ Ἑλένης, ἀπόβλητος
γίνεται, ὡς ἀγνοῶν τὰ μυστήρια. οὗτος ὁ Σίμων πολλοὺς πλανῶν ἐν
τῇ Σαμαρείᾳ μαγείαις ὑπὸ τῶν ἀποστόλων ἠλέγχθη, καὶ ἐπάρατος
γενόμενος, καθὼς ἐν ταῖς Πράξεσι γέγραπται, ὕστερον ἀπευδοκήσας
ταὐτὰ ἐπεχείρησεν· ἕως καὶ τῆς Ῥώμης ἐπιδημήσας ἀντέπεσε τοῖς
ἀποστόλοις· πρὸς ὃν πολλὰ Πέτρος ἀντικατέστη μαγείαις πλανῶντα
πολλούς. οὗτος ἐπὶ τέλει ἐλθὼν ἐν τ...τῃ, ὑπὸ πλάτανον καθεζόμενος ἐδίδασκε. καὶ δὴ λοιπὸν ἐγγὺς τοῦ ἐλέγχεσθαι γινόμενος
διὰ τὸ ἐγχρονίζειν, ἔφη, ὅτι εἰ χωσθείη ζῶν, ἀναστήσεται τῇ
τρίτῃ ἡμέρᾳ. καὶ δὴ τάφρον κελεύσας ὀρυγῆναι ὑπὸ τῶν μαθητῶν
ἐκέλευσε χωσθῆναι. οἱ μὲν οὖν τὸ προσταχθὲν ἐποίησαν, ὁ δὲ
ἀπέμεινεν ἕως νῦν· οὐ γὰρ ἦν ὁ Χριστός. οὗτος δὴ καὶ ὁ κατὰ
τὸν Σίμωνα μῦθος, ἀφ᾽ οὗ Οὐαλεντῖνος τὰς ἀφορμὰς λαβὼν ἄλλοις
ὀνόμασι καλεῖ. ὁ γὰρ Νοῦς καὶ ἡ Ἀλήθεια καὶ Λόγος καὶ Ζωὴ
καὶ Ἄνθρωπος καὶ Ἐκκλησία, οἱ Οὐαλεντίνου αἰῶνες, ὁμολογουμένως
εἰσὶν αἱ Σίμωνος ἐξ ῥίζαι, Νοῦς Ἐπίνοια Φωνὴ Ὄνομα Λογισμὸς καὶ
Ἐνθύμησις. ἀλλ᾽ ἐπεὶ ἱκανῶς ἡμῖν δοκεῖ ἐκτεθεῖσθαι τὴν Σίμωνος
μυθοποιΐαν, ἴδωμεν τί λέγει καὶ Οὐαλεντῖνος.

Inventing these things, not only did Simon abuse the words of
Moses and reinterpret them to what he wanted, but also the
words of the poets. For he also allegorises the wooden horse
and Helen with the lamp and many other things which he
adapts, and fabricates things about himself and the *Epinoia*
(Thought). And he says that (*12*) *she is the stray sheep* who (*7*) *has
always dwelt in women* and harassed the powers in the world
because of her unsurpassed beauty; (*9*) *for which reason the Trojan
war itself came about because of her.* (*8*) *For the Epinoia was dwelling
in the Helen that lived at that time,* and thus since all the powers
were suing for her, dispute and war arose in the nations in
which she appeared. (*10*) *Thus it was that Stesichorus who ridiculed
her in his poetry had his eyes blinded; but when he repented and wrote the
palinodes in which he celebrated her, his eyes were opened. But she was
reincarnated (*6*) *by the angels and the powers below, who also made the
world,* he says, (*4*) *and subsequently she was stationed in a brothel* (*11*)
in the city of Tyre in Phoenicia, where he found her when he came
there. (*13*) *For he came there for the purpose of seeking her first of all, he
said, so that he might release her from her bonds;* so he ransomed her
(*15*) *and took her round with him,* proclaiming that (*12*) *this was the
lost sheep,* (*2*) *and saying that he himself was the power over all things.*
But the weak man was taken by lust for this feeble woman,

named Helen, and bought her to have her, and being ashamed in front of his disciples he made up this story. But they again became imitators of the error and of Simon Magus and do the same things, proclaiming that one should have intercourse at random, saying: all earth is earth and it makes no difference where one sows the seed, except that one should sow the seed, but they also bless themselves in their promiscuous intercourse, saying that this is perfect love and the holy of holies ... For they are not adversely affected by anything considered evil any more, for they have been redeemed.

By redeeming Helen *(14) he thus granted salvation to mankind by means of his own recognition. For since the angels were managing the world badly because they desired supremacy, he said that he himself had come for the restoration of the world, changing his form and becoming assimilated to the principalities and powers and angels, so that he appeared as man though he was not man, and was thought to suffer in Judaea though he did not suffer, but (1) he appeared to the Jews as son, but in Samaria as Father, and in the rest of the nations as Holy Spirit, (3) but he submits to being called by whatever name men wish to call him. (15) The prophets spoke their prophecies under the inspiration of the angels who made the world; for this reason those who believe in Simon and Helen do not heed the prophets even now, and they act as they wish like free men; for they claim that they are saved by his grace. (16) There is no reason for punishment if one acts wickedly; for it is not wicked by nature but by ordinance. For the angels who made the world ordained what they liked, believing that by means of such words they could enslave those who paid attention to them. And they say that the world will pass away again at the time of the redemption of their own men.*

20. *(17) This man's disciples perform magic and spells and philtres and love-charms and they send out the* daimones *called dream-bringers to trouble whom they wish. And they exercise what are called familiar spirits, and they have an image of Simon in the form of Zeus and of Helen in the form of Athena, and they worship these,* calling the one Lord and the other Lady. And if anyone, on seeing the images, calls either that of Simon or that of Helen by name, he becomes an outcast as being ignorant of the mysteries.

This man Simon led many astray by magic in Samaria and was refuted by the apostles, and became accursed, as it is written in Acts, and subsequently having despaired he put his hand to the same practices. Until he came to Rome and came into conflict with the Apostles; and Peter stood out against him when he was leading many astray with magic. Finally he came to [Gitta?] and sat down under a plane tree and taught. And at last when he was coming near to his refutation because of the long delay he said that if he was buried alive he would rise again on the third day. And indeed he ordered a grave to be dug and that he be buried in it by his disciples. They therefore did what was commanded, but he remained there to this day; for he was not the Christ. This then is the story told by Simon, and it is from this that Valentinus took his starting points and called them by different names. For *Nous* (Mind) and *Alêtheia* (Truth) and *Logos* (Word) and *Zoe* (Life) and *Anthrôpos* (Man) and *Ecclêsia* (Church), the aeons of Valentinus are agreed to be the six roots of Simon, *Nous* (Mind), *Epinoia*, (Thought), *Phônê* (Speech), *Onoma* (Name), *Logismos* (Reason) and *Enthumêsis* (Inspiration). But since it seems to us that we have sufficiently described the myths fabricated by Simon, let us see what Valentinus says too.

Text 5. Irenaeus *Adv. Haer.* 1.23

1. Simon enim Samarites, magus ille, de quo discipulus et sector Apostolorum Lucas ait: 'Vir quidam autem nomine Simon, qui ante erat in civitate, magicam exercens [artem], et seducens gentem Samaritanorum, dicens se esse aliquem magnum, quem auscultabant a pusillo usque ad magnum, dicentes: Hic est virtus Dei, quae vocatur magna. intuebantur autem eum, propter quod multo tempore magicis suis dementasset eos.' Hic igitur Simon, qui fidem simulavit, putans Apostolos et ipsos sanitates per magicam, et non virtute Dei perficere, et per impositionem manuum Spiritu sancto adimplere credentes Deo per eum, qui ab ipsis evangelizatur Christus Iesus, per maiorem quandam magicam scientiam et hoc suspicans fieri, et offerens pecunias Apostolis, ut acciperet et ipse hanc potestatem quibuscunque velit dandi Spiritum sanctum, audivit a Petro: 'Pecunia tua tecum sit in perditionem, quoniam donum Dei existimasti pecunia possideri: non est tibi pars, neque sors in sermone hoc: cor enim tuum not est rectum coram Deo. in felle enim amaritudinis, et obligatione iniustitiae video te esse.' Et cum adhuc magis non credidisset Deo, et cupidus intendit contendere adversus Apostolos, uti et ipse gloriosus videretur esse, et universam magicam adhuc amplius inscrutans, ita ut in stuporem cogeret multos hominum: quippe cum esset sub Claudio Caesaro, a quo etiam statua honoratus esse dicitus propter magicam. hic igitur a multis quasi Deus glorificatus est, et docuit semetipsum esse (1) **qui inter Iudaeos quidem quasi Filius apparuerit, in Samaria**

autem quasi Pater descenderit, in reliquis vero gentibus quasi Spiritus sanctus adventaverit. (2) esse autem se sublimissimam virtutem, hoc est eum qui sit super omnia Pater, et (3) sustinere vocari se quodcunque eum vocant homines.

2. Simon autem Samaritanus, ex quo universae haereses substiterunt, habet huiusmodi sectae materiam. hic Helenam quandam, quam ipse (4) a Tyro civitate Phoenices quaestuariam cum redemisset, (5) secum circumducebat, dicens hanc esse primam mentis eius conceptionem, matrem omnium, per quam in initio mente concepit angelos facere et archangelos. hanc enim Ennoiam exsilientem ex eo, cognoscentem quae vult pater eius, degredi ad inferiora, et generare (6) angelos et potestates, a quibus et mundum hunc factum dixit. posteaquam autem generavit eos, haec detenta est ab ipsis propter invidiam, quoniam nollent progenies alterius cuiusdam putari esse. ipsum enim se in totum ignoratum ab ipsis: Ennoian autem eius detentam ab iis, quae ab ea emissae essent potestates, et angeli; et omnem contumeliam ab iis passam, uti non recurreret sursum ad patrem, usque adeo ut et in corpore humano includeretur, et per saecula veluti de vase in vas (7) transmigraret in altera muliebra corpora. (8) fuisse autem eam et in illa Helena, (9) propter quam Troianum contractum est bellum; (10) quapropter et Stesichorum per carmina maledicentem eam, orbatum oculis: post deinde poenitentem et scribentem eas, quae vocantur palinodias, in quibus hymnizavit eam, rursus vidisse. transmigrantem autem eam de corpore in corpus, ex eo et semper contumeliam sustinentem, (11) in novissimis etiam in fornico prostitisse: et (12) hanc esse perditam ovem. (13) quapropter et ipsum venisse, uti eam assumeret primam et liberaret eam a vinculis, (14) hominibus autem salutem praestaret per suam agnitionem. cum enim male moderarentur Angeli mundum, quoniam unusquisque eorum concupisceret principatum, ad emendationem venisse rerum, et discendisse eum transfiguratum, et assimilatum Virtutibus, et Potestatibus, et Angelis, ut et in hominibus homo appareret ipse, cum non esset homo; et passum autem in Iudaea putatum, cum non esset passus. (15) prophetas autem a mundi fabricatoribus Angelis inspiratos dixisse prophetias: quapropter nec ulterius curarent eos hi qui in eum et in Helenam eius spem habeant, et ut liberos agere quae velint: secundum enim ipsius gratiam salvari homines, sed non secundum operas iustas. (16) nec enim esse naturaliter operationes iustas, sed ex accidenti; quemadmodum posuerunt qui mundum fecerunt Angeli, per huiusmodi praecepta in servitutem

deducentes homines. quapropter et solvi mundum, et liberari eos qui
sunt eius ab imperio eorum qui mundum fecerunt, repromisit.
3. (17) igitur horum mystici sacerdotes libidinose quidem vivunt,
magias autem perficiunt, quemadmodum potest unusquisque ipsorum.
exorcismis et incantationibus utuntur. amatoria quoque et agogima,
et qui dicuntur paredri et oniropompi, et quaecunque sunt alia perierga
apud eos studiose exercentur. imaginem quoque Simonis habent factam
ad figuram Iovis, et Helenae in figuram Minervae; et has adorant:
habent quoque et vocabulum a principe impiissimae sententiae Simone,
vocati Simoniani, a quibus falsi nominis scientia accepit initia, sicut
ex ipsis assertionibus eorum adest discere.

Simon the Samaritan was that magician of whom the disciple
and follower of the Apostles Luke says: 'but there was a man,
named Simon, who had previously practised magic in the city
and amazed the nation of Samaria, saying that he himself was
somebody great. They all gave heed to him, from the least to
the greatest, saying, "This man is that power of God which is
called Great." And they gave heed to him because for a long
time he had amazed them with his magic.' This Simon
therefore who feigned faith, thinking that the Apostles
themselves also performed their cures by magic and not by the
power of God, and filled those who believed in God, through
the Christ Jesus whom they evangelised, with the Holy Spirit
by the laying on of hands – suspecting that this also was done
through some greater knowledge of magic – and offering
money to the Apostles that he too might receive this power of
giving the holy Spirit to whomsoever he wished – he it was who
heard these words from Peter: 'Your silver perish with you,
because you thought you could obtain the gift of God with
money! You have neither part nor lot in this matter, for your
heart is not right before God. For I see that you are in the gall
of bitterness and in the bond of iniquity.' And since he did not
believe in God any more he was eager to contend against the
Apostles, so that he himself might seem to be glorious, and he
studied the entire art of magic all the more so that he might
lead a great many men into amazement. He lived under
Claudius Caesar, by whom he is said to have been honoured
with a statue because of his magic. This man, therefore, was
glorified by many as a god, and he taught that he was the one
(1) *who had appeared among the Jews as Son, but descended in Samaria
as Father, and came to the rest of the nations as Holy Spirit.* But (2) *he
said that he was the highest power,* that is he who is Father *over all*

things, and *(3) submits to being called whatever men call him.*

2. But Simon the Samaritan, from whom all heresies originated, had the following theme to his sect: He redeemed a certain prostitute, Helen, *(4) from the city of Tyre in Phoenicia* and *(5) took her round with him,* saying that she was the first conception of his mind, the mother of all, through whom he first conceived in his mind to make the angels and archangels. She is the *Ennoia* (Thought), and springing forth from him, knowing what her father willed, she descended to the lower region and generated *(6) the angels and powers by whom he said this world was made.* But after she had generated them she was detained by them out of envy because they did not wish to be thought to be the offspring of any other being. He himself was totally unknown to them: but his *Ennoia* was detained by those powers and angels which had been emitted by her. And she suffered every insult from them, so that she could not return up to her father, and was even enclosed in a human body, and through the ages *(7) migrated into different female bodies* as if from vessel to vessel. *(8) And she was in that Helen (9) on account of whom the Trojan war was entered upon; (10) and it was on her account that Stesichorus who ridiculed her in his poetry had his eyes blinded; but later when he repented and wrote what are called the palinodes in which he celebrated her, his eyes were opened again.* But she was reincarnated from body to body, and undergoing every insult in them, *(11) recently was a prostitute in a brothel; and (12) she was the lost sheep. (13) For her sake he himself came for the purpose of claiming her first of all and that he might release her from her bonds;* but *(14) he granted salvation to mankind by means of his own recognition. For since the angels were managing the world badly because each one of them desired the supremacy he came for the restoration of things, and he descended changed in form, and assimilated to the principalities and powers and angels, so that he appeared as man among men, though he was not man; and was thought to suffer in Judaea, though he did not suffer. (15) The prophets spoke their prophecies under the inspiration of the angels who made the world; for this reason those who hope on Simon and Helen do not heed the prophets even now, and they act as they wish like free men; for men are saved by his grace but not by just works. (16) For there are not just works by nature, but by accident; as the angels who made the world ordained, leading men into slavery by means of such precepts. For this reason he promised that the world would pass away and those who were his own would be liberated* from the power of those who made the world.

3. *(17) Therefore the mystic priests of these men live in a licentious*

manner and perform magic to the extent that each is able. *They use exorcisms and spells; philtres also and love-charms, what are called familiar spirits and dream-bringers and whatever other curious arts there are, are studiously exercised by them. They also have an image of Simon made in the form of Jupiter and of Helen in the form of Minerva: and these they worship;* they also have a title derived from the originator of these most impious teachings, Simon, being called Simonians. From these men 'knowledge falsely so-called' received its initiation, as one can learn from their very own assertions.

A comparison between *Refutatio* 6.19.20 (text 4) and Irenaeus *Adv. Haer.* 1.23 (text 5) reveals that most of the material in Irenaeus is represented in some form, either word for word or in summary, in Hippolytus. These passages are numbered in the order in which they occur in text 5; the result in text 4 is considerably contorted. The correspondence of the individual passages is too great to be denied, yet the difference of order, at least in the first part of Hippolytus' version, is remarkable.[6] If Hippolytus took this passage directly from Irenaeus[7] why did he change the order?

The table on p. 83 summarises the order of subjects in the two texts. The most noticeable difference between the two orders is that Hippolytus starts from a point where he has been speaking of Helen, while Irenaeus starts from a point where he has been speaking of Simon. Hippolytus tells the story of Helen in chronological order from the Trojan war on, and introduces Simon and his claims at the point at which he comes into the history of Helen. Irenaeus, on the other hand, summarises Simon's claims and then mentions that he was accompanied by Helen; he then goes back to the beginning of Helen's history and tells it up to the point mentioned before, her

[6] It is important to establish that the difference of order is not due to the Latin translation of Irenaeus. All the available evidence (passages in which other authors preserve the Greek text, passages where fragments of the Syriac translation survive, the style and errors of the translation) suggest that it is an uninspired and doggedly literal translation, published less than twenty years after the original Greek. See Harvey's Introduction pp. vi and clxiv.

[7] It is hard to construct any viable alternative. Irenaeus' text was certainly known and available to Hippolytus in the remainder of *Ref.* 6.

ransom by Simon, thus reintroducing Simon and his mission. After this the two accounts roughly correspond.

Of the two accounts Hippolytus' is certainly neater: it follows a chronological sequence from the Trojan war to the present-day Simonian disciples; no event has to be mentioned twice and explanations are supplied when required; the only repetition is that Helen was the lost sheep. In Irenaeus, on the other hand, Helen as a prostitute ransomed by Simon has to be mentioned twice; Simon himself and his mission have to be partly described before the account of Helen's history and partly afterwards, and the chronology of the account is more complex. However, this does not mean that Hippolytus' order would have been better or even possible for Irenaeus: Hippolytus' order depends on starting with Helen, and this is only possible in a context in which a knowledge of Simon can already be presupposed. Hippolytus starts this new section right at the end of an extensive account of Simon's doctrines, and he can begin here with a reference to Simon's allegorisation of the poets. Irenaeus is at the beginning of a much shorter account; he has to start with the basic outline of the history of Simon, his appearance in Acts and his claim to divinity (features mentioned by Hippolytus right back in chapter 7), and he naturally comes to Helen when she appears in the life story of Simon, only then going back to explain Simon's theory about her past.

Hippolytus starts his chronological account of Helen from the Trojan war as a result of leading in from the allegorisation of the poets. This means that he omits all the details of the earlier history of Helen as the *Ennoia*[8] who generated the angels and powers who made the world and then detained her in it. He makes only a slight allusion to these events when he tells us that Helen's reincarnations were brought about by the angels and lower powers who made the world. We are, however, already familiar with the details of the generation of the *Epinoia* and the creation of the world in the *Apophasis*, whereas Irenaeus cannot presuppose such knowledge.

Irenaeus' order, and the material he includes, suit the purpose of his account. Hippolytus, because of the nature of the

---

[8] Irenaeus uses the term *Ennoia* for Helen. Hippolytus' equivalent seems to be *Epinoia*.

Hippolytus	Irenaeus
(Helen and Greek myths)	(Simon in Acts)
She is the lost sheep	(Honoured by many as a god)
Reincarnations in women	Said he appeared in Judaea as son,
Cause of Trojan war	in Samaria as Father etc.
She was in Helen then	He was the highest power
Stesichorus	He is called what men will.
She was reincarnated by angels	Ransomed Helen,
who made the world.	a prostitute of Tyre,
Recently she was a prostitute in	and took her round.
Tyre	(She was the first Ennoia:
His mission was to ransom her	she generated angels and powers;
He ransomed her	she was detained and insulted)
and took her round	reincarnated in women.
Said she was the lost sheep	She was in Helen
he was the highest power	Cause of Trojan war
(his shame before his disciples, his	Stesichorus
disciples advocate free sex).	Reincarnation of Helen
Salvation for men by knowledge	Recently she was a prostitute
Angels ruled badly, he came as	She was the lost sheep
man,	His mission was to ransom her
seemed to suffer in Judaea;	Salvation for men by knowledge.
appeared in Judaea as son, in	Angels ruled badly, he came as
Samaria as Father etc.	man,
He is called what men will.	seemed to suffer in Judaea.
Prophets were inspired by angels	
His disciples do not heed them:	Prophets were inspired by angels
they do what they wish	His disciples do not heed them:
saved by his grace.	they do what they wish
Nothing is bad by nature	saved by his grace.
but laid down by angels.	Nothing is just by nature
World will pass away.	but laid down by angels.
Disciples perform magic	World will pass away.
and have statues of Simon and	Disciples perform magic
Helen.	and have statues of Simon and
	Helen.

material he has already provided, can compress Irenaeus' account by using a more economical order of subjects and omitting or merely alluding to elements which he has already treated to some extent. The overall length of the two passages 4 and 5 is roughly equal, but Hippolytus has been able to include a certain amount of extra material not found in Irenaeus. Right at the end of the account, 6.20.2-3, is a section with a number of further references to Simon's life history and an unparalleled account of his death; in chapter 19.4-5 Hippolytus adds a section on the fact that Simon was really carried away by lust for the woman and only invented the story as a cover-up, and on the licentious beliefs of Simon's disciples.

Hippolytus seems to be particularly interested in the libertinism of the Simonian moral theory and paints a blacker picture of it than Irenaeus.[9] It is possible that he possessed another source of information on the current practices of the Simonians and the discreditable aspects of Simon's life, including the attempt at resurrection which brought about his death by mistake.[10] The second part of chapter 20 has a brief summary of Simon's life, mentioning his visit to Rome and disputes with Peter and repeating the incident reported in the Acts of the Apostles. It seems likely that these are notes from a new source that covered some of the same ground as Irenaeus, but from which Hippolytus chooses to report the story of Simon's death and the practices of the Simonians in more detail.

From this section of Hippolytus' work we are led to the conclusion that considerable care and skill has been applied to the composition. Hippolytus appears to have worked with material from more than one source to hand; the finished product shows signs of careful reorganisation to give a concise and logical account suited to the context and avoiding unnecessary repetition of material. The rearrangement of Irenaeus' text and the inclusion of items from another source suggest most plausibly that Hippolytus worked from notes rather than from the texts of these sources in this case, notes which he could then rearrange, sometimes quoting verbatim and sometimes paraphrasing, adjusting or merely alluding to what was mentioned.

---

[9] See for example Hippolytus' emphasis on their disregard of evil in place of Irenaeus' point concerning justice, *Ref.* 6.19.5; 6.19.7; *Adv. Haer.* 1.23.2.

[10] *Ref.* 6.20.3. Here again Hippolytus has a neat story to bring out the falsity of Simon's claim to be god. Christ, who really was God, was buried dead and rose up alive. Simon's 'resurrection' was the very reverse: he was buried alive and ended up dead.

Part Two:
Embedded Texts

There are two sections of Hippolytus' *Refutatio* which have been used as particularly rich hunting grounds for those whose task it has been to sniff out fragments of the Presocratics; these are the passage in book 7 in which Hippolytus compares Empedocles with the heretic Marcion, and the passage in book 9 in which Heraclitus is linked with the Noetian heresy. Although there are other sections of Hippolytus' work in which reference is made to various philosophers and quotations are often included, it is these passages which have proved most fruitful because Hippolytus has included at these points extended, detailed and copiously illustrated interpretations of the philosopher's work. There is abundant material for the fragment-seeker.

However, it is precisely in these examples that we lose most by extracting the fragments from the context, since here we are provided with the coherent interpretation to which they belong, presented in an accessible form. These passages may seem fruitful in the search for fragments, but in reality they are not so because more is lost than is gained when the text is fragmented and its structure and meaning lost. It is when they are read as a whole, as a text embedded within our present text, that they can bear fruit in accordance with the productive nature of the coherent text. Thus it is particularly important to explore these passages in detail and analyse the way in which the texts of the Presocratics are involved in Hippolytus' text.

3. Empedocles

A. Where did Hippolytus derive his information from?

Material on Empedocles occurs in a number of different sections of Hippolytus' work. The main passages are:

- (i) *Refutatio* 1.3 which includes a quotation of the couplet B117;
- (ii) *Refutatio* 6.11-12 which includes a quotation of B109 (3 lines) and the last line of B110;
- (iii) *Refutatio* 10.7 which includes B6 (3 lines) and two lines known as B17.19-20.
- (iv) *Refutatio* 7.29-31 which includes B6 (3 lines), B16 (2 lines, also quoted at *Ref.* 6.25.1), B29 (3 lines), 13 lines generally assembled as B115, B110 (10 lines) and B131 (4 lines).

Of these quotations only B16, B29,[1] B131, the first nine lines of B110, and lines 4 and 8 of B115 are not known from any other source.

The main passage of interest is the extensive account of Empedocles in book 7.[2] Some preliminary observations should be made on the source of information used by Hippolytus in the other three passages before dealing with book 7.

(i) The brief summary of Empedocles in book 1.3 is a confused account which mentions a doctrine of conflagration (*ekpurosis*), a theory of spirits (*daimones*), the principles Strife (*Neikos*) and

---

[1] Lines 1-2 of B29 are, however, also found as lines 2-3 of B134, which is quoted by Ammonius *De Interpr.* 249.1ff. and Tzetzes *Chil.* 13.80. For complete lists of the sources see M.R. Wright (1981).

[2] The material in book 7 will be taken together with the related passage from the section on Pythagoreanism in book 6.

Love (*Philia*) and the doctrine of reincarnation (*metensomatosis*).
B117 is quoted in the context of reincarnation. It is clear from
the other authorities who quote this couplet[3] that it served as
the stock proof-text for Empedocles' theory of reincarnation:
this is its function in all the authors who quote it for
doxographical purposes. This function explains its repeated use
in contexts which compare Empedocles with Pythagoras. The
couplet appears as an epigram in the *Anthologia Graeca* where it
is distinguished from another group of verses at the same entry
which are said to come from the *Katharmoi*.[4] This suggests that
B117 was widely known and quoted in its own right. Its
presence in the book 1 summary does not give any indication
that other verses were to be found in the source from which
this section derives.[5]

(ii) In book 6 the account of Simon Magus includes a
reference to Empedocles by name and two rather mutilated
quotations.[6] B109 is concerned with sense perception and is
found twice in Aristotle and three times in Sextus Empiricus,
as well as others who probably derive from Aristotle. B110 is
quoted as a whole (ten lines) by Hippolytus at *Ref.* 7.29.26, but
line 10, quoted here in a mutilated form, is also found in
Sextus Empiricus.[7]

A knowledge of Sextus Empiricus could have supplied both
the quotations in this context. However, it is clear that
Hippolytus must have had some other source for B110 when he
quotes it in full at 7.29.26. The wording of line 10 at 6.12.1
corresponds with neither Hippolytus' own later version, nor
that of Sextus Empiricus, and there are also differences in the
text of B109 from the readings of Aristotle and Sextus.[8]

---

[3] Clement *Strom.* 6.24.3; Athenaeus 8.365e; Diogenes Laertius 8.77:
Themistius *De An.* 35.13; Philoponus *De An.* 140.7; Sophonias *De An.* 24.39;
Eustathius *Comm. ad Od.* 18.79; Olympiodorus *In Phaed.* 58.17; Cyrillus *Adv.
Jud.* 872C. The couplet also appears in *Anth. Graeca* 9.569.

[4] *Anth. Graeca* 9.569; B112 lines 1-2 and 4-6.

[5] On the nature of this source see Appendix A.

[6] *Ref.* 6.11-12. B109 and B110.10.

[7] Sextus Empiricus *M.*8.286.

[8] Aristotle *De An.* 404b8; *Metaph.* 1000b6; Sextus Empiricus *M.*1.303;
7.92; 7.121. *dion* and *storgêi* are both omitted in Hippolytus, but both could
be MS. errors.

Hippolytus is not himself dependent solely on Sextus for his knowledge of Empedocles and there is no strong reason to suggest that that was his immediate source for these verses, in view of the reasons in favour of suggesting that they may have appeared in the text of the *Apophasis Megalê*.[9]

(iii) In book 10 Hippolytus claims to give a summary of the philosophers he has dealt with. The brief account is not in fact adapted to its rôle but is taken verbatim from another source. It corresponds precisely with Sextus Empiricus *Adv. Math.* 10.310-18, but it is not necessarily Sextus' own work. The format and subject matter is closely parallel to Aristotle *Physics* A, 184b15ff. The material on Empedocles in this section has no independent value, nor is there any reason to suppose that the source used by Hippolytus at this point is related in any way to the sources from which he derived the material in other sections of his work.

Two quotations from Empedocles are included: B6 and B17.19-20.[10] The context in Hippolytus book 10 and in the parallel in Sextus Empiricus concerns the number of Empedocles' principles *(archai)*, whether they are four or six. B6 is quoted as evidence for four and B17.19-20 for the addition of love and strife to make six. Two parallels should be examined.

1. The authorities who quote B6 can be divided into two groups: (i) those who include a lengthy account of the significance of the four divine names and which is to be correlated with which element;[11] in some of these the primary interest is in the use of allegory;[12] (ii) those who take for granted the symbolism and use the quotation as evidence for

---

[9] See below, Appendix B.
[10] B6 is also quoted in *Ref.* 7.29.4 but the context is entirely different.
[11] These are Probus *In Verg.* 11.4; Tzetzes *Exeg. in Iliad* 53.23; Aetius (= Plutarch *Epit.* 1.3 and Eusebius *PE* 14.14.6); Stobaeus *Ecl.* 1.10.11; Diogenes Laertius 8.76; Athenagoras *Apol.* 22.1; with these belongs Hippolytus *Ref.* 7.29.4.
[12] Particularly Tzetzes but also Probus.

four elements without further comment.[13] In both groups[14] the quotation is used with reference to Empedocles' four elements for which it seems to be the stock text, and in each case love and strife are also listed in the context although not mentioned in the quotation.

2. This tradition of the use of B6 in connection with the discussion of four- or six-element interpretations of Empedocles suggests another parallel in Simplicius' account *in Phys.* 25.14ff. Here the same question is raised: has Empedocles four elements or has he six? Simplicius does not quote B6 in this context, but he does quote B17.7-8[15] and B17.17-20.[16] Simplicius does not give a text in support of the four-element group, but had he done so that text would surely have been B6.[17]

Simplicius' material in this section of his commentary on the *Physics* is generally recognised as being derived from Theophrastus' *Doctrines of the natural philosophers*.[18] However, the arrangement of the material and Simplicius' classification of thinkers into those whose principles are (a) one or (b) more than one and various sub-classes within these divisions is not attributed to Theophrastus. McDiarmid[19] has argued that the scheme derives from the passages of Aristotle's *Physics* A on which Simplicius is commenting and has been extended by Simplicius.[20] McDiarmid concludes: 'The arrangement of

[13] These are Sextus Empiricus *M*.10.315; *M*.9.362; Hippolytus *Ref.* 10.7.3. In addition Philoponus *In Phys.* 88.4ff. uses only the first line in this context and Clement of Alexandria *Strom.* 6.17.4 uses the first line of B6 with some other lines attached.

[14] Tzetzes alone does not make explicit reference to Empedocles' four- and six-element theory.

[15] These lines are also quoted by Stobaeus in the context of B6.

[16] Of these B17.18 was used by Clement and Athenagoras, 17.20 also by Athenagoras and 17.19-20 by Sextus and Hippolytus, all in the context of B6.

[17] We should expect this at *In Phys.* 25.10-11. Simplicius does not quote B6 at all, but Philoponus refers to it in commenting on *Phys.* 1.4 (187a10), *In Phys.* 88.4.

[18] It provides the principal fragments of book 1 of the *Phusikôn Doxai* in Usener's collection, *Analecta Theophrastea*. Cf. also H. Diels (1879) pp. 475-95.

[19] McDiarmid (1953) pp. 87-9.

[20] Or extended by Alexander if the account derives from the lost commentary on the *Physics* by Alexander: Diels (1879) p. 104; cf. McDiarmid (1953) p. 90.

doctrines given by Simplicius is dictated by the passage on which he is commenting, and it is clearly not the arrangement of Theophrastus.[21] However, the arrangement based on *Physics* A is not new in Simplicius but is actually what links him with the Sextus/Hippolytus passage which has the same format. As Diels observed,[22] the similarity between the passages on Empedocles in Simplicius and in the Sextus/Hippolytus passage is so striking that their common origin is evident. Diels did not, however, proceed to observe that the *Physics* A-type construction of the whole passage in Sextus is closely parallel to that in Simplicius. Theophrastus' work was clearly already adapted to this format by the time it was used by Sextus. We may presume that if Simplicius derived his material from Alexander's commentary on the *Physics* that work probably already used the *Physics* A-type construction, but it may not have been original to Alexander either.

In both Simplicius and the Sextus/Hippolytus passage references to Aristotle and Stoic theories are included. Both must therefore be expansions or extensions of Theophrastus' material, but whether both originate from the same re-working of Theophrastus is not clear.[23]

Whatever the precise history of the material it is clear that Simplicius' account in *in Phys.* 22.22-28.31 is not original. Not only is the information included in it derived from Theophrastus but the structure stands in a tradition which takes as its model Aristotle's systematic approach exemplified in *Physics* A and *Metaphysics* A. McDiarmid has shown[24] how dependent Theophrastus is upon Aristotle's reading of the Presocratics and to what extent he fits what further material he selects into the preconceived categories of Aristotle's histories of philosophy. While this is true of the Theophrastean material, it is certainly also true of the Aristotelian interpretative format into which the Theophrastean material

[21] McDiarmid (1953) p. 88.

[22] Diels (1879) p. 93. n. 2.

[23] If they originate from the same model both must be selections from a wider range of examples.

[24] McDiarmid (1953).

has been fitted in both Simplicius and the Sextus/Hippolytus passage.

Elsewhere in his commentary Simplicius may have used an extensive text of Empedocles, and his testimony reflects that fact. In this passage, however, Simplicius is not an independent witness, but rather offers a reading of very similar origin to that found in Sextus/Hippolytus, a reading through several pairs of Aristotelian spectacles.

It is not only Simplicius and the Sextus/Hippolytus passage which manifest this common tradition. As observed above, almost all the other authorities who quote B6 do so in a context which suggests that they too have excerpted it from a passage which discussed whether Empedocles' *archai* were four or six, and thus probably stem from the same Theophrastean model. It is thus probable that none of the many testimonia for B6 is independent of this Aristotelian reading.

(iv) In book 7 Hippolytus gives an extended account of Empedocles' doctrines. The identity of the immediate source or sources from which he selected his material is a matter of some doubt.

(a) Plutarch on Empedocles

It has frequently been suggested that Plutarch may have been Hippolytus' source of information on Empedocles.[25] The main ground for this suggestion is that Hippolytus refers to a major work of Plutarch on Empedocles, the ten books *Pros Empedoklea*, at *Refutatio* 5.20.6. This must be the same work as that listed in Lamprias' Catalogue of Plutarch's works as *Eis Empedoklea* in ten books.[26] If Hippolytus knew this work directly, he might have used it for his main account of Empedocles.

The evidence certainly does not clinch the matter. Hippolytus mentions Plutarch, not in the vicinity of his account of Empedocles but in the context of a discussion of the

[25] See for example Diels (1898a) p. 399. O'Brien (1969) pp. 32-3 and 210 n. 3; Bollack (1965-9) vol. 3.1, p. 154.
[26] Lamprias catalogue number 43.

mysteries à propos a link between the Sethian heresy and
Orphic doctrines. In support of the antiquity of Orphic
mysteries he mentions some mysteries said to have existed at
Phlya in Attica before the foundation of the Eleusinian
mysteries, and refers to Plutarch on the subject: many things
are inscribed on the portico at Phlya, 'about which Plutarch
gives accounts in his ten books on Empedocles'. Plutarch may
be Hippolytus' immediate source, and the mention of his book
a bibliographical note for readers who want to follow up
material which Hippolytus is here omitting.[27] On the other
hand it is possible that the reference to Plutarch is simply
taken over from an intermediary source.[28]

The material mentioned by Hippolytus at 5.20.6 suggests
that Plutarch's work covered subjects other than Empedocles
himself, and indeed some of Hippolytus' other information on
the mysteries may derive from this work. What form did
Plutarch's work take? It is possible that a wide-ranging
commentary digressing on points suggested by verses of
Empedocles would include a detailed passage on the mysteries.

In book 7, however, Hippolytus centres on the interpretation
of Empedocles' words. The style, particularly in 7.29.16-21, is
that of a brief interpretative commentary, line by line, and
there is no tendency to digress onto subjects other than
Empedocles' own doctrines. The contrast with the digression
implied by 5.20.6 does not preclude the possibility that
Plutarch's work was the source for both, since a work in ten
books might cover a range of different topics.

Although the work on Empedocles is lost, Plutarch's other
works incorporate numerous quotations from Empedocles,
some of which may be the product of his memory, some of his
notebooks. Of the 35 verses quoted by Hippolytus in book 7,
only 8 are quoted by Plutarch in extant works, all of these
from the group collected as B115 which are the subject of close

[27] Occasional references to material omitted by choice occur at e.g. 1.5.1.
1.10.1, 7.19.1. A bibliographical suggestion for further reading occurs at
5.22.1.
[28] The difference in date between Plutarch and Hippolytus, about a
century, is sufficient for an intermediary source to be possible, although not
particularly likely.

commentary in *Ref.* 7.29.16-21.[29] Some common fund of
information for this passage of Hippolytus and certain extant
works of Plutarch might be suggested and this could be
Plutarch's lost work on Empedocles.[30]

(b) A Stoic source common to Sextus Empiricus

Hershbell, in his article on Hippolytus,[31] has argued that
Hippolytus was not clearly familiar with Plutarch's interpretations of Empedocles as exemplified by his extant works, but the
evidence is certainly not conclusive. Hershbell favours the
suggestion of Bignone[32] of a common source for Hippolytus
and Sextus Empiricus, Stoic in character, perhaps a lost work
of Chrysippus, on account of its identification of a 'right
reason' (*orthos logos*) in Empedocles. This suggestion has
certain weaknesses:

1. The passages which are supposed to be parallel in Sextus
and Hippolytus[33] both quote in support of their interpretation,
but none of the verses quoted in Sextus are found anywhere in
Hippolytus, nor vice versa.

2. The extent to which Sextus and Hippolytus have common
material on Empedocles elsewhere is very limited apart from
the verbatim parallel in *Refutatio* book 10 and *Adv. Math.*
10.310-18 which comes from an Aristotelian source.[34] B6,
which occurs in this common passage, is also quoted elsewhere
by both Sextus and Hippolytus. Other common material is
limited to that quoted in the passage on Simon Magus[35] of
which B109 is widely known from Aristotle and B110.10 is
also known to Hippolytus as part of a longer quotation at

[29] Lines 9-12 of B115 occur at *De Is. et Os.* 361C and at *De Vit. Aer.* 830F;
lines 1, 3, 5, 6 and 13 of B115 are strung together at *De Exilio* 607C; of these
line 3 does not appear in Hippolytus.

[30] The quotation (B119) at *Ref.* 5.7.30, which is not there attributed to
Empedocles, is also quoted by Plutarch at *De Exilio* 607D, just after the lines
from B115. This also may derive from Plutarch's lost work if the lines from
B115 did.

[31] Hershbell (1973) pp. 187-95.

[32] Bignone (1916) p. 647.

[33] Sextus Empiricus *M.*7.122-5; *Refutatio* 7.31.3-4.

[34] See above p. 91.

[35] *Ref.* 6.11-12. See above p. 88.

7.29.26, of which Sextus displays no awareness.

3. The interpretation said to be parallel in Sextus refers to an *orthos logos* which serves as the criterion and plays a rôle in authentic perception.[36] Although one of the quotations included by Sextus[37] includes a reference to the Muse, as well as the gods, there is no clear evidence that the Muse was taken to be the *orthos logos*. Hippolytus, by contrast, refers to a 'just reason' (*dikaios logos*), which he explicitly identifies with the Muse.[38] Its rôle is entirely different from that of the *orthos logos* in Sextus; it plays no part in perception but simply serves as an assistant to Love in the work of uniting the scattered elements. The Stoic concept of *orthos logos* seems to have little part in Hippolytus' scheme.

(c) The source common to 7.29.10 and 6.25.1

In *Refutatio* 6.24-5 Hippolytus gives an outline of Pythagorean doctrines and deals with the derivation of plurality from a monad, and the rôle of numbers in the construction of the Pythagorean cosmos. At 6.25.1 he proceeds:

> And concerning the permanence of the world the Pythagoreans issue a statement in this sort of way:
>
> > 'For indeed they were before and will be, nor ever, I think, will the ceaseless age be devoid of these two.'
>
> But what are 'these two'? Strife and Love.

The quotation here attributed to the Pythagoreans is generally known as B16 of Empedocles; Hippolytus quotes it again at 7.29.10, ascribing it to Empedocles:[39]

> About which (*sc.* Strife and Love) Empedocles [says] that they are two immortals and uncreated and that they never had an origin of their coming to birth – [speaking] in this sort of way:

[36] *M*.7.122.
[37] B3, *M*.7.125.
[38] *Ref.* 7.31.4.
[39] B16 is known only from these two passages of Hippolytus.

> 'For indeed they were before and will be, nor ever, I think,
> will the ceaseless age be devoid of these two.'

What are 'these two'? Strife and Love.

In both cases this is followed by a brief account of the activities of Love and Strife, slightly fuller in book 7 than in book 6. They do not correspond verbally but both represent the same interpretation.[40] There can be no doubt that the source used by Hippolytus is identical in these two passages, despite the fact that the attribution is to 'the Pythagoreans' in book 6 and to Empedocles in book 7. Whichever passage, if either, represents the continuous context in the source, it is clear that at least one of the two has been detached from that context and used in a passage on a different subject. This suggests a procedure of working from notes which would enable Hippolytus to include material on Empedocles in his account of Pythagoreans or vice versa.[41] If he was working from notes we do not need to work with the hypothesis that he used only one source for the whole of his account of Empedocles in book 7.

(d) Conclusion

Given that Plutarch's work on Empedocles is lost, we have insufficient evidence to determine the precise nature of Hippolytus' sources for Empedocles. From the evidence available the following scheme seems likely.

(1) The passage in book 10 is from Sextus Empiricus himself or from his immediate Aristotelian source.

(2) In book 7 the passage discussing lines of B115 at 7.29.14-23 may be from Plutarch's lost work on Empedocles.

(3) The passages incorporating B110 and B131 at 7.29.25 and 7.31.4 are unlikely to be from a source common to Sextus and Hippolytus; the interpretation is almost certainly Hippolytus' own, although it might be indirectly influenced by Stoic interpretations, including that found in Sextus.

(4) The first part of the account in book 7 (7.29.4-13), book 6.25.1, which is identical with 7.29.10, and the summary in

---

[40] Compare 6.25.2 and 7.29.11-12.
[41] Hippolytus knows of Empedocles as a Pythagorean, *Ref.* 1.3.3.

book 1.3 come from notes from one or more sources otherwise unknown which may have made a connection between Empedocles and the Pythagoreans.

B. What governed the choice and use of material in the account of Empedocles? The parallel with Marcion

The account of Empedocles in *Refutatio* 7.29-31 is juxtaposed with an account of the heresy of Marcion which is to be refuted. The importance of the comparison has been underestimated.

Among those who study Marcion, the mention of Empedocles is regarded as an irrelevant fiction: Blackman observes:[42] 'He arbitrarily derives Marcion's system from Empedocles ...'; if it has any interest it is only with regard to the question of whether Marcion was actually influenced by Empedocles.[43] Among those whose interest is Empedocles this question still curiously occurs: Hershbell comments seriously:[44] 'Hippolytus' claim that Marcion was influenced by Empedocles is suspect for at least two reasons ...'; more common is the concern that the comparison with Marcion has distorted the account of Empedocles: so Hershbell observes:[45] 'There is also some reason for thinking that Hippolytus ... read back into Empedocles doctrines peculiar to Marcion.' This concern is also the one which occupies Ramnoux,[46] and the important task for both Hershbell and Ramnoux is to detach and discard the gnostic accretions and to rid themselves of Hippolytus' distorted reading of Empedocles: the link between Marcion and Empedocles has no basis in 'fact' and hence must be dismissed as a source of error.

This approach undervalues Hippolytus' material. The question of historical 'fact' is ultimately irrelevant: whether Marcion actually intended to profess the same doctrines as Empedocles, or whether he even knew of Empedocles'

[42] Blackman (1948) p. 67.
[43] Gager (1972) p. 54.
[44] Hershbell (1973) p. 105.
[45] Hershbell (1973) p. 106.
[46] Ramnoux (1961/9) Part 2.

doctrines, are matters of no concern to Hippolytus' point. His interest is in the resemblance, whether intentional or not, which he observes between certain prominent features of Marcion's system and certain features of his own reading of Empedocles. Structurally and symbolically the systems have something in common on Hippolytus' view, and his concern is to bring out those features in his account. The worthwhile approach is not to dismiss this as distortion based upon a fiction, but to investigate the extent to which the comparison can add to our own appreciation of Empedocles. Has Hippolytus anything to offer that is of interest in his juxtaposition of Empedocles and Marcion?

(i) The choice of Empedocles

The choice of Empedocles as the parallel for Marcion is surprising in view of the existence of a tradition which associates Marcion with the Cynics. Marcion was born at Sinope in Pontus,[47] which was also the birthplace of Diogenes the Cynic,[48] and this fact is the source of extensive jokes and insults in Tertullian's work against Marcion.[49] In terms of doctrine Tertullian associates Marcion with the Cynics on the grounds of his asceticism and bestial behaviour,[50] but he also considers that Marcion's doctrines in general have been influenced by philosophy.[51]

This connection with the Cynics appears also in Hippolytus who, like Tertullian, makes repeated jokes about dogs and the dog's life.[52] There can be little doubt that Hippolytus knew the tradition that associated Marcion with the Cynics, as it

[47] Epiphanius *Haer.* 42.3.

[48] Diogenes Laertius 6.20.

[49] See particularly Tertullian *Adv. Marc.* 1.1.3-4; 1.1.5; 1.19.2; 2.5.1.

[50] *Adv. Marc.* 1.1.5.

[51] *Adv. Marc.* 2.27.6; 5. 19.7. *De Praescr.* 7.3. Epicurean influence is suggested, as well as Cynic. Clement of Alexandria also claims that Marcion was a Platonist, *Strom.* 3.3.21. On these claims see Gager (1972).

[52] *Ref.* 7.29.1: a reference to Marcion's 'dog's (Cynic's) life' (*kunikos bios*). *Ref.* 7.30.1: a reference to Marcion's 'dogs', i.e. his followers, barking against the demiurge, comparable to Tertullian *Adv. Marc.* 2.5.1. *Ref.* 10.18 and 10.19.4: Tatian and Marcion practice a 'rather doggy life' in respect of their asceticism.

appears in Tertullian; that tradition clearly dwelt on the links in terms of asceticism, and the rejection of marriage and of meat-eating, and in Hippolytus this is extended to Marcion's character and his scorn for other views.[53]

If Hippolytus' main interest in Marcion had been his rejection of marriage and meat-eating there was a ready-made precursor in Marcion's fellow-citizen Diogenes. Hippolytus does not choose to present Cynic views as the primary parallel for Marcion. Instead he offers Empedocles, and we should therefore look for a more profound comparison in Empedocles than that found in the Cynics. Empedocles also had ethical views against marriage and meat-eating, and Hippolytus does mention these teachings as parallel to those of Marcion,[54] but this is not the only, nor indeed the primary, link between Empedocles and Marcion. O'Brien,[55] in suggesting that Hippolytus is solely interested in the sexual and dietary prohibitions, and that he reads B115 as teaching these doctrines, misses the main force of Hippolytus' comparison. These parallels are an added bonus in the course of the tale, but the real story lies in the basic structures and symbols on which the two systems are founded.

(ii) Marcion

The details of the comparison with Marcion are of major importance for approaching the interpretation of Empedocles. Two points are worthy of note.

1. The historical facts about what Marcion really said are not a primary concern. The terms of the comparison are Hippolytus' understanding of Marcion's system, for which his own account of that system in book 7 of the *Refutatio* is the main evidence.

2. Evidence from the tradition concerning Marcion other than Hippolytus' own account is relevant in assessing Hippolytus' particular interests: where he stresses a point that is not prominent in other accounts, or passes over other aspects,

[53] *Ref.* 7.29.1.
[54] *Ref.* 7.29.22 and 7.30.4. See below pp. 122-3.
[55] O'Brien (1981) pp. 15-16.

we may observe the significant details of his interpretation of the traditional material with which he worked. Questions of what Marcion really believed do become relevant in those circumstances where Hippolytus might be thought to have fabricated or grossly distorted the evidence and where modern scholarship has suggested that there is no basis for his view in either the facts or the traditional accounts of Marcion: on the question of Marcion's dualism, I shall be concerned to demonstrate that there is evidence in the traditional accounts for the aspects which Hippolytus stresses; his account is an interpretation of Marcion rather than an invention.

The study of Marcion has been hampered by the out-dated but largely unchallenged work of Harnack (1924) which has been quoted as the authority from the publication of its first edition (1920) to the present day.[56] Hershbell quotes Harnack as orthodoxy throughout his article purporting to re-examine Hippolytus' presentation of Empedocles.[57] A 're-examination' of Hippolytus in the light of Harnack's Marcion gets us nowhere without a re-examination of Harnack's Marcion. Harnack presented Marcion as a proto-Luther, the first step towards the biblical theology of German protestantism. To this end he argued that Marcion based his theology on a literal reading of the bible, that he was not a Gnostic and that he was not influenced by philosophical ideas. For this interpretation Harnack found his main support in Tertullian and in the reconstruction of Marcion's biblical texts; the testimony of Hippolytus, among others, was rejected because of the extreme dualism which is attributed to Marcion. By stressing selected passages from Tertullian, Harnack suggested that Marcion's creator-god was not bad but just (*justus, dikaios*), and that there was therefore no direct *opposition* between this god and the 'stranger-god' who was wholly Love and Goodness. Texts which claimed that Marcion had an

---

[56] Lebreton (1946) pp. 523-32; Blackman (1948) p.x and passim (though with reservations). It is the basis of such general accounts as that in Evans' introduction to Tertullian's *Adv. Marc.* (1972) pp. ix-xvi. The result of the general acceptance of Harnack's exposition of Marcion was that almost no important work on Marcion was produced until two recent articles which attack Harnack's basic assumptions, Cager (1972) and Bianchi (1967b).

[57] Hershbell (1973). See particularly pp. 105-6.

antithesis between a good god and an *evil* creator-god must therefore be a corrupt later form of Marcionism which had introduced a dualism that was alien to the original position devised by Marcion.

The manipulation of the evidence involved in Harnack's reconstruction of Marcion as a biblical theologian means that his account cannot be accepted as an authority on the historical Marcion, or even the Marcion presented in the ancient tradition. Although Marcionism differs from classic gnosticism in certain fundamental respects, notably in the fact that human nature is not innately related to the divinity, the dualism upon which it depends is, if anything, more extreme than that of most gnostic systems, as Bianchi has observed.[58] Unlike most systems, Marcion's system allows no common origin to the supreme divinity and his inferior demiurge: for Marcion the two are totally alien, and the demiurge is not a corrupt emanation of the supreme but a totally distinct force.

The tendency of modern scholars to underemphasise the antithesis between Marcion's two gods as they appear in the ancient literature against Marcion is almost universal. Harnack and subsequent interpreters have stressed the fact that the Old Testament god is 'just',[59] drawing the conclusion that he cannot therefore be evil. Hence it has been maintained that the two gods are not directly opposed as forces of good and evil respectively.

The implications of the statement that the creator-god is *justus* are indeed significant, but it does not justify the conclusion that he is not evil, a conclusion which is in conflict with the very texts from which the statement that he is just comes. On the basis of what unwritten assumption are we justified in moving from the claim that he is just to the conclusion that he is not bad? 'Justice' – laws, punishments and retribution – is what is good in terms of the values of this world, by the laws and values established by the demiurge. Marcion's assertion that true goodness lies elsewhere, in a totally alien, unknown god, results in an inversion of the

[58] Bianchi (1967b) pp. 141-2.
[59] Harnack (1924) pp. 98-102; Lebreton (1946) p. 528; Blackman (1948) pp. 66-8; Hershbell (1973) p. 106.

values of this world: the values of a world ruled by a creator who is not good will not themselves be good. To miss the fundamental ambiguity of all terms such as 'justice', which results from Marcion's inversion of conventional values, is to miss the significance of the system as a whole.

The apparent contradiction observed between the statement that the creator was judicial and the frequent implications that he was evil[60] is symptomatic of this ambiguity. As Blackman observes,[61] in Marcion's view 'the gospel was not only new, but it created a transvaluation of all values. The new dispensation ushered in by the appearance of Christ was at all points in contrast with the old dispensation of the creator.' 'Just' is a term of approval in the values of the old dispensation; in the new dispensation it will be a term of abuse.

In view of the fact that scholars have denied that the creator could be evil in Marcion's system it is worthwhile reviewing the evidence. The earliest testimony for Marcion's views is that of Justin, who simply states that Marcion rejected the creator and declared that there was a greater god than him.[62] The fullest evidence comes from Irenaeus and Tertullian, in the second half of the second century, and Hippolytus writing before 235 A.D.[63] Hippolytus probably knew the work of both Irenaeus and Tertullian.[64]

(a) *The trees of good and evil*

Tertullian, Hippolytus and Origen[65] all note that the starting point in Marcion's system was the passage in Luke 6.43 about the trees of good and evil:

---

[60] A contradiction is acknowledged by Blackman (1948) p. 66, who suggests that Marcion changed his view over time (pp. 66-7). Harnack explains the 'evil-creator' evidence as a later corruption intruding into the evidence (1924) pp. 164-5.

[61] Blackman (1948) p. 109.

[62] Justin *Apology* 1.26 and 1.58.

[63] Marcion died in about 160 A.D.

[64] Hippolytus certainly knew Irenaeus' work, and the heretics reported immediately adjacent to Marcion (*Ref.* 7.32ff.) are quoted verbatim from Irenaeus. The jokes about Marcion's cynic connections suggest a knowledge of Tertullian, or a related text.

[65] Tertullian *Adv. Marc.* 1.2.1; Origen *De Princ.* 2.5.4; Hipp. *Ref.* 10.19.3.

For no good tree bears bad fruit, nor again does a bad tree bear good fruit; for each tree is known by its own fruit.

This served as a proof-text for the Marcionite division between two gods:[66] the Old Testament god, being responsible for evil actions, could not be the good god; the good god, therefore, was other than the Old Testament god. Harnack and others emphasise that this does not entail an opposition between the two gods; but Marcion employs the notion that 'by their fruits shall ye know them'. The fruits of the creator-god are the evils of this world, and this implies that the creator himself is the evil tree.

In the texts which report Marcion's use of this text the concern is not with establishing the goodness of the unknown god but with identifying the source of the evil in creation. Tertullian is explicit that Marcion's interest was in the problem of evil when he posited the two gods.[67] Tertullian claims that the creator was indeed identified as the author of evils and hence himself evil, and that a text from Isaiah 45.7 – 'I am the one who creates evils' (*ego sum qui condo mala*) – was used in support of this. Hippolytus draws the same conclusion.[68] There seems little doubt that the text from Luke 6.43 was used to draw the contrast between good and evil and to place the creator firmly in the category of evil.

(b) Evil features of creation

Tertullian suggests that Marcion emphasised the less savoury aspects of creation, and particularly unpleasant insects and '*animalia minutiora*'.[69] His hostility to birth and other natural functions is mentioned by Clement[70] and is also apparent from his treatment of the life of Jesus, from which he rejected the accounts of the birth.[71] His prohibition of marriage has a

[66] Origen *De Princ.* 2.5.4. Epiphanius *Panarion* 42.2 and Philastrius *Haer.* 17 suggest that Marcion used it in defence of his beliefs at a Synod in Rome.
[67] Tertullian *Adv. Marc.* 1.2.2: 'Languens enim ... circa mali quaestionem, unde malum ...'
[68] Hippolytus *Ref.* 10.19.3.
[69] Tertullian *Adv. Marc.* 1.13.1-1.14.5.
[70] Clement *Strom.* 3.3.12.
[71] Cf. Tertullian *De Carne* 3; *Adv. Marc.* 3.11; Hippolytus *Ref.* 7.31.5; Irenaeus *Haer.* 1.25.1. And see Bianchi (1967b) p. 145.

similar anti-cosmic motivation: the abstention from things
ordained by the demiurge and avoidance of prolonging the
created world.[72]

Harnack suggested that the evil resides in the matter
employed by the demiurge rather than the demiurge
himself.[73] This rests on the rather dubious evidence of a
chapter in Tertullian[74] in which he offers a reductio of
Marcion's system by arguing that he has in fact got not two
but nine gods: the superior and inferior gods and in addition
the place (*locus*) in which the superior god creates his heaven
and the *materia* out of which he makes, the *locus, materia* and the
evil inherent in the *materia* used by the inferior god, and two
Christs, one for each god. Tertullian's procedure in deducing
these nine principles is far from innocent. He may be justified
in suggesting that the creator used pre-existing matter, but he
quotes no support for the view that this matter was positively
evil. The phrase which he used to describe the matter, *materia
innata et infecta et aeterna*, suggests formlessness but not inherent
evil. Hippolytus also suggests that the creator used pre-existing
matter but has no suggestion that it was evil.[75] Clement does
mention 'evil matter'[76] but he does not imply that this was the
only source of evil in the 'evil nature' which results: rather he
implicates the 'just creator' as well, particularly with reference
to the absence of *logos* in the created world.[77] There are no
clear grounds for attributing evil solely to matter, since all the
texts imply at least that the demiurge is also a source of evil.[78]

[72] Hippolytus *Ref.* 10.19.4; 7.29.22; Clement *Strom.* 3.3.12.

[73] Harnack (1924) pp. 97ff.

[74] Tertullian *Adv. Marc.* 1.15.4-6.

[75] Hippolytus *Ref.* 10.19.2.

[76] Clement *Strom.* 3.3.

[77] In this respect Marcion is contrasted with Plato and the Pythagoreans,
Strom. 3.3.12.

[78] At 10.19.1 Hippolytus claims that Marcion and Cerdo had three
principles, good, just and matter, and that some followers extended this to
four, good, just, evil, matter. This contradicts the claim in book 7 that
Marcion had two principles, good and evil, and that a later version, that of
Prepon, introduced a third, just, between the two. It is possible that
Tertullian's argument in 1.15 is the basis for the statement in book 10.
Compare the variations in the accounts of Apelles at 7.38 and 10.20, which
suggest confused memory.

(c) Explicit statements that the creator is evil; association with Cerdo

Hippolytus' account in book 7 assumes that the second god of Marcion is simply wicked (*ponêros*).[79] Irenaeus, like Hippolytus, does not use the term 'just' of the creator in his account of Marcion at 1.27.2-3, although he does use the *bonus/iudicialis* antithesis at 3.25.3. No conflict is apparent between the two alternative ways of referring to the creator: in 1.27.2 the Old Testament god is *malorum factor* and *cosmocrator* and at 3.12.12 he is *malorum fabricator* and the two gods are distinguished as *alterum quidem bonum, alterum autem malum* ('one good, one bad'). Irenaeus' description of the evil god corresponds closely with that given by Tertullian.[80] Tertullian contrasts the two gods, *Adv. Marc.* 1.6.1: *alterum iudicem, ferum, bellipotentem, alterum mitem, placidum et tantummodo bonum atque optimum* ('the one judging, savage, warlike, the other gentle, peaceful and altogether good and perfect'). The characteristics listed are antithetical, and *iudex* (judging) serves as a direct opposite to *optimus* (perfect).[81] This use of judgment as a bad, rather than a good, quality is recognised in Marcion by both Tertullian and Irenaeus.[82]

All the ancient testimonies suggest that Marcion was influenced by the teaching of Cerdo.[83] Harnack denied that this could be the case;[84] he objected that Marcion's contrast was between a good god and a just god, Cerdo's between a good god and an evil god, and therefore they could have nothing in common.[85] This entirely contradicts the evidence

---

[79] E.g. *Ref.* 7.30.2.

[80] Compare Irenaeus 1.27.2 with Tertullian *Adv. Marc.* 1.6.1.

[81] This is confirmed by the use of the same antithesis at *Adv. Marc.* 2.29.1.

[82] Tertullian *Adv. Marc.* 2.24.4. Irenaeus *Haer.* 5.26.2. Tertullian *Adv. Marc.* 5.18.12 implies that Marcion called the creator 'diabolus'.

[83] Irenaeus *Haer.* 1.27.1-2; Tertullian *Adv. Marc.* 1.2.3; Hipp. *Ref.* 7.37.2; 10.19.1.

[84] Harnack (1924) pp. 28-9.

[85] 'Aber das Hauptstück der Lehre M.s, die Entgegensetzung des guten fremden Gottes und des gerechten Gottes, stammt nicht von Cerdo, der vielmehr den Gegensatz des guten und des schlechten Gottes, wie andere Gnostiker, verkündigte und ein syrischer Vulgärgnostiker war.' Harnack (1924) p. 28.

of Irenaeus and Hippolytus, both of whom ascribe to Cerdo a good god and a just god[86] while suggesting that Marcion's contrast was between a good god and a bad god.[87] Most of our evidence for Cerdo derives from Irenaeus; there are, however, no reasonable grounds for rejecting Irenaeus' testimony that Cerdo's contrast was between good and *justus*.[88] The move from Cerdo's distinction of good/*justus* to Marcion's good/*justus* = evil is the very reverse of the one Harnack considers.

(d) Marcion's book, the Antitheses; inversion of values

Ancient and modern scholars are unanimous in attributing to Marcion a book entitled *Antitheses*.[89] Tertullian gives considerable detail concerning the content: he glosses the title as meaning '*contrariae oppositiones*' and explains that the purpose of the work was to demonstrate the discord between the Law and the gospel.[90] That the work emphasised contrariety between the Old Testament and the New Testament, and hence between the two gods, is apparent from other statements of Tertullian[91] as well as being implied by the title '*Antitheses*'. Hippolytus suggests that Marcion constructed arguments on the basis of a contrast, *antiparathesis*, of good and evil.[92]

The antitheses seem to have consisted of quotations from the Old Testament juxtaposed with quotations from the New Testament to show a direct opposition between the values of the old dispensation and those advocated by Christ in the New

[86] Irenaeus *Haer.* 1.27.1 (ap. Eus. *HE* 4.11); Hippolytus *Ref.* 7.37.1.

[87] Hippolytus *Ref.* 7.29.1; 7.30.1-2; 7.31.1; Irenaeus 1.27.2; 3.12.12.

[88] Harnack's suggestion that Irenaeus' evidence should be rejected and that of later sources (Epiphanius *Haer.* 41.1, Filastrius *Haer.* 44, both of whom ascribe to Cerdo a theory indistinguishable from that which they ascribe to Marcion) should be preferred, Harnack (1924) pp. 34*-39*, is untenable, as Blackman has shown (1948) pp. 67-70. Cf. also Gager (1972) p. 53.

[89] Tertullian *Adv. Marc.* 1.19.4; 4.1.1; 4.4.4; 4.6.1. Cf. Hippolytus *Ref.* 7.30.1-2; Irenaeus *Haer.* 1.27.3.

[90] Tertullian *Adv. Marc.* 1.19.4.

[91] E.g. *Adv. Marc.* 4.6.1; 4.1.1; 2.29.1.

[92] *Ref.* 7.30.1; 7.30.2; cf. also 7.37.2. The reference to *antiparathesis* is a joke: Hippolytus' own *antiparathesis* of Marcion and Empedocles will show up Marcion as evil by contrast with Empedocles: *Ref.* 7.29.3; 7.30.2-4.

Testament.[93] As Blackman observed,[94] Marcion's view is that the new dispensation has brought about an inversion of all values. Further indication that this was the point of Marcion's teachings is the evidence for his account of Christ's descent into Hades:[95] those who offended against the Law and against the god of the Old Testament are saved by Marcion's Christ; those who were good and righteous (note the word *justos*, Irenaeus 1.27.2) by the terms of the Old Testament are left in Hell; the wicked are saved, the righteous are damned. By the values of the good god, that is by the true values, the wicked are good and the righteous are bad. The values of the old dispensation are reversed.

(e) Hippolytus' account of Marcion

It is clear from the evidence set out here that the tradition concerning Marcion sometimes claimed that the creator-god was evil as well as just. This is true not only of Irenaeus and those who follow him but also of Tertullian, despite the fact that his argument requires that he minimise the evil attributed to the creator-god.[96] Hippolytus, by contrast with Tertullian, is concerned to emphasise the evil and maximise the antithesis between the two gods, but this is a choice of emphasis of a feature already present in the tradition and does not represent an unwarranted import on Hippolytus' part. Hippolytus alone brings out clearly the force of Marcion's inversion of values: if this world, and the god who defines the values of this world, are evil then what is commended by the values of this world is also evil: marriage, procreation, meat-eating[97] – all that belongs to this cosmos and to the Old Testament Law.

---

[93] For detailed examples of the contradictions see Tertullian *Adv. Marc.* 3.21; 4.20.3; 5.3; 4.12; 4.34.1; Theodoret *Haer. Fab.* 1.24; Irenaeus 4.8.2.

[94] Blackman (1948) 109.

[95] Irenaeus *Haer.* 1.27.3. Cf. also Theodoret *Haer. Fab.* 1.24; Epiphanius *Haer.* 42.4.

[96] Tertullian's attempt at refutation of Marcion consists of an argument that the two gods identified by Marcion are but two aspects of the one supreme god: that there is no incompatibility between the two characters which Marcion thinks are contrasted.

[97] *Ref.* 7.30.3-4.

Irenaeus and Tertullian may not have seen the force of this point: Irenaeus describes Marcion's creator as primarily evil, Tertullian sees him as just but not evil. Modern scholars have likewise assumed that just and evil must be mutually exclusive alternatives. The recognition of the ambiguity of terms such as 'just' depends upon a detachment from the values of this world which identify just with good; Hippolytus, who sets Marcion's anticosmic dualism alongside Empedocles' alternation of opposed regimes, recognises the reversal of values which it implies. In both Marcion and Empedocles the reversal of jurisdiction between gods of opposed characters is intimately bound up with the need to question the values of the present world.

C. What reading of Empedocles does this lead to?

(i) The unity of Empedocles' work

It has been argued above[98] that the traditional concern with assigning verses to distinct poems of Empedocles is misguided and arbitrary. Hippolytus, like the other ancient interpreters, treats Empedocles' thought as a unity and knows of no division into separate poems. He knows of an association of *katharmoi* (purifications) with Empedocles,[99] but he does not restrict the application of this term to any particular group of doctrines. Many of his comments defy the division made by modern scholars between religious and scientific doctrines. All of this is good evidence that no such distinction was envisaged in his day.

The interpretation which follows works on the assumption that Empedocles wrote only one major work and that all his doctrines were closely related and interdependent. No attempt will be made to assign verses to different poems. Hippolytus finds no problems in combining Empedocles' themes, and this interpretation, which takes Hippolytus' material as its starting point, aims to make sense of Hippolytus' reading and to build upon it.

[98] Above pp. 24-31.
[99] *Ref.* 7.29.3.

(ii) Hippolytus and the 'neoplatonic' interpretation

Hippolytus identifies in Empedocles a distinction between the cosmos under strife and the cosmos under love.[100] An understanding of the precise nature of this distinction will be basic for the understanding of Hippolytus' interpretation as a whole.

On two occasions O'Brien claims that Hippolytus' interpretation of Empedocles is 'the earliest and longest example' of what was to become the standard neoplatonic interpretation.[101] The interpretation to which he refers is the identification of the world ruled by love as the intelligible world and the world ruled by strife as the sensible world. The implication of this interpretation is that the two worlds are not consecutive, nor destructive of each other, but simultaneous. Classic examples of this interpretation are found in Proclus[102] and Syrianus,[103] and Simplicius proposes a modification of a similar view.[104] This interpretation differs in certain important respects from the account found in Hippolytus, and the contrast between the two highlights the structure of that of Hippolytus.

The basis of O'Brien's claim that Hippolytus' interpretation is the same as that of the later neoplatonic writers is the term *noêtos* (intelligible), occurring with reference to the world brought about by love, at one point in Hippolytus' account.[105] O'Brien appears to conclude that this is equivalent to a statement of the identity of 'the intelligible world' and Empedocles' 'sphere', in contradistinction to a 'sensible world' which would be the world under strife.[106] Is this justified? Hippolytus makes no reference to 'the sensible world' and he does not use the word *aisthêtos* (sensible) at all in expounding Empedocles. It is not clear that *noêtos* is to be understood in

---

[100] E.g. *Ref.* 7.29.8; 7.29.11-14; 7.29.21-2 etc.
[101] O'Brien (1969) p. 100; (1981) 79-80.
[102] Proclus *In Tim.* 160D (2.69.18-27).
[103] Syrianus *In Metaph.* 43.6-23; 187. 19-27.
[104] E.g. Simplicius *In Phys.* 160.12-161.20. This retains the idea that Empedocles has two distinct worlds, the sensible and the intelligible.
[105] *Ref.* 7.29.17.
[106] O'Brien (1981) p. 79.

opposition to *aisthêtos* at this point. Furthermore Hippolytus does not refer to 'the intelligible world'; the world under love is, perhaps, intelligible but is it 'the intelligible world'?

Hippolytus' main emphasis is on the distinction between one and many. Initially he identifies not two worlds but two forces, love and strife, operating on the elements which constitute the 'world'.[107] Both forces operate on the same materials but to opposite effect, Love making the world one and Strife making it many.[108] There is thus one *kosmos* (world) which is sometimes one and sometimes many. As the account proceeds the terminology shifts so that *kosmos*, either alone or more precisely designated as 'this world', is used with reference to the world in a state of plurality, as is *ktisis* (creation), or *ktisis hautê* (this creation).[109] Nevertheless the unity produced by Love is still 'the cosmos' under a different guise;[110] the 'one' which Love produces is the world at a different stage, of which the contents differ only in arrangement from those of this present world. The contrast which Hippolytus derives between 'this world' and 'that world' is a temporal one: this world is the world as we know it now, all the parts of the world that we perceive (7.29.12); that world is the world that comes about when Love gains control.

The emphasis on the distinction between many and one is important. Hippolytus does not distinguish 'this world' and 'that world' as sensible and intelligible respectively, but as many and one.[111] The present world is plural in all its aspects, intelligible as well as sensible, and Strife is responsible for all these.[112] On the other hand the one brought about by Love is not the neoplatonic intelligible world, which not only itself includes plurality, as Simplicius observed,[113] but must also be eternal. The one brought about by Love, on Hippolytus' view, is certainly not eternal.

The distinction between many and one, as opposed to

---

[107] *Ref.* 7.29.7.
[108] *Ref.* 7.29.8.
[109] *Ref.* 7.29.9, 7.29.15.
[110] *Ref.* 7.29.13-14.
[111] *Ref.* 7.29.9, 11, 12, 14, 15, 16, 18, 21, 23, 24; 7.30.4; 7.31.3; 6.25.2, 3.
[112] *Ref.* 7.29.12.
[113] Simplicius *In Phys.* 31.18-34.17, esp. 34.8-12; cf. *In De Caelo* 294.10-13.

sensible and intelligible, links Hippolytus' passage with
passages in Syrianus' and Asclepius' commentaries on the
Metaphysics.[114] Both of these know of a connection of Love
and Strife with Pythagorean principles, whereby Strife is the
indefinite dyad, the principle of plurality, and Love is the one,
the principle of unity. Syrianus makes it clear that Strife is
responsible for the plurality in *noêta* as well as the sensible
cosmos. Love is responsible for the sphere which is the primary
being (*to prôtôs on*).[115]

It is a Pythagorean account of this sort, in terms of many
and one, rather than the neoplatonic version, which we find in
Hippolytus. The link with Pythagorean principles is not explicit
in book 7, but in the parallel passage in book 6 the same
interpretation appears in the context of the account of the
Pythagoreans.[116]

(a) The account of Pythagorean doctrine, 6.23-7

The summary of Empedoclean doctrine at 6.25.1-4 occurs in
an account of the Pythagoreans in which Hippolytus' interest
is in numerology and Pythagorean accounts of the generation
of the world from numbers. His aim is to link the Pythagorean
number system with the system of aeons in Valentinian
gnosticism. The one and the indefinite dyad are described,
6.23.1-2, followed by an account of the derivation of the
tetraktys from which the series point, line, plane and solid are
said to derive, 6.23.3-4. Bodies, i.e. the physical world, have as
their *archê* (principle) the tetraktys, while numbers as a whole
have as theirs the monad. A distinction between two worlds,
intelligible and sensible, having the monad and tetraktys as
their respective *archai*, is made in 6.24.

It is worth noting that the tetraktys, and not the indefinite
dyad, is responsible for the sensible, three-dimensional world.
Love and Strife, on the other hand, are introduced at 6.25.1 in
connection with mathematical processes applied to the number

[114] Syrianus *In Metaph.* 11.25-31; 43.11-16; Asclepius *In Metaph.* 198,25-6.
[115] Syrianus *In Metaph.* 11.32-3.
[116] On the common source for these passages see above pp. 95-6.

system as a whole, and not in connection with a division between sensibles and intelligibles. Strife is simply a principle of plurality, corresponding with the dyad.

It is clear that two separate distinctions are made in the account of Pythagorean doctrine and that the distinction between unity and plurality is not the same as that between intelligible and sensible. Unity and plurality have as their *archai* the one and the indefinite dyad; the intelligible and sensible worlds have as their *archai* the one and the tetraktys. This allows for plurality to exist within the intelligible world, since the dyad and the numbers up to ten belong to the intelligible world, as do mathematics and plane geometry which concern incorporeals (6.23.3).

Love and Strife are presented as principles of unity and plurality, and this distinction does not coincide with that between intelligible and sensible. The neoplatonic interpretation of the later passage of Syrianus[117] conflates the two distinctions so that Strife is the principle of plurality and of the sensible world. This is the interpretation to which Simplicius objects,[118] pointing out that the spheres of operation of Love and Strife do not correspond with the intelligible and sensible worlds respectively; but this is not the interpretation found in Hippolytus. The 'Pythagorean' interpretation, found in Hippolytus, Asclepius and the earlier passage of Syrianus, identifies two separate divisions.

←————ONE |———— MANY————→

←————INTELLIGIBLE | SENSIBLE ——→

(b) The cosmos under Love
It is now clear why Hippolytus refers to the cosmos under Love as intelligible: it is indeed *an* intelligible or spiritual world in the 'Pythagorean' interpretation, for the sensible world falls entirely within the realm of plurality; but it is not *the* 'intelligible world', nor, indeed, is it part of the present

[117] Syrianus *In Metaph.* 43.14-20.
[118] Simplicius *In Phys.* 31.31-32.1.

intelligible world – it is temporally distinguished from the present world which is a world of plurality under Strife in both its sensible and its intelligible aspects. The one, which is the world under Love, does not at present exist since its existence is only brought about at the dissolution of the present world of plurality.

(iii) Exiles

Hippolytus' account of the system of Empedocles is constructed upon this basic division between 'this world' and 'that world', and their respective ruling principles Love and Strife. The cycle of alternation of one and many which this entails is normally regarded as the central theme of Empedocles' 'physical poem';[119] Hippolytus' use of the material defies such classification: a distinction between 'this world' and 'that world' on these lines is the basis for the history of the *daimones* which appears in B115 and related texts. Hippolytus works with both sets of texts as a single group.

The lines assembled by Diels Kranz as B115 derive from several groups quoted in various combinations by a considerable number of authors.[120] Hippolytus, who is an

---

[119] See for example O'Brien (1969) p. 88; Wright (1981) pp. 22-56; Hippolytus quotes B6 and B16 which are normally assigned to the 'Physics', and also B29, which is, however, partly the same as B134.

[120] (a) B115.1-2 Hippolytus *Ref.* 7.29.23
                    Simplicius *In Phys.* 1184.9.
                    Stobaeus 2.8.42 (quoting Porphyry).
        (b) B115.4-5 Hippolytus *Ref.* 7.29.16.
        (c) B115.6-8 Hippolytus *Ref.* 7.29.17.
                    Origen *Cels.* 8.53.
        (d) B115.9-12 Hippolytus *Ref.* 7.29.19 and 21.
                    Plutarch *De Is. et Os.* 361C (= Eusebius *P.E.* 5.5.2).
                    Plutarch *Vit. Aer.* 830F.
        (e) B115.13-14 Hippolytus *Ref.* 7.29. 14-15.
                    Asclepius *In Metaph.* 197.20.
                    Philoponus *In G.C.* 266.4.
                                In De An. 73.32.
                                In Phys. 24.20.
                    Plotinus 4.8.1.19.
                    Hierocles *In Carmen Aureum* 54.
        (f) B115.1,3,5,6,13 Plutarch *De Exil.* 607C.

authority for almost all the lines, uses them with running commentary to expound the basic outline of Empedocles' work.

Hippolytus begins with a couplet that is normally placed at the end of B115:

> And I am now one of these, a fugitive from god and a wanderer relying on raving strife.[121]

The couplet is quoted alone in the six other texts in which it occurs[122] and in no case is its precise association with other verses of B115 indicated. All the sources, including Hippolytus, associate it with the exchange of rule between Love and Strife and the 'descent' of the soul as a result of its banishment from the one by Strife. If 'of these' (*tôn*) is to be read at the beginning[123] it requires an antecedent, and the banished *daimones* of B115.5-6 provide a suitable candidate. Whatever the proper context for this couplet, its prominent position in Hippolytus' exposition is significant. Here we get explicit reference to the present life as an exile: we are now fugitives.

The second line of Empedocles' couplet, 'Relying on raving strife', implies a present state in which the fugitive is obedient to and trusting in Strife, emphasised by the 'now' in the first line.[124] The reason why the fugitive banished from god trusts in 'raging strife' will become apparent only if the cycle of incarnation is related to the cycle of alternating Love and Strife, as Hippolytus and the other authorities for this couplet suggest that it is. His dependence on Strife is bound up with the fact that it is the world ruled by Strife that is the place of his exile.

---

[121] νῦν is omitted by Hippolytus and supplied from Plutarch, who reads τὴν instead of Hippolytus' τῶν, and εἰμι for εἰμι. εἰμι should perhaps also be read in Philoponus and Asclepius who have ὡς καὶ ἐγὼ δεῦρ'εἰμί as the first part of line 13.

[122] The authorities listed in note 120 section (e).

[123] The alternative reading, τὴν...εἰμι, requires a different antecedent, presumably meaning 'the way I now travel'. This is not so easily supplied from the plural ἀργαλέας...κελεύθους of B115.8. The reading of Philoponus and Asclepius gives a similar sense.

[124] Cf. P. Kingsley (1979) p. 95 on the present force of *pisunos* (relying).

The fugitives have undergone ritual banishment as a result of pollution. The nature of the deed committed is intimated in lines 3-4 of B115, but of these Hippolytus quotes only line 4, while Plutarch quotes among his selection of lines at *De Exilio* 607C line 3 but not line 4. No authority quotes both, but there is no reason to suggest that Plutarch is quoting all the lines he knows, nor similarly in the case of Hippolytus who starts a new quotation with line 4.[125] Both lines fit into a context strongly reminiscent of Hesiod's account of Styx and the consequences of sin among the gods, *Theogony* 782-805. Hippolytus' line is almost a quotation of *Theogony* 793 and identifies the sin in general terms as the breaking of an oath. Plutarch's line specifies *phonos*, blood-guilt, according to the generally accepted emendation of Stephanus.[126] Together the lines take up Hesiod's reference to an outbreak of strife among the gods,

When dispute and strife arise among the immortals,[127]

and make it specific: that strife and the oath-breaking[128] which are punished by banishment from the company of the gods are constituted by murder and result in the expulsion of victims condemned to wander for three thousand years. When someone defiles his limbs with blood-guilt, and thereby breaks a fundamental oath of the gods, the *daimones* are banished from the company of the blessed:

When someone defiles his own limbs with blood-guilt,
and also ... forswears himself, breaking his oath,
the *daimones* who are blessed with a long life
wander thirty thousand seasons far from the place of the
    blessed ...

[125] The text is not perfect and a word is missing from line 4. It is also possible that a line has dropped out of Hippolytus' text.

[126] The MS. reading *phobôi*, (fear) leeaves it unclear what is the source of pollution behind 'defiles' or what constitutes the breaking of the oath; nor is there any reason why a *daimôn* should sin 'from fear' (Wright (1981) p. 273). In view of the prohibition on bloodshed which is prominent in Empedocles, *phonôi* (blood-guilt) gives a much more satisfactory reading.

[127] *Theogony* 782.

[128] *Theogony* 782, 784, 793.

Who commits the deed and who is the victim banished for the sin? There is no doubt that one individual is guilty of blood-guilt and oath-breaking. Most translators attempt to make the ensuing punishment fall upon the guilty individual, by translating as if the ensuing lines, 6-12, were in the singular;[129] but the banishment is not of one *daimôn* but of the *daimones* as a group:

> The *daimones* who are blessed with a long life
> wander thirty thousand seasons far from the place of the blessed,
> they are born as all forms of mortal creatures in the course of time,
> creatures who change, traversing the rugged paths of life.

All the *daimones* suffer for the sin of one individual. Hippolytus makes it clear in his commentary that he understood the punishment to fall upon all souls and not just a guilty one. Was the individual who committed the deed one of the number of *daimones*? The text is not explicit: *daimones* in the nominative does not provide a genitive for 'someone' (*tis*) to mean 'one of the *daimones*.'[130] It is probable that *tis* would be a *daimôn*[131] but the fact is not important nor stressed: *tis* means anyone, and the important point is that whoever commits the deed – and it might be anyone – all the *daimones* suffer for it. The outbreak of strife does not affect only the individual responsible for it, but the whole society. In order to defuse the chain of retribution initiated by murder – to purge the pollution – victims are required, ritual victims to serve as *pharmakoi* (scapegoats). Such is the rôle of the banished *daimones*.[132]

---

[129] E.g. Wright (1981) p. 270; Van der Ben (1975) p. 107 (fr. 6); Kirk, Raven, Schofield (1983) p. 315; West (1966) p. 374.

[130] The impossibility of the genitive *daimonôn* for metrical reasons should not be stressed (contra Wright (1981) p. 273) since had the relation of *tis* and *daimones* been important it could certainly have been expressed.

[131] There is no indication that other beings exist.

[132] In order to serve in this rôle the *daimones* must be in a position to take the guilt upon them; hence there must be some relationship between them and the one whose sin initiates the guilt. This further suggests that the guilty individual iṣ *daimôn*, but which one precisely is unimportant.

The *daimones* are expelled from their place of blessedness in expiation of pollution by blood-guilt to become wanderers with no resting place, expelled from one element to another, always thrown out and hated:

> For the fury of *aithêr* drives them to the deep,[133]
> the deep spits them out onto the ground, earth to the rays
> of the brilliant sun, and the sun casts them into the whirlwinds
>   of the *aithêr*;
> one receives them from another, but all of them hate.

One might compare the situation of Oedipus in Sophocles' *Oedipus at Colonus*, who has been wandering in exile from place to place, never acceptable; even when he reaches Colonus which he hopes to make his resting place he is initially rejected.[134]

The ritual purification which involves banishment of the *daimones* into the cycle of incarnation and reincarnation is fixed by a decree of necessity (B115.1.2):

> There is an oracle of necessity, the ancient decree of the gods
> eternal, sealed down with broad oaths.

The association of these lines with the rest of B115 is not entirely clear. The main authority is Plutarch, who only quotes line 1 followed by line 3. Hippolytus quotes the couplet at the very end of his commentary on B115, but refers the 'decree of necessity' back to the regular alternation of Love and Strife, one and many. The same interpretation is given by Simplicius[135] who quotes them in association with B26 and B30, both normally assigned to the 'physics'. Plutarch's selection of lines at *De Exilio* 607C is not strong evidence on which to base an argument for attaching the couplet to B115, but the lines do belong to the same Hesiodic context of the rest of B115, and should fit with the oath-breaking mentioned in

[133] This version of line 9 comes from Plutarch. The second half is corrupt in the manuscript of Hippolytus and the first part is quoted loosely.
[134] Sophocles *OC* 36-7, 148-91.
[135] Simplicius *In Phys.* 1184.9. Stobaeus 2.8.42 includes them in a discussion of ethics and fate.

line 4. The repeated association of the 'decree of necessity' with the alternation of Love and Strife is another example of the impossibility of dividing the so-called physical doctrines from the ritual banishment of the *daimones* described in the rest of B115.

What is the decree of necessity which declares that blood-guilt on the hands of one individual entails the banishment of all the *daimones* as *katharmoi*?[136] Hippolytus refers it to the alternating rules of Love and Strife[137] and the resultant changes from unity to plurality and vice versa. In Hesiod the introduction of violence and strife among the gods

When dispute and strife arise among the immortals ...

resulted in the banishment of the sinner for nine years. For Empedocles the introduction of strife is the start of a new era of division and violence: it results in a world of plurality because violence differentiates and sets apart. The expiation of blood-guilt involves the initiation of a world of plurality such as our own; hence the decree which lays down the punishment for sin is the same decree as that which ensures the alternating reigns of Love and Strife. The *phonos* which starts it all is the beginning of a new reign of Strife.

We, therefore, and all creatures in the present world, are fugitives condemned to wander in expiation of an original pollution by blood-guilt on the hands of one individual. We come under the rule of Strife since that regime begins and ends with the period of exile; as exiles we are subject to and dependent upon Strife in whose world we wander. Thus B115.14, 'Relying on raving strife', makes sense, for although Strife is mad and hostile the fugitive relies upon him as an exile relying upon the ruling powers of the land in which he must briefly lodge.[138]

---

[136] Note that the term *katharmos* can refer to an individual banished as a ritual victim in expiation of blood-guilt. The term is frequently associated with pollution from the murder of kin, and in a context where purification required is either human sacrifice or exile. Cf. Herodotus 7.197, Plutarch *De Curiositate* 518B and the irony implied by these associations in Euripides *IT* 1332, Sophocles *OT* 1228 and Aeschylus *Choephoroi* 968.

[137] *Ref.* 7.29.23.

[138] See above p. 114. Compare Sophocles *OC* 294-309; 549-68.

(iv) The inversion of values

The consequences of viewing the soul's presence in this world as an exile from a world that is wholly other are momentous. Hippolytus' interpretation draws out these consequences, but they can be identified in other material from Empedocles which derives from other sources also.

The regimes of Love and Strife involve opposed forces producing opposite effects: Strife produces difference, plurality, and violence, which provokes and prolongs differences; Love breaks down differences and works to produce an undifferentiated unity. The resultant values associated with the two regimes will be opposed, the one set an inversion of the other. This feature is brought out by Hippolytus' juxtaposition of Empedocles with Marcion whose two-world system involves a similar inversion of values.[139]

Love, Hippolytus explains,[140] is a sort of peace and agreement and affection which chooses to make the world one, perfect, restored. Strife, on the other hand, always disperses the one and chops it up to produce many. Strife is the cause of the *ktisis* – this present created world – and is concerned that this creation should remain. But Strife is said to be *oulomenon*, glossed by Hippolytus as meaning *olethrion* (destructive).[141] The contradiction implied by the claim that the one who maintains and preserves this world is 'destructive' is fundamental to the whole structure: from the point of view of the *daimôn* in exile, Strife who stands for the preservation of the values of this world is destructive. All that is good in the world of Strife prolongs the exile of the *daimôn*, and according to the values of his true home under Love that is destructive.

(v) Violence and sacrifice

Given that it was violence which initiated the new reign of Strife, and that it is the continuation of such violence and strife which prolongs and maintains the differences of the world under Strife, we should expect that violence should be

---

[139] See above pp. 101-8.
[140] *Ref.* 7.29.8.
[141] *Ref.* 7.29.9.

classified as good in the value system of this world, according
to Empedocles. An example of Empedocles' comments on this
subject can be found in his attitude to sacrifice, since sacrifice
is a feature of the conventional religious system which belongs,
on Empedocles' view, to this world and contributes to its
stable existence. Sacrifice is ritual violence sanctioned by the
regime of Strife, and Empedocles sees it as a re-enactment of
the original act of murder which initiated this regime. The
animals selected for sacrifice correspond to the original victim
of the initial outbreak of violence, since they are kin to those
who perform the sacrifice – the reincarnated souls of their
children and parents – and their fellow *daimones* banished with
them from the world of Love. The repetition of the original act
of violence is the essence of the religious system of this world,
because it again results in the renewed exile of the *daimones* in
expiation of the blood-guilt, and hence it prolongs the rule of
Strife.

Men commit these deeds unwittingly because they are
indoctrinated in the values of this world under Strife.
Empedocles' outcry against sacrifice is a remonstration at
those who cannot see what they are doing:

> Will you not cease from ill-famed bloodshed? Do you not see
> that you are devouring each other in the carelessness of your
> hearts?[142]

They are unwittingly killing their children and their parents in
sacrifice:

> The father takes up his own dear son, now changed in form,
> and slaughters him while offering prayer, the overgrown fool;
>   but they can see no way out
> as they offer the imploring victim in sacrifice; not heeding the
>   warning cries
> he completes the slaughter and devotes his care to an evil
>   banquet in his hall.
> In the same way son seizes father, children their mother,

---

[142] B136 (from Sextus Empiricus *M*.9.127). Note the recurrence of the key
word *phonos* as in B115.3.

depriving them of their life-force and feeding on their own flesh.[143]

Thus Hippolytus observes that Empedocles instructed his followers not to eat living things, because they were the bodies inhabited by souls undergoing punishment.[144] Empedocles explains the consequences of the sacrificial practices:

> Accordingly maddened by troublesome evils
> you will never release your heart from dreadful torments.[145]

The result is prolonged misery and exile for the *daimones*.

(vi) Misunderstanding and deception

Men fail to see what they are really doing. When they think they are doing what is right and dutiful they are really murdering their own kin. The deception suffered by the majority of mankind is the result of their refusal to allow for the existence of anything beyond the present world of experience.[146] Because they think that so long as men are alive (that is, what they call life), so long they exist and suffer good and bad things, but before they were born and after they die they are nothing,[147] therefore they fail to perceive any possibility that what seem to be 'bad things and good things' (B153) in this life might in reality be the very opposite. Men cannot appreciate even the possibility that the values with which they are familiar might be false, if they cannot conceive of any existence other than the familiar one.

The very words men use are part of the deception and reveal their misunderstanding: they speak of birth (B8), of death, 'coming to be' and 'the ill-fated lot' (B9). In terms of this

[143] B137 (from Sextus Empiricus *M*.9.129).
[144] *Ref.* 7.29.22 and 7.30.4.
[145] B145 (from Clement *Protr.* 2.27).
[146] Cf. B15, B11, B9, B8. On men's self-deception by their involvement with the world of experience see Kingsley (1979) pp. 115-17; Kingsley fails to perceive the connection between this deception and their delusion concerning sacrifice, due to his suggestion that the deception originates from Aphrodite.
[147] B15 (from Plutarch *Adv. Colot.* 1113D).

present world one cannot avoid using such terms: Empedocles himself must use them in order to conform to the conventions of communication;[148] but they represent a misunderstanding if they are taken to indicate the finality which men think they imply.

Because they are deceived by their involvement with the world of Strife, men find it impossible to believe what Empedocles has to say.[149] These men who cannot believe are in fact bad men

> But it is to the bad men who hold the sway that it matters
> strongly that they disbelieve.[150]

These are the ones who are so bound up in doing what is good and right in the eyes of this world that they cannot see where they are wrong. Such are the men of Acragas, proud of their good deeds,[151] whom Empedocles addresses in conventional terms, before revealing their misunderstanding. Such men are only persuaded of what belongs to their present experience; understanding of Empedocles' teaching is reserved for the more discerning.[152]

(vii) Prohibitions

In the context of a theory that identifies souls in their present state of incarnation as *katharmoi* banished for the ritual purification of an original deed of violence, the prohibition of bloodshed, both for sacrifice and meat-eating, is plausible. The killing of any creature is an act of violence against another *daimôn* and, because of the cycle of reincarnations, the murder of one's own kin; it is a repeated source of pollution which prolongs the period of catharsis for the exiled souls.[153]

---

[148] B9 (from Plutarch *Adv. Colot.* 1113A-B).

[149] B114 (from Clement *Strom.* 5.9).

[150] B4 (from Clement *Strom.* 5.18).

[151] B112 (from Diogenes Laertius 8.62).

[152] B2 (from Sextus Empiricus *M.* 7.122-4.)

[153] Note that the objection to sacrifice is to sacrifice in its functioning state, as part of conventional religion, and not in a degenerate and ineffective state. Contra Girard (1972/1977).

Hippolytus links the prohibition on meat-eating with a prohibition on sexual relations: he claims that Empedocles demanded sexual abstinence 'so that they should not aid and prolong the works which Strife creates, dividing and dissolving the work of Love'.[154] No direct quotations on this subject have been preserved,[155] and scholars have reviled Hippolytus for this claim. Zuntz suggests that it is entirely fabrication: 'Need one still elaborate its incompatibility with the whole of Empedocles', and indeed all Greek thought?'[156] Is it really incompatible with Empedocles' thought? The prohibition on sacrifice and meat-eating arises from the recognition that all bloodshed is the murder of kin, the blood-guilt which pollutes. If all creatures are kin, every sexual act will be incestuous and similarly polluting: all fall within the prohibited class of the familiar. Like ritual violence in sacrifice and meat-eating, sexual violence in the form of incestuous relations prolongs the world of Strife: sex requires differentiation, distinctions which belong to the regime of Strife.

There are two levels to the prohibition of sex. Superficially it leads to reproduction, multiplication and the furthering of the incarnate life. This level scholars reject as banal: it would be too simple to suggest that the rule of Strife is furthered merely by the multiplication of offspring in this world. This, however, is only the outward sign, dependent on the underlying reason why sex prolongs this world: incest is comparable with murder in producing the prolonged banishment of the *katharmoi*. The effect of both is to drive the *daimones* into new reincarnations, visible as the reproduction of offspring.

(viii) The rôles of Love and Strife

Hippolytus emphasises the rôles of Love and Strife in terms of

---

[154] *Ref.* 7.29.22. Cf. 7.30.4.

[155] It is possible that B141, on the prohibition on beans, 'Wretches, utter wretches, keep your hands from beans', should have some sexual implication, as Gellius (*Noct. Att.* 4.11.9) insists. It is certainly unsatisfactory to start seeking 'medical reasons' for objecting to beans (as does e.g. Wright (1981) p. 289): Empedocles was not that sort of medic, nor 'reasonable' in the way that Wright suggests.

[156] Zuntz (1971) p. 261n1.

producing 'many' and producing 'one',[157] and this interpretation corresponds to the terms found in the verses of Empedocles quoted by other writers.[158] It seems clear that Love eliminates all differences and Strife promotes and creates difference.[159] To suggest that Love eliminates the differences characteristic of the world of Strife is not to say that there is no continuity between the two worlds: it is clear that Empedocles assumes that the *daimôn* is eternal and persists through the change of regime, and that the components of the two worlds are the same. Nothing comes to be out of what was not.[160]

Empedocles takes as basic the four elements, earth, air, fire and water, which are divine[161] and may represent the *daimones*. Under Love all the differences which make it possible to distinguish between and enumerate these divinities cease to apply, and this may be true of Love and Strife also.[162] The components of the 'sphere' under Love are the elements but no divisions or distinctions can be identified.

With the outbreak of blood-guilt[163] Strife is differentiated again. The identification of a particular individual as guilty of the deed is impossible since the elimination of the differences under Love means that no distinct *daimôn* is identifiable.[164] Given that nothing was set apart as other, the act of blood-guilt was necessarily upon a victim within the familiar group and constitutes fratricide, the murder of a kinsman. The result is the establishment of differentiation and the renewed dominance of Strife, which causes the banishment of the *daimones*, now differentiated, into the world of plurality. The initial set of four elements and two ruling powers becomes further differentiated to form the extreme plurality of the

[157] *Ref.* 7.29.8-14, 22-5.

[158] E.g. B17.1-2, 7-8, 16-17; B20.2-5; B26.

[159] Kingsley's distinction (1979, pp. 12ff.) between attraction of like to like and unlike to unlike is therefore in danger of misleading since under Love there are no likes and unlikes but an undifferentiated unity.

[160] B12.

[161] B6.

[162] The effect on these is unclear; cf. Aristotle *Metaph.* B, 1000b1 (on B36). The question is insoluble given the evidence.

[163] B.115.3. This is necessitated by the alternation of Love and Strife.

[164] Hence the unspecified *tis* of B115.3. See above p. 116.

kosmos:[165] additional differentiation is produced by juxtaposi-
tions which form mixtures of different sorts,[166] ultimately
resulting in a situation where even the various limbs of
creatures are of different natures, such that monsters
occur.[167] After such extreme plurality the differentiation
begins to break down again under the force of returning Love,
producing coherent creatures progressively less differentiated.
There will thus be two periods when normal non-monstrous
creatures occur, both in the period leading up to total
difference and in the period of breakdown of difference:

> Twofold is the genesis of mortals, twofold their passing away;
> for the one is brought to birth and also destroyed by the
>   combination of all things,
> and the other springs up at the dissolution of things again, and
>   then vanishes.[168]

(ix) The sinless men of Aphrodite, B128

The ten verses of B128 are preserved in Porphyry *De Abstinentia*
2.20, and less fully in other authorities;[169] they are not
quoted by Hippolytus, but they have caused some difficulty for
previous attempts to interpret the material we have been
concerned with, particularly the banishment of the *daimones*.
The text describes a time when men[170] kept themselves free of
defilement, did not shed blood in sacrifice and did not worship
various violent gods but only Cypris. It does not describe the
activities of *daimones* in their disincarnate state but of men,
which means incarnate *daimones*. This should mean that it
comes after the 'fall' since incarnation is part of the
punishment undergone by the fallen *daimones*.

B128 is set in the past and Porphyry includes it in a
historical excursus on sacrificial practice in ancient times.

---

[165] See Hippolytus *Ref.* 7.29.12.

[166] B17.34-5; B21.13-14.

[167] B61. There is insufficient evidence to suggest a stage when even the
coherence required for complete limbs is impossible.

[168] B17.3-5 (from Simplicius *in Phys.* 157.25).

[169] See Wright (1981) p. 143.

[170] *anthrôpoisi*, B128.9.

Porphyry's information derives from Theophrastus and we
have no indication of the context from which Theophrastus
extracted the ten lines. The problem is why men just after
expulsion from heaven for pollution should be described as
living apparently sinless lives? One possible answer is offered
by Kingsley[171] who suggests a 'double fall': the men in B128
were already polluted from the original blood-guilt, but in
consequence of their horror at that sin they scrupulously
avoided further defilement in the first period of their
incarnation; at some later stage they 'fell' again into defiling
themselves with blood.

This solution is not wholly satisfactory in that it breaks the
cycle of alternating Love and Strife. After the initial outbreak
of Strife in heaven there is an ensuing period in which men
behave as if under the rule of Love before a second outbreak of
Strife at the second fall. If Strife is responsible for this
incarnate world this is anomalous, while the deception which
prevents men from seeing that they are polluting themselves
would be expected to afflict men from the first stages of their
incarnation, just as it does now.

There is, however, an alternative explanation. Although the
text is set in the past this does not preclude it from describing
the end of a period of banishment rather than the beginning.
Since the cycle of Love and Strife is eternal and continuous it
is possible to describe the return to the rule of Love in the past
as well as in the future. The end of a period of exile comes
when men come to their senses and cease to pollute themselves
with blood-guilt: only then is there no prolongation of the
period of catharsis, and men have only to live out the
remaining period of banishment for the pollution already on
their hands before returning to their state of blessedness. Such
a period of pure living must have occurred at the end of a reign
of Strife in the past: at that time men did not have the violent
gods but only Cypris, they poured libations but did not defile
their altars with blood, and the killing and eating of living
things – known to them from their past history – was the
greatest pollution in their eyes.[172]

[171] Kingsley (1979) pp. 66-72.
[172] B128.

With this text we may link others. B129: there was among them a man who knew a great deal and who was master of wise tasks – he saw things as they really are, in ten and twenty generations of men.[173] Men must clearly be enlightened to their true plight before they will be able to reform their behaviour, and the man who recognises and reveals the truth will be one who perceives the long-term effects of their actions over a series of generations. This must have occurred in the past, in the period described in B128.[174]

B146: At the end they are prophets, poets, doctors, leaders among men upon earth, and thence they spring up as gods, highest in honours.[175] This appears to be a description of the men who accept the truth and live pure lives, followed by their return to the 'gods'.[176]

B147: Sharing the same hearth as other immortals, having the same table, freed from the troubles of men, unwearied.[177] Clement quotes this as evidence that 'if we live piously and justly we shall be blessed here but even more blessed after the transfer hence, not having happiness in time but able to relax eternally'. There are no tensed verbs to locate the quotation in the past or the future; this could therefore be a description of the state subsequently attained by the men of the past age of B128.

(x) Hippolytus as reader of Empedocles

The effect of a system of alternating regimes such as has been described here, in which the values of 'this world' are inverted in 'the other world', is to produce a fundamental ambiguity in Empedocles' discourse. The words he has to use are the conventional terms to describe the value system of this world,

[173] B129 from Porphyry *Vita Pyth.* 30.
[174] The same will be required if the present age of Strife is to be brought to an end, and it is possible that Empedocles sees himself as such a figure, or that he saw Pythagoras as such, witness the tradition concerning B129.
[175] B146 from Clement *Strom.* 4.150.
[176] The reference to prophets, poets, doctors, again suggests Empedocles' own rôle.
[177] B147 from Clement *Strom.* 5.122.

the system which is to be questioned and undermined. Sometimes Empedocles specifies that a word is used in the sense understood by men in their ignorance;[178] he admits that he is forced to adopt conventional usages.[179] Every value-loaded term that he uses will in fact be necessarily ambiguous, and the possibility of such ambiguity in Empedocles' discourse is rarely appreciated.[180]

Hippolytus' interpretation stresses the contrast between 'this world' and 'that world' and the soul's status as fugitive whose home is not in 'this world'. This gives prominence to the opposed value systems implied by the alternating rules of Love and Strife. The comparison with the anti-cosmic dualism of Marcion's system brings out the ambiguity of the values of this world. Hippolytus does not however make Empedocles' system into an anti-cosmic dualism such as Marcion's: it is clear from his account that the contents of both worlds are the same; the cosmos is not inherently evil, but only in so far as it embodies the values of Strife; only the power shifts, and with it the value systems alternate. Hippolytus is clear that there is one world, now a unity, now a plurality, now under Love, now under Strife.[181] He stresses that the other creatures in this world are also *daimones* suffering exile under the rule of Strife.[182] The parallel with Marcion is the inversion of values which the change of regime entails, while in other respects the two systems differ, as Hippolytus makes clear.

The system of Empedocles is presented as more subtle than the crude dualism of Marcion. Hippolytus offers a relatively sensitive account of the cycle of banishment of the polluted *daimones* and draws out the significance in terms of the status

[178] B8, B9, B11, B15, B17.22.

[179] B9.5.

[180] An ambiguity in these value-terms is suggested by Kingsley (1979) p. 93, but he, I believe, determines the sense in the wrong direction in identifying the term *oulomenon* as a feature simply of men's mistaken terminology. On my view it is a feature of their ignorance that they fail to observe the conflict between their actions (which suggest that Strife is valuable and preservative) and their words (which name Strife as destructive).

[181] *Ref.* 7.29.8-9; 6.25.2-4.

[182] *Ref.* 7.29.22; 7.30.4.

of this world as a place of exile and punishment. These features
are not found in Marcion, for whom the soul belongs to this
world and is a creature of the demiurge, ultimately removed to
the realm of the good god by no right of its own. Hippolytus
offers a reading which stresses both the relationship between
the cycle of banishment and return and the alternation of
regimes, and the conflicting values which the banishment
entails.

(xi) Hippolytus on B110

A puzzling feature of Hippolytus' account of Empedocles is his
use of B110 at the end of the passage.[183] It stands apart from
the main interpretation, and according to the accepted text
Hippolytus identifies in it a third, intelligible, power in
addition to Love and Strife:

> But he says that there is also a third intelligible power, which it
> is possible to invent from these things, saying thus ...[184]

B110 itself consists of instructions to the listener to study what
he has heard carefully, in which case he will reap great benefit,
and a warning against the dangers of being led astray by the
interests of men and forgetting or corrupting the words he has
learnt. A.A. Long[185] remarks that Hippolytus' introduction
gives no help at all on the interpretation of the fragment.
Bollack[186] appears to suppose that Hippolytus identifies the
'third intelligible power' as being 'la puissance que confère
l'Amour dans notre monde'; evidently Bollack finds a
reference to such a power in B110, but which words might
have been read thus by Hippolytus is far from clear.[187]

Hippolytus has occasion to refer to the presence of a third
power in Empedocles again two chapters later when dealing

[183] Ref. 7.29.26.
[184] Ref. 7.29.25.
[185] A.A. Long (1966) p. 268.
[186] Bollack (1965/9) vol. 3 p. 577.
[187] Line 4 might be suggested: ἄλλα τε πόλλ' ἀπὸ τῶνδ' ἐκτήσεαι. But
ἐκτήσεαι is a conjecture, and this would give Hippolytus 'many other things'
rather than one third power.

with a later form of Marcionism which he regards as corrupt
and the innovation of Prepon.[188] This form of Marcionism
had an intermediary principle between good and evil, and
Hippolytus suggests that a comparable principle is found in
Empedocles' Muse, for which he quotes B131.[189] It is
unsatisfactory to suggest that Hippolytus had already
identified a third power in B110, in which there is no reference
to the Muse, and subsequently changed the identification for
no clear reason.

The problem is in fact a false one and results from the fact
that the text has been emended, following a suggestion of
Miller in the original edition. The reference to *kai noêtên tritên
tina dunamin* ('also a third intelligible power') at *Ref.* 7.29.25 is
not in the manuscript, which reads *kainon tên tritên tina dunamin*
('the third power is an innovation'). Hippolytus claims that in
B110 Empedocles is warning that the introduction of a third
power which can be invented from the doctrines outlined
already is an innovation. There is no doubt that Hippolytus
saw Prepon's third principle as an innovation (7.31.1):

> But since now in our own times a certain Marcionite named
> Prepon has attempted an innovation ...

In B110 he finds Empedocles warning of the dangers of
corruption of his words by those who are distracted by the
cares of men: the passage represents Empedocles' comment on
what people will subsequently make of his teaching.

In chapter 31 Hippolytus is concerned to ensure that
Prepon's system can also be shown to derive from Empedocles.
This leads him to suggest that the introduction of the third
principle does appear in Empedocles' poem as the Muse on
which Empedocles calls for aid. The Muse is an addition
which has no place in the list of divine beings which constitute
the contents of the world; thus it is in some sense an
'innovation' on Empedocles' part, a contamination of the pure
Empedoclean system. This 'third power' is not itself to be

[188] *Ref.* 7.31.1.
[189] *Ref.* 7.31.4.

located in B110 but only in B131; B110 merely gives a general warning concerning the possibility of corruption of Empedocles' doctrines.[190]

---

[190] B110 appears to suggest two possible results: the one who takes to heart Empedocles' words will 'gain many things' since the doctrines 'increase themselves'; the one who is distracted will forget, because the doctrines 'seek their own kind'. It is possible that the 'innovation' should belong in the first category of the legitimate developments of Empedocles' doctrines.

4. Heraclitus

A. Where did Hippolytus derive his information from?

The significant material on Heraclitus occurs in *Refutatio* 9.9.1-9.10.8. This section of text supplies nineteen quotations classified by Diels as fragments of Heraclitus, namely B1 and B50-67. Sixteen of these are not cited explicitly in any other extant text. According to Marcovich's division[1] between citation, paraphrase and reminiscence only B1 and B54 are *cited* by other authors and B52 is *paraphrased*.[2] Marcovich gives varying numbers of possible reminiscences of varying accuracy, but there is no other evidence at all for B55, B57, B59, B63 or B66. Hippolytus is thus the unique source for a considerable number of famous Heraclitean sayings.

The material used by Hippolytus falls into two classes: (1) quotations which include reference to knowledge and ignorance or employ verbs often or usually associated with cognition; (2) quotations concerned with the identification of opposites or the denial of distinctions between them, and statements of unity. Those which include references to cognition are B1, B51, B54, B55, B56, B57, B66; those with reference to the unity of opposites, or of all things, are B50, B51, B52, B53, B57, B58, B59, B60, B61, B62, B63, B67. The predominance of these two themes may reflect the interests of the source from which Hippolytus made his selection of material.

The likely context for a collection of material bearing on the means of access to knowledge and the inability of men in

---

[1] Marcovich (1967) p.xv.

[2] B1: cited by Sextus Empiricus *M* 7.132 and Clement *Strom.* 5.3.7; paraphrased by Aristotle *Rhet* Γ5. 1407b14. B54: cited by Plutarch *De An. Procr.* 1026c. B52: paraphrased by Lucian *Vit. Auct.* 14.

general to achieve it is a discussion of Heraclitus' epistemology.[3] Hippolytus' own interests in quoting the material are not in the epistemology *per se* but in the resultant denial of distinctions (for instance between the visible and invisible) and in what it is that men fail to recognise. On the other hand the collection of material on opposites does reflect a particular interest of Hippolytus; but Hippolytus must have selected this theme on the basis of knowledge of some texts, and he must have had access to a collection which included these texts.[4] If this was not Heraclitus' own book it will already have been selected with a particular reading in mind.

Aristotle[5] notes that Heraclitus was associated with violation of the principle of contradiction. Subsequently we find Heraclitus taken as the example of someone who asserted that contradictories are true of the same thing by the 'Followers of Aenesidemus', or perhaps Aenesidemus himself, who are attacked by Sextus Empiricus for suggesting a close link between Heracliteanism and Scepticism.[6] One place where Heraclitus' doctrine of opposites must have been stressed was the book, presumably by Aenesidemus, from which Sextus derived his information on Aenesidemus' association with Heraclitus, and from which he may have derived much of the information on Heraclitus which he uses elsewhere in his own work.[7] From Sextus' use of this work we know that Aenesidemus had discussed Heraclitus' theory of knowledge in his book, as well as the doctrine of opposites, in which case it combined the two interests which are most

[3] A possible alternative would be a passage concerning Heraclitus' disdain for other men, a theme prominent in the biographical literature (cf. Diogenes Laertius 9.1-3 and 6), but there is no evidence for any biographical interest in this passage.

[4] There is no evidence that this theme was observed by Stoic doxography, and it is unlikely that Hippolytus' material came from a Stoic source.

[5] *Metaph.* Γ, 1005b23ff.

[6] Sextus Empiricus *PH* 1. 210ff. It is clear that Sextus' opponents based their case on Heraclitus' assertion of the unity of opposites.

[7] Sextus ascribes doctrines to Heraclitus which he elsewhere assigns to Aenesidemus: compare *Adv. Math.* 9.360 and 10.230 with *PH* 3.138 and *Adv. Math.* 10.216; 10.233; also compare *Adv. Math.* 8.286 with *Adv. Math.* 7.349. The clearest example is the account of Heraclitus' epistemology, *Adv. Math.* 7.126ff. and 8.8.

prominent in Hippolytus' own account of Heraclitus.

These facts suggest that a possible area in which Hippolytus might have found a predominance of texts on these themes would have been among the Sceptical followers of Aenesidemus. We cannot conclude that Hippolytus' source was a work of Aenesidemus himself,[8] and his selection may only reflect a choice from a much more extensive range of material. However, it is worth noting that Hippolytus' own interest is not specifically in epistemology, while the texts he quotes reflect precisely the combination of epistemology and contradiction which interested Aenesidemus.[9]

B. What governed the choice and use of Heraclitean material? The parallel with Noetus and Callistus

In accordance with Hippolytus' method elsewhere, the force of his interpretation of Heraclitus is brought out by the juxtaposition with the parallel system of thought identified in the monarchian Noetus. Hippolytus gives a brief account of the doctrines of Noetus immediately after the passage on

[8] Janacek (1959) has argued that the passages common to Hippolytus and Sextus Empiricus do not represent Hippolytus copying Sextus but both using a common source. Elsewhere (Janacek 1980) he argues that there is a common source where Sextus Empiricus and Diogenes Laertius have parallel passages, and that the source was probably Aenesidemus. Janacek's arguments are not compelling but it is certainly the case that Hippolytus had access to literature and probably lectures, of the sceptical school and may well have known Aenesidemus' work.

[9] An attempt to name Hippolytus' source for his account of Heraclitus was made by Reinhardt (1916) pp. 158ff. who proposed (apparently seriously) that the source was Simon Magus' *Apophasis Megalê*. Few have taken this absurd suggestion seriously (though Kirk does (1954) p. 193); there is no evidence that Simon Magus knew anything substantial of Heraclitus, and Hippolytus' reference to Heraclitus in connection with him is clearly (see below p. 221), merely an inference from the prominence of fire in Simon's doctrines. Fire is significantly *not* prominent in the quotations available and used by Hippolytus in book 9. Reinhardt's case rested entirely on his assertion (pp. 158-9) that the material on Heraclitus does not fit Hippolytus' comparison with Noetus and is largely superfluous. The analysis which follows aims to demonstrate that, on the contrary, every item included is relevant to the theme.

Heraclitus, 9.10.9-12. This is followed by a detailed account of the life of Callistus, Hippolytus' own rival and a follower of Noetus, which includes another very brief summary of Noetian doctrines, 9.12.16-19. The initial impression that the life story of Callistus is irrelevant to the comparison with Heraclitus is unjustified: his life continues the theme of the breakdown of values and conventional distinctions; once an incompetent slave but now head of the church at Rome, once a liar, trouble-maker and convict but now the moral leader of the people, Callistus represents the disastrous results of the theory of indifference to which he adheres in his theology and in his ethical teaching. It is this theme of the confusion of opposed values which Hippolytus stresses in Heraclitus.

Noetus' position, classified as Modalist Monarchian or Patripassianist, is characterised by the claim that there is no distinction between God the Father and God the Son. The distinction between two 'persons' evolved later by Trinitarian theology is, on the Patripassianist view, incorrect, and Jesus Christ is simply the Father in a different mode. Thus all the experiences undergone by Christ during his incarnation can be directly referred to God *simpliciter* (rather than being restricted to one person of the Trinity) and any predicate applicable to the son is *ipso facto* applicable to God the Father or God as a whole.

These tenets are prominent in other texts which recount Noetian doctrines, particularly Hippolytus' *Contra Noetium*, Epiphanius' *Panarion* and Tertullian's *Adversus Praxean*,[10] and these texts can be used to complement the material presented in the *Refutatio*. Hippolytus begins at *Refutatio* 9.10.9 with Noetus' insistence on the unity of god: god is one and the same

---

[10] Praxeas is attacked by Tertullian for doctrines very similar to those ascribed to Noetus by Hippolytus. Some relation between them is suggested by the fact that Praxeas also appears as the last heretic in Ps. Tertullian *Adversus Omnes Haereses*. This short work seems to be a Latin paraphrase of the lost work of Hippolytus, the *Syntagma*. Photius at *Bibl.* 121 states that the *Syntagma* was against 32 heresies starting with the Dositheans and finishing with Noetus and the Noetians. Ps. Tertullian *Adv. Omn. Haer.* mentions 32 names of heretics and schools of thought and names Dosithus first and Praxeas last. Praxeas, whose doctrines are certainly Noetian, may represent Photius' 'Noetians' although the name of Noetus is not actually mentioned.

(*hena kai ton auton*), a phrase which is familiar from the material on Heraclitus; he is the creator of all things (*pantôn dêmiourgos*) and he is father. Noetus' single god is the subject of contrasting characteristics which Hippolytus proceeds to enumerate (9.10.9-10): he originally chose to be revealed to just men of old as being invisible;[11] at different periods of time he was visible and invisible,[12] spatially unconfined and spatially confined, unmastered and mastered, uncreated and created, immortal and mortal.[13]

Hippolytus' interests focus on questions of identity and difference implied by this succession of opposite characteristics: Noetus claims that it is 'one and the same god' who is described first by one set of predicates and then by the set of contrary predicates. In what sense can it be one and the same god when it has changed in all its principal characteristics? In particular the one set of characteristics, invisible, spatially unconfined, not subject to another authority, not subject to genesis, and immortal, are those normally taken as the proper attributes of the divine, whereas their contraries properly characterise what is non-divine. Noetus' claim that god comes to be characterised entirely by these non-divine attributes violates the conventional distinctions which mark out what is divine from what is not divine.

The Noetian assertion of the identity of Father and Son, which is the one most widely discussed in other texts,[14] is mentioned by Hippolytus as being generally known (9.10.10). Hippolytus quotes or paraphrases the formulation given by Noetus, which specifies the reciprocal relationship: the father

[11] This is a reference to the Old Testament period and should be compared with the discussion of Isaiah 45.14-15 in Hippolytus' *Contra Noetum* 4.

[12] Part of this contrast is missing from the text as it stands, but there can be no doubt that it should be supplied, p. 244 line 14.

[13] The three latter pairs have specific application to theological issues raised by the Noetian controversy: subjection to another authority, birth and mortality are central concepts in the birth, passion and death of Christ, and the importance of these issues can be identified in the *Contra Noetum* 6 (the question of *kratos*), 16.3 (*genesis*), 18.4 (mortality) and 8.1-3 (all three).

[14] *Contra Noetum* 1.1 and Ps. Tertullian *Adv. Omn. Haer.* 8 suggest that the characteristic doctrine was that Christ was the Father. It is discussed in detail by Tertullian *Adv. Prax.* 10.

is his own son, not the son of another, and the son is his own father (9.10.11). The change of name from father to son depends on a temporal distinction, and the choice of the father to undergo birth at will.[15] Again Hippolytus suggests that Noetus' doctrine ignores an important distinction of rôles; on conventional terms the father cannot be his own son and remain the same person.

Refutatio 9.10.12 concludes this account of Noetus with a series of paradoxes designed to highlight the absurdities which result from ignoring these distinctions and supposing that the terms 'father' and 'son' refer to the same individual. These paradoxes derive from scriptural passages which pose difficulties for the Noetian view. The first concerns the crucifixion: Christ's words from the cross, 'Father, into thy hands I commend my spirit',[16] are addressed to himself if he is the father. The second, 'dying and not dying', raises some difficulty about the death of Christ. It may be based on the texts discussed at *Contra Noetum* 18.4 concerning Christ's ability to lay down and take up his life of his own accord.[17] The third concerns the raising of Christ from the dead which is a central issue in the discussion of the Noetian position: if Christ and the father were one and the same, who raised Christ from the dead? The prominent term for the raising of Christ in the New Testament is the transitive verb *egeirô*, I rouse, usually either the passive *êgerthê* or *egertheis* (having been raised) with Christ as the subject,[18] or the active *egeiras* (having raised) with the father as subject and Christ as object.[19] This latter construction was clearly of particular importance for establishing a case against the Noetian position and is discussed in several of the anti-Monarchian texts.[20] In this context, however, Hippolytus uses the verb

[15] 9.10.11. The will of god is central in Noetus, cf. *Ref.* 9.10.9, 9.10.10, 9.10.11; *Contra Noetum* 8.3, 9.2, 10.1-3.

[16] Luke 23.46. cf. *Contra Noetum* 18.4.

[17] John 10.18.

[18] E.g. Romans 6.4, 6.9; 1 Cor. 15.12-20; John 2.22, 21.14; Luke 24.6, 24.34, etc.

[19] See Romans 8.11, 1 Cor. 15.15, Acts 13.30, 13.37 in particular, but compare Acts 2.24 and John 5.21.

[20] Romans 8.11 and parallel phrases from Isaiah 45.13 are discussed by Epiphanius *Panarion* 57.7 and Hippolytus *Contra Noetum* 4.6. and 18.5.

anistêmi (I raise) which may reflect Noetus' own terminology,[21]
but in the section on Heraclitus there is almost certainly
evidence of the significance of the term *egeirô* in connection
with this issue of the resurrection of Christ.[22]

The series of absurdities in the Noetian position is
concluded with three points concerning the passion. Again the
emphasis is on the breakdown of important distinctions
between what can be and what cannot be predicated of the
absolute divinity: Hippolytus finds it absurd that god himself
– 'this, the god and father of all things' (9.10.12) – should have
been buried in a tomb, pierced with a lance and fastened with
nails. These criticisms advert to the same problems of spatial
confinement, subjection to authorities and passibility that
were raised in 9.10.10, characteristics which belong only to
what is not-divine in conventional religion.

The summary of Callistus' position at *Refutatio* 9.12.16-19
dwells on the same points of Noetian doctrine, and
particularly the identity of father and son. The term *logos* is
used in this context:

> Saying that the *logos* was himself son, and himself also called
> by the name father, but that the spirit was one and undivided.

The term *logos* becomes prominent in the Heraclitus passage
in what appears to be a similar rôle. We also find a reference
to a claim that both the regions above and those below
(9.12.17) are full of the spirit of god, a point which appears to
deny the conventional association of 'higher' with 'more
divine': Callistus claims instead that there is no distinction
between up and down as regards divine attributes. One point
in which Callistus differs from Noetus is mentioned at 9.12.19:
Callistus denied that the father actually suffered (*peponthenai*),
preferring the ambiguity of 'being in sympathy with'
(*sumpeponthenai*). He is thus less extreme than Noetus in his
denial of the distinctions that mark out divinity, in that he

---

[21] The intransitive form of *anistêmi* would suit Noetus' case better.
Hippolytus' use of the transitive form here is paralleled in the reference to
God's raising of Christ at Acts 2.24.

[22] See below p. 176.

does allow that god cannot properly be said to suffer. It is Noetus' extreme position that constitutes the parallel for Heraclitus.

Callistus' ethical position is of greater significance and is elaborated in some detail at 9.12.20-6. The theoretical position which denies that one attribute rather than its opposite has any value or particular association with divinity results likewise in a permissive attitude on moral questions. For the followers of Noetus, value terms such as good and bad, sinner or sinless, have no significance in distinguishing what can or cannot be associated with divinity; such distinctions are meaningless and irrelevant to religion. Hippolytus dwells on the fact that Callistus offered easy forgiveness of sins to Christians after baptism and allowed sinners to remain in the Church, and clergy to remain in office after committing major sins. He revels in relating the shocking behaviour resulting from such a permissive society. Callistus' justification for allowing sinners to enjoy an equal status in the Church refers to scriptural phrases[23] which imply the expectation of a subsequent judgment by god: it is not up to men to decide what is or is not acceptable to god; but the expectation of a final judgment is not made explicit and is not implied at all by the use of the example of Noah's Ark.[24] If an absolute judgment is envisaged, Callistus' position will be an attack not on distinctions as such but on the distinctions imposed by men in their conventional beliefs.

C. Past work on the comparison between Heraclitus and Noetus

Two articles must be mentioned here:

(i) C. Ramnoux, 'Commentaire à la refutation des hérésies' (1961/9) 67-94

In this part of her two-part article Ramnoux considers the

---

[23] *Ref.* 9.12.22: 'Who art thou that judgest another man's servant?' (Romans 14.4) and 'Let the tares grow together with the wheat.' (cf. Matthew 13.29-30).
[24] *Ref.* 9.12.23.

account of Heraclitus at *Refutatio* 9.9-10, recognising the importance of presenting the context in which the fragments are preserved. The article has not been influential, and some of its inadequacies are noted by Marcovich (1966) 256n.3 and 259.

Ramnoux's approach is an attempt to 'strip off' (*dépouiller*, pp.68 and 81) the interpretative strata superimposed upon the 'genuine fragments' of Heraclitus in order to get back to some authentic body of unadulterated material. Although this shows a misconception, on my view,[25] as to what is of interest and helpful in dealing with such a text,[26] the major problem in Ramnoux's study is the fact that the 'interpretative strata' which she attempts to strip off do not correspond with what is actually found in the text.

The major difficulty concerns the identity of the heresy to which Heraclitus is assimilated. The technique of linking a heretic with a philosopher is noted by Ramnoux, but she curiously seems to ignore, or fail to observe, the account of the doctrines of Noetus which provide the parallel. Although she translates the main summary of Noetus' doctrines, her dismissal of the rest as interesting solely for the history of heresy[27] means that she ignores important material concerning Hippolytus' view of the Noetians. She appears unaware of the fact that the doctrines outlined as those of Noetus and his followers[28] *are* the doctrines to which Hippolytus is comparing Heraclitus in chapters 9 and 10. She mentions Noetus three times in passing towards the very end of her paper, as if his doctrines were irrelevant to the analysis of the passage under discussion.

The heresy which Ramnoux does describe is one which she attempts to 'reconstruct' by reading into Hippolytus'

[25] See above, Introduction pp. 12-13.

[26] Ramnoux professes awareness (p. 82) of the danger of letting the baby out with the bathwater (though the question of identifying *which* is the baby requires some consideration) but her approach is also liable to result in a process of 'peeling the onion'. In rejecting certain interpretations as 'fallacious' (p. 68) she is simply stripping away part of the most valuable evidence, in that these are the interpretations which we can analyse in detail.

[27] Ramnoux (1961/9) p. 67.

[28] *Ref.* 9.10.9 and again in chapter 12 (which she entirely ignores).

comments on Heraclitus the doctrines she considers he might have in mind. She describes the heresy as a type of gnosticism,[29] which is fundamentally misleading since the majority of the doctrines which she then describes are directly opposed to the basic tenets of gnosticism.

There are considerable problems with the 'heresy' constructed by Ramnoux, the main one being that many of its points cannot be adequately distinguished from an orthodox position. Hippolytus' supposed *objection* to the theories she lists would place him firmly on the side of the gnostics against whom he has been arguing for the previous eight books of the *Refutatio*. This conclusion is unacceptable: the Church to which Hippolytus adhered had defined itself primarily by contrast with gnosticism. A major part of Ramnoux's position rests upon her interpretation of the terms 'god', 'just' (*theos, dikaios*) as a contrasting gnostic pair, which is discussed below.[30] Ramnoux lists the features of her heresy under six points on page 73:

(1) confusion between the immanent and the transcendent both in the realm of being and of knowledge;
(2) confusion of good and bad, or the rejection of ethical dualism;
(3) the resurrection of this lower mortal flesh;
(4) the final judgment as a conflagration and apotheosis;
(5) the identity of Father and Son, that is Christ and the Father;
(6) identification of the supreme god with the demiurge, creator of the world.

Of these only (2) and (5) could be considered objectionable *per se* to Hippolytus' orthodoxy. (1) would allow for heresy precisely in so far as it allows for the detailed Monarchian doctrines attributed to Noetus in the later chapters, but is not in itself heretical.

In combination with a number of other features of the

---

[29] Ramnoux (1961/9) pp. 67-8.
[30] See below pp. 146-7.

work,[31] this preoccupation with an irrelevant heresy means that Ramnoux's comments are of little value for the study of Heraclitus.

(ii) M. Marcovich, 'Hippolytus and Heraclitus' (1966)

Marcovich treats a number of themes of interest in the relationship between the Noetian heresy and Hippolytus' material on Heraclitus, and does so in the light of his knowledge of Hippolytus and of the Patristic period which leads to more satisfactory results than those of Ramnoux. He notices particularly Noetus' insistence on the identity of God the Creator and God the Father (an anti-gnostic point) and quotes a number of texts.[32] Although it seems likely that this was a concern of Noetus, it does not seem to me so prominent in Hippolytus' concern with the parallels in Heraclitus. Marcovich also simplifies the account of Heraclitus to a single concern with the equation God = world (or creation), attacking his second thesis of Noetus (Father = Son);[33] this equation is certainly prominent but is not, on my view, the only relevant theme. Marcovich does not explore the implications of the parallel with Noetus in depth since he takes the view that (p.263) 'in spite of the context Hippolytus is a reliable source for Heraclitus, thanks to his habit of copying his sources ...' Thus his interest in the passage is the traditional concern with identifying accurate 'fragments' rather than with anything we might gain in interpretation from the comments offered by Hippolytus.

D. What reading of Heraclitus does Hippolytus' juxtaposition lead to?

In dealing with Hippolytus' reading of Heraclitus we are

[31] E.g. the failure to give any precise references to the numbering of the Greek text, which obscures the order of the text (esp. p. 72), the use of translation which obscures important differences of terminology (esp. pp. 70, 90, 91) and is sometimes tendentious (e.g. the translation of *Ref.* 9.10.1 on p. 81); the assumption that Hippolytus' arrangement of the fragments is archaising (p. 85). See below, p. 148n.47.

[32] Marcovich (1966) p. 256.

[33] Marcovich (1966) pp. 258-60.

naturally dealing with only one of the many interpretations which go to make up the mosaic of our current knowledge of Heraclitus' thought. As mentioned above, the characteristic pattern of Diels' arrangement of Heraclitean fragments arose from the fact that each ancient interpreter concentrates on a different theme in Heraclitus and quotes material in support of that theme. Hippolytus' reading of Heraclitus is partial and biased in so far as it gives prominence to some aspects to the exclusion of others, and our own study of his material will admittedly be similarly partial.

Whereas with Empedocles we could make provisional use of material quoted by other writers which was clearly relevant to the same theme, with Heraclitus the evidence is more difficult to handle. Short of embarking upon a complete analysis of the other interpretations in which texts are embedded, we are not in a position to use them extensively in connection with Hippolytus' material. Such juxtaposition is precisely the interpretative game played by the modern editors who rearrange the text without regard to the context in which it occurs.

Thus the primary concern in what follows will be to draw as much out of Hippolytus' own text as is possible and explore his interpretation in depth, as one among many possible readings of the text, and one which is founded upon a particular selection of material, the texts actually found embedded in Hippolytus' work. This reading is incomplete so far as our total knowledge of Heraclitus goes, but it is the first stage in the process of reading the text.

(i) Opposites undermined

Heraclitus' use of opposites, which occupies a large part of Hippolytus' account of Heraclitus, constitutes a major theme. As in his account of Noetus, Hippolytus focuses on questions of identity and difference and the application of contrasting predicates to the same thing: Heraclitus also questions the conventional distinctions which these terms import.

(a) The subject of these different terms

In Noetus' theory the unity to which the contrasting

characteristics belong has so far been termed 'god', but this is not a consistent usage of Hippolytus'. Although he starts with the statement 'that god is one and the same' (9.10.9), the term *theos*, god, is not used again until the very end of the chapter. The terminology is fluid, and father, demiurge, son, as well as descriptive phrases such as 'the one who dwelt among men as man' (9.10.11) are all used indiscriminately and said to be 'one and the same thing' (9.10.11). In the case of Heraclitus the position is similar: there is no single term which Hippolytus consistently uses to designate the subject to which all the contrasting descriptions apply. Instead he builds up a cumulative list of terms which are identified in successive sayings of Heraclitus: *logos*, child, father, aeon, etc. The only candidate as the term by which he would identify the subject to which these terms apply is 'the all' (*to pan*), which he uses in this rôle in the first sentence of his account (9.9.1) and again on two subsequent occasions to identify *logos* (9.9.3) and child (9.9.4) as being 'the all'. Apart from the list of terms in the first sentence (9.9.1) the term god is not introduced as a description of this subject in Heraclitus until 9.9.5 at least, and perhaps later if Wendland's conjectural reading at that point is rejected.[34] Thus although Hippolytus introduces Heraclitus' doctrine of opposites as parallel to Noetus' doctrine of god, and clearly takes it to be applicable, among other things, to matters concerning god (cf. the final passage on B67 at 9.10.8), it is clear that both Heraclitus' and Noetus' doctrines are taken to have wider implications; as a result of the breakdown of distinctions between god and other things, both theories concern the whole range of values in the world as a whole, and hence Hippolytus chooses the phrase 'the all' to express the general implications of Heraclitus' theory.

(b) The opening sentence

The opening sentence of the account of Heraclitus is programmatic:

---

[34] According to Wendland three letters are illegible in the manuscript. For my suggestions concerning the state of the text at this point see below pp. 160-1.

> Heraclitus says that the all is divisible indivisible, created uncreated, mortal immortal, *logos*, aeon, father, son, god, just.

Each term in this list adverts to a point made later in the course of the account of Heraclitus,[35] and they are also terms which pick out significant themes in the parallel with Noetus.[36] Since this list of terms has occasioned intense discussion in the past, the main difficulties must be dealt with briefly here.

It has been usual to assume[37] that these should be divided into six pairs of opposites, and commas are always inserted in the text in accordance with this reading, with complex explanations given for the problematic pairs *logos*, aeon and god, just. The difficulties are simply resolved when it is recognised that Hippolytus' concern is with a breakdown not only of distinctions between opposites but of all differences: he is introducing the key phrase from B50, *hen panta einai*: one thing is all things and all things are one thing;[38] and the one thing is all things in that it can be called by any one of a range of various terms which may be opposites or may import distinctions in their own right in conventional usage. There is no indication that 'all things' should be restricted to pairs of

[35] divisible indivisible: cf. ?9.9.3, B1, and B50.
created uncreated: cf. 9.9.4, B52, B53, and B67 (9.10.8).
mortal immortal: cf. 9.10.6, B62.
logos: cf. 9.9.1-3, B50 and B1.
aiôn: cf. 9.9.4, B52.
father: cf. 9.9.4, B53.
son: cf. ?9.9.4, B52.
god: cf. 9.10.8, B67.
just: cf. 9.10.7, B64-66.
[36] This is particularly clear for created, uncreated, mortal, immortal, *logos*, father, son, god. The pair divisible indivisible may refer to the question of the Noetians' denial of divisions between the persons of the Trinity. The significance of *aiôn* and just will be discussed below.
[37] Kirk (1954) pp. 65-6 reviews earlier suggestions by Kranz, Diels, Bergk, Gomperz, Heidel and Wendland, all based on the assumption that six (or more) contradictory pairs must be found here. Ramnoux (1961/9) follows the same tradition (p. 75) but it is questioned by Marcovich (1966) who suggests that *theos dikaios* (god just) should be taken as *one* idea (p. 259).
[38] The ambiguity should not be resolved (contra e.g. Marcovich (1967) p. 116: 'Of course, *panta* is the subject here ...').

relative opposites: some terms such as 'god' imply difference such that certain other terms such as mortal, created, and the› like could not be ascribed to the same individual. No single opposed term need be sought for the inclusion of this term to represent a breakdown of distinction.

Gnostic distinctions have figured as the main explanation for those who seek a contrast in the pairs *logos*, aeon and god, just. Ramnoux[39] proposes that the significance of the pair *logos*, aeon can be explained from Irenaeus' account of gnostic emanations, but in what sense she can identify a contrast from this source is unclear: in all gnostic systems the *logos* is an aeon and both are derivative from the Father. The suggestion of a gnostic antithesis between god and just was made by Wendland[40] and taken up by Kirk and Ramnoux.[41] It is founded upon the Marcionite distinction between a bad but judicial god, the Creator of the Old Testament, and the true good god who is supreme. The extent to which a straight contrast could be drawn between the simple terms 'god' and 'just' even in Marcionism is far from clear,[42] and there is no reason to look for allusions to Marcion's doctrines in this passage where the Noetian heresy is under discussion. Hippolytus himself recognised no such division between god and creator, and to suggest that he is objecting to the denial of such a distinction by Noetus or Heraclitus is to place him on the wrong side of the heretical fence. There is no evidence from Hippolytus' own account of Noetus that Noetus made any important comments on the status of the Old Testament god apart from his insistence that he was identical with the

[39] Ramnoux (1961/9) p. 75.

[40] Wendland ad loc. p. 241.

[41] Kirk (1954) p. 66; Ramnoux (1961/9) p. 75. Kirk betrays his lack of understanding of the point by cashing out Wendland's reference the wrong way round (*theos* must be the true god and *dikaion* the Old Testament creator; not vice versa). Kirk is followed in this mistake by Ramnoux who does not acknowledge her debt to Kirk.

[42] On the question of whether the inferior god was bad or just or both, and on the possible intermediate 'Just' principle, see above pp. 101-8. See also Marcovich (1966) p. 259.

god revealed in Christ.[43]

Taken as separate ideas, these four terms present less problem: all of them have strong associations of theological or ethical value, and hence import implications of distinctions which are undermined by Heraclitus' denial of all differences.

(c) Hen panta einai

This key theme of the whole section on Heraclitus' doctrine of opposites occurs in the first quotation given by Hippolytus, B50.[44] The one thing ('the all') is all things (all the things listed in the preceding sentence, *logos*, aeon, father, etc). Hippolytus will proceed to build up a collection of material which identifies the terms listed in the first sentence and others which import similar notions of degree as 'one and the same'. The terms in the list can serve as markers for us in the cumulation of identities, but they are not the only terms which are identified as one and the same.

Logos occurs in the first part of B50:

Listening not to me but to the *logos*, it is wise to agree (*homologein*) that one thing is all things/all things are one thing (*hen panta einai*).

Is this significant in Hippolytus' use of the words? *Logos* is actually a correction by Bernays of the manuscript reading *dogmatos* (doctrine), and Marcovich's argument in favour of the correction is not conclusive.[45] However, the possibility that

[43] Marcovich (1966) p. 259 suggests that *theos dikaios* should be taken as a single idea in opposition to *to pan*, thus producing the identity God = world. This makes it obscure how the rest of the list of terms identified with *to pan* fit into the scheme: although one of Hippolytus' conclusions is that god and creation must be indistinguishable for Heraclitus, I do not think that that point can be located in any contrast between *to pan* and *theos dikaios* here; why *dikaios*?

[44] *einai* is Miller's correction of the ms. reading *eidenai*. The two words are confused elsewhere by the scribe. See Marcovich (1967) 113 against e.g. Ramnoux (1959) and Bollack-Wismann (1972) 175.

[45] Marcovich (1967) p. 113. I see no reason why the scribe's illiteracy should result in his changing *logos* to *dogmatos*, though it does seem plausible that *dogmatos* might have originated as an explanation of what *logos* meant in this context, and took the place of *logos* in the text as a result.

Hippolytus read and wrote *logos* and saw the significance of its relation to *homologein* is strong. *Logos*, as one of the terms which name 'the all', is itself identical with the one, *hen*. 'Listening not to me but to the *logos* (one) it is wise for us to agree (make the *logos* one and the same) that all things are one.' The one thing itself communicates its own nature, is itself the articulate *logos*.[46]

Hippolytus picks up a pun[47] in *homologein* which becomes prominent in an accumulation of words emphasising unity, agreement, cohesion in the following sentence: *homologousin* (they agree), *xuniasin* (they understand), *homologeei*, (it agrees), *harmoniê* (harmony). The stress is on sameness, unity and identity, but the term *homologein* has particular significance in connection with Noetus' assertion that the *Logos* was 'the same' as the father. Heraclitus complained that all men do not agree with him, *oude homologousin*: here Hippolytus picks up the use of *homologein* in B50 – it is wise to agree.[48] But in B51 *homologeei* is used of 'it', the one which agrees with itself, *heautôi homologeei*, while the listeners of B50 are the subject of *ou xuniasin* – they fail to understand. It differs from itself,

---

[46] The same would be true of Noetus' *logos* which is itself the one (god) and is also that aspect of god which communicates itself (as the incarnate *logos* and as the word of god in scripture). Scripture and the incarnate *logos* are the means by which god persuades men that he is one thing and all things, for Noetus (cf. *Contra Noetum* 3-7, Epiphanius *Panarion* 57, and *Ref.* 9.10.11). Thus Hippolytus may have used B50 for a parallel with Noetus as well as for the theme of unity in Heraclitus. On the multiple implications of *logos* and problems of translating it see Tertullian *Adv. Prax.* 5.

[47] Hippolytus' interest in puns and etymological symbolism is evident in many contexts (cf. e.g. *Ref.* 6.6.1). Ramnoux (1961/9) attempts to argue that Hippolytus' construction of the account of Heraclitus, on the basis of association of words, symbolism, alliteration and word-play, is archaising since words ceased to be magic in the time of Heraclitus. This view is untenable, since there is no evidence that words lost their magic in popular and poetic contexts with the advent of syllogistic argument, and we do not have to suppose a tradition of neo-orphism reviving the word-play of the Heraclitean age to explain its presence in the theosophical and pseudo-scientific popular writing of the age of gnosticism (as Ramnoux proposes, p. 85). This type of play on words is a feature of Hippolytus' style in those passages where he is not copying but composing in his own right (the beginnings and ends of books, connecting passages between different subjects and between a philosopher and his related heretic).

[48] Is there a significance in relation to the question of whether the heretic can persuade men to agree with his assertion of the unity of the *logos*?

diapheromenon heautôi, and it agrees with itself, *heautôi homologeei*:
is it many or is it one? Heraclitus, Hippolytus suggests,
answers one, *hen panta einai*, and that the difference is
irrelevant to its unity and sameness,[49] but the rest of mankind
believes that the differences are fundamental and signal the
need to distinguish a plurality, to apply many *logoi*.

Doubts have been cast on the word *homologeei* in the text at
this point.[50] The main reason behind the preference for
reading another word for 'it agrees', *sumpheretai*, is Plato
Symposium 187a:

> For he says that the one differing from itself agrees
> (*sumpheresthai*) with itself, like the *harmonia* of the bow and the
> lyre.

which almost certainly refers to the same passage in
Heraclitus, and the natural tendency to trust Plato as the
earlier witness. However, B10, which includes the phrase
sumpheromenon diapheromenon (agreeing, disagreeing), would be
sufficient explanation for Plato, who almost certainly quotes
from memory, to have 'misquoted' by assimilation of more
than one passage, whereas Hippolytus must have had some
text before him.[51] The likelihood of confusion with previous
occurrences of the word in Hippolytus' passage is not so
strong as has been suggested.[52] If I am right to suggest that the

---

[49] Compare Noetus' claim that the different manifestations of his god,
despite involving contrasting characteristics, are simply modes of the same
individual, *Ref.* 9.10.9-10.

[50] See in particular Kirk (1954) pp. 204-6 who quotes a list of authorities
on his side, Vlastos (1955) p. 348 and Marcovich (1967) pp. 124-5.

[51] Cf. Vlastos (1955) p. 348, arguing in favour of Hippolytus' reading,
palintropos, in the second part of the fragment. Marcovich's accusation that
homologeei derives from a Stoic source used by Hippolytus will not stand up to
the evidence concerning Hippolytus' source (see above section (a) and below
on *Ref.* 9.10.7).

[52] Cf. Kirk (1954) p. 204. It is not true (contra Kirk, Raven, Schofield,
(1983) p. 192) that *homologein* had been used twice in the infinitive in the
preceding passage. The preceding sentence included *homologousin* but the ms.
reading in B51, *homologeein* (with final v) would suggest corruption with
homologein three lines above. In neither case does any similarity of context
lead to the (rather surprising) substitution of *homologeein* for *sumpheretai* being
any more likely.

significance of the word *homologein* for Hippolytus' purpose was a major reason for his quoting this text, we should naturally suppose that Hippolytus himself read *homologeei*: if Heraclitus' text originally read *sumpheretai* we must then suppose that Hippolytus had a corrupt text, in which case the occurrence of *homologein* in the context in Hippolytus' commentary cannot be used to explain the corruption.

As regards the meaning of the words I cannot see Kirk's difficulty[53] with the reading *homologeei*. He claims that the word *homologei* had a special meaning in fragment 50 dependent on the word play with *logos* and that 'there is naturally no such motive in fr. 51'. This claim begs the question, for we have no original context for B51 and hence cannot judge what motive there might have been for a play on the word *logos*.[54] All we know is that Hippolytus used it with just such a play on *logos* as a primary theme, and that he quoted it in the same context as B50. There are insufficient grounds for supposing that Plato's testimony should carry greater weight than Hippolytus', and the sound procedure is to see what can be made of Hippolytus' reading rather than to change the text to a less challenging reading.

In differing from itself it leads men to apply different words to things and it becomes many in their eyes, but in agreeing with itself it makes those *logoi* the same, *homologeei*. What men think are fundamentally different descriptions all amount to the same thing, because there is but one thing. For Hippolytus' purpose Noetus holds the same view: other men think that the different manifestations of the divine amount to a plurality of persons; they distinguish differences. But in fact there is but one, and the *logos* is indeed the same as the father.

The quotation B51 includes an image to illustrate the 'harmony' which differs from itself and agrees with itself:

[53] Kirk (1954) p. 205.
[54] Similarly Kirk's statement that the idea of correspondence of words 'is certainly not present in fr. 51' (Kirk (1954) p. 206) again begs the question as to the possible range of meanings that might be explored in the use of *homologeei* in B51.

They do not understand how in differing from itself it agrees with itself: a back-turning (*palintropos*) construction (*harmoniê*) like that of the bow and lyre.

Harmoniê is one of the terms which emphasise unity and agreement, but Hippolytus' interest in the image may extend further than the one term: his interest is in questions of identity, but particularly in what sort of identity can be ascribed to something which is described by opposite features. The term *harmoniê* itself implies a conjunction of different things, and in the case of the bow or lyre it is only the *harmoniê*, construction, that holds together the opposed forces as a functioning and efficient unity: if taken apart the different components are useless.[55]

The word *palintropos* describing *harmoniê* may well suggest strong associations for Hippolytus' demonstration of a similarity of ideas between Heraclitus and Noetus. In terms of Noetus' system *tropos* would be a natural usage for the mode of existence or manifestation of god at the various stages of history;[56] in addition to its meaning of 'mode' it carries associations with change, *tropê*, which is used of the different manifestations of fire in Heraclitus, B31. The implication of change is the basis of a possible criticism of Noetian doctrine in Tertullian's account[57] and Hippolytus may be suggesting the same criticism in recording the Heraclitean term *palintropos* in this context.[58] *Palin-* serves to emphasise the

[55] The bow, whose name is life and whose function death (B48), is a prime example of that which links opposed forces. What holds them together is the word *bios* ('bow' and 'life'): the *logos* is the same, it agrees (*homologeei*).

[56] This is sense D of *tropos* in Lampe. The history of the use of this term for the mode of being of god in Christ, and other theological issues, is a long and complex one, but it becomes particularly prominent in the Arian controversy (e.g. Athanasius *Ar.* 3.15). We have no evidence for any particular term used by the Monarchian heretics for the modes in which god was manifested – indeed the absence of any such term may suggest that they avoided terms which might imply change.

[57] Tertullian *Adv. Prax.* 27 (cf. *kata chronôn tropên, Ref.* 9.10.11).

[58] Further criticism might be implied by the association of the term *tropos* with figurative speech and a suggestion that for Noetus (and perhaps Heraclitus also) the terms used to distinguish different characteristics are merely used metaphorically (*tropikôs*) and carry no real meaning. The 'son' was not really the son but only called 'son' (*Ref.* 9.10.11).

associations of changeability: it is a reciprocal change back-and-forth between one mode and another, and the implications of continuous repetition, or at least of reversion to a former mode, are strong. Noetus' god, transformed from one character to a fashion characterised by opposite features and back to its original characteristics again, was certainly *palintropos*. What of the implications of the word in Heraclitus' reference to the *harmoniê*?

The word *palintropos* has been doubted,[59] although most recent opinion has favoured *palintropos* as against the variant *palintonos* (back-stretching) found in some, but not all, of the other authorities who quote part of this saying.[60] *Palintonos* is a standard epithet for the bow in Homer, and hence the *lectio facilior* in citations of the Heraclitean saying, while the variant *enantiotropês hêrmosthai* ('having been harmonised in an opposite-turning way') quoted from Theophrastus by Diogenes Laertius 9.7 clearly suggests that *palintropos* was known to Theophrastus.[61] Kranz (1958) p.253 has pointed out the parallel in Euripides' *Hippolytus* 161ff., which suggests that the musical significance of the combination of *-tropos* and *harmonia* did not pass unnoticed in antiquity.

The term *palintropos*, alternating between one state and another, applies to the bow and lyre with respect to the process involved in using them. In the case of the lyre the tuning is literally changed from one mode to another in playing; in both bow and lyre the natural state is an equilibrium of opposed tensions[62] which is disturbed and altered by the action of drawing the bow string and plucking

---

[59] Kirk (1954) p. 211, Marcovich (1967) p. 125 and further references in Vlastos (1955) p. 348.

[60] Plutarch *De Is.* 369B and one ms. at *De tranq. an.* 473F, and Porphyry *De Antr. Nymph.* 29 have *palintonos*; Plutarch *De an. procr.* 1026B and all the other mss at 473F have *palintropos* as in Hippolytus. Hippolytus alone gives a complete citation.

[61] These and further arguments which constitute a convincing case for retaining *palintropos* are set out in Vlastos (1955) 348-51.

[62] 'Tensions' are a feature of accounts discussing the reading *palintonos* and are not explicit in the reading *palintropos*. However the familiarity of the Homeric *palintonos* as an epithet of the bow enables us to read *palintropos* as a comment on and sophistication of the same observation.

the lyre string until the release of the string allows it to return to its original state. The use of the instrument involves a continuous succession of alternating states, with the force of a spring, resulting from the construction (*harmoniê*) of the instrument, drawing them back to their original state after each disturbance. Each is *palintropos* in the same way as Noetus' god is *palintropos*: it exists in a succession of different states, drawn back to its original state after a period in which it had adopted a form foreign to its natural tendencies.[63]

Hippolytus' reading suggests that we might see the differentiation of the 'one' in Heraclitus as a change of state comparable with the change of state undergone by a bow when the string is drawn, while its internal forces draw it back to its normal state. Distinctions (perhaps the *tropai* of B31) are merely distortions of a state of equilibrium; they are part of the working of the world but they do not mark out a plurality of things in the world as men think.

(d) Logos, child, aeon, king, father, creation, creator

Hippolytus proceeds to give a detailed account of the material on which he based his claim in the first sentence of his summary (*Ref.* 9.9.1) that Heraclitus identified 'the all' with a range of different ideas.[64] At *Ref.* 9.9.3-4, B1 and B52-53 are used to give an accumulation of identities of the following form:

B1   The all = *logos*
B52   The all = child, child = aeon, aeon = king
B53   king = father, father = creation, creation = creator

This yields the conclusion that all these terms can be identified.[65] This group of identifications is followed by a more

---

[63] Vlastos (1955) also sees the point of *palintropos* in the bow and lyre as being in their modus operandi despite the fact that he emphasises the idea of turning, *tropê*, rather than that of mode, *tropos*, in *palintropos*.

[64] See above, pp. 144-7.

[65] Note the contrast with Marcovich's suggestion that the argument is only designed to conclude that 'creation' and 'creator' are identified (Marcovich (1966) p. 258), for which only the last pair is required and hence the majority of the analysis of these passages is superfluous. A single narrow reading of B53 or B67 would have served his entire purpose.

complex argument concerning the denial of distinctions between a range of opposite qualities which carry implications of value, which will be dealt with separately below.[66] However, one further point is made at *Ref.* 9.10.8 which belongs in this earlier group:

B67   creation = creator.

The importance of the term *logos* in Hippolytus' scheme has already been noted,[67] and its prominence in *Refutatio* 9.9.1-2 continues into the commentary on B1 where Hippolytus claims that Heraclitus identifies 'the all' as logos, and hence marks out B1 as the basis for the inclusion of *logos* in the list of terms at 9.9.1.[68] Hippolytus' introductory words to B1 are particularly important for discerning how he understood the words which he then quotes.

Hoti de logos estin aei to pan reads, on the analogy with the first sentence at 9.9.1, as a statement 'that the one thing (the all) is always *logos*'. Hippolytus' *estin aei* (is always) suggests that he almost certainly took it that *aei* (always) in B1 could be taken with *eontos* (being): *tou de logou toud'eontos aei* ..., 'this logos being always ...'. It does not, however, imply that he did not recognise it as ambiguous, nor that he would not also have taken it to govern the words which follow it at the same time, nor that he would have felt it necessary to opt for one or the other exclusively.[69]

More important is the interpretation of the whole phrase *tou de logou toud'eontos aei* ... Hippolytus concludes that Heraclitus said that the one thing (the all) is always *logos*: clearly he reads in this phrase a reference to 'the all', the one thing, and the most likely reference is to the word 'this', *toude*: 'This thing

[66] Below pp. 160-70.

[67] Above p. 148 and n. 46.

[68] Hippolytus does not comment on the continued theme of the ignorance of men, on which see above pp. 132-3.

[69] Kirk's comment (1954, p. 34) implies that Hippolytus must have understood *aei* (always) exclusively with *eontos* (being), a conclusion which is not justified by the text. Aristotle, as he points out, at *Rhet.* Γ5, 1407b14, had noted the ambiguity without committing himself to one or the other interpretation. Kahn (1979, pp. 92-5) argues in favour of studied ambiguity in which neither interpretation is exclusively 'the correct one'.

always being the *logos* ...' That Heraclitus should refer to his one thing as 'this' implies that it had already been mentioned. It has been mentioned in Hippolytus' context, but has he any grounds for suggesting that it had been mentioned in the original context of B1? The quotation is apparently based on words which occurred 'at the beginning of Heraclitus' book'.[70] If nothing occurred before these words, the reference of 'this' could only be '*logos*'. Several suggestions have been made in the past as to what words might have come immediately before B1 as the opening words of the book,[71] but Hippolytus' suggestion as to the reference of *toude* would lead us to expect not a mention of *logos* or *legei*[72] but a reference to *hen* (one) or some similar term. The apparent prominence of *xunon* (common) in B1 and B2 (and cf. B114) might suggest that Heraclitus' treatise began with some such concern:

> One thing is common; but of this thing which is always the *logos* men are always uncomprehending (*axunetoi*).[73]

Hippolytus' introductory comment continues with a phrase qualifying *logos*, *kai dia pantos ôn* (and being through everything), a suggestion that the *logos* is in some way universal. The relevance of this comment to B1 must be located in the words *ginomenôn gar pantôn kata ton logon tonde* (all things coming to be according to this *logos*), which, however, would be more valuable to Hippolytus as a point about creation.[74] The fact that the point about the universality of the

---

[70] Sextus Empiricus *Adv. Math.* 7.132. Cf. Aristotle *Rhet.* 1407b14.

[71] See the discussion in Kirk (1954) p. 36.

[72] The suggestions of Capelle, Aall, Gilbert, Zeller, Wilamowitz, Diels et al.

[73] The *de* in B1 thus becomes a normal usage, and *axunetoi* a clear pun as in B114. Neither Sextus Empiricus nor Aristotle gives any indication of having a text which included any words before those they quote, but their text need not have been complete. Whether Hippolytus had any justification for his understanding of 'this' as a reference to 'the all' is unclear, but his source may itself have included exegetical commentary expounding the texts which were relevant to the unity of opposites.

[74] Creation of all things in accordance with the *Logos* would be a promising starting point for a comparison with Noetus in view of the significance of the pre-incarnate *Logos* and its rôle in creation in discussions of Monarchian doctrines e.g. *Contra Noetum* 10.

logos seems to have little justification and is not supported directly by the quoted text suggests that the text of Hippolytus' comment may be more corrupt than has been recognised.[75] We should expect a comment that related Heraclitus' phrase to that of John 1.3 *panta di'autou egeneto* (all things came to be through him).

Hippolytus' interest is in the identification of *logos* as a term for the one thing and this is the primary rôle which B1 plays in his argument, although the remainder of the text continues two themes: (1) the assertion that all distinctions are denied by Heraclitus' doctrine: all things fall under the scheme – all things are *kata ton logon*; (2) the failure of other men to recognise this universal fact, a theme introduced in B51 and continued in B1, although Hippolytus does not comment again. In addition the reference to dividing each thing in B1 may be one basis for the presence of divisible, indivisible in the opening list at 9.9.1: Heraclitus who asserts the unity of all things nevertheless divides them in his own use of words, 'according to nature'. On the one hand there is no distinction, on the other hand Heraclitus' own discourse imports the distinctions which are necessary for describing things *kata phusin*.

B52 is introduced with a comment parallel to that used for B1, and again it indicates the distinctions which are the focus of Hippolytus' interest. The all, the one thing, is identified as child, as it was identified as *logos* in B1, but a further breakdown of differences is suggested in the references to eternal and king. As *logos* in B1 picked up the term *logos* in the list at 9.9.1, so ought child in B52, as another term for the all, and the principal candidate is son, a term with stronger implications for the parallel with Noetus.

Hippolytus reads B52 as a claim that the one thing, the all, is a child. The quotation gives him the statement *aiôn pais esti* (*aiôn* is a child), in which case he regards *aiôn* (age) as a substitute for the all, a claim already made in the opening list

---

[75] The ms. reads ὦν instead of ὤν; Bernays proposed αἰῶνος.

of terms for the all at 9.9.1, but not explicitly justified. In the juxtaposition of *aiôn* and *pais* (child) a polarity is apparent which Hippolytus emphasises by his association of *aiôn* with *di'aiônos aiônios* (eternal through eternity), in his commentary: *aiôn* carries associations of eternity in the sense of a long period of time, *pais* those of short-lived youthfulness; eternity, the everlasting, has associations of importance and value, it belongs to the divine and what is honourable; *pais* is of no worth, a child playing commands no respect. The contrast is underlined by Hippolytus' use of *aiônios* to characterise *basileus*, king, again with associations of importance and influence.

'Eternity is a child playing at draughts; the kingdom is the kingdom of a child.' Two contrasts are undermined here: that between child's play and kingly rule, and that between eternity and childhood. Both are relevant to the parallel with Noetus, who attributed the temporal childhood of Christ to the eternal god the Father and hence maintained that the 'king of all things' was for a time nothing else than a child playing.[76]

The introduction to B53 is not parallel with the two previous points made by Hippolytus. This time he does not mention 'the all', and the definite article for *patêr* (father) suggests that we should translate: 'that the father of all things created is created and uncreated, creation and creator ...'. The quotation B53 itself gives us the equation of king and father and the previous stages in the argument had provided an equation between king and 'the all'. Hence B53 serves as the basis of the claim that father is a term for 'the all' at 9.9.1, as well as the inclusion of created, uncreated in the list at this point.

The identification of father and king implies an identification of father with the child who was also king in B52. This identity is one we should expect Hippolytus to have an interest in as a parallel to Noetus' identification of Father and Son. The confusion between father and son may be one basis for the mention of *genetos agenetos* (begotten, unbegotten) in this context, but the link with creation, creator suggests

[76] For the use of the 'kingdom of a child' paradox in orthodox Christianity, on the other hand, cf. Matthew 18.1-4.

that the primary reference is to a confusion between created and uncreated. The confusion between creator and creature is not a prominent theme in Noetus' system, but clearly came over strongly from Hippolytus' reading of B53.

What interpretation of the words of B53 leads Hippolytus to this impression of the confusion of the rôle of creator and created, of cause and effect, originator and consequence? Kirk reconstructs what he takes to be the argument by which Hippolytus 'evidently derived his conclusion' as follows:[77] 'War is described as a supreme god, and yet he creates the gods as well as men; therefore *qua* god he is both creator and created' – an argument which Kirk then dismisses as 'childish'. The 'childishness' of the argument arises from the dubious move '*qua* god he is both creator and created' which can hardly be justified from the text, in which the important term seems to be father, not god.

We should do better to attend to the significance for Hippolytus the Christian of the term *polemos*, war. War for him is something originated by mankind;[78] it is not only created, but is the creature of created beings itself, the product of man's fallen state. War must be *genetos* – originated, caused, part of the changing world, a feature of the *ktisis*. If Heraclitus characterises war as the creative father and supreme god with control over the destiny of man he is displaying a profound confusion between created and uncreated things. The irony identified by Hippolytus in this description of war as the one with power to make men slave or free, immortal or mortal, is a striking feature of the Heraclitean text.

The interpretation of *polemos* as the basis for Hippolytus' reading of the text is confirmed by his use of B67, which is included right at the end of the account, *Ref.* 9.10.8, but points out precisely the same confusion of creator and created

---

[77] Kirk (1954) p. 245.

[78] Marcovich (1966) p. 258 suggests that 'war' is confused with Empedocles' 'Strife' as equivalent to the world. An association of 'this world' with the reign of strife is found in Hippolytus' view of Empedocles (see above pp. 119f.) but Strife is particularly identified as the demiurge, the *creator* of this world, so that the point does not explain an association with the *created* world. The reference to Empedocles is not necessary to an understanding of Hippolytus' point here.

world.[79] In B67 the point about war being a feature of the created world seems to be the same as in B53. Hippolytus says that the created cosmos is itself creator:

> For the made world has itself become creator and maker of itself ...

In the quotation which follows, the reference to the created cosmos must be located in the list of opposites 'day, night, winter, summer, war, peace, satiety, hunger (all the opposites, that is the intention) ...'; it is in the identification of god[80] with these features of the created world-order, and the suggestion that he changes from one to the other, *all_oioutai*,[81] that Hippolytus sees the identification of creator and his own creation.

Did B67 stand last in Hippolytus' account of Heraclitus? If it did we can perhaps see why it did, and why it was set apart from B53. Not only does B67 make the point which Hippolytus' comment makes explicit, but it sums up the theme of the breakdown of distinctions which has been running through the whole account. There is no difference between god and his created world and there is no difference between the opposites which mark out the created world: day and night are one and the same (B57) as also are winter and

---

[79] This passage appears to be an afterthought. p. 244.5 'he says' (*legei*) must mean Heraclitus despite the fact that it follows a reference to Noetus. It is conceivable that the text is at fault and the passage has been transposed out of its proper context.

[80] The word 'god' at the start of the quotation seems to be required by Hippolytus' interpretation. Some subject has to be supplied for the second part of the quotation to fit the simile of spices and smells, for which 'god' is not ideal. Either *pur* (fire) or some similar term should be supplied in the second part (Diels); or fire was originally the subject throughout, 'god' being an inference by Hippolytus (a suggestion put to me by Professor Owen, which, however, devalues the meaning and also probably maligns Hippolytus' integrity); or thirdly the two parts of B67 were unconnected and from different contexts. We are dependent on Hippolytus' judgment that the subject in the second part was equivalent to 'god' in the first part, and that the two texts could be connected.

[81] The term is incompatible with a totally impassible god, but must be applicable to Noetus' god; see above p. 136.

summer, war and peace, satiety and lack. The contrasting values which are applied to these pairs mark no real distinctions: god is any of them and all of them in turn.

(e) Dissolute values

The last part of chapter 9 presents a problem as a result of gaps in the text. The point of the passage seems to be to argue that Heraclitus ascribed equal honour to apparent and non-apparent things in such a way as to treat them as one and the same thing: this is the claim made in the summary at the beginning of chapter 10, which is also supported by references back to two of the quotations used in the argument in chapter 9, B54 and B55. The discussion of Heraclitus concerns matters of epistemology, although the conclusion drawn concerns the ascription of honour and status to things visible or invisible.[82]

The passage starts with the repetition of *part* of B51: 'But that (it) is ... "a *harmoniê* like that of the bow and lyre".' Part of Hippolytus' introductory comment is lost. Against the suggestion[83] that the quotation simply supported an identification of the all (it) with a harmony, 'But that it is a *harmoniê* he says in these words ...' we may observe that such an identification is of no direct value to Hippolytus' purpose of juxtaposing parallels from Heraclitus and Noetus, while all previous and subsequent points of this form are directly relevant. It is possible that the earlier part of B51, as at 9.9.2, might have been quoted here also, thus introducing the ignorance of mortals concerning the harmony, and not simply the reference to harmony. In this case the introductory comment which follows the quotation would fit better as the introduction to B51; in its present position it does not apply to B54, which it precedes: B54, 'The invisible *harmoniê* is better

---

[82] The parallel in Noetus is probably not primarily epistemological, but the identification of god in visible and invisible modes as the same, and hence equally worthy of honour in both. (Compare *Ref.* 9.10.9-10). It also forms part of the general denial of value distinctions in moral and religious contexts which follows.

[83] Implied by Wendland's suggestion ad loc. p. 242.

than the visible' does not constitute a statement that 'it' (the harmony?) is unknown, but rather an implication that there are two sorts of harmony, one invisible and the other visible. B54 in fact has its own exegesis following *after* the quotation; this exegesis belongs to B54 but in the present text hangs unconnected either grammatically or by a particle to the quotation it explains.

All this evidence suggests that the sentence which now leads into B54 is the one which belongs in the lacuna before B51, having slipped a line down. The text would perhaps run as follows (9.9.5):

9. 9. 5. ὅτι δέ ἐστιν ἀφανής ἀόρατος ἄγνωστος ἀνθρώποις, ἐν τούτοις λέγει· 'οὐ ξυνιᾶσιν ὅκως διαφερόμενον ἑωυτῶι ὁμολογέει· παλίντροπος ἁρμονίη ὅκως περ τόξου καί λύρης' (B 51). ἐν δὲ τούτοις 'ἁρμονίη ἀφανής φανερῆς κρείττων' (B 54), ἐπαινεῖ καί προθαυμάζει πρό τοῦ γινωσκομένου τό ἄγνωστον αὐτοῦ καί ἀόρατον τῆς δυνάμεως. ὅτι δέ ἐστιν ὁρατός...

But that it is invisible, unseen, unknown to men he says in these words: 'they do not understand how in differing from itself it agrees with itself; a back-turning construction (*harmoniê*) like that of the bow and lyre' B51. But in these words 'the invisible *harmoniê* is better than the visible' B54 he praises and extols the unknown part of it and the unseen part of its power more highly than the known part. But that it is visible ...

In the passage as a whole we should then have a clear argument running as follows:

1. It (the one thing) is non-apparent, invisible, unknown to men (supported by B51 entire).
2. Its non-apparent and unknown aspect is honoured as superior to the known (supported by B54). '
3. It is also visible and comprehensible to men (supported by B55). Visible things are preferred to the invisible.
4. Some conclusion (or further premise) lost in the lacuna at p.242 line 16 and supported by B56.

The lacuna in the introduction to B56 leaves it very unclear what is its status in the argument. The point being argued is the equal status, and ultimately the identity, of the apparent and the non-apparent. It is clear that B56 deals in paradoxes concerned with knowledge and visible and invisible things, but the implications read there by Hippolytus are far from clear. In view of the lacuna, Kirk (1950) is surely wrong to suggest (p.158) that it is plain that B56 'must be quoted as an additional confirmation of the same point' as B55.[84] There is *no* indication in the text of whether Hippolytus' point was the same as B55, or the opposite again (as in B54), or the conclusion of the argument. The very fact that the quotation B56 does *not* satisfactorily support the point made in B55[85] argues that that was probably *not* the point which Hippolytus was making.[86]

In the first part of the quotation there is a paradox arising from the position of Homer as the wisest of the Greeks: he, if anyone, knew plain truths; but he was blind – hence knowledge of truths, wisdom, does not consist in knowledge of *phanera* (apparent things) in the normal sense because Homer could not see ordinary *phanera*. Men are deceived if they think knowledge is of what is plainly visible, because wise man Homer did not possess that. Men are blind to this truth, like Homer. But then on the other hand (here the second half of the quotation comes into play),[87] perhaps Homer did not

[84] Kirk suggests (1950) p. 158 that 'there is no doubt' that Wendland's proposed supplement is correct.

[85] See Kirk (1950) p. 158.

[86] I do not feel that it is necessary to demonstrate in detail the reasons why Kirk's account of this passage in his article (1950) seems to me inaccurate and superficial. My own exegesis offers an alternative view.

[87] There is an initial impression that the second part of the quotation does not belong with the first; the sense in which Homer was deceived is surely different from the sense in which men are deceived, and the riddle does not seem to concern knowledge of *phanera*. As regards Heraclitean authorship these objections were satisfactorily dismissed by Kirk (1950) p. 159; there remains the possibility that the two parts were unconnected in their original context in Heraclitus. The contorted reasoning, word play, and use of the same words with disparate implications in adjacent sentences are, however, not unfamiliar features of Heraclitus' work. Cf. Kahn (1979) p. 112 for unacknowledged use of the ambiguity of the vocabulary of catching lice.

understand the question of the superiority of the invisible to the visible and vice versa. In the riddle, which Homer could not understand, the boys do not want or care for the *phanera* – once they have seen and grasped what is visible they cast it away and seek what is not visible, *aphanês*; yet the *aphanês* is no better than the *phaneron*, and when they grasp it they will cast it away again. It is the boys who are wise and Homer is left puzzled. Men are deceived, blind like Homer, if they think Homer was wise, for he was no wiser than boys. There is a threefold paradox as to why men are deceived: (a) because they think knowledge is of the apparent; (b) because they think knowledge of the apparent is significantly different from knowledge of the non-apparent; (c) because they think Homer was wise when he was himself deceived.

Such a reading of B56 would serve Hippolytus as an example of not just one of the two positions that he claims Heraclitus maintains, but of the contradiction or indifference in his position. This quotation argues for both positions: (a) knowledge of what is apparent is not superior because Homer, the wisest man, did not have it; (b) Homer was not wise because he did not know what was obscure either – hence it is wrong to suppose that knowledge of the obscure is superior. What the riddle demonstrates is that the seen and the unseen, the known and the unknown, are actually all the same and equally worthless, and that is what Homer failed to see. The quotation illustrates Heraclitus' treatment of the visible and invisible as equal in status and equivalent to one another.

The conclusion of the argument, expressed at 9.10.1, is that the visible and invisible are given equal value in Heraclitus' system:

> Thus Heraclitus places the visible things in the same rank as the invisible things and honours them equally ...[88]

The result is as if they were one and the same thing, 'on the grounds that the visible and the invisible are undoubtedly one

---

[88] This passage is incorrectly translated by Ramnoux (1961/9) pp. 77 and 81, who appears to find in it a suggestion that certain fragments occurred in the same context in Heraclitus.

thing'. The passage which follows, 9.10.2-5, offers a series of further examples in which opposites with associations of value are said to be one and the same, thus denying the traditional distinctions of value.

Two preliminary points should be made concerning the parallel with Noetian doctrine to be identified in this section. Both can be seen to contribute to Hippolytus' understanding of Heraclitus.

1. The assertion that good and bad are the same is picked up in Callistus' ethical position[89] which treated good and bad alike. Similar implications of value can be identified in the other opposites mentioned in this passage, all of which can be used in ethical contexts as value-loaded contrasts. Pure/impure and straight/crooked both fit the parallel with Callistus' failure to discriminate between sinners and the morally upright.[90] In the case of light and dark Hippolytus' introductory comment makes explicit the association with good and evil, 9.10.2. The contrast above/below has similar associations in the context of rewards and punishments, heaven and hell.

2. The presence of above/below can also be linked with the summary of Callistus' Monarchian doctrine, in which above and below do not have distinct values as regards relationship with divinity, *Ref.* 9.12.17.[91] As the conclusion of the argument at the end of book 9, chapter 9 was that visible and invisible are equally honourable, so the opposites in chapter 10 continue the theme. Differences of status are inappropriate for these terms. The denial of differences both of moral value and of status amount to a single theme in Hippolytus' interpretation of these sayings.

In B57 Hippolytus finds denial of any difference between light and dark, and hence between good and evil.[92] In

[89] See above p. 139.

[90] *Ref.* 9.12.23: the church is likened to Noah's ark in which 'all pure and impure things' are included.

[91] See above p. 138.

[92] In Hippolytus' introduction at 9.10.2 the ms. reads ἐπιτιμᾷ γοῦν Ἡσιόδῳ, ὅτι ἡμέραν καὶ νύκτα οἶδεν.. The Göttingen edition (followed e.g. by Kirk (1954 p. 155) suggested οὐκ οἶδεν, which might be preferable in view of οὐκ ἐγίνωσκεν in the quotation which follows. No difference of meaning hangs on the text, and there could be some point to the criticism that Hesiod 'knew' day and night, i.e. recognised them as two things.

identifying day and night 'for they are one' Heraclitus was denying the difference between light and dark. The use of the verb *epitimâi* (downgrades) in Hippolytus' introduction to B57 picks up the theme of honour and status which runs through the passage; it echoes *timâi* (honours) in the first sentence of chapter 10 and *protimeô, protimêsas* (honouring more) at the end of 10.1. While Heraclitus honoured the visible and invisible equally, he did not honour the teacher of men, Hesiod (by contrast he rebuked and dishonoured him), evidence of Heraclitus' rejection of conventional estimations of worth and honour. Hippolytus' comment captures an irony that can be detected in B57 itself which suggests the honour paid to Hesiod by the majority of men, and momentarily implies that they were right to suppose that he knew many things: *touton epistantai pleista eidenai* – they understood that he knew many things – only to undercut this respect immediately with a rebuke: it was actually in knowing many things that he was wrong, since in treating day and night as a plurality he proved himself not to know them. Thus men did and did not understand the sense in which Hesiod was *didaskalos pleistôn*, a teacher of many things (as well as of many men), for they rightly saw that he recognised many things, but they were wrong to suppose that he knew them.[93]

Hippolytus does not suggest any answer to the riddle, namely why it is that day and night are actually one, and there is no indication as to whether an answer was suggested by the original context of the quotation. In so far as Hippolytus has any interpretation to offer it must be that night and day can only be distinguished in terms of light and dark, and since different values cannot be applied to light and dark any more than to good and evil it is foolish to distinguish between day and night. It has, however, been generally assumed that Heraclitus was making some specific 'scientific' point about night and day as such, and that this must have to do with the discovery of the 24-hour day: it is this which is the true unity and night and day are merely aspects of it.[94] But

[93] Note the use of three different verbs for cognition in one sentence. On the prominence of material with epistemological implications see above p. 132.
[94] See e.g. Kahn (1979) pp. 109-10; Kirk (1954) p. 156.

this unity is surely not strong enough for Heraclitus' assertion that 'they are one', since it is clear that he is not averse to using the terms 'day' and 'night' significantly and recognising that night differs from day by the absence of sunlight (B99). Why should Hesiod be said to have abused the natural unity of the 24-hour day simply by using the terms 'night' and 'day' significantly?

The reference to Hesiod is surely to *Theogony* 744-57,[95] but what precisely is Hesiod's mistake? Kahn suggested that Hesiod was wrong to see day and night as 'separate and irreconcilable powers', but it is not clear on what grounds this should be objectionable. Day and night are indeed 'irreconcilable' in that they are mutually incompatible. It is impossible that both should exist at the same time in the same place. Hesiod's mistake was rather in violating this incompatibility by envisaging the *two* existing together, meeting, greeting one another (*Thg.* 748-9), one being inside the house while the other is out and about (750). Heraclitus' point is that it is impossible that day and night are two things, since it is impossible to envisage both together. This incompatibility of opposites shows that they are in fact one: there is not a plurality that might logically be envisaged together in the same place at the same time. There is one thing which turns into day when it ceases to be night and into night when it ceases to be day. This explains the reliability of the 24-hour day rather than being a conclusion from it: despite the fact that the length of day and night constantly varies it never happens that day comes up too soon before the night has gone or that night mistakes its length and stays around too long. It is an absolute law (*dikê*) that the sun cannot transgress its measure for any particular day (B94), in that it will never happen that it fails to go down when night arrives; and this law is unbreakable because day and night are one thing and cannot both be present together. This gives a strong sense to Heraclitus' claim: it is in virtue of being one and the same that night and day are alternatives since this alone explains the

[95] Correctly identified as such by Kahn (1979) p. 110. It has been usual to see the primary reference as being to *Theogony* 123f. (see e.g. Kirk (1954) pp. 155-7) which, however, does not yield any profound insights as the object of Heraclitus' disapproval.

logical impossibility of their occurring as two together.

In B58 Hippolytus finds the claim that good and bad are the same. A simple, but relatively uninteresting, explanation of his interpretation is that it is a statement that the effects of medical treatment are both good and bad, cures which are good and further illnesses which are bad. This gives a confusion of good and bad in the sense of benefits and harm. The context in Hippolytus suggests, however, that there should also be moral significance in the identification of good and bad.

The vocabulary of B58 includes a number of emotive terms: *epaiteontai*, begging, is a word normally associated with mendicants; *basanizontes*, torturing; *tous arrôstountas*, the weak, the infirm; *mêden axioi*, good for nothing, dishonourable. The doctors, supposedly good, worthy and honourable men who give benefit to the sick and deserve their fee, turn out to be morally base: their victims are the weak and the infirm and these they subject to the severest tortures; they beg for money like dishonourable beggars who have done nothing to earn their wage; and it is from the weak and infirm that they beg – an ironical reversal of rôles since it is normally the disabled who must beg.

> The doctors cut, burn, torture the weak badly in every way, and beg for money though they do not deserve to take a fee from the weak, when they produce the same effects, good things and diseases.

Heraclitus casts doubt on all the conventional distinctions of status and moral worth which are applied to the activities of the medical profession: their supposedly good deeds are as shameful and harmful as those which are normally condemned. There is no meaningful difference between good and bad, morally worthy and morally base, and the doctors exemplify this breakdown of differences.

The same breakdown of moral judgments can be observed in B59, concerning straight and crooked. Hippolytus' explanatory gloss must be the basis of any interpretation of the obscure claim that the way for the fuller's shop is straight and crooked. Hippolytus' suggestion refers to the processes involved in the fulling industry, and he identifies the instrument as the one 'called *kochlias*' whose rotation is both straight and twisted. This instrument clearly involved a screw or roller, but was not necessarily the screw press.

The first word used by Hippolytus to mean crooked is *streblon*. This sets the tone of the ensuing passage since in addition to its metaphorical implications of perverse or wicked dealing it is connected with a whole series of terms based on the stem *strebl-*, some of which have connections with the fuller's shop,[96] and many of which are used in connection with torturing and the 'rack'.[97] *Kochlias*, which Hippolytus says is the instrument to which Heraclitus refers, is a term used for the 'rack' or some similar instrument of torture in the Acts of the Martyrs.[98] Hippolytus' introduction, and his gloss on the precise instrument involved, both suggest a reading which identifies the straight and crooked paths as a reference to 'straight' and 'crooked' uses of the same machine in the fulling industry and in torture. Whether or not Hippolytus' *kochlias* is actually the correct instrument,[99] his idea that the dual rôle of a machine in the fullers' shop is in question may be a suggestion of some value.[100]

A single machine with two motions and two functions undermines the conventional distinctions of morality:

[96] *Streblê* is a device for squeezing or wringing clothes in Plutarch (*Mor.* 950a) and cf. *streblôsis* of wringing or twisting clothes in Gregory of Nyssa *De Hominis Opificio* 13.4.

[97] *Streblê* is an instrument of torture or torture in general in the Septuagint, as well as other authors (LSJ s.v. στρέβλη II) and *strebloô* is the verb of such torture; in Patristic writers the term for the 'rack' is *streblôtêrion*, *streblôtêr* or *streblôma* of the process of 'racking' (Lampe s.v.).

[98] *Martyrum Persarum Acta* 1.16; 1.17; *Martyrium Nicephori* 4.

[99] Kahn (1979) p. 191 suggests that Hippolytus' idea is anachronistic on the grounds that *kochlias* is a screw-press, which is not demonstrated. It may, however, be an instrument of Hippolytus' own day which fits the double rôle of some other instrument of Heraclitus' day.

[100] This would actually favour Kahn's suggestion (1979, pp. 192-3) that the carding wheels were also an instrument of torture. The Heraclitean text at present leaves the identification of the instrument vague, but it is possible that the context indicated that the contrast straight/crooked had moral overtones connected with torture. Hippolytus' suggestion, based, perhaps, on some hint from this context, may be true to the spirit of the original words.

Heraclitus implies that the difference between the straight and the crooked uses of the instrument is no more than the difference between the straight and curved motions which constitute a single movement in the operation of the machine.

The distinctions denied in B60 and B61 follow similar lines: one thing is the subject of both value terms. It is the same road that goes up and down,[101] and both in virtue of the same feature, its slope, just as the doctors in virtue of one set of practices are both honourable and base. It is the same water that is pure and impure, not because of a difference between salty and fresh water, but simply in virtue of being salty. The value terms do not mark a difference identifiable in the object itself.

The entire argument from 9.9.5 to 9.10.5 has been constructed as evidence of Heraclitus' denial of distinctions of dignity and moral value in his epistemological statements concerning the visible and the invisible and in his use of opposites which undermine conventional value judgments. At 9.10.6 one further quotation is added to the list, B62. Here again distinctions of dignity and superior or inferior relationship with divinity are undermined by the identification of 'mortals' and 'immortals'. 'Mortal' and 'immortal' are terms from the initial list of predicates applicable to 'the all' in 9.9.1 and hence this quotation links up not only with the moral indifference of the immediately preceding passage but also with the earlier theme of the unity of all things. Mortality and immortality are significant features in the controversy with Noetus, and are mentioned with reference to Noetus' god in 9.10.10. The apparent contradictions involved in the second part of the quotation, which follow from the notions of life and death – how can the immortals have a death? – are precisely the paradoxes brought out in the Noetian position – how can god cease to be immortal and undergo death?

---

[101] Hippolytus gives no suggestion that B60 was read with a cosmological significance in Heraclitus' context. His interest in the value-associations of 'up' and 'down' (see above p. 164), suggests rather that he reads the terms literally.

(ii) Judgment reasserted

Refutatio 9.10.7 deals with a new theme in which opposites are not prominent as they are in the main part of the account of Heraclitus. The passage concerns the judgment of the world by fire.

The whole of the passage, and the immediately preceding comment on B63,[102] were regarded by Kirk as not only an afterthought on Hippolytus' part, but as entirely irrelevant to his purpose of refuting Noetus.[103] Kirk suggests that Hippolytus has simply been carried away by his interest in anticipations of Christian themes in Heraclitus. The same suggestion is made by Marcovich.[104] The results of such a suggestion are problematic:

1. It means that Hippolytus is a muddle-headed old fool, which, as Kirk noted, is uncharacteristic. If we accept that Hippolytus is here identifying Christian doctrines in Heraclitus, he gives a very confused account since his next comment is that the material just quoted represents the ideas of both Heraclitus and Noetus, thus suggesting that these doctrines are heretical and objectionable in his view. This fact led Ramnoux to the conclusion that the last judgment and resurrection of the flesh were actually heretical doctrines to which Hippolytus was objecting.[105]

2. The material Hippolytus has to hand does not easily yield the conclusions he attempts to draw from it, so that we need to identify some stronger reason for his interest than that he was struck by a similarity with his own ideas.[106] He seems to find difficulty in locating any references to fire at all, and

---

[102] On this point see below pp. 173-9.

[103] Kirk (1954) pp. 349-52.

[104] Marcovich (1966) p. 261. Marcovich, unlike Kirk, does not appreciate the careful construction of Hippolytus' composition of these parallels.

[105] Ramnoux (1961/9) p. 73.

[106] See Marcovich (1966) p. 262. Attempts to rearrange the order of quotations to make the conclusion follow more easily from the examples quoted such as were offered by Fränkel, and by Marcovich (1966), do not provide any satisfactory explanation of the obvious paucity of Hippolytus' material and the difficulty with which he has to draw the point out of recalcitrant quotations.

the best he has initially for the notion of judgment of the world is a reference to 'thunderbolt' (*keraunos*) which he then has to explain as being a reference to the eternal fire. The next point concerning the intelligence of the fire and its rôle in the *dioikêsis* is not supported by any quotation at all. This is followed by a statement that Heraclitus called the fire 'need' (*chrêsmosunê*) and 'satiety' (*koros*), but again there is no explicit mention of fire in the words of Heraclitus which are given. Finally in B66 we are given the first and last mention of 'fire' (*pur*) in a Heraclitean quotation; but B66 should have been used in support of the original reference to judgment by fire, instead of hanging loose at the end.[107]

Judgment, like fire, is identified with difficulty in the material Hippolytus quotes. He has to extract this notion from *oiakizei* (steers) in B64 which he glosses by the term *kateuthunei*, a term in which the notion of guiding is combined with that of examination and judgment of past actions; this was the term used for the examination of public magistrates with regard to the correct conduct of their office.[108] This is an ideal term with which to catch the implications of a last judgment, and bridges the gap between *oiakizei*, which does not carry those associations, and *krisis* (judgment) in the introductory comment.

In B66 Hippolytus has a quotation[109] which does provide a reference to universal judgment and consummation by fire. Was it used as such in his source book? It is possible that it was, but the verbs are verbs of cognition and it is quite possible that the words were used in a very different context, with reference to the rôle of fire in perception: 'Fire will attend to all things in turn, distinguish them and comprehend.' This

---

[107] This curious misplacement of B66 was the basis of the rearrangements mentioned in n. 106.

[108] *IG* ii²1193.10; cf. *euthunô* in Aristotle *Politics* 1271a6, 1274a17, etc. *euthunos* is the technical term for official public examiners at Athens. *euthunê* is used of Judgment Day by Basil *Ep*. 174 and John Chrysostom *De Sacerdotio* 4.2, both later than Hippolytus.

[109] This discussion is based on the assumption that B66 is a quotation from Heraclitus (questioned by Reinhardt (1942) but reinstated by later scholars. cf. Marcovich (1959) and Kahn (1979) p. 271ff.) Note the presence of *phêsi*.

would be fire characterised as *phronimon*, as the cognitive element, but not necessarily associated with *ekpurôsis* (conflagration).

The points which Hippolytus makes here have affinities with the Stoic interpretation of Heraclitus, but Hippolytus shows no awareness of the selection of quotations which supported the Stoic account.[110] The one useful text he has may have been used for an epistemological point in his source, which may explain his failure to introduce it in connection with his initial comment on *ekpurôsis*. His source does not have Stoic interests, and his own interest in these doctrines cannot be explained by his discovery of striking material on the subject in his source.

Hippolytus has argued that Heraclitus denied all conventional distinctions, undermined the associations of dignity and moral value of the whole range of terms used in normal discourse and denied that there are differences to constitute a plurality such as men commonly believe in. Now he argues that Heraclitus did allow for an absolute discrimination, such as could not be envisaged between the conventional opposites just listed. The judgment of the majority of men on matters of moral value, and all the differences which they take to mark out the world, are based on nothing. The only true judgment is that of fire which 'discriminates and comprehends'.

Why should Hippolytus suggest that Heraclitus' apparently universal denial of differences is actually undermined by a claim that there is an absolute judgment, albeit not the conventional judgments made by men? The answer surely lies in the parallel with Noetian doctrines which he seeks to support in quoting this material: Callistus' denial of conventional distinctions of moral and theological value was a denial that men were competent to do the judging, but implied that ultimately the day of Judgment would come.[111]

Was Hippolytus right to suggest that Heraclitus envisaged such a restoration of difference in an absolute judgment by fire? We have noticed that the material available to him on

---

[110] E.g. perhaps B30, 31, 76, 90.
[111] *Refutatio* 9.12.22-23. See above p. 139.

this theme is scarce and with difficulty supports his view. There is more interpretation and less quotation in this section than elsewhere. References to thunderbolt, need and satiety could have come from any context, and there is little to suggest that they were originally associated with judgment by fire. B66, however, is more problematic since even in a purely epistemological context, rather than a cosmic rôle, it seems to imply discrimination and judgment of a plurality such as should be precluded by the denial of difference. Clearly we are left in the realm of speculation, but a possible explanation is that fire was identified as cognitive in the conventional distinctions which characterise the world view of men in general: fire is that which is responsible for discerning a plurality and grasping distinctions; but its distinctions are erroneous and its judgments misleading, for the 'all things' (*panta*) which it discriminates are in fact one: *hen panta einai*.

(iii) Whose resurrection?

The passage on judgment follows a reference to resurrection and the quotation of B63. This point, which has also been identified as part of Hippolytus' digression on anticipations of Christian doctrines, poses a similar challenge. If judgment is in fact directly relevant to the refutation of Noetus, this single sentence will be the only irrelevant point in the entire account of Heraclitus. Such a verdict must be questioned.

We are faced with a threefold problem in dealing with this section of the text, *Ref.* 9.10.6: (1) the meaning of the quotation from Heraclitus is opaque without help from the context; (2) the connection of the material in the quotation with the subjects supposedly identified in it by Hippolytus and mentioned in his comment is obscure; (3) Hippolytus' interest in identifying these subjects in the Heraclitean text is not immediately apparent.

Hippolytus claims to find in B63 a reference to resurrection, and in particular resurrection of the ordinary visible flesh 'in which we were born', and also a reference to God as the one who effects the resurrection. B63 appears to contain no reference to resurrection, no reference to the flesh of any sort, and no reference to God.

It has been usual to suppose that Hippolytus is primarily making an observation about the Christian doctrine of the resurrection of the flesh as applied to men in general. This certainly seems to be implied by the insistence that the flesh which is raised is 'this visible flesh in which we are born'. Scope for reading this doctrine into B63 is limited, but we may note the presence of the phrase 'of the living and the dead' (*zôntôn kai nekrôn*) at the end of the quotation. This phrase is standard in Christian texts with reference to the general resurrection of the dead at Judgment Day.[112] It also gives Hippolytus his necessary reference to the resurrection of the flesh since *nekroi* are not dead souls but dead bodies, corpses.[113]

However, the general resurrection of the dead is not a significant point in the Noetian controversy, still less the question of god's responsibility for this resurrection. The point applies much more significantly to the question of the resurrection of Christ, on which subject there certainly is a problem about God's responsibility, given the difficulty of explaining how God the Father raised Christ if Christ and the Father are one and the same.[114] Thus, although we cannot deny that Hippolytus' first comment does identify a reference to the general resurrection, his second comment must be taken to apply particularly to the resurrection of Christ as the first and chief example of the resurrection of the flesh.[115]

Heraclitus' position, illustrated by this text, should correspond in Hippolytus' interpretation with the problematic position maintained by Noetus, rather than with the orthodox position; in Noetian doctrine the one raised from the dead and the one responsible for raising him were the same, both god.

[112] This phrase is particularly prominent as a formula in the creeds produced at much the time when Hippolytus was writing but it occurs from the very earliest Christian literature (Barnabas *Ep.* 7.2, 2 Clem. 1.1) onwards.

[113] Note the prominence of the term with associations of the material, inanimate, the bodies of the unbaptised dead etc. Lampe s.v.

[114] See above, p. 137.

[115] The question of whether Christ's resurrection was a resurrection of this everyday visible, mortal, passible flesh would have major consequences for Noetus' denial of the distinction between Father and Son, since the risen body must belong to Christ after his release from the temporary 'mortal' mode.

When Hippolytus remarks that the text suggests that god is responsible for the resurrection, we should take it that he understands it to mean that god is also the one raised.

Given these considerations what can be made of Hippolytus' interpretation of the text: *entha d'eonti epanistasthai kai phulakas ginesthai egerti zôntôn kai nekrôn*? His suggestion that God is both the subject and object of the raising requires that he identified a singular subject in the text. *Epanistasthai kai phulakas ginesthaï* appears to assume a plural: 'They rose up and became guards.' *Eonti* (being), however, is dative singular, and, as Marcovich noted,[116] this is the most likely candidate for Hippolytus' recognition of a reference to God. He has already argued that Heraclitus' discourse concerns a single subject, the referent of the term *theos* (god) among a whole range of others; here the single subject of *eonti* is not expressed: it is not clear whether Hippolytus infers that it is 'god' from any information in his context. One possibility is that *logos* (word) was implied by the context, a term which Hippolytus justifiably regards as interchangeable with *theos*, following his earlier argument equating terms for *to pan* ('the all'). This would suit his reading of the text as parallel to the resurrection of the incarnate *logos* in Noetus.

The dative *eonti* fits with *epanistasthai*, which carries a sense of hostile rising, while *entha* (here), or *enthade*,[117] clearly belongs with *eonti*. The first part of the text might be understood by Hippolytus: 'When he (god) was here in this world they rose up against him and set themselves as guards ...' To Hippolytus, interpreting in terms of parallels with Noetus' account of the resurrection of Christ, this recalls the doctrines concerning the death and burial of Christ: the *Logos*, on Noetus' terms simply 'God', was here in this world and men rose up against him, put him to death and then set themselves as guards at the tomb.[118] These points are some of

[116] Marcovich (1967) p. 396.

[117] It is normal to read ἔνθα δ' ἐόντι, but it is possible that the sense would be better conveyed by *enthade eonti*. *Enthade* has a standard use in referring to 'this world' by contrast with the 'other world' which would fit Hippolytus' reading particularly well. This reading is preferred by Ramnoux (1961/9) p. 90.

[118] Cf. Matthew 27.66; 28.4.

the absurdities mentioned in the account of Noetus: Did God die? Could God be buried in a tomb? Could God be subject to a guard of mortal men?[119] The point which Hippolytus actually mentions in connection with this text is, however, that concerning his raising himself from the dead,[120] and we must seek the basis for his point in the second part of the quotation, *egerti zônton kai nekrôn*. This is actually an emendation of the MS. reading *egertizonton* which must be wrong. *Zônton kai nekrôn* is a probable reading in view of Hippolytus' mention of the resurrection of the flesh,[121] but is *egerti* right? This reading, 'wakefully', would describe the attitude of the guards, but Hippolytus' comment requires a reference to a resurrection caused, and perhaps also undergone, by the god who appears in *eonti*.

We have noted the prominence of the verb *egeirô* in connection with the raising of Christ,[122] and it is plausible that the presence of a related term in this text suggested to Hippolytus a reference to the resurrection of Christ. However, *egerti* describing the guards is not a satisfactory basis for such a reading, and some alternatives should be explored. Initially plausible is the suggestion *egerthenti* (having been roused), an easy emendation and a common word in Heraclitus, who uses it to describe those who are awake to his discourse.[123] *Egerthenti*, in agreement with *eonti*, would give the required identification of God himself with the one who was roused from the dead. There are problems, however, with the contorted construction of the text since *zônton kai nekrôn* hangs apparently dependent upon *egerthenti* and with no very clear relation to it. It would be necessary at least to understand *ek zônton kai nekrôn*, 'he who was roused from among the living and the dead'.

Following the lines of this suggestion and the possibility that *egerti* hides a dative in apposition with the subject of *eonti*, an alternative may be suggested. Hippolytus finds *theos* (in

---

[119] Cf. *Ref.* 9.10.10 and 9.10.12, and see above p. 138.
[120] Cf. *Ref.* 9.10.12.
[121] See above p. 174.
[122] Above pp. 137-8.
[123] B1, B21; *egrêgoros* (awake) in B26, B88, B89.

eonti) identified with the cause of the resurrection: God is the quickener of the dead. No clear term for an 'awakener' presents itself, but *egersis*, the awakening,[124] is a strong candidate. If Hippolytus read *egersi* and understood it as a dative in apposition with the dative at the opening of the quotation it would give him the point he needs:

> When god was here in this world men rose up against him and set themselves as guards against him who was the awakening of the living and the dead.

Hippolytus' point might be: Noetus would have held that the *logos* was present on earth and men in their folly turned against him and thought they could set a guard against the one who was in fact God, the cause of the resurrection of the living and the dead; for Noetus the incarnate *logos* was god himself, and hence was himself the one who raises the dead; Heraclitus' saying implies the same identification.

Can Hippolytus' interpretation aid our appreciation of Heraclitus' own point? The answer must be that it can, though clearly not in terms of the resurrection of Christ.

(a) We may free ourselves from the concern with a supposed parallel at Hesiod *Works and Days* 122-3. This parallel is based upon one word, *phulakas* (guards). In Hesiod men of the golden age become *phulakes thnêtôn anthrôpôn* (guards of mortal men),[125] and the old reading which took *zôntôn kai nekrôn* as dependent on *phulakas* could argue for some sort of parallel construction, although the change of vocabulary needed explanation. This slight parallel withers to nothing if *zôntôn kai nekrôn* is dependent on *egersi*, not on *phulakas*. Furthermore Hesiod has no reference to these spirits rising from the dead,[126] and there is certainly no parallel for the hostility implied by *epanistasthai*. Heraclitus is consistently critical of Hesiod, and it is inadequate to assume that he is here taking over much of Hesiod's view of an afterlife and constructing one on the same

---

[124] Cf. the personification of *egersis* in Empedocles B123.1.

[125] *Works and Days* 123 and 253.

[126] They do not rise any more than the silver generation which become the spirits of the underworld, 141.

lines, as Kahn seems to do.[127]

(b) Although Hippolytus naturally interprets the awakening of the living and the dead as a literal resurrection, we are not obliged to do so. The material recording Heraclitus' emphasis on the links between sleep and death, and ignorance and sleep is extensive. Ignorant men go around as if they were asleep (B1); supposedly awake, all they see is death or sleep (B21); as if death or sleep would help them to see what they cannot see when alive and awake (B26); one should not behave like sleepers (B73).[128] It is in fact only those who are awake who appreciate Heraclitus' point concerning the unity of the world. The living are no better than the dead until they have been woken up by Heraclitus' discourse (B89).

In B63 we have suggested that the context supplied a reference to *logos*. Heraclitus' *logos* is itself communicative of itself, as we have seen from B50;[129] it is the means of awakening ignorant men to an awareness of itself. The subject of *eonti* is *logos*, that to which men should be alert if they are to discover the truth that all things are one (B50). Heraclitus remarks on the hostility of men to his words and their refusal to be awakened:

The *logos* is here among them but foolish men rise in hostility against it and set themselves as guards against an awakening of the living and the dead.

Not only do men resist the truth but they attempt to ward off any possibility that men might be awakened to it, men who, though alive, are like the dead or the sleeping in their ignorance.

We have, then, no Hesiodic spirits of the righteous, no resurrection of guardian souls, no heroes and demons, watchers and holy ones; only another reference to the ignorance of men and their resistance to the discourse of

---

[127] Kahn (1979) p. 255.

[128] Cf. also B88: there is a parallel between living and dead, awake and sleeping; B75: it is those who are asleep who are responsible for the occurrence of things in the world.

[129] See above p. 148.

Heraclitus which would rouse them from their stupor. No doubt the vocabulary may be modelled on traditional accounts of life after death, since an awakening to the truth is a life after death, but it is an awakening to the fact that the life lived before was but sleep-walking.

Hippolytus' comment is inadequate in that it does not spell out clearly what is the doctrine to be found in the passage, but it is not irrelevant to his purpose. His identification of a general 'quickening of the dead' is not entirely misleading: though not a 'resurrection' it is an awakening from oblivion that Heraclitus recommends for men in general.

(iv) Appendix: whose chapter?

In this chapter all things together (*panta homou*) have set forth (*exetheto*) Heraclitus' own idea, and at the same time also that of the heresy of Noetus, (whom) I have briefly demonstrated (*epedeixa*) to be a disciple (*mathêtên*) not of Christ but of Heraclitus. (*Ref.* 9.10.8)

Panta homou is a common phrase in Hippolytus' *Refutatio*.[130] In every case listed by Wendland *panta* is plural and the phrase means 'all (things) together'. The phrase is also one which occurs in the Presocratics, three times in Anaxagoras (B1, B4 and B6). In each case *panta* is neuter plural and the phrase means 'all things together'. *Panta homou*, if not actually a Heraclitean phrase, is a Hippolytean phrase with which to sum up his understanding of Heraclitus' doctrine that all things are one. In this sentence its rôle is clearly as neuter plural subject of the main verb *exetheto*: 'all things together have set forth ...' But it serves a double rôle since *panta homou* also expresses the proper meaning of Heraclitus' discourse: the doctrine 'all things together' has set forth the proper meaning.

'In this chapter' (*en de toutôi tôi kephalaiôi*) therefore clearly refers to the summary which Hippolytus has just given of Heraclitus' doctrines and which he is now concluding: 'In this

[130] It merits inclusion as a separate entry in Wendland's index (under ὁμοῦ) where he lists four occurrences at pp. 127.18, 158.7, 159.11, 220.7, not including the present instance on p. 244.2. Clearly there may be others which have also been omitted.

summary all the points together have set forth his particular idea …' there is no reason to suggest a reference to any chapter in any other work, whether Heraclitus' book or Hippolytus' source, neither of which has been mentioned to constitute 'this summary'.[131]

The second part of the sentence is corrupt. If *mathêtên* is correct at the end of the sentence *hon* (whom) must be supplied as the object of *epedeixa*; but this is a stop-gap emendation and far from satisfactory since *hon* must refer to Noetus, not his idea nor his heresy, which makes the order of the Greek most improbable.[132] Omitting *hon*, as in the manuscript, the object of *epedeixa* becomes 'the idea of the Noetian heresy', in which case we must reject *mathêtên* which is unecessary and does not fit. This correction is much more satisfactory than the supplement *hon*.[133] The whole sentence then reads without difficulty:

ἐν δὲ τούτῳ τῷ κεφαλαίῳ πάντα ὁμοῦ τὸν ἴδιον νοῦν ἐξέθετο, ἅμα
δὲ καὶ τὸν τῆς Νοητοῦ αἱρέσεως δι᾽ ὀλίγων ἐπέδειξα οὐκ ὄντα
Χριστοῦ ἀλλὰ Ἡρακλείτου.

In this summary all things together have set forth his (Heraclitus') particular idea, and at the same time I have briefly shown that the particular idea of the heresy of Noetus is not Christ's idea but Heraclitus'.[134]

Central to this passage is the *idios nous* (particular idea), common to Heraclitus and Noetus; it is picked up in B67

---

[131] Many implausible arguments have been hung on the phantom mention of 'Heraclitus' chapter' at this point, e.g. Kirk (1954) pp. 184-5 and 350-1; Kahn (1979) p. 201; Ramnoux (1961/9) p. 79.

[132] We should expect it to read … ἅμα δὲ καὶ τὸν τῆς αἱρέσεως νοῦν τῆς τοῦ Νοητοῦ, ὃν δι᾽ ὀλίγων …

[133] It is readily explained as an insertion by someone who had not understood the point being made. The point about Noetus' followers being disciples of Heraclitus is made twice later in the chapter, 9.10.9 and 9.10.10, taking up the introductory point at 9.8.2. It need not have been made a fourth time here.

[134] This has the advantage of placing Heraclitus last in the sentence instead of Noetus (*mathêtês*); the following quotation is introduced by 'he says' and appears to be a quotation from Heraclitus, not Noetus.

which follows – 'God is all the opposites, this is the idea' – this is the special idea of Heraclitus which we find in Noetus' heresy.

(v) Conclusion: Heraclitus' idios nous

Hippolytus' account has presented a build-up of material which he claims expresses the 'particular idea' of Heraclitus. Two themes have emerged as prominent: the assertion that all things regarded by men as a plurality are in fact one, and the rejection of all conventional distinctions in theology, ethics and social value systems. The juxtaposition with the Noetian position in which theological and ethical values are called into question brings out something of the force of Heraclitus' point: not only does he question the values of other men; he actually denies that such distinctions of value are appropriate at all.

The point concerns theology: god is no different from the ordinary processes of this secular world (B67) and men are entirely confused in their religious practices; they pollute themselves in trying to purify themselves (B5) as if pure and impure marked significant distinctions (B61); they are like pigs who bath in mud (B13). God recognises no such distinctions of value: to him all things are alike and it is men who have constructed the distinctions (B102). It also concerns the whole range of conventional status symbols: just as priests and prophets who care for the religious system held in honour by men are actually unholy (B14) so doctors who have honour among men are really beggars and dishonourable (B58); Homer, Hesiod and the other favourite teachers are as ignorant as the rest of men (B40, B42, B56, B106); the value placed on wealth and gold is meaningless (B9, B22, B4); even the honour paid to corpses might as well be paid to dung: corpses are more useless than dung (B96).

The world is not divided up as men think: all their distinctions which mark it out as a plurality import meaningless differences which govern their attitudes and make them see the world in terms of opposites. Until men can escape from this enslavement to polarities which determine their actions and speech (B73) and can see the world as one undifferentiated unity without contrasting values, they live as if in a dream, in a private understanding (B2). Only Heraclitus' private understanding (*idios nous*) can become a common account by breaking down the differences between men's ideas as well as between the things to which they apply them.

Thus Hippolytus offers us Heraclitus as a figure who rejects the traditional values of the society in which he lived: he rejects the polarities between good and bad maintained by traditional ethics, those between divine and non-divine maintained by traditional religion, and those between honour and dishonour maintained by the culture taught with the models of Homer and Hesiod. Difference and distinctions form the basis of that culture. Heraclitus denies that basis altogether.

Conclusion

The aim of this book has been to justify a new method of approach to the reading of the Presocratics, centring on the analysis of ancient interpretations. Three justifications for the method have been offered here.

1. The theoretical arguments in favour of reading the text of the Presocratics as embedded texts within the context of the interpretations they were selected to illustrate are set out in the introduction. I have argued that the traditional approach is both unsound in its assumptions and limited in confining its attention to a small sample of disjointed phrases. It is the interpretations, based on informed readings of a fuller text than we possess, which can form the basis of a fuller and less restricted exploration of possible meanings of the text.

2. The studies in Part One, and particularly that concerning Hippolytus' account of Aristotle, demonstrate some of the weaknesses of the traditional use of excerpted fragments and the advantages of considering the interpretation as a whole. It has been shown that relatively little of interest can be derived from the limited amount of material that is quoted directly from Aristotle's own works, while Hippolytus' interpretation is not difficult to handle: despite the fact that it represents a polemical view of Aristotle, there is ample evidence in the text itself to indicate the extent of this influence and the interests which inspired it.

3. The chapters in Part Two exemplify the results of the method, when applied to the interpretation of Presocratic thought. Heraclitus' sayings are riddled with oppositions and fragmented by the traditional approach. Hippolytus' reading provides a framework within which they fall into a coherent pattern of thought. The dismemberment of Empedocles' verses into two discrete poems is healed by the recognition of the single system of alternating values which emerges from

Hippolytus' work. These represent new readings of the text and demonstrate the fruits of a close analysis of the interpretative context in which the text is read.

The value of these readings

While new readings of the Presocratics may be justified, they need not be of any particular interest. What have these new readings to offer?

(i) The contrast with the Aristotelian approach

As has been observed above (p.14) modern interpretation of the Presocratic philosophers has been dominated by the influence of Aristotle's approach, which has given prominence to doctrines concerning 'Physics' and an emphasis on the development of science. Empedocles' views concerning the physical process of generation and change have been studied in isolation from the story of the *daimôn*; Heraclitus' concern with opposites has been taken at face value as an observation about the way the physical world works.

Hippolytus' interest in identifying in the philosophers' work comments comparable to the theological views of his heretics leads him to seek further implications in the doctrines he reports. Empedocles' cycle of Love and Strife, and the incarnation of the *daimôn*, while they do constitute some sort of explanation of processes in the physical world, have much more profound implications from the point of view of human values. The questioning of values and of religious practices implied by the alternation of Love and Strife is a whole area of Empedocles' thought which merits exploration. Heraclitus' observations on opposites are similarly pressed to yield not only comments on the nature of things and on the application of language to the natural world, but also implications concerning the structure of society and the values upon which its conventions are founded. Hippolytus' interpretation thus prompts us to explore not simply an alternative reading to Aristotle's, and one which offsets his bias towards natural science, but a more profound one which looks beyond the straightforward accounts of physical phenomena.

(ii) The advantages of this approach

It might be claimed that there is nothing in these readings which could not have been derived from an imaginative reading of the context-free fragments: we do not actually need Hippolytus' interpretation in order to be able to think along these lines. It is indeed true that these readings ultimately centre on the same passages of text as the traditional 'context-free fragments' approach, and it is conceivable, if unlikely, that despite our current preconceptions one might string them together and interpret them in precisely the same way independently of the prompting of Hippolytus.

Were we to do so, however, this reading would have no claim to authority. It would be a wild conjecture, an imaginative reconstruction, and would have no greater claim to be a reading of the text of the philosopher concerned than any other arbitrary hypothesis. Our aim is indeed to make the text perform (above, p.9) but in order to make it do anything interesting we need more of the text than the fragments provide. We need to fill up the gaps. The advantage of Hippolytus' reading is that he fills up the gaps in order to make the text perform, partly on the basis of a greater knowledge of the context than we possess, and partly on the basis of his interests which can be analysed from his text. Thus whereas our independent reading could not be based on more of the text than we now possess, Hippolytus' reading can claim that authority; and while our filling of the gaps would be arbitrary, Hippolytus' concerns are open to analysis and the effects of his use of the material can be assessed. In juxtaposing philosophers and heretics his concern is to make them fit; where they do not fit, that concern has not significantly restricted his reading.

In one sense Hippolytus' reading has a claim to authority as well as offering us a context in which the embedded text functions. In another sense it has no claim to authority, since it is but one of many alternative readings of the text which may be represented in the ancient interpretations. Those who had access to more of the text than we do made it mean many different things. Our appreciation of that text depends upon a full exploration of as many as possible of those readings. The fact that Hippolytus' reading differs from the Aristotelian tradition does not mean that either should be set forth as definitive to the exclusion of the other. Hippolytus' interpretation has served as the basis for an exploration in the thought of Heraclitus and Empedocles. It has not been set forth as the truth.

Appendix A
Hippolytus on the *phusikoi*

Book One of Hippolytus' *Refutatio* consists of outlines or summaries of the doctrines of twenty philosophers or philosophical schools from Thales to Pyrrho and the Academics, two chapters on barbarians and one section on Hesiod. Of these, chapters 1 to 16 deal with the fourteen Presocratic philosophers which Hippolytus classes as the *phusikoi* (natural philosophers), starting with Thales and finishing with Hippon.

Diels (1879) pp.144-56 examined the whole of Book 1 in some detail in an attempt to identify the possible sources from which Hippolytus derived the information he gives. His main conclusions can be summarised as follows: he identifies two works of significantly different character, which should not be confused: (a) a slim volume of the succession type containing mainly anecdotal material about the lives of the philosophers and discussing a number of characters in a single chapter; this was a work of very little doxographical value; (b) a Theophrastean work of much greater value which recounted the doctrines of a single thinker per chapter. The overall pattern that Diels identifies is that Hippolytus started work with only the meagre epitome of lives (a) and wrote the first five chapters from this, whereupon, depressed by the inadequacy of his source book, he acquired book (b) from which he wrote chapters 6-16, possibly turning back to (a) for the chapters on Socrates, Plato, Aristotle, and the post-Aristotelians and the barbarians (18-26).

However, the division is not quite as simple as this. In chapter 2 (on Pythagoras) Diels notes that there is possible evidence of more than one source, in that the same facts are mentioned in paragraphs 6-18 as had been alluded to in 1-5. Furthermore Hippolytus does not simply change sources at chapter 5: he frequently turns back to his (a) material for one sentence at the end of 6, one sentence at the end of 7, one sentence at the end of 8, one sentence of 10, part of the first paragraph of 13, the last sentence of 13, and the first paragraph of 14. At all these points Hippolytus records information which Diels considers more in character with the epitome of lives. These conclusions have remained the almost unchallenged orthodoxy since their publication.[1]

There are, however, certain questions that need to be raised about the model of Hippolytus' method of working which Diels assumes and the extent of the evidence which he considers in constructing his account. In the first place there are certain very general considerations which make Diels' model as it stands somewhat implausible. On his reconstruction we find Hippolytus sitting down with his book (a) to copy out as and when he comes to them such doctrines as he can find of the Greek philosophers, with apparently no criterion of selection since he has very little information from which to select. After writing four chapters and discovering that his book has caused him to write a highly confused account of Empedocles and Heraclitus he goes to the trouble of procuring a better book of Theophrastean excerpts. He does not, however, choose to revise or re-write the two muddled chapters, despite the fact that these will in fact turn out to be two of the most significant thinkers in the later books; instead

---

[1] Mejer (1978) pp. 83-6 questions Diels' assignment of the two sources to distinct genres, one a biographical type of 'successions' literature (the (a) source) and the other a doxographical work (the (b) source). He argues that both sources could have contained biographical as well as doxographical material, but that the difference is one of quality, the second source being Theophrastean and much more valuable. Thus he does not question Diels' identification of a single division of sources at chapter 5 and the Theophrastean character of the whole of 6-16, nor does he question Diels' assessment of the relative merits of the two sources such that source (b) is much better than source (a). The advantage of Mejer's view is that it avoids the necessity of supposing that Hippolytus mixed up two sources in chapters 6-16 as Diels had suggested. (On the distinction of genre suggested by Diels, cf. also Von Kienle (1961) pp. 23-4).

he proceeds to copy out the doctrines of further philosophers in some detail, all the while diligently taking care to keep opening up his old source book to record minor and irrelevant details and anecdotal material. This process continues until the Theophrastean book (b) comes to an end with Hippon.

This reconstruction clearly raises a number of doubts. To begin with, it seems clear that Hippolytus had already worked out at least a general idea of the plan of his work: it was primarily intended as an anti-heretical treatise. He had previously written at least one other work on the heresies (the *Syntagma*, to which he refers in the first section of the prooemium), so that he was already familiar with the doctrines with which he would be dealing on that side of the comparison in the later books. Evidently at some stage before starting the work he must have conceived the idea that the heretical doctrines could be closely compared with and shown to derive from the doctrines of the philosophers, which implies at any rate a minimal acquaintance with the relevant philosophers.

In this respect it is relevant to consider the preface in which Hippolytus makes a number of general points about the reluctance of heretics to be refuted and the necessity of sparing no effort to correct them and to set forth the truth, which do not apply closely to the work as we have it, but only in a general sense. He also refers several times to the fact that he envisages that the extent and depth of the study required may mean that it runs to some length, but that he intends to go into the necessary detail none the less: *Praef.* 5 'It seems good not to give up even if the discussion is rather long.' In *Praef.* 10 he envisages that the work will require much research. All these references suggest that the introduction and Book 1 were written in the order in which they stand in the work. Yet already Hippolytus has planned the structure of the remainder of the work, that he will compare each heresy with a philosopher from whom it can be shown to derive.[2] It is clear that he has already some idea of some possible combinations based on a preliminary knowledge of the philosophers. Apart from Plato and Aristotle the philosophers of whom he makes

[2] *Praef.*: 9.

most use in the later books are the Pythagoreans, Empedocles and Heraclitus; yet even a basic knowledge of these sufficient to suggest them as possible sources of heretical doctrines should have enabled him to write a more accurate account than that provided by Diels' (a) source or to excerpt more coherently from a chapter which discussed more than one thinker together; but they are the very three on which his account appears most deficient.

It is very difficult to suppose that Hippolytus wrote Book 1 either without having in mind his ultimate purpose as a criterion for selecting which doctrines he chose to report, or without already having come into contact with the doctrines of the philosophers in a work of better quality than that described by Diels as his first source. The motive for Book 1 seems to be to establish the work as a scholarly one and to impress the reader with its learning. It is unlikely that Hippolytus would have been content to use Diels' (a) source for such a purpose.

This brings us on to a preliminary point concerning the extent of the evidence used by Diels. According to his assignment of Book 1 to the two sources, all the passages that include any verbatim quotation (Pythagoras, Empedocles, Xenophanes para (i), and Plato (?)) are assigned to source (a). The excerpts from the Theophrastean work contain no quotations. The very small number of quotations in Book 1 mean that it is not impossible to envisage them incorporated into an epitome of lives such as he describes. But in the later books Hippolytus has access to a significantly large number of quotations for Empedocles and Heraclitus, not restricted to those that might be used to illustrate a biographical work. These can hardly be referred to the Theophrastean work since they certainly do not fit in with the pattern of the excerpts from it in Book 1. We have to assume either that Hippolytus has acquired yet another source for these thinkers or that the (a) source in fact contained a lot more doctrinal material than appeared from Book 1.

It is within Book 1 that the main doubts about Diels' division arise. The first part of Book 1 (chs 1-16) divides into three sections between each of which Hippolytus reconsiders his plan of action. In chapter 5 he says that there were some other *phusikoi* (other than Thales, Pythagoras, Empedocles and Heraclitus) whom he had not thought it necessary to include because they said nothing different from the ones he has mentioned. He decides, however, to include them in view of the fact that many later *phusikoi* derived from this school. It is clear from this that he is not so interested in the next group of philosophers as he was in the previous group, nor perhaps as he is in the group that follows.[3] He merely intends to record their views as relevant to the influence which they had on the succession of later thinkers, not as relevant to his own interests in the origins of heresy. This is not the point at which he would look for a new and better source in order to have more material for a more thorough treatment than he gave to the previous four philosophers.

More plausible is the idea that, having acquired a new (and, in Diels' view, better) source, Hippolytus discovers that these philosophers are more interesting than he thought and is thus persuaded to include them after all; on the other hand it does not look any more likely that he was looking for more material for the third group starting from Parmenides (supposing that he had intended to proceed immediately to them after Heraclitus, and was only then diverted into writing chapters 6-9 as a summary of the background material). Chapters 11-16, when we do come to them, are somewhat shorter and markedly less thorough and organised than the intervening chapters 6-9. They are summaries of a few significant beliefs in each case, and again they are not thinkers of whom he will make extensive use in the later books.

The second division of Book 1 comes in chapter 10, this time at a point where Diels does not recognise a change of source (although the stylistic evidence strongly suggests that we should look for some such change).[4] Here Hippolytus suddenly seems to finish the *phusikoi* and write his closing sentence, preparing to proceed to Socrates and the *êthikoi* (moral philosophers). This was exactly what he said he was going to do in his little plan of action at chapter 5. There he said 'We think that after setting forth philosophy in succession from Pythagoras [i.e. those he has just written up,

---

[3] Section 3, Parmenides to Hippon.
[4] See Table 1 and discussion below.

Pythagoras, Empedocles and Heraclitus] we should go back to
the opinions of those who followed Thales' (chs 6-9). He starts
6 by claiming that Anaximander was a disciple of Thales, 'and
after refuting these we should go on to ethical and logical
philosophy of which the ethical was originated by Socrates and
the dialectical by Aristotle'.

However, this plan does not after all proceed smoothly.
Hippolytus appears suddenly to discover that, far from his
having finished the Presocratics, there are a whole lot more
who say 'different things about the divine and the nature of
the universe'; so many in fact that he would have to procure
more writing materials to write about them all in detail.[5]
They are, however, so significant for later thinkers that he will
have to go on to deal with them. He proceeds to give brief
paragraphs on Parmenides, Leucippus, Democritus, Xenophanes, Ecphantus and Hippon.

From the structure of the book it thus appears that
Hippolytus wrote section 1 (chs 1-4) from a source from which
he chose to omit any others than Thales, Pythagoras,
Empedocles and Heraclitus, the four most interesting from his
point of view. At this point something, possibly the acquisition
of another source,[6] suggested that he should have included
Anaximander, Anaximenes, Anaxagoras and Archelaos. He
therefore proceeded to write section 2 (chapters 6-9). At the
end of these he thought he had completed the Presocratics,
whereupon some other discovery made him change his plan
again and realise that he should add six more chapters (section
3).

It is matters of style and subject that give us the clearest
evidence for three marked divisions, rather than the two
constructed by Diels, in the first sixteen chapters of the book.
These show that chapters 6-9, the central section, form a
homogeneous group quite unlike the material preceding or
following them.[7] Chapters 6-9 are clearly constructed on a

---

[5] 1.10.

[6] Alternatively Hippolytus may have sought another simpler source
because he realised for some other reason that it would be desirable to
include brief outlines of these four. Cf. n. 23 below.

[7] See Tables 1 and 2. Table 1 (pp. 194-5) shows the topics dealt with for
each of the philosophers in chapters 1-16. Table 2 (pp. 198-205)

strict system: each discusses the views of the philosopher in question on topics concerned with cosmology, the material, shape and movement of the earth and heavenly bodies, various meteorological phenomena, the development of animal life and of man. In each chapter the topics discussed are almost exactly the same, just one or two being omitted in each case (e.g. weather is not mentioned in 9 and animal life is omitted in 7). The order in which these topics are dealt with is precisely the same in each chapter, with one minor exception.[8] Many of these topics are mentioned nowhere else and none of them occurs in connection with more than one or at the most two other thinkers, of which some occurrences are in section 1 (e.g. movement of stars, earthquakes) and some in section 3 (e.g. material character of heavenly bodies).[9] In no other chapter are topics dealt with in this strict sequence.[10] The views of these four philosophers are reported impersonally, in a straightforward list of facts. No comments are made, and there is no discussion of the reasons why each came to hold these views. In this the chapters differ in character from some at least of the later chapters: in 11 Hippolytus notices that Parmenides contradicts himself and does not escape the popular belief in plurality; in 12 he criticises the fact that Leucippus fails to explain what necessity is.

Another noticeable feature of these four chapters 6-9 is that, despite their being substantially longer than most and apparently complete and thorough in their account, they make no mention of a number of subjects which he mentions reasonably frequently in other much shorter summaries. For example god or the divine (*to theion*) is considered in each of the first four chapters and again in 14 and 15 as well as frequently after Socrates. It is not surprising that this is a subject that interests him, when he has information on it. But neither

---

demonstrates how closely the four chapters in section 2 correspond in style and structure to form a homogeneous group.

[8] Animal life and man are found before instead of after the meteorological phenomena in chapter 6 (see Table 2).

[9] See Table 1.

[10] In the latter part of chapter 14 on Xenophanes (14.3-6) it is perhaps possible to detect something of the same approach.

Table 1. Distribution of subjects per chapter in Hippolytus, *Refutatio*, book 1

	Patronymic	City	Date by king	Details of life	Arché	Material arché	Kinesis	Hot & cold	Position of earth	Shape of earth	Rivers etc.	Stars (character)	Stars (distance)	Stars (movement)	Sun (size)	Sun (height)	Paths of heavenly bodies
SECTION I																	
Ch.1 Thales		●	●	●	●	●									●		
Ch.2 Pythagoras		●		●	●			○							●		
Ch.3 Empedocles						●											
Ch.4 Heraclitus		●			●	●											
SECTION II																	
Ch.6 Anaximander	●	●			●	●	●		●	●		●	●		○	●	
Ch.7 Anaximenes	●	●			●	●	●	●	●	●		●	●				●
Ch.8 Anaxagoras	●	●			●	●	●	●	●	●	●	●	●	●	●	●	●
Ch.9 Archelaus	●	●			●	●	●	●	●	●		●			●		●
SECTION III																	
Ch.11 Parmenides					●	●											
Ch.12 Leucippus													●				
Ch.13 Democritus	●	●		●										●		●	
Ch.14 Xenophanes	●	●	●								●	●					
Ch.15 Ecphantus		●					●		●								
Ch.16 Hippon		●			●			●									

● subject appears in this chapter.

○ subject appears in this chapter but in a rather different context.

Moon (character)	Eclipses	Winds	Precipitation	Lightening & thunder	Earthquakes	Origin of life	Reproduction	Man	God/divine	Metensomatosis	Soul	Daimones	Knowledge & ignorance	Evil	Full & void	Olympiad date	Reference to source	Quotations	WORD USAGE	ἄπειρον	κόσμος	οὐρανός	στοιχεῖον	σῶμα
					●				●				●									●		
									●	●	●	●	●				●	●		●	●			
									●	●	●	●						●						
									●				●	●										
●	●	●	●	●		●		●									●			●	○	●	○	
●		●	●	●	●												●			●				
●	●	●		●	●	●	●										●			●		●		
●						●	●	●														●		
																					●			
															●					●	●		●	●
●															●					●	●		●	
●									●									●			●			
									●		●		●							●	●			●
									●												●			

theology, nor *daimones*, the soul, the nature of evil, or epistemology, all of which occur occasionally in sections 1 and 3, occurs at all in chapters 6-9.[11] It looks as though chapters 6-9 are an almost verbatim copy of a brief systematic report which included only the physical theories of the four philosophers without reference to theology, psychology or epistemology, and that Hippolytus has given us more or less all that it contained on these thinkers.

A number of other features suggest a strongly distinctive source for this section. As Diels noticed, we have a relatively high frequency of close Theophrastean parallels in these chapters: we are almost certainly dealing with a source reasonably closely derived from Theophrastus, which perhaps accounts for the strict order of topics. Diels also indicates some passages in chapters 11-16 which he thinks are Theophrastean, but these are very loose parallels, in most cases a single word which may derive from the words of the original formulation of the theory, or be merely a chance echo.[12] Another feature is the use of dates. Dates are given at the ends of chapters 6, 7 and 8 for Anaximander, Anaximenes and Anaxagoras, by Olympiads. In no other chapters are dates given by Olympiads. Diels thought these Apollodoran dates smacked of his epitome of lives; hence he proposed that the pedantic Hippolytus struggled back[13] to his old useless source to dig out a single date each time, despite the fact that he had not included dates anywhere else in his work. It seems far more likely that the

---

[11] This does not count the uninformative passing reference to *theoi* (gods) and *theia* (divine things) in 7.1: they are mentioned as being among the things (i.e. all things) that come from air.

[12] The passages which Diels lists as Theophrastean are the whole of chapters 11 and 12, the first sentence of 13.1, 13.2-4 (but not the last sentence of 13.4), 14.2-6, and the whole of chapters 15 and 16. However, his parallel texts of the other Theophrastean writers derived from Aetius along with Hippolytus book 1 show that the parallels in these chapters are markedly less than those in chapters 6-9, and amount to only a very small proportion of the text. If it was the case, as I am suggesting, that Hippolytus' (a') source was really much more extensive and contained a whole range of material, there is no reason why it might not have included occasional items ultimately of Theophrastean origin.

[13] Quite a task if the book is in roll form. For the inclusion of this material in the Theophrastean work, cf. Mejer (1978) p. 84.

new source he was using included Olympiad dates, which he mechanically included in copying out these three chapters, but left out as irrelevant in chapter 9.[14] The only other indications of date are in chapter 1 where Thales is dated as contemporary with Croesus and chapter 14 where Xenophanes is dated as contemporary with Cyrus. Again a common source seems probable, and again the dates may be Apollodorus',[15] but it would appear that only the source of section 2 gave Olympiads, while the source he used for the dates of Thales and Xenophanes only gave dates by reference to other significant figures.

Another feature is the use of the patronymic in introducing a character. This occurs in chapters 6, 7, 8, 9, 13 and 14. These last two present a problem on any interpretation. Diels was tempted to see it as a Theophrastean feature, but had in fact to assign the last two occurrences to his (a) material because they were so closely associated with such material. They remain a problem for a view that identifies distinct sources for sections 2 and 3. In either case it has to be assumed that the source of section 2 gives the patronymic in every case, while the other source does not consistently omit it, or may in fact include it in some cases where Hippolytus does omit it. This, together with the wide range of topics included in sections 1 and 3 as compared with section 2, suggests that there may be considerably more material available to Hippolytus for sections 1 and 3 than there is for section 2, and that he is making selective excerpts. This is also suggested by the fact that he has direct quotations to hand for chapters in which he gives unusually brief summaries (and also has considerable numbers of quotations available for these thinkers in later books), but apparently derives no quotations from the source of section 2.

---

[14] In general Hippolytus does not seem to have been much worried about the precise chronology of his characters.

[15] Cf. Thales, DK 11 A 1, section 37.

Book 1, Chapter 6   Chapter 7

Ia   Anaximander was a pupil of   Anaximenes, who was also a
      Thales. Anaximander, son of   Milesian, the son of Eurystratus,
      Praxiades, a Milesian. He said   said that the principle was infinite
      that the principle of all things air
      was a certain nature of the
      infinite.

II   from which the universes come   from which come the things that
      into being and the cosmic   come into being and the things
      systems in the universes. This   that have come into being and the
      nature is eternal and unageing   things that will be and gods and
      and it surrounds all the cosmic   divine things, and the remaining
      systems. But he speaks of time   things come from the offspring of
      in that coming to be and being   this air. The form of this air is like
      and passing away are marked   this: when it is most equable it it
      out.   not evident to sight, but it is
                                        revealed by the cold and the hot
                                        and the damp and that which is in
                                        motion.

Ib   He said that the principle and
      element of things was the
      infinite (*apeiron*), being the first
      to use this name for the
      principle. [see above, section Ia]

III   In addition to this he said that There is always motion; for the
      there is eternal motion in which things that change would not
      it happens that the universes   change if they were not moved.
      come into being.

IV   For when it is condensed and
                                        rarefied it appears different. For
                                        when it is dispersed into what is
                                        rarer it becomes fire, condensed
                                        again into air it becomes winds,
                                        cloud is produced out of air by
                                        felting, and then as it is condensed
                                        more water, even more so earth,
                                        and at its most dense stones. So
                                        that the opposites which have chief
                                        control of generation are hot and
                                        cold.

Chapter 8	Chapter 9
After him came Anaxagoras, son of Hegesibolus, of Clazomenae. He said that the principle of the universe was mind and matter, mind as producing, matter as product.	Archelaus, Athenian by birth, son of Apollodorus. He said there was a mixture of matter like Anaxagoras and that the principles were just the same. But he said that a mixture was inherent in mind from the start.
For when all things were together, mind came upon them and set them in order.	
But he says the material principles are unlimited and the smaller of these he calls 'infinites'.	
All things partake of motion, being moved by mind, and the things that are alike come together. And the things in the universe are set in order by the cyclical motion.	The origin of motion is the separating-out of the hot and the cold from each other, and the hot moves while the cold stays still.
The dense and the wet and the dark and cold and all the heavy things come together into the middle, and the earth is made of these things solidified. But the opposites of these – the hot and the bright and the dry and the light – proceeded to the further part of the aither.	But water, when melted, runs into the middle, where it also becomes air, when it is burnt up, and earth, of which the former is carried upwards and the latter settles below.

Book 1, Chapter 6   Chapter 7

V   But the earth is on high, held up   And the earth is flat, borne aloft
      by nothing, but staying where   upon air,
      it is because of the similar
      distance of everything. The
      shape of it is curved, round, just
      like a column drum. And of its
      surfaces we walk on one and
      there exists another on the
      other side.

VI

VII   But the stars come into being as   In the same way the sun and moon
      a circle of fire separated off from   and the other stars, being all of
      the fire in the world and   them fiery, float on the air
      encompassed by air. There are   because of flatness. The stars came
      sort of breathing passages like   out of earth because of the fact that
      pipes through which the stars   a secretion was given off from the
      are seen; for this reason eclipses   earth and when the secretion
      occur when the breathing holes   vapourised fire was produced, and
      are blocked up. The moon   out of the fire when it was raised
      sometimes appears waxing and   on high the stars were composed.
      sometimes waning in   But there are also earthly natures
      accordance with the blocking   in the region of the stars, carried
      up or opening of the passages.   round with the stars. But he says
      The circle of the sun is twenty-   that the stars do not move under
      seven times that of the moon,   the earth, as others have supposed,
      and the highest is the sun,   but round the earth just as a felt
      lowest the circles of the fixed   cap turns round our head. The sun
      stars.   is hidden not because it has gone
                                             under the earth but because it is
                                             concealed by the loftier parts of the
                                             earth and because the distance
                                             between it and us is increased. The

Chapter 8

Chapter 9

And the earth is flat in shape and stays up on high because of its size and there being no void. And because of this the air is extremely strong and carries the earth aloft.

Therefore the earth is still and comes into being for these reasons, but it lies in the middle being no fraction to speak of in proportion to the whole universe.

Of the wet things on the earth the sea existed originally and then the waters in it evaporated and settled out again so that it also derives from the rivers that flow into it. The rivers derive their substance both from the rain and from the waters in the earth; for the earth is hollow and it has water in the cavities. But the Nile rises in summer when waters are carried down to it from the snows in the antarctic regions.

The sun and moon and all the stars are fiery-hot stones carried round with the rotation of the aither. Below the stars there are some bodies carried round with the sun and the moon, invisible to us. We do not feel the heat of the stars because the distance from the earth is great. Also they are not so hot as the sun because their region is colder. The moon is lower than the sun and nearer to us. The sun exceeds the Peloponnese in size. The moon does not have light of its own, but from the sun. The rotation of the stars goes under the earth. The moon is eclipsed when the earth gets in the way, but sometimes also when the bodies below the moon get in the way and the sun is eclipsed at the new moon when the moon gets in the way.

But (the air) produced from the burning (controls the universe) and the nature of the stars derived from this when it was first burnt up. The greatest of the stars is the sun, the second the moon, and of the rest some are smaller, some larger. He says the universe is inclined and hence the sun gives light to the earth, makes the air transparent and the earth dry. For at first it was a marsh in that it is lofty round the edge and concave in the middle. As evidence of its being concave he adduces the fact that the sun does not rise and set at the same time for everybody, which ought to be the case if it was level.

stars do not provide heat due to the
extent of the distance.

VIIIa Living things come into being
***by evaporation by the sun.
Man was originally similar to
another creature, that is to a
fish. [see below section VIIIb]

IX   Winds occur when the finest   Winds are created when the air
      vapours of the air are separated   which has been condensed a bit,
      off and when they are set in   having been rarefied, is set in
      motion and gather together,   motion

X   and rain comes from the vapour   but when it comes together and is
      given off by the things under   even more condensed it gives rise
      the sun,   to clouds and thus changes to
                                         water. Hail occurs when the water
                                         brought down from the clouds
                                         freezes and snow when the clouds
                                         themselves being wetter become
                                         frozen.

XI   but lightning occurs when wind   Lightning is produced when the
      strikes the clouds and breaks   clouds are broken up by the force
      them up.   of the winds. For when they are
                                         broken up the flash is bright and
                                         fiery. The rainbow is produced
                                         when the sun's rays fall upon
                                         solidified air.

XII   Earthquakes are a result of the
                                         earth being excessively altered by
                                         heating and cooling.

Chapter 8   Chapter 9

The sun and moon perform
turnings because they are pushed
back by the air. But the moon
turns frequently because it is
unable to overcome the cold.
Anaxagoras was the first to define
matters regarding eclipses and
sources of light. He said that the
moon is earthy and has plains and
ravines in it. The milky way is a
reflection of the light of the stars
that are not lit by the sun.
Shooting stars are like sparks flying
off from the rotation of the axis.

Winds occur when the air is
rarefied by the sun and when
things are burnt and make their
way towards the pole and are
carried off.

Thunder and lightning come from
heat striking the clouds.

Earthquakes occur when the air
from above strikes the region
under the earth. For when this is

VIIIb [see above, section VIIIa]

XIII Anaximander was born in the   These are the theories of
third year of the forty-second   Anaximenes. He flourished
Olympiad.   around the first year of the fifty-
                                       eighth Olympiad.

Chapter 8   Chapter 9

moved the earth that rests on it is
shaken by it.

Living things originally came into
being in water, but subsequently
from each other, and males occur
when the seed is secreted from the
parts on the right and cleaves to
the parts on the right of the womb,
and females in the opposite way.

Concerning living things he says
that when the earth was first
warmed up in the lower part where
the hot and the cold were mixed,
there appeared the other living
things in great number and also
men, all having the same life-style
taking nourishment from the slime
– but they were shortlived and
subsequently generation from each
other was established. And men
were distinguished from the others
and established rulers and laws
and crafts and cities and so on.
And he says mind is innate to all
creatures alike. But each of the
creatures uses mind, some more
slowly and some more quickly.

Anaxagoras flourished in the first
year of the eighty-eighth
Olympiad in which year they say
Plato was also born. They say
Anaxagoras foretold the future as
well.

There seems to be one item of linguistic evidence that tells in favour of a source for section 3 distinct from that of section 2, and against Diels' view that the Theophrastean source continued to chapter 16. In chapters 6, 8 and 9 the word *ouranos* is used to refer to the ordered structure of earth, moon, sun, stars, etc. The word *kosmos* is used only once, in chapter 6, when it refers to the *kosmos*, or *kosmoi*, *in* the *ouranoi* which seems to be the arrangement or ordering of the bodies, not a term that can refer to the ordered physical structure itself. The word *ouranos* does not occur at all in chapters 11-16, and the only other occurrence in the first sixteen chapters is in chapter 1 in an anecdote about Thales quoted from Plato's *Theaetetus* in Plato's words.[16] It is clear from this that the term *ouranos* is not characteristic of sections 1 and 3 but is characteristic of section 2. The term *kosmos*, on the other hand, occurs in every chapter of section 3 in the sense of an ordered physical structure, as *ouranos* was used in section 2. It would be fair to say that *kosmos* in this sense was not characteristic of section 2 but was characteristic of section 3. The phrase *to pan* meaning the universe (with or without order) seems to be common to the whole work and may well be Hippolytus' own preferred term.

All the evidence seems to suggest a strong distinction between chapters 6-9 and the rest of the book, but no significant distinction between chapters 1-4 and 11-16. It seems unlikely that Hippolytus was using more than one book at a time in these chapters, and the following strategy is plausible. He started off with a single source (call it a') from which he wrote chapters 1-4. This probably started with Thales as the first *phusikos*, and in view of the general scarcity of information on his theories it is unlikely to have contained much more information than Hippolytus gives. The information is mainly doxographical: in terms of biography we are given only his date (*kata Kroison*, in the time of Croesus) and the anecdote from Plato, which is likely to have been included in many doxographical works in the absence of more useful data on Thales. The interest in his theories is confirmed by the

---

[16] 1.1.4, Plato *Theaetetus* 174a. It is not impossible that this anecdote was added by Hippolytus from Plato.

fact that a belief in condensation and rarefaction from water is attributed to him to augment the meagre statement that the origin of things was water.

Hippolytus turns to Pythagoras after Thales, but it looks as though they may well not have been adjacent in his source. He gives only a very vague indication that this philosophy was not very far distant from the same period by way of connection with the previous chapter. It seems likely that a passage on the Milesians may well have come after Thales in the source, but having found Thales already fairly unpromising for his purposes Hippolytus may have chosen to omit Anaximander and others, as he says in chapter 5.

On Pythagoras Hippolytus has a large quantity of information and gives him the longest chapter of any of the Presocratics. There are no marked signs of confusion to suggest that the source contained Pythagoras, Heraclitus and Empedocles indiscriminately in a single chapter.[17] The repetitions within the Pythagoras chapter that Diels remarked on are not in fact repetitions at all: in 2.2 he notes that Pythagoras said that god was *monas*; in 2.6 he reports that he said the origin of numbers was the first *monas*. In 2.3 he reports Pythagoras' custom of expecting his disciples to keep silence; in 2.16 in recounting the details of the course of discipleship he refers in passing to the fact that, in the first stage, the disciple remained silent, as if this was a fact already explained; in 2.18 he discusses whether Pythagoras picked up this habit of ordaining silence from the Egyptians. In 2.4 he reports the fact that Pythagoras divided his disciples into two classes and called some *esôterikoi* and others *exôterikoi*; in 2.17 he tells us that the *esôterikoi* were called *Puthagoreoi* and the others were called *Puthagoristai*, a different fact which presupposes knowledge of the first point. The fact that sections 1-5a of the chapter seem to give a brief summary of life and work and 5a-15 discuss his doctrine in some detail may well reflect the combination of a number of authorities in the source used by Hippolytus. That his source compared a number of different doxographers is supported by the fact that he quotes two for the same fact in 2.12: both Diodorus Eretrieus and Aristoxenus

[17] Contra Diels (1879) p. 145.

Musicus refer to Pythagoras' association with Zaratas the Chaldaean.

Hippolytus' source seems to consider itself a work of some scholarly pretensions: it gives a fairly detailed account of Pythagorean number-terminology and the theory behind it, it discusses at length the origin of some of his ideas concerning the cosmos and life, the soul and the conduct he prescribed for the individual. The fact that a fair proportion of the material is concerned with Pythagoras' own life, the characteristic features of his school, his claims to reincarnation and the Pythagorean life-style is more to be attributed to the religious nature of the Pythagorean sect and its emphasis on matters of life-style and on the legends concerning the life and miracles associated with Pythagoras, than to a particularly 'biographical' interest in the source.

For Empedocles, we are given a few very brief statements on his doctrines which are compared with the Stoics and Pythagoras. We are offered another account of an incident connected with Pythagoras' claim to have been reincarnated which occupies a considerable portion of the brief chapter. This suggests on the one hand that the passage discussing Empedocles' belief in *metensômatôsis* (reincarnation) did not follow so close upon the same subject in Pythagoras in the source as it does here: it is introduced in its own right without reference to the account already given. On the other hand it seems that the source Hippolytus used was interested in discussing the relations of the doctrines of different philosophers and schools with one another.[18] Empedocles' belief in reincarnation is illustrated by a quotation such as one might expect to find in a much more detailed discussion of the doctrine. It may be that what Hippolytus had in his source was an attempt by the author to make sense of these notoriously difficult philosophers by an extensive discussion of quotations from their work and comparison with doctrines found in other thinkers. Hippolytus would thus be faced with a large quantity

---

[18] This is borne out by the account of Heraclitus in chapter 4 which compares Heraclitus and Empedocles.

of very diverse and scarcely coherent material[19] from which he tried unsuccessfully to extract a suitably brief summary of the beliefs of each on the subjects that interest him for Book 1. Perhaps because he realised that he would use the detailed material later he is not prepared to work out a detailed and lengthy account; but it need not be a lack of accurate information that leads to the confused and cryptic reports of these two characters, but rather a superfluity of quotations, interpretation and comparison.

The accounts of the thinkers given in chapters 11-16 seem similar in character though much less confused. The account of Parmenides is very brief, but hints at a discussion of the relationship between the two parts of his poem in the twofold repetition of the fact that the same man said two incompatible things. Similarly a fragment of Xenophanes is given with an interpretation that is influenced by a comparison with sceptical doctrines.[20] A link between the source of section 3 and that of section 1 is suggested by the references to Democritus as the laughing philosopher in 13.4, and Heraclitus as the weeping philosopher in 4.1.[21]

All this evidence suggests that we should regard Hippolytus' (a') source as the more extensive and more interesting of the two: far from being the slim volume of lives that Diels proposed, it probably contained a wealth of information, commentary and quotations from various sources, and may have included some of the material that Hippolytus used in later books. The inadequacy of the accounts Hippolytus composes is to be attributed more to the difficulty of extracting

[19] It is possible that much of the material used by Hippolytus in the later books could have come from a similar context.

[20] 1.14.1 'He was the first to say that all things were incomprehensible, speaking as follows ...' (DK 21 B 34). The fragment is used in the same context by Sextus Empiricus (*Adv. Math.* 7.49 and 110) and the comparison between Xenophanes' thought and scepticism is discussed by Sextus at *PH* I 224-5. Mejer (1978) suggested that Hippolytus' source here was within the sceptical tradition (p. 84).

[21] Hippolytus' source for section 3 must have included Zeno the Eleatic after Parmenides and before Leucippus since Leucippus is said to be a disciple of Zeno's in a position which would normally refer to a teacher who had already been included, and usually the one immediately preceding. Hippolytus, however, has chosen to omit Zeno completely.

a brief coherent summary from such a quantity of interpretation and discussion. Hippolytus may well have worked from notes taken from the book, which might have aggravated the difficulty of reconstructing a coherent account.[22] His (b') source on the other hand was clearly much simpler in construction and provided him with a basic factual summary of each thinker in turn; however it does not deal with the theological and ethical subjects in which he is really interested, nor does it give him the detailed information he would need for discussing the philosophers in later books of the *Refutatio*. He finds it convenient to use this simplistic work for a few thinkers who are of little importance to his final purpose. From this source he can simply copy the account exactly as he finds it.[23] The (b') source certainly adheres very closely to the Theophrastean tradition, as Diels has shown, but we cannot claim that it adheres closely to the original texts of the philosophers whose doctrines it reports. It is readily apparent that they have been forced into conformity with a strict doxographical sequence of topics and a view on each topic has been sought from each of them.

Hippolytus has indeed used two sources for his account of the Presocratics and it is important to make the distinction between the two since they are very different in character. As regards their relative quality, however, Diels' verdict is unacceptable. The (a') source contains a wider range of material, and probably a greater cross-section of interpretations and influences, but as such the influences at any particular point are more difficult to assess. Hippolytus' own criteria of selection also have more influence here. The (b')

[22] On the technique of excerpting in ancient authors, see e.g. Skydsgaard (1968) ch. 7 and Mejer (1978) pp. 16-18.

[23] Hippolytus seems to have selected Pythagoras, Empedocles and Heraclitus as most interesting originally and chosen to omit Anaximander and Anaximenes. At chapter 5 he changes his mind. This may mean that he only discovered his Theophrastean pamphlet (b') at this point. With this book the main burden of his task was done for him, and it was easier to include the less interesting characters after all. Having included the four for which the pamphlet gave summaries he feels duty bound at chapter 10 to go back to his (a') source and include a few more who were significant for the history of philosophy, although not for his own purpose.

source is easier to assess since it clearly is Theophrastean, but its interests are narrower and the influence of interpretation and of the self-imposed structure are very great. It looks through the tinted spectacles of Theophrastus.

Appendix B
The *Apophasis Megalê* of Simon Magus

Work on Simon Magus tended in the past to concentrate on constructing doctrines for Simon on the basis of the hints in the biographical accounts and rejecting the testimony of the *Apophasis Megalê*. This was largely in the wake of the work of Salmon[1] in 1885 (which cast doubts on the authenticity of the majority of Hippolytus' reports on heretics and suggested that he had been taken in by a forger), and the continued debate on the subject up to about 1925.[2] This meant that the *Apophasis Megalê* received almost no attention either in its own right or as a work of Simon Magus. Even after the forgery theory had subsided there remained the question of whether the *Apophasis Megalê* could really be ascribed to Simon Magus himself; it was suggested that its gnosticism was not sufficiently primitive[3] and it continued to receive little or no attention. More recently, however, the *Apophasis Megalê* has been the subject of two studies in its own right, both of which attempt to re-establish the credentials of the *Apophasis* and demonstrate that Hippolytus' report must ultimately derive from a work that stands very early in the history of gnosticism.

Frickel took as his starting point an examination of the nature of the immediate source used by Hippolytus for his report. In 1967 he published a brief summary of his results, omitting the details of his study, and argued for the conclusion that Hippolytus copied, more or less word for word, from a source which was already a paraphrase of, or commentary on,

[1] Salmon (1885) pp. 389-402.
[2] For a summary of the debate, see Frickel (1968).
[3] See e.g. E. de Faye (1925).

the *Apophasis* and not the work itself; hence the *Apophasis* itself was somewhat older than the source Hippolytus used. In 1968 Frickel published the detailed study on which these conclusions were based. This includes an extensive examination of Hippolytus' method of work and the extent to which he quotes his sources verbatim or summarises them, concluding that Hippolytus' work is almost entirely verbatim quotation and very rarely if ever includes what can properly be termed summarising of his sources.[4] He also examines the frequent use of the word *phêsin* in the *Apophasis* report, which he suggests is normally seen as an indication that Hippolytus is summarising or explaining the meaning of a passage. This he claims is not necessarily the case since it may have been taken over from the model where it marked such an explanatory passage or may have been inserted by Hippolytus when he was still copying word for word from his model.

In 1969 Salles-Dabadie published *Recherches sur Simon le Mage*: I. *L'Apophasis Megalê* which concentrates not so much on the transmission of the *Apophasis Megalê* as on its doctrinal content.[5] It therefore assumes the economical hypothesis that the vast majority of the material provided by Hippolytus comes from the authentic *Apophasis* (though he does posit a wicked Christian to insert the New Testament quotations which he finds unacceptable). After reconstructing a cosmogony from the fragments he argues that the theory and language suggest that its author was of semitic origin, knew little Greek but in learning what Greek he knew had been inspired by Greek

---

[4] Frickel's criterion of verbatim quotation of a source leads him into some confusion. He criticises earlier scholars who attempted to identify certain passages as verbatim quotations from the *Apophasis* on the grounds that if, as he believes, Hippolytus' model was a paraphrase and not the *Apophasis* itself then the whole passage, including parts which appear to be paraphrases or comments, may be verbatim quotation of the model. He fails to observe that what these earlier scholars were seeking was a criterion of verbatim quotation from the *Apophasis* itself for which his own criterion of verbatim citation of some other hypothetical model is irrelevant. On his own account the extent to which the *Apophasis* itself is quoted word for word in Hippolytus' text must be very similar to that suggested by those he criticises.

[5] Salles-Dabadie knows of Frickel's paper of 1967 but apparently not the monograph of 1968.

philosophy, especially Stoicism, and dreamed up theories which are primitive in comparison with developed gnostic systems, a characterisation designed to suit the traditional Simon Magus.

Both scholars are inclined to agree that in origin the *Apophasis* is both doctrinally and chronologically relatively early in the history of gnosticism. Two questions however still need further investigation if we are adequately to assess Hippolytus' contribution to the report on Simon Magus: (1) what exactly was the nature of the source and its relationship to the original *Apophasis*, and (2) who was responsible for the references to Greek philosophy and why?

The first question falls into two parts: (a) how does what Hippolytus actually wrote compare with what he had in his immediate source, and (b) how does (or did) what was in his source compare with the original text of the *Apophasis*, supposing there was one? Frickel devotes a considerable proportion of his work to considering the first of these questions on the basis of comparison with other sections of Hippolytus' work: he argues that the evidence of Book 10 (the 'Epitome') suggests that Hippolytus generally quotes verbatim from his sources and that where he wants to shorten the account he does so by omitting sections rather than summarising the whole. He cites the report on Marcus (Book 6.39-54) from Irenaeus and the quotations from Sextus Empiricus as supporting the claim that Hippolytus generally copies word for word, and the Naassene report which follows the order of the hymn to Attis (5.7-9) as suggesting that Hippolytus' order follows that of his source. He is also inclined to conclude that because large parts are left out in Book 10, the main reports in Books 5-9 must quote the original sources in full.[6]

Frickel's conclusion that the report on the *Apophasis* reproduces Hippolytus' model exactly without re-arrangement or omission is not adequately supported. He himself has to deal with cases in which the report in the 'Epitome' in Book 10 is in fact fuller than the equivalent report in the main book,[7] and

[6] See Frickel (1967) p. 201. This argument seems to me to prove nothing.
[7] E.g. *Ref.* 10.11, 10.16.6, and 10.17.2.

also mentions that where Hippolytus copies from Irenaeus it is not without Hippolytus' own digressions in the form of explanatory material. Furthermore it is not the case that we can assume that Hippolytus' practice in epitomising his own work in Book 10 is necessarily a guide to his practice in writing the main books.[8] It is more likely that Hippolytus' practice in the immediate vicinity of the *Apophasis* report, within the same account of Simon Magus, will serve as a control for this section of his work. The passages concerning the life of Simon, before and after the *Apophasis* report, offer a clear example of Hippolytus' handling of his material. The analysis in chapter two demonstrates that there is nothing in these sections to suggest that Hippolytus was committed to a policy of copying out a single source, word for word, without omission, summary, digression or re-arrangement. Indeed if the supposition that he may have used notes is correct, we might expect that he will have been selective in quoting passages from the *Apophasis*, if that work was extensive, and may well have re-arranged them in what he considered a logical sequence.

(i) The arrangement

The problem with analysis of the *Apophasis* report itself is that the subject matter seems to be intentionally mysterious and obscure, and is expressed in an oracular style. It is difficult to tell how much of the obscurity might have been caused by omission of intervening material and re-arrangement by Hippolytus. In so far as one can determine the main subjects in the account it appears that references to fire are recurrent; this may be because fire was a major interest in the *Apophasis*, or it may mean that Hippolytus was using it as a criterion for

[8] Frickel's argument depends upon the claim that book 10 was in fact written before the main books and from the same original sources, rather than as an epitome of the main books. The thesis is implausible, and impossible to demonstrate. Book 10 has no argument and hence no point as a work in its own right; the sections on the philosophers certainly are not taken from the same original sources. It seems more probable that it was written as a summary of the earlier books, but written from Hippolytus' notebooks containing his extracts from source-works, rather than from his written-up work. See Koschorke (1975) Appendix II arguing against Frickel's view.

Table 1. Summary of subject matter, *Ref.* 6.9-17

	The *archê* is fire, equivalent to the infinite power.
	Fire is two-fold, visible and invisible, potential and actual.
	Fire contains everything: the visible perishes, the invisible actualised fruit is preserved (from the consuming fire).
10	Digression on perishable man: all flesh is grass.
11	Empedocles.
12	The created cosmos came from ungenerated fire.
	Six roots generated in pairs.
	Infinite power is in roots, and hence in everything, potentially.
	If the potential power is actualised (*exeikonisthêi*) it is the same as the infinite power = *hestôs, stas, stêsomenos*.
	If it remains potential it perishes.
13	The three pairs of roots are equivalent to heaven, earth, sun, moon, air, water.
14	Allegorisation of six days' creation.
	God makes man in image and likeness. He must be made into the image (*exeikonisthêi*) or he will perish.
	God makes man in Paradise = womb. Allegory of Paradise.
15-16.4	Allegory of books of bible as senses of foetus.
16.4-	Man must be made into the image (*exeikonisthêi*) and become the perfect fruit.
17	There are three aeons, that have stood, one power divided.
	Fire is the origin of generation and desire. Changes of fire.
	The tree of life guarded by a flaming sword turning and changing.

selection of passages. If the latter is the case we may also suggest that he was interested in passages which allegorised or re-interpreted quotations from scripture, or referred to Greek philosophers, since these account for the main passages which digress or go into particular detail.

Table 1 gives a summary of the order of subjects in chapters 9-17. At the beginning of chapter 18 there is a break followed by further quotations from the *Apophasis* dealing with the derivation of *nous* (mind) and *epinoia* (thought) to become plurality out of unity. This passage seems to belong with the generation of the six roots in chapter 12, and this may be an indication of how Hippolytus has constructed the account. In chapter 12 he lists the six roots in a summary manner stating that Simon called them *nous* and *epinoia, phônê* (speech) and *onoma* (name), *logismos* (reason) and *enthumêsis* (inspiration); he does not give details of the process of generation. In chapter 13 he returns to the first pair, now already characterised as heaven and earth, male and female: his purpose seems to be to introduce the quotation from Isaiah which Simon interpreted as referring to his *hestôs, stas, stêsomenos* power (that stood, stands and will stand). Between these two stages should surely come the complex and mystical derivation of plurality from unity, and of male and female from the bi-sexual principle, which is the subject of the long quotation in chapter 18. Hippolytus chose to omit this passage in chapter 12; this is not surprising if we envisage that there was an equally long and involved passage concerning the derivation of each of the other two pairs of roots as well. His concern was to summarise, and the important fact was that Simon derived six roots from fire, comparable with Empedocles' system. However, when he comes to chapter 18 and is due to sum up and conclude the report on the *Apophasis*, in a manner which allows him to lead into the story of the relationship between Simon and Helen, the detailed account of the generation of *epinoia* becomes relevant: it represents the prehistory of Helen and the necessary background to that story as he tells it. For this reason it is worthwhile for him to include the detailed account of the generation of this particular pair of roots at this particular point.

If this conclusion is correct it suggests that Hippolytus had far more of the *Apophasis* text available than he actually sees reason to quote and that his selected quotations were originally separated by some intervening material rather than being a continuous passage.

(ii) The use of phêsin

Hippolytus' presentation of the *Apophasis* material is characterised by a very high frequency of the insertion of the word *phêsin*. As has been argued above,[9] the thesis of Frickel (1968) that the usage was no indication of whether or not Hippolytus was following his model closely is untenable. A likely hypothesis seems to be that *phêsin* is inserted every time there is a new quotation that is not a direct continuation from the

---

[9] See above p. 17.

preceding words; this avoids the initial objection that the passage in chapter 18 appears to be a continuous quotation of a section from the *Apophasis* but has no occurrences of the inserted *phêsin*.[10]

On this hypothesis the high frequency of this use of *phêsin* in the report as a whole would indicate that it was largely composed of brief extracts from the *Apophasis*, rather than continuous passages, and that these were strung together with the minimum of explanatory material. This conclusion would fit well with the stilted style and difficult structure of the report. We should thus expect *phêsin* with direct speech to occur in sentences which could be taken as quotations from the *Apophasis Megalê*, such that *phêsin* could mean 'it says'. There are also a number of other verbs that suggest that a word or words are quoted from the book, for example *kalei* (call) (p.136 line 25) and *prosagoreuei* (name) (p.137 line 6). The results of understanding *phêsin* as an indication that Hippolytus is quoting from the *Apophasis* are promising: the vocabulary and phraseology of the sentences marked out in this way form a pattern and fit well with the long passage in chapter 18. Some of the recurrent features are listed in Table 2.[11]

[10] It is introduced unambiguously as a precise quotation from the *Apophasis*. The use of the word *diarrêdên* (explicitly) here need not imply that this quotation is more 'exact' or 'explicit' than others since it seems to characterise Simon's manner of dealing with the subject in question rather than the nature of the quotation: 'Simon deals explicitly with this subject in the *Apophasis* thus ...' rather than 'Simon deals with this subject in the *Apophasis* exactly thus ...'

[11] One occurrence of *phêsin* (at 6.17.4) is problematic, but equally so for any interpretation of *phêsin*. The sentence does not make good sense, and we must perhaps allow that *phêsin* has been inserted by mistake or misplaced. Other examples which might seem problematic are not so on closer examination: (a) 6.13: the subject of *legôn* is the person speaking in the quotation from Isaiah. (b) 6.14.2 and 6.14.3: the subject of *legôsin* is clearly 'they', i.e. the scriptures, the authorities. (c) 6.14.7: *autôi* refers to God, not Simon; *thelei* probably refers to the scriptural quotation and the phrase *houtô thelei gegraphthai* should be translated 'is usually written like this'. (d) 6.17.2: *kat' autous* may refer to the three aeons or to followers of Simon. The subject of *legousin* seems almost certainly to be the three aeons. Hence this phrase is part of the direct quotation. (e) There are also a number of occurrences of 'as I said' (*hôs ephên*, p. 139 line 10, p. 140 line 13; *has ephêmen*, p. 140 line 23; *hôs eirêkamen*, p. 143 line 25. It is not clear whether these are inserted by Hippolytus or derive from his source. See above p. 60 and note 47 on comparable examples in the Aristotle report.

Table 2. Patterns of phraseology in the *Apophasis* material

I   Ref. 6. 9. 4   τοῦτο τὸ γράμμα ἀποφάσεως
          10. 1   τοῦτο ἐστι τὸ γεγραμμένον ἐν τῇ γραφῇ
          15. 2   ἐπιγραφή
          16. 4   ἐπιγεγραμμένον
          18. 2   γράφω ἅ γράφω, τὸ γράμμα τοῦτο

II   Ref. 6.14. 4   αὕτη ἐστι ἡ ἑβδόμη
               τουτέστι τὸ πνεῦμα
          14. 6   τοῦτό ἐστι τὸ εἰρημένον
          15. 1   τουτέστιν εἰς τέσσαρες
               οὗτος ἐστιν ὁ νόμος
          15. 2   αὕτη γὰρ ἐστίν
          17. 3   αὕτη ἐστὶ δύναμις
          17. 5   αὕτη ἐστὶν ἡ φλογίνη
          18. 2   ἥτις ἐστὶ δύναμις
          18. 3   ἥτις ἐστὶ μεγάλη δύναμις
          18. 6   τουτέστι τὴν δύναμιν

III   Ref. 6.11   οὕτως ὡς
              οὕτως ὡς
          12. 4   οὕτως ὡς
          14. 7   οὕτως γὰρ
          15. 4   ὅτι ταῦθ᾽ οὕτως ἔχει
          18. 6   ὡς ... οὕτως
          18. 7   ἔστιν οὖν οὕτως
              οὕτως ἐστι

IV   Ref. 6.12. 1   τοῦτον τὸν τρόπον
          14. 7   πῶς οὖν καὶ τίνα τρόπον

V   Ref. 6. 9. 9   ἅπαντα ταῦτα
          12. 1   πάντα γὰρ
          14. 4   τὸ πάντα ἔχον
               κοσμοῦσα μόνη πάντα
          17. 6   ἡ πάντας ἔχουσα
          18. 3   διέπων τὰ πάντα
          18. 4   ὁ βαστάζων πάντα

VI   <u>Ref.</u> 6. 9. 4 ἡ ῥίζα

            12. 1 ἐξ ῥίζας

            15. 5 ῥίζῃ μέν

            16. 6 τὰς ῥίζας τοῦ δένδρου

            18. 2 ἀπὸ μιᾶς ῥίζης

VII   <u>Ref.</u> 6.10. 2 πρὸς διδασκαλίαν ἀρκεῖ

            15. 2 ἤρκει πρὸς γνῶσιν ... ἡ ἐπιγραφή

            16. 1 ἀρκεῖ τὸ λεχθέν ... πρὸς ἐπίγνωσιν

We may conclude from the use of *phêsin* that there is no evidence in the text to suggest that Hippolytus was using anything other than what he considered to be the original *Apophasis Megalê* as his immediate source; there is no reason to suppose that the use of *phêsin* is not Hippolytus' own indication of when he is starting a new quotation, as it appears to be in other parts of the work. The frequency of *phêsin* suggests that he has included a large number of short extracts, and probably indicates that the book he had to hand was considerably longer than his summary of it.

(iii) The references to Greek philosophy

Frickel does not consider the possibility that *phêsin* might be an indication of direct quotation of the *Apophasis* itself; similarly Salles-Dabadie identifies genuine 'fragments' of the *Apophasis* without regard to the occurrence of *phêsin*. For both authors the result would be ruled out by other considerations: Frickel would prefer to argue that citations from scripture, Homer and Greek philosophy are all features of the 'commentary' material in Hippolytus' model, and not features of Simon's original *Apophasis*;[12] Salles-Dabadie is prepared to admit the Greek influences and Old Testament references, but excludes the New Testament from the original *Apophasis* of Simon.[13] On

[12] Frickel (1967) Sect. 26.

[13] Salles-Dabadie (1969) p. 66: 'Mais la pensée primitive, exprimée par l'auteur dans des passages disparus, devait être suffisament claire, puisque, plus tard, un disciple chrétien – il est à peine besoin de dire que la doctrine de notre auteur n'a rien de commun avec le christianisme – n'a pas craint de la commenter à l'aide d'une citation empruntée à Saint Paul.' One supposes that Salles-Dabadie's 'Christian' did find something in common since he was supposedly reminded of St. Paul by Simon's similar ideas (ibid.).

the hypothesis that *phêsin* indicates a quotation from the *Apophasis* itself both Greek influences and a few hints of contact with Christianity have to be included in the original work. In 9.10 a saying of Jesus found in Matthew and Luke appears to be included and in 14.6 a phrase from 1 Corinthians is likewise. In 16.6 another saying found in Matthew and Luke is quoted.[14] In 15.4 to 16.1 the quotation from Homer was clearly in Hippolytus' source and the physiological section on the embryo in the womb, chapter 14, looks as if it almost certainly derived from a Greek medical source.[15]

The position with regard to the references to Heraclitus, Empedocles, Plato and Aristotle is not quite so clear. The first of these is to Heraclitus, 6.9.3. It occurs in a passage which is certainly not verbatim quotation, but summary, at the start of the report on the *Apophasis*. Hippolytus is criticising Simon for misinterpretation of Moses, and for stealing from Heraclitus. The passage comes before what are generally held to be the opening words of the *Apophasis*, quoted at 6.9.4,[16] and it is therefore probable that these criticisms in 6.9.3 are Hippolytus' own introduction specifying two grounds on which he wishes to refute Simon, first for intentionally misinterpreting the scriptures and second for stealing his ideas from the philosophers, which is the usual crime. Hippolytus illustrates the crimes with a particular example, which he has presumably found in the text but clearly not necessarily as the first words of his text.[17] Hippolytus objects to finding the words from Deuteronomy 4.24 used by Simon to support the view that the foundation of all the material world is fire; the demonstration (which is somewhat unclear) of the inaccuracy of this interpretation is surely Hippolytus' own. It seems probable that the idea that Simon derived his views from Heraclitus was inspired by the claim that the principle was fire rather than any explicit reference to Heraclitus in the text.

---

[14] The quotation from Isaiah at *Ref.* 6.10.2 is also found in 1 Peter but this does not prove that Simon knew it from there.
[15] Cf. Galen, *In Hipp. de Alim.* 15.387 (Kuhn) (quoted by Wendland ad loc.).
[16] Cf. *Ref.* 5.9.5.
[17] Contra Frickel (1968).

This sentence is the sum total of any indication given by Hippolytus as to how his account of Simon Magus serves as a refutation. He does not explicitly demonstrate elsewhere in the report that Simon's thought derives from the Greeks. However, the choice of quotations in the remainder of the report serves as evidence for both crimes; there is a high concentration of extracts which tell of the rôle of fire, extracts where statements are supported by interpretations of scriptural quotations and extracts which quote from, or show the influence of, Greek thought. Hippolytus first hints at the clue to the refutation of Simon and then provides the texts as evidence.

Apart from the passage employing Homer *Odyssey* 9.304-6 (15.4-16.1) and the passage derived from Greek medicine (14.8-11) there are two passages that merit discussion: (1) the reference to Plato and Aristotle at 9.6.; (2) the reference to Empedocles at 11-12.1.

1. At 9.5 we are told that the fire, according to Simon, is nothing simple; it has a two-fold nature of which Simon calls one *krupton* and the other *phaneron*. These terms are then glossed (9.6): 'This is the same as Aristotle calls "what is in potentiality" and "what is in actuality", or Plato calls the intelligible and sensible'. We can be sure that the terms *krupton* and *phaneron* were used in Simon's text, but what about the two pairs of equivalents? The gloss is certainly accurate and helpful: the Platonic terms indicate the sense in which the hidden aspect of fire is the superior one, the one destined to be preserved for eternity, while the manifest aspect is the imperfect and destined to perish; thus *krupton* corresponds with *noêton*, and *phaneron* corresponds with *aisthêton*; the Aristotelian equivalents, on the other hand, apply only to the process involved in the relationship between the two terms, namely the actualisation which enables that which had been merely on the level of sense-perception and the material, evident world to attain its state of full perfection, namely existence on the spiritual or intellectual level in detachment from the material sensible world.[18] It is clear that what is *dunamei*, not as yet

[18] The normal associations of *dunamei* and *energeia* with non-evident and evident respectively do not apply in this comparison. In both the image of the

brought to perfection, corresponds with that which is *phaneron* (the as-yet unproductive parts of the tree in the image at 6.9.9) and the perfected actuality with that which is *krupton*. The Aristotelian *dunamei* is also used to explain why that which remains only potential will perish 'just as potential knowledge perishes with a man when he dies' (12.4 and again at 16.5).

The term *dunamei* is very closely bound up with the fundamental details of Simon's theory.[19] The word *dunamis* is central to his doctrines in other ways,[20] and this is a strong reason for suggesting that the Aristotelian term was known and used by Simon for this purpose.

2. In 6.11 and 6.12.1 we have references to Empedocles including two quotations. At the start of chapter 12, as Diels observed,[21] *phêsin* must refer to Simon, or the book from which Hippolytus is quoting, and *enomize* (he thought) to Empedocles: 'For, Simon says, Empedocles thought all the parts of fire ...' This reference to Empedocles' opinion thus appears in the text of the *Apophasis*, and follows straight on from the previous quotation in which Empedocles had been named. It is therefore necessary to suppose that the phrase 'thus as Empedocles says' and the verses of B109 also appeared in the source to which *phêsi* at 6.12.1 refers, presumably the text of the *Apophasis* which Hippolytus is using.

Why should the *Apophasis* have quoted these fragments from Empedocles here? The first, B109, is used twice by Aristotle[22] to illustrate Empedocles' theory of perception: in the *Metaphysics* he uses it to illustrate the fact that Empedocles had a theory of perception of like by like; in the *De Anima* he concludes from it that the soul is made of all the elements, since it perceives like by like. In the *Apophasis* there may also be a connection with perception. The sentence following B109

---

tree and the use of the Aristotelian terms the comparison applies *qua* process of attaining the perfect state of which the individual is capable and not *qua* evident or non-evident.

[19] The term *energeia* is not so central since Simon has a term of his own for actualisation, *exeikonizesthai*.

[20] The word *dunamis* occurs 52 times in the *Apophasis* report.

[21] Diels Kranz (1951) p. 352 (ad B110).

[22] *De Anima* A2, 404b8; *Metaph.* B4, 1000b5.

For, Simon says, Empedocles thought all the invisible parts of
fire had intelligence and equal understanding,

suggests some point concerning a theory of perception and
knowledge: the apparent parts of the elements are perceived by
the intelligible, hidden parts, since the intelligible parts have
intelligence.[23]

This fits well with the theory which Hippolytus proceeds to
describe in chapter 12: from the fire come six roots, each of
which contains the unlimited power in potentiality. This power
must be actualised;[24] if it is not, but remains in potentiality, it
perishes like the potential knowledge of grammar or geometry
in a man's soul.[25] The unlimited power is in some sense
equivalent to knowledge, and since all the six roots which
come from fire have this power in potentiality we can conclude
that 'all the ... parts of fire have intelligence and equal
understanding'. Potentiality (*dunamei*) is equivalent to *phaneron*
(6.9.6). Hence each of the six roots is twofold: those in which
the power is only potential are the *phaneron* part, the sensible
and visible part; those in which the power is actualised are the
krupton part, the intelligible and invisible part. It therefore
becomes clear that in the quotation of Empedocles we should
understand that we perceive the sensible, evident parts of fire
by means of the intelligible parts in which the potential
knowledge has been actualised.

It is apparent that this passage including the fragments of
Empedocles is tremendously compressed until the reasoning
behind it is scarcely recoverable. It is not unlikely that this is
the result of the extraction of the passage which referred to
Empedocles without adequate explanation and summary of
the context in the *Apophasis* which must have been a theory of
knowledge based on the actualisation of the *dunamis*. We might
also suggest that an account of such a theory of knowledge
would be more likely to come after the material in chapter 12
concerning the derivation of the six roots and the presence in

---

[23] If we adopt the emendation 'visible and invisible' we have to suppose
that both parts have intelligence and hence perceive each other.

[24] The term used is *exeikonisthêi*.

[25] Cf. Aristotle *De Anima* 417a21ff.

them of the unlimited power in potentiality; the comparison with Empedocles' six roots and his theory of knowledge would then be intelligible.

This suggests, first, that Hippolytus has selected the passage which includes the fragments of Empedocles because he is interested in passages which refer to the Greeks and not because he is interested in the theory which it illustrated; for this reason he has omitted its context almost completely and left it more or less incomprehensible;[26] secondly that he has perhaps changed the order of the passages he quotes, either because the Empedocles passage was particularly important to him and was picked out first for that reason, or possibly because it would have interrupted the course of his summary of the origins of the roots.

(iv) Conclusion

If this assessment of Hippolytus' work in the account of Simon Magus is correct it implies that the extent of his own influence on the choice of passages included, the arrangement of them and the composition of intervening exegetical summary is probably much greater than was allowed by either Frickel or Salles-Dabadie. We do not have to suppose that he simply copied mechanically and fully from a work that was already in a fragmentary condition or largely second-hand summary.

This analysis also implies that the *Apophasis* text used by Hippolytus included, as an integral part of it, considerable influence from Greek thought, both specific quotation and complex inheritance of ideas, and also some influence from Christianity. The latter influence may mean that the final composition of the text that Hippolytus used was later than the possible limits for the end of the life of the Simon Magus of Acts, but it need not necessarily do so. We know that Simon came into contact with Christianity at a very early stage of its career, if the chronology of Acts bears any relation to the truth, and there is no reason to suppose that Samaria did not continue to be a centre for Christianity throughout the period

[26] The words immediately preceding B109 remain apparently incomprehensible.

of Simon's life. The sayings of Jesus, of which the *Apophasis* quotes two, must have been part of the oral teaching for new converts from the very start, and were probably circulating in writing before the composition of the Gospels. Hence we do not have to suggest that the Gospels themselves were in existence when these words were quoted in the *Apophasis*.[27]

Even if we argue that the immediate source from which Hippolytus worked was a version of the genuine *Apophasis* itself, this need not imply that the work was a simple text comprising only one type of material and constructed by a single process of composition. The work is, according to its title, a 'revelation' and much of the material recounted by Hippolytus is the sort of mystical mumbo-jumbo that one would expect to form the 'core' of a revelation. It is, however, frequently the case that a revelation also includes an explanation of itself in simpler terms or without the complex imagery[28] and we may well expect that some of the exegetical passages might be material from this part of the revelation. Furthermore there will be the exegesis of the visionary in his own report of the vision when he writes it down or recounts it orally.[29] Finally the visionary himself may not write his revelation down, but it may be recorded by a pupil, perhaps years later; or even if he did write, the definitive edition may have been prepared by a pupil. The authentic *Apophasis Megalê* need not have been written by the hand of Simon Magus to be the genuine and most authoritative record of the Revelation of Simon. Hence we may well expect to find numerous strands of explanation and exegesis within what can accurately be called the original text, and we do not need to suppose that there was an earlier and more authentic text which included only the 'revelatory mumbo-jumbo'.[30] The interpretation incorporated by the

---

[27] The phrase from 1 Cor., quoted at 14.6, suggests a later date, but this need not be significantly later, given that the *Apophasis* may date from a later period of Simon's life than the encounter recorded in Acts.

[28] Cf. for example *Corp. Herm.* 1 (*Poimandres*): the author sees a vision and then Poimandres, who is part of the vision, explains its meaning at length. Cf. also the Revelation of St. John 7.14.

[29] E.g. the sections of the *Poimandres* where the author describes his own reactions to the vision, his awareness that it was his *nous*, and the hymn at the end.

[30] Contra e.g. Frickel, among many others.

visionary himself, and by the man who wrote the record if he is different, in a sense forms part of the revelation itself.

These conclusions concern the work of Simon Magus and call for a totally new approach to the study of the material from the *Apophasis*, rejecting the premise that because it stands early in the history of gnosticism and as in some sense 'primitive' it must therefore be 'simple' and unitary in character, composition and influence.

Appendix C

Hippolytus, *Refutation of All Heresies*

Text and translation

Text edited by P. Wendland, *Die Griechischen Christlichen Schriftsteller*, vol. 26 (Leipzig 1916).

⟨ΤΟΥ ΚΑΤΑ ΠΑΣΩΝ ΑΙΡΕΣΕΩΝ ΕΛΕΓΧΟΥ

ΒΙΒΛΙΟΝ ϛ′⟩. 5

1. Τάδε ἔνεστιν ἐν τῇ ἕκτῃ τοῦ κατὰ πασῶν αἱρέσεων ἐλέγχου·
2. Τίνα τὰ Σίμωνι τετολμημένα, καὶ ὅτι ἐκ μαγικῶν καὶ ποιη-
τικῶν τὸ δόγμα κρατύνει.
3. Τίνα ὁ Οὐαλεντῖνος δογματίζει, καὶ ὅτι ἐκ γραφῶν οὐ συνί-
σταται αὐτοῦ τὸ δόγμα, ἀλλὰ ἐκ τῶν Πλατωνικῶν καὶ Πυθαγορικῶν 10
δογμάτων.
4. Καὶ τίνα τὰ Σεκούνδῳ καὶ Πτολεμαίῳ καὶ Ἡρακλέωνι δοκοῦντα, ὡς καὶ αὐτοὶ τοῖς αὐτοῖς, οἷς οἱ Ἕλληνες σοφοί, ἐχρήσαντο
⟨δόγμασιν, ἀλλ'⟩ ἄλλοις ῥήμασι.
5. Τίνα τὰ Μάρκῳ καὶ Κολαρβάσῳ νομισθέντα, καὶ ὅτι τινὲς 15
αὐτῶν μαγείαις καὶ ἀριθμοῖς Πυθαγορείοις † ἔσχον.
6. Ὅσα μὲν οὖν ἐδόκει τοῖς ἀπὸ τοῦ ὄφεως τὰς ἀρχὰς παρειλη-
φόσι καὶ κατὰ τελείωσιν τῶν χρόνων εἰς φανερὸν τὰς δόξας ἐκου-
σίως προενεγκαμένοις, ἐν τῇ πρὸ ταύτης βίβλῳ οὔσῃ πέμπτῃ τοῦ
ἐλέγχου τῶν αἱρέσεων ἐξεθέμην· νυνὶ δὲ καὶ τῶν ἀκολούθων τὰς 20
γνώμας οὐ σιωπήσω, ἀλλ' οὐδὲ μίαν ἀνέλεγκτον καταλείψω, εἴ γε δυνατὸν πάσας ἀπομνημονεῦσαι καὶ τὰ τούτων ἀπόρρητα ὄργια, ἃ δικαίως ὄργια κλητέον· οὐ γὰρ μακρὰν ἀπέχουσιν ὀργῆς τοιαῦτα τετολ-
μηκότες, ἵνα καὶ τῇ ἐτυμολογίᾳ χρήσωμαι.

1 7. Δοκεῖ οὖν καὶ τὰ Σίμωνος τοῦ Γιττηνοῦ, κώμης τῆς Σαμα- 25
ρείας, νῦν ἐκθέσθαι, παρ' οὗ καὶ τοὺς ἀκολούθους δείξομεν ἀφορμὰς

---

4 Titel fehlt P, aber eine Zeile
frei und rote Initiale T (freilich dieselbe Art des Absatzes Z. 17)   13 ⟨καὶ⟩ ὡς
We.   Ἑλλήνων We.   14 ⟨ ⟩ Diels (S. 135, 1 u. V 23, 3 ἄλλοι ἄλλως τὰ αὐτὰ
διηγούμενοι): ἀλλ' Gö.   16 ἐσχόλαζον oder ἐνέσχον Miller, προσέσχον Gö., ἐχρήσαντο Pasquali   17 f περιειληφόσι falsch als Lesart P Miller   18 τελείωσιν
Bunsen, Hipp. and his age I² 350 (I 35): μείωσιν P   18 f ἀνοσίως Bunsen
a. a. O.   19 προσενεγκαμένοις P, verb. Gö.   19 f τοὺς ἐλέγχους P, verb. Gö.
25 Γιττηνοῦ Gö.: γειττηνοῦ aus γειττινοῦ P

[Book six of the *Refutation of All Heresies*]

1. The following items are contained in the sixth book of the Refutation of All Heresies:

2. The things ventured by Simon, and that he supports his doctrine from magical and poetical sources.

3. What Valentinus teaches, and that his doctrine is not established from the scriptures but from Platonic and Pythagorean doctrines.

4. And the opinions of Secundus and Ptolemaeus and Heracleon, how they also used the same notions as the Greeks but in different words.

5. The beliefs of Marcus and Colabasus, and that some of them used magic and Pythagorean numbers.

6. I have set out in the previous book, the fifth book of the Refutation of All Heresies, the opinions of those who took their principles from the serpent and in the fullness of time brought their doctrines into the open. Now I shall not remain silent concerning the ideas of those who followed, but I shall not leave even one idea unrefuted, if indeed it is possible to remember all of them and the unmentionable 'rites' of these men, which are rightly termed '*orgia*'; for those who have ventured such things are not far distant from fury (*orgê*), to use the etymology.

7. It seems right now to set out the doctrines of Simon of Gitta (a village in Samaria). We shall show that it is from him that those who followed took their starting points / and

135W λαβόντας ἑτέροις ὀνόμασιν ὅμοια τετολμηκέναι. οὗτος ὁ Σίμων
μαγείας ἔμπειρος ὢν καὶ τὰ μὲν παίξας πολλοὺς κατὰ τὴν Θρασυμή-
δους τέχνην, ᾧ τρόπῳ ἄνωθεν ἐξεθέμεθα, τὰ δὲ καὶ διὰ δαιμόνων
κακουργήσας, θεοποιῆσαι ἑαυτὸν ἐπεχείρησεν, | ἄνθρωπος γόης καὶ ς
5 μεστὸς ἀπονοίας, ὃν ἐν ταῖς Πράξεσιν οἱ ἀπόστολοι ἤλεγξαν. οὐ ς
πολλῷ σοφώτερον καὶ μετριώτερον Ἄφεθος ὁ Λίβυς ὀρεχθεὶς θεὸς
νομισθῆναι ἐν Λιβύῃ ἐπεχείρησεν· οὗ τὸν μῦθον οὐ πολύ τι ἀπεμ-
φαίνοντα τῆς Σίμωνος τοῦ ματαίου ἐπιθυμίας, δοκεῖ διηγήσασθαι
ὄντα ἄξιον τῆς τούτου ἐπιχειρήσεως.
10 8. Ἄφεθος ὁ Λίβυς ἐπεθύμησε θεὸς γενέσθαι· ὡς δὲ πολυπραγ- ι
μονῶν πάνυ ἀπετύγχανε τῆς ἐπιθυμίας, ἠθέλησε κἂν δοκεῖν γεγονέναι,
καὶ ἔδοξέ γε ὡς ἀληθῶς χρόνῳ πλείονι γεγονέναι θεός. ἔθυον γὰρ
οἱ ἀνόητοι Λίβυες αὐτῷ, θείᾳ τινὶ [δυνάμει,] νομίζοντες ἄνωθεν ἐξ
οὐρανοῦ πεπιστευκέναι φωνῇ. συναθροίσας γὰρ εἰς ἕνα καὶ τὸν αὐ-
15 τὸν οἰκίσκον ὄρνιθας πλείστους ψιττακοὺς κατέκλεισεν· εἰσὶ δὲ πλεῖ-
στοι κατὰ τὴν Λιβύην ψιττακοὶ καὶ ἐναργῶς μιμούμενοι πάνυ τὴν
ἀνθρωπίνην φωνήν. οὗτος χρόνῳ διαθρέψας τοὺς ὄρνεις ἐδίδαξε
λέγειν· Ἄφεθος θεός ἐστιν. ὡς δὲ ἤσκησαν οἱ ὄρνιθες χρόνῳ πολλῷ
καὶ τοῦτο ἔλεγον, ὅπερ ᾤετο [τὸ] λεχθὲν θεὸν εἶναι ποιήσειν νομί-
20 ζεσθαι τὸν Ἄφεθον, τότε ἀνοίξας τὸ οἴκημα εἴασεν ἄλλον ἀλλαχόσε
τοὺς ψιττακούς. πετομένων δὲ τῶν ὀρνίθων ἐξῆλθεν ὁ φθόγγος εἰς
πᾶσαν τὴν Λιβύην, καὶ τὰ ῥήματα αὐτῶν διῆλθε μέχρι τῆς Ἑλληνι-
κῆς γῆς, καὶ οὕτως οἱ Λίβυες καταπλαγέντες ἐπὶ τῇ τῶν ὀρνίθων
φωνῇ τό τε πραχθὲν ὑπὸ τοῦ Ἀφέθου πανούργευμα μὴ ἐννοήσαντες
25 θεὸν εἶχον τὸν Ἄφεθον. τῶν δὲ Ἑλλήνων τις ἀκριβῶς ἐννοήσας τὸ
σόφισμα τοῦ νενομισμένου θεοῦ διὰ τῶν αὐτῶν ἐκείνων ψιττακῶν
οὐκ ἐλέγχει μόνον, ἀλλὰ καὶ ἀφανίζει τὸν ἀλαζόνα καὶ φορτικὸν ἐκεῖνον ἄνθρωπον. μετεδίδαξε δὲ ὁ Ἕλλην καθείρξας πολλοὺς ἀπὸ τῶν
ψιττακῶν λέγειν· Ἄφεθος ἡμᾶς κατακλείσας ἠνάγκασε λέγειν· Ἄφεθος
30 θεός ἐστιν. | ἀκούσαντες δὲ οἱ Λίβυες τῆς παλινῳδίας τῶν ψιττακῶν,
πάντες ὁμοθυμαδὸν συνελθόντες κατέκαυσαν τὸν Ἄφεθον.

1—3 *Iren.* *I* 23, 1 *S.* 190. 191 *H.* et universam magicam adhuc amplius scru-
tans ita ut in stuporem cogeret multos hominum . . . ebenda Citate aus Apostel-
gesch. — 3 ἄνωθεν] IV 28 ff — 4 *Iren.*: a multis quasi deus glorificatus est
— 5 Act. 8, 9—24 — 10 ff dieselbe Geschichte von Psaphon Maximus Tyrius
XXXV 4 S. 344 Hobein, von Hanno Älian Var. hist. XIV 30, von Apsephas Scholion
zu Dion Chrys. I 14 (A. Sonny, Ad Dionem Chrys. Analecta, Kiew 1896 S. 96. 92)

2 μαγείαν P   13 ⟨ὡς⟩ θείᾳ Gö.   δυνάμει > Miller (Maximus θείαν τινὰ
νομίσαντες εἶναι φήμην)   19 τὸ > Miller   24 ἐνοήσαντες P

ventured similar things under different names. This man Simon was experienced in magic and, on the one hand, tricked many according to the art of Thrasymedes (in the manner we have described above) and, on the other hand, working evil through *daimones* he tried to make himself a god – although he was a human sorcerer and full of craziness, the one whom the Apostles refuted in the Acts. Much more wisely and moderately than he, Apsethos the Libyan had aimed to be considered a gŏd and made an attempt in Libya. His story does not differ a great deal from the desire of the unsuccessful Simon, and it seems right to tell it as being worthy of his attempt.

8. Apsethos the Libyan set his heart on becoming a god. But when despite having taken much trouble he was disappointed in his desire, he conceived a wish that at least he might seem to have become one, and indeed after a long time he did seem to have actually become a god. For the foolish Libyans offered sacrifice to him, in the belief that they were placing their trust in a divine voice from heaven above. For he gathered together into one cage a large number of parrots and locked them up. There are many parrots in Libya and they imitate human speech very clearly. Apsethos kept the birds for some time and taught them to say 'Apsethos is god'. When the birds had practised for a long time and were saying this phrase, which he thought would make Apsethos be believed to be a god when it was said, then he opened the cage and allowed the birds to go to different places. As the birds flew off their voice went out into all Libya and their words reached unto the land of Greece, and thus the Libyans, being struck by the speech of the birds and having no conception of the unscrupulous deed done by Apsethos, held Apsethos to be a god. But one of the Greeks, accurately noting the artifice of the supposed god, by means of the very same parrots not only refuted that charlatan and crude man but also brought about his demise. The Greek confined a lot of the parrots and retaught them to say 'Apsethos shut us up and compelled us to say "Apsethos is a god" '. When the Libyans heard the parrots' palinode, all with one accord came together and burnt Apsethos. /

1   9. Οὕτως ἡγητέον Σίμωνα τὸν μάγον ἀπεικάζοντας τῷ Λίβυΐ †
136W τάχιον, ἀνθρώπῳ γενομένῳ οὕτως θεῷ. εἰ δὲ ἔχει τὰ τῆς εἰκόνος
ἀκριβῶς καὶ πέπονθεν ὁ μάγος πάθος τι παραπλήσιον Ἀψέθῳ, ἐπι-
χειρήσωμεν μεταδιδάσκειν τοῦ Σίμωνος τοὺς ψιττακούς, ὅτι Χριστὸς
2 οὐκ ἦν Σίμων ὁ ἑστώς, στάς, στησόμενος, ἀλλ᾽ ἄνθρωπος ἦν ἐκ
σπέρματος, γέννημα γυναικός, ἐξ αἱμάτων καὶ ἐπιθυμίας σαρκικῆς
καθάπερ καὶ οἱ λοιποὶ γεγεννημένος· καὶ ὅτι ταῦθ᾽ οὕτως ἔχει,
3 προϊόντος τοῦ λόγου ῥᾳδίως ἐπιδείξομεν. λέγει δὲ ὁ Σίμων μετα-
φράζων τὸν νόμον Μωϋσέως ἀνοήτως τε καὶ κακοτέχνως. Μωσέως
γὰρ λέγοντος, »ὅτι ὁ θεὸς πῦρ φλέγον ἐστὶ καὶ καταναλίσκον«, δε-
ξάμενος τὸ λεχθὲν ὑπὸ Μωσέως οὐκ ὀρθῶς, πῦρ εἶναι τῶν ὅλων
λέγει τὴν ἀρχήν, οὐ νοήσας τὸ εἰρημένον, ὅτι θεὸς οὐ πῦρ, ἀλλὰ πῦρ
φλέγον καὶ καταναλίσκον, οὐκ αὐτὸν διασπῶν μόνον τὸν νόμον Μω-
4 σέως, ἀλλὰ καὶ τὸν σκοτεινὸν Ἡράκλειτον συλαγωγῶν. ἀπέραντον
δὲ εἶναι δύναμιν ὁ Σίμων προσαγορεύει τῶν ὅλων τὴν ἀρχήν, λέγων
οὕτως· »τοῦτο τὸ γράμμα ἀποφάσεως φωνῆς καὶ ὀνόματος ἐξ ἐπινοίας τῆς μεγάλης δυνάμεως τῆς ἀπεράντου. διὸ ἔσται ἐσφραγισμένον,
κεκρυμμένον, κεκαλυμμένον, κείμενον ἐν τῷ οἰκητηρίῳ, οὗ ἡ ῥίζα
5 τῶν ὅλων τεθεμελίωται«. οἰκητήριον δὲ λέγει εἶναι τὸν ἄνθρωπον
τοῦτον τὸν ἐξ αἱμάτων γεγεννημένον, καὶ κατοικεῖν ἐν αὐτῷ τὴν
ἀπέραντον δύναμιν, ἣν ῥίζαν εἶναι τῶν ὅλων φησίν. ἔστι δὲ ἡ ἀπέραντος δύναμις, τὸ πῦρ, κατὰ τὸν Σίμωνα οὐδὲν ἁπλοῦν, καθάπερ
f. 60ᵛ οἱ πολλοὶ ἁπλᾶ λέγοντες εἶναι τὰ τέσσαρα στοιχεῖα | καὶ τὸ πῦρ
ἁπλοῦν εἶναι νενομίκασιν, ἀλλὰ γὰρ εἶναι [τὴν] τοῦ πυρὸς διπλῆν τινα
τὴν φύσιν, καὶ τῆς διπλῆς ταύτης καλεῖ τὸ μέν τι κρυπτόν, τὸ δέ τι
6 φανερόν· κεκρύφθαι δὲ τὰ κρυπτὰ ἐν τοῖς φανεροῖς τοῦ πυρός, καὶ
τὰ φανερὰ τοῦ πυρὸς ὑπὸ τῶν κρυπτῶν γεγονέναι. ἔστι δὲ τοῦτο,
ὅπερ Ἀριστοτέλης δυνάμει καὶ ἐνεργείᾳ καλεῖ ἢ Πλάτων νοητὸν καὶ

1–S. 145, 5 zu diesem System des Simon vgl. Redlich, Archiv f. Gesch. der
Philos. XXIII, 374. 537 — 6 vgl. Joh. 1, 13? — 9 ff vgl. Clemens, Ecl. proph. 26, 1
S. 144, 10 ff St. — 10 Deut. 4, 24 κύριος ὁ θεός σου πῦρ καταναλίσκον ἐστίν 9, 3
Exod. 24, 17 τὸ δὲ εἶδος τῆς δόξης κυρίου ὡσεὶ πῦρ φλέγον vgl. Orig. De prin-
cipiis I 1, 1. 2 S. 16, 19 ff K. — 11 f vgl. Heraklit bei Diels, Vorsokr.³ I 72, 36 ff
— 14 f. 21—27 vgl. X 12, 1 — 16—19 vgl. V 9, 5

1 οὕτως] τούτῳ? We.   2 τάχιον] μάταιον We., vgl. S. 135, 8   τάχιον ⟨ἢ⟩ ἀνθρώπῳ γενομένῳ ὄντως θεῷ (Christus) Miller   3 f ἐπιχειρήσομεν Miller   8 f μετα-
φράσσων P, verb. Gö.   9 μωνσέος P (ο aus ω?)   10 zuerst φλέγων und καταναλίσκων P   13 φλέγων (aber καταναλίσκων [so] P)   οὐδ᾽ αὐτὸν We.
14 συλλαγωγῶν P   16 ἀπόφασις? Miller   17 τῆς² (nicht τοῦ) P   24 τὴν
> Miller, vgl. H   25 τι² > H   27 ἀπὸ Hilg. S. 458   28 πλάττων P

9. It is in this way that we must regard Simon Magus, likening him (more swiftly) to the Libyan man who became a god thus. But if the details of the analogy apply accurately and the Magus suffered anything comparable to Apsethos, let us try to reteach Simon's parrots that Simon, 'he that stood and stands and will stand', was not Christ but a man born of seed, the offspring of a woman, born of blood and the will of the flesh just like the rest of us. And that this is so we shall easily demonstrate as the argument proceeds. Simon interprets the law of Moses foolishly and badly in what he says. For while Moses says 'that God is a flaming and consuming fire', Simon takes Moses' saying incorrectly and says that fire is the principle of all things, not noticing that what is said is that God is not fire but a flaming and consuming fire; he does not only tear apart the Law of Moses but also plunders from Heraclitus the obscure. Simon states that the principle of all things is an unlimited power, saying thus:

'This is the writing of the revelation of voice and name from the mind of the great power, the unlimited. Therefore it will be sealed, concealed, buried, lying in the dwelling where the rest of all things has its foundation.'

The 'dwelling' he says is this man born of blood, and that the unlimited power dwells in him, which he says is the root of all things. But the unlimited power, the fire, is, according to Simon, nothing simple, in the way that most people who say the four elements are 'simple' have considered fire to be simple, but the nature of fire is a double one and of this double nature he calls the one 'hidden' and the other 'evident'; the hidden parts of the fire are hidden in the evident parts, and the evident parts are generated by the hidden parts. This is just what Aristotle calls 'in potentiality' and 'in actuality', or Plato calls

137W αἰσθητόν. καὶ τὸ μὲν φανερὸν τοῦ πυρὸς πάντα ἔχει ἐν ἑαυτῷ ὅσα 7
ἄν τις ἐπινοήσῃ ἢ καὶ λάθῃ παραλιπὼν τῶν ὁρατῶν· τὸ δὲ κρυπτὸν
πᾶν ὅ τι ἐννοήσει τις νοητὸν καὶ πεφευγὸς τὴν αἴσθησιν ἢ καὶ
παραλείπει μὴ διανοηθείς. καθόλου δὲ ἔστιν εἰπεῖν, πάντων τῶν 8
5 ὄντων αἰσθητῶν τε καὶ νοητῶν, ὧν ἐκεῖνος κρυφίων καὶ φανερῶν
προσαγορεύει, ἔστι θησαυρὸς τὸ πῦρ τὸ ὑπερουράνιον, οἱονεὶ δένδρον
μέγα ὡς ⟨τὸ⟩ δι᾽ ὀνείρου βλεπόμενον τῷ Ναβουχοδονόσορ, ἐξ οὗ πᾶσα
σὰρξ τρέφεται. καὶ τὸ μὲν φανερὸν εἶναι τοῦ πυρὸς νομίζει τὸ 9
πρέμνον, τοὺς κλάδους, τὰ φύλλα, τὸν ἔξωθεν αὐτῷ περικείμενον
10 φλοιόν· ἅπαντα, φησί, ταῦτα τοῦ μεγάλου δένδρου ἀναφθέντα ὑπὸ
τῆς παμφάγου τοῦ πυρὸς ἀφανίζεται φλογός. ὁ δὲ καρπὸς τοῦ δέν- 10
δρου ἐὰν ἐξεικονισθῇ καὶ τὴν ἑαυτοῦ μορφὴν ἀπολάβῃ, εἰς ἀποθήκην τίθεται, οὐκ εἰς τὸ πῦρ. γέγονε μὲν γάρ, φησίν, ὁ καρπός,
ἵνα εἰς τὴν ἀποθήκην τεθῇ, τὸ δὲ ἄχυρον, ἵνα παραδοθῇ τῷ πυρί,
15 ὅπερ ἐστὶ πρέμνον, οὐκ αὐτοῦ χάριν ἀλλὰ τοῦ καρποῦ γεγενημένον.
    10. Καὶ τοῦτό ἐστι, φησί, τὸ γεγραμμένον ἐν τῇ γραφῇ· ›ὁ γὰρ 1
ἀμπελὼν κυρίου Σαβαὼθ οἶκος τοῦ Ἰσραήλ ἐστι, καὶ ἄνθρωπος τοῦ
Ἰούδα νεόφυτον | ἠγαπημένον‹. εἰ δὲ ἄνθρωπος τοῦ Ἰούδα νεόφυτον f.
ἠγαπημένον, δέδεικται, φησίν, ὅτι ξύλον οὐκ ἄλλο τι ἀλλ᾽ ἢ ἄνθρω-
20 πός ἐστιν. ἀλλὰ περὶ τῆς ἐκκρίσεως αὐτοῦ καὶ διακρίσεως ἱκανῶς, 2
φησίν, εἴρηκεν ἡ γραφή, καὶ πρὸς διδασκαλίαν ἀρκεῖ τοῖς ἐξεικονισμέ-
νοις τὸ λεχθέν· ›ὅτι πᾶσα σὰρξ χόρτος, καὶ πᾶσα δόξα σαρκὸς ὡς
ἄνθος χόρτου. ἐξηράνθη ὁ χόρτος, καὶ τὸ ἄνθος αὐτοῦ ἐξέπεσε· τὸ
δὲ ῥῆμα κυρίου μένει εἰς τὸν αἰῶνα‹. ῥῆμα δέ, φησίν, ἐστὶ κυρίου
25 τὸ ἐν στόματι γεννώμενον ῥῆμα καὶ λόγος, ἄλλη δὲ χωρίον γενέσεως
οὐκ ἔστι.
    11. Τοιούτου· δὲ ὄντος, ὡς δι᾽ ὀλίγων εἰπεῖν, κατὰ τὸν Σίμωνα
τοῦ πυρὸς καὶ πάντων τῶν ὄντων ὁρατῶν καὶ ἀοράτων, ὧν αὐτὸς
ἐνήχων καὶ ⟨ἀν⟩ήχων, ἀριθμητῶν καὶ ⟨ἀν⟩αρίθμων ἐν τῇ Ἀποφάσει

1—4 s. zu S. 116, 20 — 7 Daniel 4, 7—9 — 9 vgl. VII 21, 3 — 13f Matth.
3, 12; Luk. 3, 17 — 16—18 Jes. 5, 7 — 22—24 I Petr. 1, 24 (διότι und δόξα
αὐτῆς) = Jes. 40, 6. 7

    2 τὸν ἀόρατον P, verb. Miller   3 πεφευγὼς P   ἢ Gö.: εἰ P   5 ὄντων
Miller: ὅλων P   κρυφίως καὶ φανερῶς P, verb. Gö.   7 + τὸ Miller   τῷ]
τὸν P   9 τὸν] τῶν P   αὐτῷ] Gö.: αὐτῶν P   10 ⟨τὰ⟩ τοῦ We. (oder ἀνα-
φθέντος?)   ὑπὸ (nicht ἀπὸ) P   12 ἀπολαύῃ P   15 γεγενημένον P   19 ⟨τὸ⟩
ξύλον We.   25 δὲ steht in P (> Miller)   27 ὀλίγον P   28 ὡσαύτως Gö.,
doch s. Z. 4. 5   28f ἀορ. νοῦν αὐτὸ ἐνεργὸν καὶ ἦχον καὶ ἀναρίθμητον ἀφιθμὸν
Hilg. S. 458   29 ἀνήχων Gö.: ἤχων P   ἀριθμητῶν καὶ Gö.: καὶ ἀριθμητῶν P
ἀναρίθμων Cruice: ἀριθμῶν so P

'intelligible' and / 'sensible'. And the evident part of the fire has within itself everything which one might conceive even if one leaves aside visible things and forgets them. But the hidden part has all that one will think of that is intelligible and has escaped perception, or that one passes over without thinking. In general one may say that of all things both perceptible and intelligible, which he calls hidden and evident, the supercelestial fire is the treasure store – like a great tree, such as that seen by Nebuchadnezzar in a dream, from which all flesh is nourished. And he thinks that the evident part of the fire is the trunk, the branches, the leaves, the bark round the outside of it; all these parts of the great tree, he says, are burnt by the all-consuming flame of the fire and destroyed, but the fruit of the tree, if it is made into the image and takes on its own form, is put into the store, not onto the fire. For the fruit was created, he says, to be put into the store, but the chaff to be delivered over to the fire – that is the trunk which is created not for its own sake but for the sake of the fruit.

10. And this is, he says, what is written in the scripture: 'For the vineyard of the Lord of hosts is the house of Israel, and the man of Judah is his beloved seedling'. But if the man of Judah is the beloved seedling it has been demonstrated, he says, that the tree is nothing else than man. But concerning the selection and discrimination of it enough has been said, he says, by scripture and for the instruction of those made into the image this saying is sufficient: 'that all flesh is grass and all the glory of the flesh as the flower of the grass. The grass withereth and the flower thereof falleth away. But the word of the Lord endureth for ever.' The word of the Lord, he says, is the word and *logos* begotten in the mouth, and there is no other place of begetting.

11. Such, to put it briefly, is the fire according to Simon, and all things seen and unseen, which he calls resounding and sounds (soundless), numerable and numbers (innumerable),

138W τῇ μεγάλῃ καλεῖ, τελείων νοερῶν, οὕτως ὡς ἕκαστον τῶν ἀπειράκις
ἀπείρως ἐπινοηθῆναι δυναμένων καὶ λαλεῖν καὶ διανοεῖσθαι καὶ ἐνερ-
γεῖν, οὕτως ὥς φησιν Ἐμπεδοκλῆς·

gαίη μὲν γὰρ γαῖαν ὀπώπαμεν, ὕδατι δὲ ὕδωρ,
αἰθέρι δ᾽ αἰθέρα ⟨δῖον⟩, ἀτὰρ πυρὶ πῦρ ἀίδηλον,   5
καὶ ⟨στοργῇ⟩ στοργήν, νεῖκος δέ τε νείκεϊ λυγρῷ.

1   12. Πάντα γὰρ, φησίν, ἐνόμιζε τὰ μέρη τοῦ πυρὸς τὰ ⟨ὁρατὰ καὶ
τὰ⟩ ἀόρατα »φρόνησιν ἔχειν καὶ γνώμην ἴσην«. γέγονεν οὖν ὁ κόσμος
ὁ γεννητὸς ἀπὸ τοῦ ἀγεννήτου πυρός. ἤρξατο δέ, φησί, γενέσθαι τοῦτον τὸν τρόπον, ἐξ ῥίζας τὰς πρώτας τῆς ἀρχῆς τῆς γεννήσεως λα- 10
2   βὼν ὁ γεννητὸς ἀπὸ τῆς ἀρχῆς τοῦ πυρὸς ἐκείνου. γεγονέναι δὲ τὰς
ῥίζας φησὶ κατὰ συζυγίας ἀπὸ τοῦ πυρός, ἅστινας ῥίζας καλεῖ νοῦν

f. 61ᵛ καὶ ἐπίνοιαν, | φωνὴν καὶ ὄνομα, λογισμὸν καὶ ἐνθύμησιν· εἶναι δὲ ἐν
ταῖς ἓξ ῥίζαις ταύταις πᾶσαν ὁμοῦ τὴν ἀπέραντον δύναμιν δυνάμει,
3   οὐκ ἐνεργείᾳ. ἥντινα ἀπέραντον δύναμιν φησὶ τὸν ἑστῶτα, ⟨στάντα⟩, 15
στησόμενον. ὃς ἐὰν μὲν ἐξεικονισθῇ ὢν ἐν ταῖς ἓξ δυνάμεσιν, ἔσται
οὐσίᾳ, δυνάμει, μεγέθει, ἀποτελέσματι μία καὶ ἡ αὐτὴ τῇ ἀγεννήτῳ
καὶ ἀπεράντῳ δυνάμει, [καὶ] οὐδὲν ὅλως ἔχουσα ἐνδεέστερον ἐκείνης
4   τῆς ἀγεννήτου καὶ ἀπαραλλάκτου ⟨καὶ⟩ ἀπεράντου δυνάμεως· ἐὰν δὲ
μείνῃ τῇ δυνάμει μόνον ἐν ταῖς ἓξ δυνάμεσι καὶ μὴ ἐξεικονισθῇ, ἀφα- 20
νίζεται, φησί, καὶ ἀπόλλυται οὕτως ὡς ἡ δύναμις ἡ γραμματικὴ ἢ
γεωμετρικὴ ἐν ἀνθρώπου ψυχῇ· προσλαβοῦσα γὰρ ἡ δύναμις τέχνην
φῶς τῶν γινομένων γίνεται, μὴ προσλαβοῦσα δὲ ἀτεχνία καὶ σκότος,
καὶ ὡς ὅτε οὐκ ἦν, ἀποθνήσκοντι τῷ ἀνθρώπῳ συνδιαφθείρεται.
13. Τῶν δὲ ἓξ δυνάμεων τούτων καὶ τῆς ἑβδόμης τῆς μετὰ τῶν 25
ἓξ καλεῖ τὴν πρώτην συζυγίαν νοῦν καὶ ἐπίνοιαν, οὐρανὸν καὶ γῆν·
καὶ τὸν μὲν ἄρσενα ἄνωθεν ἐπιβλέπειν καὶ προνοεῖν τῆς συζύγου,

3 Empedokles Fr. 109 D. — 7—23 vgl. X 12, 2—4 — 8 Empedokles Fr. 110, 10
πάντα γὰρ ἴσθι φρόνησιν ἔχειν καὶ νώματος αἶσαν — 19—22 vgl. S. 116, 20—24
u. VII 22, 1

1 τέλειον νοερὸν Gö.   οὕτως ὡς > Cruice (ὡς ἕκ. Atticismus)   5 + δῖον
nach Emp. (bei Aristot.) Miller   6 καὶ ⟨στοργῇ⟩ στοργήν Miller: στοργὴν
δὲ στοργῇ oder στοργῇ δὲ στοργὴν Aristot.   δέ τε nach Aristot. Miller:
ἐπὶ P   7 νόμιζε Meineke, Z. f. Altertumswiss. X 375   7f ⟨ ⟩ (nach H) Gö.,
vgl. Meineke a. a. O.   8 γνώμην ἴσην P: νώματος αἶσαν nach Sext. Miller,
γνώματοσ ἴσον Hipp. VII 29, 26   11 γεννητὸς ⟨γέγονεν⟩ Miller, doch s. H
12 συζυγίαν H   15 στάντα H Miller, vgl. S. 136, 5. 139, 7. VI 17, 1   16 ὃς
H Gö.: ὡς P   ὢν > H Miller, νοῶν Hilg. S. 459   18 καὶ a. Rande zugefügt
P, > H   19 ἀπαραλάκτου P   + καὶ H Gö.   21 ἢ Gö.: ἡ P H, vgl. VI 16, 5,
ἢ ἤ? We.   24 ὅτι P

in the *Apophasis* / *Megalê*, perfect, intellectual, just as each of the things able to be conceived in infinitely many ways and to speak and to think and to act, thus as Empedocles says:

> 'For with earth we have seen earth, with water water, with *aithêr* (heavenly) *aithêr*, with fire destructive fire and (with love) love, and strife with baneful strife.'

12. For, he says, all the parts of fire, (both the visible parts and) the invisible parts, he believed 'have wisdom and equal intelligence'. Therefore the generated world came to be from the ungenerated fire. It began to come into being, he says, in this way, the generated world taking the first six roots of the principle of generation from the principle of that fire. And he says that the roots were generated in pairs from the fire, and these roots he calls mind and thought, speech and name, reason and inspiration. There is in these six roots the entire unlimited power all together but in potentiality not in actuality. He says that this unlimited power is he who stood (and stands) and will stand. If he is made into the image, being in the six powers, he will be in essence, in power, in magnitude and in effect one and the same as the ungenerated and unlimited power, having nothing at all lacking in comparison with that ungenerated and unchanging and unlimited power. But if it remains only in potentiality and is not made into the image, it is destroyed, he says, and perishes just as the grammatical or geometrical power in a man's soul; for when the power takes on the skill it becomes a light for the things that come to be, but when it does not take on skill it becomes lack of skill and darkness, and when the man dies it perishes with him, just as when it did not exist.

13. Of these six powers and the seventh which belongs with the six he calls the first pair, that is mind and thought, heaven and earth; and the male one looks down from above and takes

139W τὴν δὲ γῆν ὑποδέχεσθαι κάτω τοὺς ἀπὸ τοῦ οὐρανοῦ νοεροὺς κατα-
φερομένους τῇ γῇ συγγενεῖς καρπούς. διὰ τοῦτο, φησίν, ἀποβλέπων
πολλάκις ὁ λόγος πρὸς τὰ ἐκ νοὸς καὶ ἐπινοίας γεγεννημένα, τουτέστιν ἐξ οὐρανοῦ καὶ γῆς, λέγει· »ἄκουε, οὐρανέ, καὶ ἐνωτίζου, γῆ,
5 ὅτι κύριος ἐλάλησεν· υἱοὺς ἐγέννησα καὶ ὕψωσα, αὐτοὶ δέ με | ἠθέτη- f.
σαν«. ὁ δὲ λέγων ταῦτα, φησίν, ἡ ἑβδόμη δύναμίς ἐστιν, ⟨ὁ⟩ ἑστώς,
στάς, στησόμενος· αὐτὸς γὰρ αἴτιος τούτων τῶν καλῶν, ὧν ἐπῄνεσε
Μωσῆς καὶ εἶπε καλὰ λίαν. ἡ δὲ φωνὴ καὶ τὸ ὄνομα ἥλιος καὶ σελήνη, ὁ δὲ λογισμὸς καὶ ἡ ἐνθύμησις ἀὴρ καὶ ὕδωρ. ἐν δὲ τούτοις
10 ἅπασιν ἐμμέμικται καὶ κέκραται, ὡς ἔφην, ἡ μεγάλη δύναμις ἡ ἀπέραντος, ὁ ἑστώς.

14. Μωσέως οὖν εἰρηκότος· »ἓξ ἡμέραις ἐν αἷς ὁ θεὸς ἐποίησε 1
τὸν οὐρανὸν καὶ τὴν γῆν, καὶ τῇ ἑβδόμῃ κατέπαυσεν ἀπὸ πάντων
τῶν ἔργων αὐτοῦ«, τὸν εἰρημένον τρόπον μετοικονομήσας ὁ Σίμων
15 ἑαυτὸν θεοποιεῖ. ὅταν οὖν λέγωσιν, ὅτι εἰσὶ τρεῖς ἡμέραι πρὸ ἡλίου 2
καὶ σελήνης γεγεννημέναι, αἰνίσσονται νοῦν καὶ ἐπίνοιαν, τουτέστιν
οὐρανὸν καὶ γῆν, καὶ τὴν ἑβδόμην δύναμιν τὴν ἀπέραντον· αὗται
γὰρ αἱ τρεῖς δυνάμεις εἰσὶ πρὸ πασῶν τῶν ἄλλων γενόμεναι. ὅταν 3
δὲ λέγωσι· »πρὸ πάντων τῶν αἰώνων γεννᾷ με«, περὶ τῆς ἑβδόμης,
20 φησί, δυνάμεως τὰ τοιαῦτα λέγεται εἶναι. ἑβδόμη δὲ αὕτη δύναμις,
ἥτις ἦν δύναμις ὑπάρχουσα ἐν τῇ ἀπεράντῳ δυνάμει, ἥτις γέγονε
πρὸ πάντων τῶν αἰώνων. αὕτη ἐστί, φησίν, ἡ ἑβδόμη δύναμις, περὶ 4
ἧς λέγει Μωσῆς· »καὶ πνεῦμα θεοῦ ἐπεφέρετο ἐπάνω τοῦ ὕδατος«,
τουτέστι, φησί, τὸ πνεῦμα τὸ πάντα ἔχον ἐν ἑαυτῷ, εἰκὼν τῆς ἀπε-
25 ράντου δυνάμεως, περὶ ἧς ὁ Σίμων λέγει· »εἰκὼν ἐξ ἀφθάρτου μορφῆς, κοσμοῦσα μόνη πάντα«. αὕτη γὰρ ἡ δύναμις, ἡ ἐπιφερομένη 5
ἐπάνω τοῦ ὕδατος ἐξ ἀφθάρτου, φησί, γεγενημένη μορφῆς κοσμεῖ
μόνη πάντα. τοιαύτης οὖν τινος καὶ παραπλησίου τῆς κατασκευῆς
τοῦ κόσμου γενομένης παρ' αὐτοῖς, »ἔπλασε«, φησίν, »ὁ θεὸς τὸν
30 ἄνθρωπον χοῦν ἀπὸ | τῆς γῆς« λαβών· ἔπλασε δὲ οὐχ ἁπλοῦν, ἀλλὰ f.
διπλοῦν »κατ' εἰκόνα καὶ καθ' ὁμοίωσιν«. εἰκὼν δέ ἐστι τὸ πνεῦμα 6

4 Jes. 1, 2, vgl. V 26, 36 — 7f Gen. 1, 31 — 12 Exod. 20, 17 ἐν γὰρ ἓξ
ἡμέραις ἐποίησε κύριος τὸν οὐρανὸν καὶ τὴν γῆν καὶ τὴν θάλασσαν καὶ πάντα τὰ
ἐν αὐτοῖς καὶ κατέπαυσε τῇ ἡμέρᾳ τῇ ἑβδόμῃ Gen. 2, 2 καὶ κατέπαυσε τῇ ἡμέρᾳ
τῇ ἑβδόμῃ ἀπὸ πάντων τῶν ἔργων αὐτοῦ — 15 vgl. S. 121, 12 — 19 vgl. Prov. 8, 23
πρὸ τοῦ αἰῶνος ἐθεμελίωσέν με 8, 25 πρὸ δὲ πάντων βουνῶν γεννᾷ με — 23. 27.
30 Gen. 1, 2, vgl. V 19, 17 — 29 Gen. 2, 7 — 31 Gen. 1, 26 — man vermißt
die Erklärung von καθ' ὁμοίωσιν (Clem. Exc. 50, 1 S. 123, 9ff., 54, 2 S. 125, 1 St.)

1 ὑποδέχεται P   6 + ὁ Gö.   12 ἡμέραι We.   18 ⟨αἱ⟩ πρὸ We.   20 εἶναι
> We.   24 τῶ πάντα ἔχειν P

thought for his spouse, / and the earth takes upon herself down
below the intellectual fruits borne down from the heaven,
which are akin to the earth. For this reason, he says, the *Logos*
looks away frequently towards the things begotten of mind
and thought, that is of heaven and earth, and says 'Hear, O
heaven, and give ear O earth, for the Lord hath spoken: sons I
have begotten and brought up, but they have rebelled against
me'. The one who says these things, he says, is the seventh
power, he who stood and stands and will stand. For he is cause
of these good things, which Moses praised and said they were
very good. But the speech and name are the sun and moon,
and the reason and inspiration are air and water. But in all
these is mixed and mingled the great power, the unlimited one,
he that stood, as I said.

14. Therefore when Moses said 'Six days in which god
made the heaven and the earth, and on the seventh he rested
from all his works', changing the set up in the said manner
Simon makes himself a god. When they say that there are
three days before the sun and moon are created, they hint at
mind and thought, that is heaven and earth, and the seventh
power, the unlimited one; for these three powers are come into
being before all the others. But when they say 'before all the
ages he begat me' these things are said about the seventh
power, he says. But this is the seventh power, which was the
power subsisting in the unlimited in potentiality, which came
into being before all ages. This is, he says, the seventh power,
about which Moses speaks: 'And the spirit of god moved on the
face of the water', that is, he says, the spirit which has all
things in itself, the image of the unlimited power, about which
Simon says: 'The image from an imperishable form, alone
ordering all things.' For this power, the one which moves on
the face of the water, coming from an imperishable form, he
says, alone orders all things. Some such, or similar,
construction of the cosmos occurred according to them, and
'God fashioned man', he says 'by taking dust from the earth';
he fashioned him not simple but twofold 'in the image and in

140W τὸ ἐπιφερόμενον ἐπάνω τοῦ ὕδατος· ὃ ἐὰν μὴ ἐξεικονισθῇ, μετὰ τοῦ κόσμου ἀπολεῖται, δυνάμει μεῖναν μόνον καὶ μὴ ἐνεργείᾳ γενόμενον — τοῦτό ἐστι, φησί, τὸ εἰρημένον· »ἵνα μὴ σὺν τῷ κόσμῳ κατακριθῶμεν« —· ἐὰν δὲ ἐξεικονισθῇ καὶ γένηται ἀπὸ στιγμῆς ἀμερίστου, ὡς γέγραπται ἐν τῇ Ἀποφάσει, τὸ μικρὸν μέγα γενήσεται. τὸ δὲ μέγα 5 ἔσται εἰς τὸν ἄπειρον αἰῶνα καὶ ἀπαράλλακτον, τὸ μηκέτι γινόμενον.
7 πῶς οὖν καὶ τίνα τρόπον, φησί, πλάσσει τὸν ἄνθρωπον ὁ θεός; ἐν παραδείσῳ, οὕτως γὰρ αὐτῷ δοκεῖ. ἔστω, φησί, παράδεισος ἡ μήτρα, καὶ ὅτι τοῦτό ἐστιν ἀληθὲς ἡ γραφὴ διδάξει ὅτε λέγει· »ἐγώ εἰμι ὁ πλάσσων σε ἐν μήτρᾳ μητρός σου«· καὶ τοῦτο γὰρ οὕτω θέλει γε- 10 γράφθαι. τὸν παράδεισον, φησίν, ἀλληγορῶν ὁ Μωσῆς τὴν μήτραν
8 εἴρηκεν, εἴπερ δεῖ τῷ λόγῳ πιστεύειν. εἰ δὲ πλάσσει ὁ θεὸς ἐν μή- τρᾳ μητρὸς τὸν ἄνθρωπον, τουτέστιν ἐν παραδείσῳ, ὡς ἔφην, ἔστω παράδεισος ἡ μήτρα, Ἐδὲμ δὲ τὸ χόριον, »ποταμὸς ἐκπορευόμενος ἐξ Ἐδὲμ ποτίζειν τὸν παράδεισον« ὁ ὀμφαλός. οὗτος, φησίν, »ἀφορί- 15 ζεται« ὁ ὀμφαλὸς »εἰς τέσσαρας ἀρχάς«· ἑκατέρωθεν γὰρ τοῦ ὀμφα- λοῦ δύο εἰσὶν ἀρτηρίαι παρατεταμέναι, ὀχετοὶ πνεύματος, καὶ δύο
9 φλέβες, ὀχετοὶ αἵματος. ἐπειδὰν δέ, φησίν, ἀπὸ τοῦ Ἐδὲμ χορίου ἐκπορευόμενος ὁ ὀμφαλὸς ἐμφυῇ τῷ γενομένῳ κατὰ τὸ ἐπιγάστριον,
f. 63r ὃ κοινῶς | πάντες προσαγορεύουσιν ὀμφαλόν * * * αἱ δὲ δύο φλέβες, 20 δι᾽ ὧν ῥεῖ καὶ φέρεται ἀπὸ τοῦ Ἐδὲμ τοῦ χορίου τὸ αἷμα, κατὰ τὰς
10 καλουμένας πύλας τοῦ ἥπατος, αἵτινες τὸ γεννώμενον τρέφουσιν· αἱ ἀρτηρίαι, ἃς ἔφημεν ὀχετοὺς εἶναι πνεύματος, ἑκατέρωθεν περιλαβοῦ- σαι τὴν κύστιν κατὰ τὸ πλατὺ ὀστοῦν, πρὸς τὴν μεγάλην συνάπτου- σιν ἀρτηρίαν, τὴν κατὰ ῥάχιν καλουμένην ἀορτήν, καὶ οὕτως διὰ 25 τῶν παραθύρων ἐπὶ τὴν καρδίαν ὁδεύσαν τὸ πνεῦμα κίνησιν ἐργά-
11 ζεται τῶν ἐμβρύων. πλαττόμενον γὰρ τὸ βρέφος ἐν τῷ παραδείσῳ

---

3 I Kor. 11, 32, vgl. V 12, 7 — 4f vgl. V 9, 5 E. — 9 vgl. Jes. 44, 2 ὁ πλάσας σε ἐκ κοιλίας V. 24 ὁ πλάσσων σε ἐκ κοιλίας? — 14 ff Gen. 2, 10, vgl. V 9, 14 — 16 ff Galen, In Hipp. De alim. Bd. XV 387 Kühn ἔστι γὰρ ἐν αὐτῷ ἀγγεῖα τέτταρα, δύο μὲν ἀρτηρίαι, δύο δὲ φλέβες μέσον ἑαυτῶν ἔχουσαι τὸν οὐραχόν . . . . καὶ διὰ τούτων οἷον ἐκ πρέμνων τινῶν ἐκ τῆς μήτρας ἕλκει τὸ ἔμβρυον αἷμα καὶ πνεῦμα

1 τοῦ ἐπιφερομένου P 6 ἀπαράλακτον P τὸν μηχ. Hilg. S. 459 nach S. 144, 3 7 πλάσεις P, spatium hinter ἁ 10 πλάσων P 14 χωρίον P, verb. Cruice, ebenso Z. 18. 21 ποταμὸς ⟨δ᾽⟩ We. 15 ποτίζει P 17 παρατε- ταγμέναι, verb. Gö. 18 f ἔπειτα — ἐμφύεται Petersen bei Gö. 19 nach ἐπι- γάστριον Lücke Miller 20 ὃ Cruice: ὃν P Lücke Gö. 23 f περιλαβοῦσαι Gö.: μὲν λαβοῦσαι P

the likeness'. The image is the spirit / moving on the face of the water; which if it is not made into the image perishes with the world, remaining only in potentiality and not coming to be in actuality – this is, he says, the saying 'that we may not be condemned with the world' – but if it is made into the image and comes to be from an indivisible point, then the small becomes great, as it is written in the *Apophasis*. The great will be unto the infinite and changeless age, which no longer comes to be. How then, and in what manner, did God fashion man? In Paradise, for so it seemed to be good to him. Let Paradise be the womb, he says, and that this is true scripture teaches when it says 'I am he that fashioned thee in thy mother's womb'; for this is usually written thus. Moses allegorising Paradise, he says, said the womb if one is to believe the argument. But if God fashioned man in his mother's womb, that is in Paradise, as I said, let Paradise be the womb and Eden the placenta, and the 'river flowing out of Eden to water the garden' the umbilical cord. This umbilical cord, he says, 'divides into four heads'. For on each side of the umbilical cord there are two arteries extended, channels for breath, and two veins, channels for blood. But since the umbilical cord flowing out from Eden the placenta is embedded in the offspring at the abdomen, which all generally call the umbilicus, ... but the two veins through which the blood flows and is carried from Eden the placenta, through what are called the portal fissures of the liver, and they nourish the foetus. The arteries which we said were channels for breath, encompass the bladder on either side at the broad bone and join on to the great artery, the one along the spine called the aorta, and hence the breath makes its way to the heart via the ventricles and brings about movement of the embryo. For the foetus fashioned in Paradise / neither takes

141W οὔτε τῷ στόματι τροφὴν λαμβάνει οὔτε τοῖς ῥισὶν ἀναπνέει· ἐν ὑγροῖς
γὰρ ὑπάρχοντι αὐτῷ παρὰ πόδας ἦν ὁ θάνατος εἰ ἀνέπνευσεν· ἐπε-
σπάσατο γὰρ ἂν ἀπὸ τῶν ὑγρῶν καὶ ἐφθάρη. ἀλλὰ γὰρ ὅλον περιέ-
σφιγκται τῷ καλουμένῳ χιτῶνι ἀμνίῳ, τρέφεται δὲ δι᾽ ὀμφαλοῦ καὶ
5 διὰ τῆς ⟨ἀορτῆς τῆς⟩ κατὰ ῥάχιν, ὡς ἔφην, τὴν τοῦ πνεύματος οὐσίαν λαμβάνει.

15. Ὁ οὖν ποταμός, φησίν, ὁ ἐκπορευόμενος ἐξ Ἐδὲμ εἰς τέσσαρας
ἀφορίζεται ἀρχάς, ὀχετοὺς τέσσαρας, τουτέστιν εἰς τέσσαρας αἰσθήσεις
τοῦ γεννωμένου, ὅρασιν, [ἀκοήν,] ὄσφρησιν, γεῦσιν καὶ ἁφήν. ταύτας
10 γὰρ ἔχει μόνας τὰς αἰσθήσεις ἐν τῷ παραδείσῳ πλασσόμενον τὸ παι-
δίον. οὗτος, φησίν, ἐστὶν ὁ νόμος, ὃν ἔθηκε Μωσῆς, καὶ πρὸς τοῦτον
αὐτὸν τὸν νόμον γέγραπται τῶν βιβλίων ἕκαστον, ὡς ⟨αἱ⟩ ἐπιγραφαὶ
δηλοῦσι. τὸ πρῶτον βιβλίον Γένεσις· ἤρκει, φησί, πρὸς γνῶσιν τῶν
ὅλων ἡ ἐπιγραφὴ τοῦ βιβλίου. αὕτη γάρ, φησίν, ἐστὶν ἡ Γένεσις
15 ὅρασις, εἰς ἣν ἀφορίζεται ποταμοῦ σχίσις ἡ μία· ἐθεάθη γὰρ ὁ κόσμος
ἐν ὁράσει. ἐπιγραφὴ βιβλίου δευτέρου Ἔξοδος· ἔδει γὰρ τὸ γεννηθέν,
τὴν Ἐρυθρὰν | διοδεῦσαν θάλασσαν, ἐλθεῖν ἐπὶ τὴν ἔρημον — Ἐρυ-
θρὰν δὲ λέγει, φασί, τὸ αἷμα —, καὶ γεύσασθαι πικρὸν ὕδωρ. πικρὸν
γάρ, φησίν, ἐστὶ τὸ ὕδωρ τὸ μετὰ τὴν Ἐρυθρὰν θάλασσαν, ὅπερ ἐστὶν
20 ὁδὸς τῆς κατὰ τὸν βίον γνώσεως τῶν ἐπιπόνων ὁδευομένη καὶ πι-
κρῶν. στραφὲν δὲ ὑπὸ Μωσέως, τουτέστι τοῦ λόγου, τὸ πικρὸν
ἐκεῖνο γίνεται γλυκύ. καὶ ὅτι ταῦθ᾽ οὕτως ἔχει, κοινῇ πάντων ἐστὶν
ἀκοῦσαι κατὰ τοὺς ποιητὰς λεγόντων·

ῥίζῃ μὲν μέλαν ⟨ἔσκε⟩, γάλακτι δὲ εἴκελον ἄνθος·
25   μῶλυ δέ μιν καλέουσι θεοί· χαλεπὸν δέ τ᾽ ὀρύσσειν
ἀνδράσι γε θνητοῖσι· θεοὶ δέ τε πάντα δύνανται.

16. Ἀρκεῖ, φησί, ⟨τὸ⟩ λεχθὲν ὑπὸ τῶν ἐθνῶν πρὸς ἐπίγνωσιν τῶν
ὅλων τοῖς ἔχουσιν ἀκοὰς (τῆς ἀκ)οῆς· τούτου γάρ, φησίν, ὁ γευσάμενος
τοῦ καρποῦ ὑπὸ τῆς Κίρκης οὐκ ἀπεθηριώθη μόνος, ἀλλὰ καὶ τοὺς

2 ff vgl. [Galen] Abh. Akad. Berl. 1895 S. 37, 1 ff — 7 Gen. 2, 10, vgl. V
9, 14 — 17 Exod. 15, 22—26, vgl. V 7, 39 — 24 Homer ι 304—306

5 ⟨ ⟩ Cruice   9 ἀκοήν < Miller. Das Gehör fehlt im folgenden, und sein
Fehlen wird Z. 10 begründet   12 + αἱ Gö.   15 σχίσις, über ι ein Buchst.
(υ?) P   16 ἐπιγραφὴ We. (ἡ ἐπιγραφὴ Gö.): αὖ γραφὴ P? aber obere Hälfte
von ῦ unkenntlich, dann Riß, αὖ ἐπιγραφὴ? Miller   18 φησί? Miller   20 ⟨διὰ⟩
τῶν Cruice   20 f πικρῶς P   26 δύναταιτε P   27 + τὸ Miller   28 (τῆς
ἀκ)οῆς Gö. (ο in P nicht ganz kenntlich) nach alttest. ἀκοῇ ἀκούειν (Mark 4, 23
u. ö. εἴ τις ἔχει ὦτα ἀκούειν): (ὑπακ)οῆς Miller

food with the mouth nor breathes with the nostrils; it exists in fluids and death would be upon it at once if it breathed, for it would draw in from the fluids and perish. But it is entirely wrapped round with what is called the foetal membrane, but it is nourished through the umbilicus, and through the (aorta) along the spine, as I said, it obtains the substance of breath.

15. The river flowing out of Eden, he says, divides into four heads, four channels, that is into four senses of the foetus, sight, (hearing), smell, taste and touch. These senses alone the child being fashioned in Paradise has. This, he says, is the law which Moses set down, and with regard to this same law is written each of the books of the bible, as the titles show. The first book is Genesis. The title of the book is sufficient for knowledge of all things. This, he says, Genesis, is sight into which the first section of the river divides; for the world was viewed with sight. The title of the second book is Exodus; for it is necessary for the child that is born to pass through the Red Sea and come into the desert – 'Red' means the blood, they say – and taste bitter water. For, he says, the water beyond the Red Sea is bitter, that is the highway of sufferings and bitter things of the knowledge that is in this life. But turned about by Moses, that is by the *Logos*, that bitter becomes sweet. And that this is so one can hear everyone saying through the poets:

> 'It is black at the root but its flower is like milk; the gods call it moley; it is difficult to dig up for mortal men, but the gods can do anything.'

16. The saying of the gentiles is sufficient for knowledge of all things to those who have ears for hearing. For he who tasted of this fruit, he says, was alone not turned into a beast by Circe and also / using the power of this fruit even

142W ἤδη τεθηριωμένους τῇ δυνάμει χρώμενος τοῦ τοιούτου καρποῦ εἰς
τὸν πρῶτον ἐκεῖνον τὸν ἴδιον αὐτῶν ἀνέπλασε καὶ ἀνετύπωσε καὶ
2 ἀνεκαλέσατο χαρακτῆρα. πιστὸς δὲ ἀνὴρ καὶ ἀγαπώμενος ὑπὸ τῆς
φαρμακίδος ἐκείνης διὰ τὸν γαλακτώδη καὶ θεῖον ἐκεῖνον καρπόν,
φησίν, εὑρίσκεται. Λευϊτικὸν ὁμοίως τὸ τρίτον βιβλίον, ὅπερ ἐστὶν
ἡ ὄσφρησις ⟨ἢ⟩ ἀναπνοή. θυσιῶν γάρ ἐστι καὶ προσφορῶν ὅλον
ἐκεῖνο τὸ βιβλίον. ὅπου δέ ἐστι θυσία, ὀσμή τις εὐωδίας ἀπὸ τῆς
θυσίας διὰ τῶν θυμιαμάτων γίνεται· περὶ ἣν εὐωδίαν ὄσφρησιν εἶναι
3 δ(. . .)ριον. Ἀριθμοὶ τὸ τέταρτον τῶν βιβλίων· γεῦσιν λέγει, ὅπου
λόγος ἐνεργεῖ· διὰ γὰρ τοῦ λαλεῖν πάντα ἀριθμοῦ τάξει καλεῖται. 1(
f. 64ʳ Δευτερονόμιον δέ, φησίν, ἐστὶ πρὸς | τὴν ἀφὴν τοῦ πεπλασμένου παι-
4 δίου ἐπιγεγραμμένον. ὥσπερ γὰρ ἡ ἀφὴ τὰ ὑπὸ τῶν ἄλλων αἰσθήσεων ὁραθέντα θιγοῦσα ἀνακεφαλαιοῦται καὶ βεβαιοῖ, σκληρὸν ἢ θερμὸν ἢ γλίσχρον δοκιμάσασα, οὕτως τὸ πέμπτον βιβλίον τοῦ νόμου
ἀνακεφαλαίωσίς ἐστι τῶν πρὸ αὐτοῦ γραφέντων τεσσάρων. 1
5 Πάντα οὖν, φησί, τὰ ἀγέννητά ἐστιν ἐν ἡμῖν δυνάμει, οὐκ ἐνεργείᾳ, ὡς ἡ γραμματικὴ ἢ γεωμετρική. ἐὰν οὖν τύχῃ τοῦ λόγου τοῦ
προσήκοντος καὶ διδασκαλίας καὶ στραφήσεται τὸ πικρὸν εἰς γλυκύ,
τουτέστιν »αἱ ζιβύναι εἰς δρέπανα καὶ αἱ μάχαιραι εἰς ἄροτρα«, οὐκ
ἔσται ἄχυρα καὶ ξύλα τὰ γεννώμενα ⟨ἀφανιζόμενα⟩ πυρί, ἀλλὰ καρ- 2
πὸς τέλειος ἐξεικονισμένος, ὡς ἔφην, ἴσος καὶ ὅμοιος τῇ ἀγεννήτῳ
6 καὶ ἀπεράντῳ δυνάμει. ἐὰν δὲ μείνῃ δένδρον μόνον, καρπὸν μὴ
ποιοῦν, ⟨μὴ⟩ ἐξεικονισμένον ἀφανίζεται. »ἐγγὺς γάρ που«, φησίν, »ἡ
ἀξίνη παρὰ τὰς ῥίζας τοῦ δένδρου· πᾶν δένδρον, φησί, μὴ ποιοῦν
καρπὸν καλὸν ἐκκόπτεται καὶ εἰς πῦρ βάλλεται.« 2
1 17. Ἔστιν οὖν κατὰ τὸν Σίμωνα τὸ μακάριον καὶ ἄφθαρτον
ἐκεῖνο ἐν παντὶ κεκρυμμένον δυνάμει, οὐκ ἐνεργείᾳ, ὅπερ ἐστὶν ὁ
ἑστώς, στάς, στησόμενος· ἑστὼς ἄνω ἐν τῇ ἀγεννήτῳ δυνάμει, στὰς

9f Gemeint ist die Zunge als Organ der γεῦσις und des λόγος — 16f vgl.
V 19, 1. 2. VI 12, 3 — 18 vgl. VI 15, 4 — 19 Jes. 2, 4 — 19—24 vgl.
VI 9, 9 — 20ff vgl. VI 12, 3 — 23—25 Matth. 3, 10; Luk. 3, 9, vgl. V 8, 31 —
26 μακάριον καὶ ἄφθαρτον] vgl. Epicurea p. 71 Usener — 28 ff vgl. Clem. Recogn. II 7

2 ἐνέπλασε P   6 + ἢ Miller   9 δ . . . ριον P, ρ nicht ganz sicher, der
auf δ folgende Buchstabe hatte den Accent: δοκιμαστήριον Gö., δεῖ κριτήριον
Cruice, beides zu lang; κριτήριον (δ statt κ) We., nach S. 123, 13; δ' μόριον Diels
als Glossem des Folgenden   14 γλίσχρον ⟨ἢ ψυχρὸν⟩ Cruice   17 ἢ] ἡ P, vgl.
S. 138, 21, ἢ ἡ We.   20 + ἀφανιζόμενα We., vgl. VI 9, 11   23 + μὴ Gö.

remoulded those already turned into beasts and re-struck them and recalled them back to their original form. But the trustworthy man loved by that sorceress is discovered by means of that milky and divine fruit, he says. Similarly Leviticus the third book, which is smell, inhalation. That whole book is of sacrifices and offerings. When there is a sacrifice a good smell comes from the sacrifice because of the incenses; concerning which good smell the sense of smell is ... The fourth of the books is Numbers. It means taste, where the *logos* is active; for it is by speaking that all things are named in the order of number. But Deuteronomy, he says, is named with respect to the sense of touch of the child that is being formed. For just as the sense of touch, touching upon the things seen by the other senses, sums up and confirms, testing hard or hot or sticky, so the fifth book of the Law is a summing-up of the four books written before it.

Therefore, he says, all the ungenerated things are in us in potentiality, not in actuality, like grammar or geometry. If therefore one should light upon the fitting *logos*, and upon teaching, and the bitter is turned to sweet, that is 'the spears to pruning hooks and the swords to ploughshares', then the generated things will not be chaff and wood for the fire, but the perfect fruit made into the image, as I said, equal and like to the ungenerated and unlimited power. But if it remains only a tree, not producing fruit, it will perish because it is not made into the image. 'For the axe is close to the roots of the tree,' he says. 'Every tree which does not bear good fruit will be cut down and thrown into the fire.'

17. According to Simon that blessed and imperishable thing is hidden in potentiality in everything, but not in actuality – this is the one who stood and stands and will stand: he stood above in the ungenerated power, stands / below in the flowing of

143W κάτω ἐν τῇ ῥοῇ τῶν ὑδάτων ἐν εἰκόνι γεννηθείς, στησόμενος ἄνω
παρὰ τὴν μακαρίαν ἀπέραντον δύναμιν, ἐὰν ἐξεικονισθῇ. τρεῖς γάρ, ₂
φησίν, εἰσὶν ἑστῶτες, καὶ ἄνευ τοῦ τρεῖς εἶναι ἑστῶτας αἰῶνας οὐ
κοσμεῖται ὁ ⟨ἀ⟩γέννητος ὁ κατ᾽ αὐτοὺς ἐπὶ τοῦ ὕδατος φερόμενος, ὁ
5 καθ᾽ ὁμοίωσιν ἀναπεπλασμένος τέλειος ἐπου(ράνιος), κατ᾽ οὐδεμίαν
ἐπίνοιαν ἐνδεέστερος τῆς ἀγεννήτου δυνάμεως γενόμενος. | τοῦτ᾽ ἔστιν ₁
ὃ λέγουσιν· ἐγὼ καὶ σὺ ἕν, πρὸ ἐμοῦ σύ, τὸ μετὰ σὲ ἐγώ. αὕτη,
φησίν, ἐστὶ δύναμις μία, διῃρημένη ἄνω κάτω, αὑτὴν γεννῶσα, αὑτὴν
αὔξουσα, αὑτὴν ζητοῦσα, αὑτὴν εὑρίσκουσα, αὑτῆς μήτηρ οὖσα, αὑτῆς
10 πατήρ, αὑτῆς ἀδελφή, αὑτῆς σύζυγος, αὑτῆς θυγάτηρ, αὑτῆς υἱός,
μήτηρ πατήρ, ἕν, οὖσα ῥίζα τῶν ὅλων.
Καὶ ὅτι, φησίν, ἀπὸ πυρὸς ἡ ἀρχὴ τῆς γενέσεώς ἐστι τῶν γεν- ₅
νωμένων, τοιοῦτον κατανόει τινὰ τρόπον. πάντων, ὅσων γένεσίς
ἐστιν, ἀπὸ πυρὸς ἡ ἀρχὴ τῆς ἐπιθυμίας τῆς γενέσεως γίνεται. τοι-
15 γαροῦν πυροῦσθαι τὸ ἐπιθυμεῖν τῆς μεταβλητῆς γενέσεως ὀνομάζεται.
ἓν δὲ ὂν τὸ πῦρ τροπὰς στρέφεται δύο. στρέφεται γάρ, φησίν, ἐν
τῷ ἀνδρὶ τὸ αἷμα, καὶ θερμὸν καὶ ξανθὸν ὡς πῦρ τυπούμενον, εἰς
σπέρμα, ἐν δὲ τῇ γυναικὶ τὸ αὐτὸ τοῦτο αἷμα εἰς γάλα. καὶ γίνεται
ἡ τοῦ ἄρρενος τροπὴ γένεσις, ἡ δὲ τῆς θηλείας τροπὴ τροφὴ τῷ
20 γεννωμένῳ. αὕτη, φησίν, ἐστὶν ἡ ›φλογίνη ῥομφαία ἡ στρεφομένη
φυλάσσειν τὴν ὁδὸν τοῦ ξύλου τῆς ζωῆς‹. στρέφεται γὰρ τὸ αἷμα
εἰς σπέρμα καὶ γάλα, καὶ γίνεται ἡ δύναμις αὕτη μήτηρ καὶ πατήρ,
πατὴρ τῶν γινομένων καὶ αὔξησις τῶν τρεφομένων, ἀπροσδεής, αὐ-
τάρκης. φυλάσσεται δέ, φησί, τὸ ξύλον τῆς ζωῆς διὰ τῆς στρεφομέ-
25 νης φλογίνης ῥομφαίας, ὡς εἰρήκαμεν, ἡ δύναμις ἡ ἑβδόμη ἡ ἐξ αὐτῆς,
ἡ πάντας ἔχουσα, ἡ ἐν ταῖς ἓξ κατακειμένη δυνάμεσιν. ἐὰν γὰρ μὴ
στρέφηται ἡ φλο|γίνη ῥομφαία, φθαρήσεται καὶ ἀπολεῖται τὸ καλὸν
ἐκεῖνο ξύλον· ἐὰν δὲ στρέφηται εἰς σπέρμα καὶ γάλα, ὁ δυνάμει ἐν
τούτοις κατακείμενος λόγου τοῦ προσήκοντος καὶ τόπου κυρίου, ἐν ᾧ

---

4 Gen. 1, 2, vgl. zu S. 139, 23 — 5f vgl. S. 139, 31 — 15 πυροῦσθαι]
I Kor. 7, 9 — 20f Gen. 3, 24 — 23f ἀπροσδεής, αὐτάρκης] s. Norden, Agnostos
Theos S. 17 ff

4 ἀγέννητος P, verb. Gö.   5 κατ᾽ οὐδεμίαν (nicht κατὰ δὲ μίαν) P   7 τὸ
Miller: τῷ P   8f αὑτὴν viermal P   9 αὐτῆς P, so stets im folgenden
11 ἐνοῦσα P   13 κατανοεῖ P   14 γενέσεως P   16 ἐνδέον P, verb. Gö.
τροπὰς στρέφεται δύο Gö.: τροφὰς τρέφεται. διὸ P   19 γένησις P   τροφὴ
(nicht τρυφὴ) P   23 πατὴρ Gö.: παρὰ P   25 αὐτῆς P   26 πάντα Cruice
(vgl. S. 137, 1; 139, 24)   27 στρέφεται P   29 λόγου Gö. (vgl. 142, 17): λόγος P

the waters born in the image, and will stand above alongside the blessed unlimited power, if he is made into the image. For there are three that have stood, he says, and without the existence of the three aeons that have stood the ungenerated one who, according to them, moves upon the face of the water, is not set in order – the one who is formed in the likeness, perfect heavenly, not falling short of the ungenerated power in respect of any thought. This is what they say: I and thou are one, before me, thou, after thee, I. This, he says, is the one power, divided above and below, generating itself, increasing itself, seeking itself, finding itself, mother of itself, father of itself, sister of itself, spouse of itself, daughter of itself, son of itself, mother father, one, being the root of all things.

And that the origin of genesis for the things that are created, it says, is from fire, he thinks in some way such as this. Of all things of which there is genesis, the origin of the desire for genesis comes from fire. Hence the desire for transitory genesis is called 'burning'. But while the fire is one thing it turns in two ways; for in the man, he says, the blood, which is hot and orange like fire, turns to seed, but in the woman this same blood turns to milk. And the change in the male becomes begetting and that of the female becomes nourishment for that which is begotten. This, he says, is the 'flaming sword which turns to guard the way to the tree of life'. For the blood turns to seed and milk, and this power becomes mother and father, father of the things that are begotten and growth of the things that are nourished, lacking nothing, self-sufficient. But, he says, the tree of life is guarded by means of the turning flaming sword, as we said, the seventh power derived from itself, the one which holds all things, lying within the six powers. For if the flaming sword does not turn, that fine tree will be destroyed and perish; but if it turns to seed and milk then the one that lies in these things in potentiality, lighting upon the fitting *logos* and the proper place in which / *logos* is begotten,

144W γεννᾶται λόγος, τυχών, ἀρξάμενος ὡς ἀπὸ σπινθῆρος ἐλαχίστου παν-
τελῶς μεγαλυνθήσεται καὶ αὐξήσει καὶ ἔσται δύναμις ἀπέραντος,
ἀπαράλλακτος, ⟨ἴση καὶ ὁμοία⟩ αἰῶνι ἀπαραλλάκτῳ μηκέτι γινομένῳ
εἰς τὸν ἀπέραντον αἰῶνα.

1 18. Γέγονεν οὖν ὁμολογουμένως κατὰ τοῦτον τὸν λόγον τοῖς
ἀνοήτοις Σίμων θεός, ὥσπερ ὁ Λίβυς ἐκεῖνος ὁ καὶ Ἄψεθος, γεννητὸς
μὲν καὶ παθητός, ὅταν ᾖ ἐν δυνάμει, ἀπαθὴς δὲ ἐκ γεννητοῦ, ὅταν
ἐξεικονισθῇ καὶ γενόμενος τέλειος ἐξέλθῃ τῶν δυνάμεων τῶν πρώ-
2 των δύο, τουτέστιν οὐρανοῦ καὶ γῆς. λέγει γὰρ Σίμων διαρρήδην
περὶ τούτου ἐν τῇ Ἀποφάσει οὕτως· »ὑμῖν οὖν λέγω ἃ λέγω καὶ
γράφω ἃ γράφω, τὸ γράμμα τοῦτο· δύο εἰσὶ παραφυάδες τῶν ὅλων
αἰώνων, μήτε ἀρχὴν μήτε πέρας ἔχουσαι, ἀπὸ μιᾶς ῥίζης, ἥτις ἐστὶ
3 δύναμις σιγὴ ἀόρατος, ἀκατάληπτος· ὧν ἡ μία φαίνεται ἄνωθεν, ἥτις
ἐστὶ μεγάλη δύναμις, νοῦς τῶν ὅλων, διέπων τὰ πάντα, ἄρσην, ἡ δὲ
ἑτέρα κάτωθεν, ἐπίνοια μεγάλη, θήλεια, γεννῶσα τὰ πάντα. ἔνθεν
ἀλλήλοις ἀντιστοιχοῦντες συζυγίαν ἔχουσι, καὶ τὸ μέσον διάστημα
4 ἐμφαίνουσιν ἀέρα ἀκατάληπτον, μήτε ἀρχὴν μήτε πέρας ἔχοντα. ἐν
δὲ τούτῳ πατὴρ ὁ βαστάζων πάντα καὶ τρέφων τὰ ἀρχὴν καὶ πέρας
ἔχοντα. οὗτός ἐστιν ὁ ἑστώς, στάς, στησόμενος, ὢν ἀρσενόθηλυς
f. 65v δύναμις κατὰ τὴν | προϋπάρχουσαν δύναμιν ἀπέραντον, ἥτις οὐ εἶ
ἀρχὴν οὔτε πέρας ἔχει, ἐν μονότητι οὖσα· ἀπὸ γὰρ ταύτης προελ-
5 θοῦσα ἡ ἐν μονότητι ἐπίνοια ἐγένετο δύο. κἀκεῖνος ἦν εἷς· ἔχων
γὰρ ἐν ἑαυτῷ αὐτὴν ἦν μόνος, οὐ μέντοι πρῶτος, καίπερ προϋπάρ-
χων, φανεὶς δὲ αὐτῷ ἀπὸ ἑαυτοῦ ἐγένετο δεύτερος. ἀλλ᾽ οὐδὲ πατὴρ
6 ἐκλήθη, πρὶν αὐτὴν αὐτὸν ὀνομάσαι πατέρα. ὡς οὖν αὐτὸς ἑαυτὸν
ἀπὸ ἑαυτοῦ προαγαγὼν ἐφανέρωσεν ἑαυτῷ τὴν ἰδίαν ἐπίνοιαν, οὕτως
καὶ ἡ φανεῖσα ἐπίνοια οὐκ ἐποίησεν, ἀλλὰ ἰδοῦσα αὐτὸν ἐνέκρυψε
τὸν πατέρα ἐν ἑαυτῇ, τουτέστι τὴν δύναμιν, καὶ ἔστιν ἀρσενόθηλυς
δύναμις καὶ ἐπίνοια· ὅθεν ἀλλήλοις ἀντιστοιχοῦσιν — οὐδὲν γὰρ δια-

---

1 vgl. S. 140, 4 — 3f vgl. S. 140, 5f — 14 vgl. Anaxagoras Fr. 12 D.
πάντα διεκόσμησε νοῦς

1 τυχών Gö. (vgl. S. 142, 17): ψυχῶν P   ὡς Gö.: ὢν P   3 ἀπαράλακτος P
⟨ ⟩ Gö., vgl. S. 142, 21   ἀπαραλάκτω P   γινομένη? We., s. zu S. 140, 6
7 ὅτε ἂν P   11 τὸ γράμμα τοῦτο] H. hat vielleicht das Original, in dem auf
τοῦτο τὸ γράμμα dieselben Worte wie S. 136, 16 folgten, gekürzt   13 ὢν ἡ
μία P   18 πατὴρ ὁ Gö.: πατέρα P   τρέφοντα ἀρχὴν P   21 οὖσα Cruice:
οὖσαν P   24 αὐτῷ P, αὐτὸς Miller, doch s. Z. 26   25 αὐτὴν Gö.: αὐτὴ P
ὀνομάσαι Gö.: ὀνομάσει P   26 ὑπὸ falsch als Text von P Miller, vgl. Hilg. S. 458
27 ἐπίνοιαν P, ⟨ἐπίνοια⟩ ἐπίνοιαν? We.

starting as it were from the smallest spark, will be entirely enlarged and will grow and will be an unlimited power, unchanging, (equal and similar) to the unchanging aeon that no longer undergoes change unto the unlimited age.

18. Hence in accordance with this theory Simon undoubtedly became a god to the foolish, as that Libyan Apsethos also did, being on the one hand begotten and subject to passion while he is in potentiality, but impassible instead of begotten when made into the image and become perfect he emerges from the first two powers, that is heaven and earth. For Simon speaks explicitly concerning this in the *Apophasis* thus:

'Unto you, therefore, I speak what I speak and I write what I write, this writ: two offshoots there are of all the aeons, having neither beginning nor limit, rising from one root, which is the power silence invisible incomprehensible; of these two offshoots the one appears from above – this is the great power, mind of all things, controlling all things, male – and the other from below the great thought, female, giving birth to all things. Then standing over against each other they have intercourse, and reveal the intervening space, air incomprehensible, having neither beginning nor limit. In this space is the father who holds all things and nourishes the things that have beginning and limit. He is the one who stood and stands and will stand, being a male-female power in accordance with the pre-existing unlimited power, who has neither beginning nor limit, being unique. For it is from this power that the unique thought came forth and became two. And he also was one; for having her within him he was alone, but not, however, first despite pre-existing, but appearing to himself from himself he became second. Nor was he called father before she called him father. Therefore just as he, bringing forth himself from himself revealed to himself his own thought, so also the thought that was revealed did not create, but seeing him hid the father, that is the power, in herself, and she is a male-female power and thought. Hence they stand over against each other – correspond to each other – for power differs not at all / from thought – and they are one: power is

145W φέρει δύναμις ἐπινοίας — ἐν ὄντες· ἐκ μὲν τῶν ἄνω εὑρίσκεται δύ- 7
ναμις, ἐκ δὲ τῶν κάτω ἐπίνοια. ἔστιν οὖν οὕτως καὶ τὸ φανὲν ἀπ᾽
αὐτῶν· ἓν ὂν δύο εὑρίσκεται, ἀρσενόθηλυς ἔχων τὴν θήλειαν ἐν
ἑαυτῷ. οὕτως ἐστὶ νοῦς ἐν ἐπινοίᾳ, ἀχώριστα ἀπ᾽ ἀλλήλων, ἓν ὄντες
5 δύο εὑρίσκονται.«
  19. Ταῦτα μὲν οὖν ὁ Σίμων ἐφευρὼν οὐ μόνον τὰ Μωσέως κα- 1
κοτεχνήσας εἰς ὃ ἐβούλετο μεθηρμήνευσεν, ἀλλὰ καὶ τὰ τῶν ποιητῶν.
καὶ γὰρ τὸν δούρειον ἵππον ἀλληγορεῖ καὶ τὴν Ἑλένην ἅμα τῇ λαμπάδι καὶ ἄλλα πλεῖστα ὅσα μετάγ(ων τά) τε αὐτοῦ καὶ τῆς ἐπινοίας
10 πλαστολογεῖ. εἰπέ τε ταύτην τὸ πρόβατον τὸ πεπλανημένον, ἥτις 2
ἀεὶ καταγινομένη ἐν γυναιξὶν ἐτάρασσε | τὰς ἐν κόσμῳ δυνάμεις διὰ f.
τὸ ἀνυπέρβλητον αὐτῆς κάλλος· ὅθεν καὶ ὁ Τρωϊκὸς πόλεμος δι᾽ αὐτὴν γεγένηται. ἐν γὰρ τῇ κατ᾽ ἐκεῖνον καιρὸν γενομένῃ Ἑλένῃ ἐνῴκησεν [ἐν αὐτῇ] ἡ ἐπίνοια, καὶ οὕτως πασῶν ἐπιδικαζομένων αὐτῆς
15 τῶν ἐξουσιῶν, στάσις καὶ πόλεμος ἐπανέστη ἐν οἷς ἐφάνη ἔθνεσιν.
οὕτως γοῦν τὸν Στησίχορον διὰ τῶν ἐπῶν λοιδορήσαντα αὐτὴν τὰς 3
ὄψεις τυφλωθῆναι· αὖθις δὲ μεταμεληθέντος αὐτοῦ καὶ γράψαντος

8ff vgl. Iren. I 23, 2 S. 192ff H.; Clem. Homil. II 34f; Filastrius C. 29, 5ff M.;
Epiph. XXI 3 S. 9,2ff D. ἀναγκάζεται αὐτὴν διαγράφειν Ὅμηρος ἐπὶ πύργου ἑστηκέναι
καὶ διὰ λαμπάδος ὑποφαίνειν τοῖς Ἕλλησι τὴν κατὰ τῶν Φρυγῶν ἐπιβουλήν. ἐχαρακτή-
ριζε δὲ διὰ τῆς λαμπάδος (λαμπηδόνος V) ... τὴν τοῦ ἄνωθεν φωτὸς ἔνδειξιν. διὸ καὶ
τὸν παρ᾽ Ὁμήρῳ δούρειον ἵππον μεμηχανημένον .... ἔλεγε πάλιν ὁ γόης ὅτι ἄγνοιά
ἐστι τῶν ἐθνῶν, Schneidewin, Gött. Nachr. 1852 S. 99f; Gruppe, Griech. Myth.
S. 686⁵ — 10. S. 146, 6f Luk. 15, 4; Iren. I 23, 2: et hanc esse perditam ovem;
Tert. De anima 34; Epiph. XXI 3 — 11 Filastrius 29, 7: in figura feminea
apparens — 12—14 Iren. I 23, 2: hanc esse primam mentis eius conceptionem
.... fuisse autem eam (sc. Ennoian) et in illa Helena, propter quam Troianum
contractum est bellum — 17—S. 146, 4 Iren.: quapropter et Stesichorum per
carmina maledicentem eam orbatum oculis; post deinde paenitentem et scribentem
eas quae vocantur palinodias, in quibus hymnizavit eam, rursus vidisse. transmigrantem autem eam de corpore in corpus, ex eo et semper contumeliam sustinentem in novissimis etiam in fornice prostitisse .... (vorher die angeli erwähnt)

2 ἔστιν] ἔτι? We., dann Z. 3 keine Interpunction ἀπ᾽ Miller: ἂν P
3 εὑρίσκεται Hilg. S. 459: εὑρίσκεσθαι P 4 οὕτως Gö.: οὗτος P ἃ χωριστὰ
Gö., ἀχώριστα δ᾽ oder γὰρ Miller 5 δύο ⟨δ᾽⟩ We. 7 τὰ] τὰς P 9 μετά-
γ(ων τά) τε We.: μετάγ · ·ˊ τε P, μετάγων εἰς τὰ Gö. αὐτοῦ P 10 πλαστολογεῖ Roeper: πλείστους λέγει P, πλείστους ἀνάγει Cruize εἰπέ τε We.: εἴμ᾽ε
τε P, εἶν(αι δ᾽ ἔλ)εγε Miller, den Raum überschreitend 13 ἐκεῖνον καιρὸν (oder
ἐκεῖνα καιροῦ) Miller: ἐκείνον καιροῦ P γενομένου P 14 ἐν > Scott
αὐτῇ P: αὕτη Scott, > We. 17 μεταμεληθέντα αὐτὸν καὶ γράψαντα We.
Hippolyt III.
10

discovered from the things above and thought from the things below. And that which is revealed from them is also thus: being one it is found as two, male-female having the female within itself. Thus mind is in thought, indivisible from each other, being one they are found as two.'

19. Inventing these things, not only did Simon abuse the words of Moses and reinterpret them to what he wanted, but also the words of the poets. For he also allegorises the wooden horse and Helen with the lamp and many other things which he adapts, and fabricates things about himself and the Epinoia. And he says that she is the stray sheep who has always dwelt in women and harassed the powers in the world because of her unsurpassed beauty; for which reason the Trojan War itself came about because of her. For the Epinoia was dwelling in the Helen that lived at that time, and thus since all the powers were suing for her, dispute and war arose in the nations in which she appeared. Thus it was that Stesichorus who ridiculed her in his poetry had his eyes blinded; but when he repented and wrote / the palinodes in which he celebrated her,

146W τὰς παλινῳδίας ἐν αἷς ὕμνησεν αὐτήν, ἀναβλέψαι· μετενσωματουμένην
⟨δὲ⟩ ὑπὸ τῶν ἀγγέλων καὶ τῶν κάτω ἐξουσιῶν, οἳ καὶ τὸν κόσμον,
φησίν, ἐποίησαν, ὕστερον ἐπὶ τέγους ἐν Τύρῳ τῆς Φοινίκης πόλει
4 στῆναι, ἣ κατελθὼν εὗρεν. ἐπὶ γὰρ τὴν ταύτης πρώτην ζήτησιν
ἔφη παραγεγονέναι, ὅπως ῥύσηται αὐτὴν τῶν δεσμῶν· ἣν λυτρωσάμενος ἅμα ἑαυτῷ περιῆγε, φάσκων τοῦτο εἶναι τὸ ἀπολωλὸς πρόβατον, ἑαυτὸν δὲ λέγων τὴν ὑπὲρ πάντα δύναμιν εἶναι. ὁ δὲ ψυχρὸς
ἐρασθεὶς τοῦ γυναίου τούτου, Ἑλένης καλουμένης, ὠνησάμενος εἶχε,
5 καὶ τοὺς μαθητὰς αἰδούμενος τοῦτον τὸν μῦθον ἔπλασεν. οἱ δὲ αὖθις
μιμηταὶ τοῦ πλάνου καὶ Σίμωνος μάγου γινόμενοι τὰ ὅμοια δρῶσιν, 1
ἀλογίστως φάσκοντες δεῖν μίγνυσθαι, λέγοντες· πᾶσα γῆ γῆ, καὶ οὐ
διαφέρει ποῦ τις σπείρει, πλὴν ἵνα σπείρῃ, ἀλλὰ καὶ μακαρίζουσιν
ἑαυτοὺς ἐπὶ τῇ (ξένῃ) μίξει, ταύτην εἶναι λέγοντες τὴν τελείαν ἀγά-
f. 66ᵛ πην, καὶ τὸ ἅγιος ἁγίων . . λλη . ος ἁγιασθήσεται· | οὐ γὰρ μὴ κρα-
τεῖσθαι αὐτοὺς ἔτι τινὶ νομιζομένῳ κακῷ, λελύτρωνται γάρ. τὴν 1
δὲ Ἑλένην λυτρωσάμενος οὕτως τοῖς ἀνθρώποις σωτηρίαν παρέσχε

4f. 15-S. **147**, 6 *Iren. I 23, 3*: quapropter et ipsum venisse, uti eam assumeret
primam et liberaret eam a vinculis, hominibus autem salutem praestaret per suam
agnitionem (vgl. Theod. I 1). cum enim male moderarentur angeli mundum,
quoniam unusquisque eorum concupisceret principatum, ad emendationem venisse
rerum et descendisse eum transfiguratum et assimilatum virtutibus et potestatibus
et angelis, ut et in hominibus homo appareret ipse, cum non esset homo, et
passum autem in Iudaea putatum, cum non esset passus. Über Hippolyts Syntagma·
s. Lipsius, Zur Quellenkritik des Epiph. S. 75ff — **5. 6. 8** *Iren. I 23, 2*: hic
Helenam quandam, quam ipse a Tyro civitate Phoenices quaestuariam cum
redemisset, secum circumducebat — **7** *Iren. I 23, 1*: esse autem se sublimissimam virtutem, hoc est eum qui sit super omnia pater; *Clem. Recogn. II 7; Filastrius 29, 1*: dicens se esse virtutem dei quae supra omnes virtutes est, s. Act. 8, 10
— **13f** Holl vergleicht Epiph. XXVI 4 S. 43, 8 D. 5 S. 44, 26. 16 S. 57, 30ff —
14f vgl. Clemens Strom. III 30 S. 209, 32f St. (οἱ ἀπὸ Προδίκου) ζῶσιν ὡς βούλονται. βούλονται δὲ φιληδόνως, κρατηθῆναι ὑπ᾽ οὐδενὸς νενομικότες.

---

1 παλινῳδίας P   **2** + δὲ Roeper   **3** τέγους Gö. Theodoret I 1 (s. Iren.)
und Justin Apol. I 26: τε τοὺς P, τούτοις Harvey Iren. I 192   **4** ἣ We. (»wo
Simon sie fand«): ἣν P   **7** ψυδρὸς Roeper, μιαρὸς Bunsen I 351 (I 37)
10 ⟨τοῦ⟩ καὶ Cruice   μάγου Σίμωνος ∽ We.   **12** ποῦ τι P   **13** ξένῃ
Miller, ξ wohl kenntlich, Accent auf 2. Buchst.: κοινῇ Gö., ἀδιαφόρῳ Cruice un-
möglich   **14** ἁγίῳ Klost.   λλη ᵒˢ P, vorher können 1—2 Buchst. fehlen: ἐπάλληλος
We., κολληθεὶς Klost.   ἁγιασθή P, στ nicht sicher kenntlich   **15** ἔτι We.: ἐπὶ P

his eyes were opened. But she was reincarnated by the angels and the powers below, who also made the world, he says, and subsequently she was stationed in a brothel in the city of Tyre in Phoenicia, where he found her when he came there. For he came there for the purpose of seeking her first of all, he said, so that he might release her from her bonds; so he ransomed her and took her round with him, proclaiming that this was the lost sheep, and saying that he himself was the power over all things. But the weak man was taken by lust for this feeble woman, named Helen, and bought her to have her, and being ashamed in front of his disciples he made up this story. But they again became imitators of the error and of Simon Magus and do the same things, proclaiming that one should have intercourse at random, saying: all earth is earth and it makes no difference where one sows the seed, except that one should sow the seed, but they also bless themselves in their promiscuous intercourse, saying that this is perfect love and the holy of holies ... For they are not adversely affected by anything considered evil any more, for they have been redeemed.

By redeeming Helen he thus granted salvation to mankind /

147W διὰ τῆς ἰδίας ἐπιγνώσεως. κακῶς γὰρ διοικούντων τῶν ἀγγέλων 6
τὸν κόσμον διὰ τὸ φιλαρχεῖν αὐτούς, εἰς ἐπανόρθωσιν ἐληλυθέναι
αὐτὸν ἔφη μεταμορφούμενον καὶ ἐξομοιούμενον ταῖς ἀρχαῖς καὶ ταῖς
ἐξουσίαις καὶ τοῖς ἀγγέλοις, ὡς καὶ ἄνθρωπον φαίνεσθαι αὐτὸν μὴ
5 ὄντα ἄνθρωπον, καὶ παθεῖν δὲ ἐν τῇ Ἰουδαίᾳ [καὶ] δεδοκηκέναι μὴ
πεπονθότα, ἀλλὰ φανέντα Ἰουδαίοις μὲν ὡς υἱόν, ἐν δὲ τῇ Σαμαρείᾳ
ὡς πατέρα, ἐν δὲ τοῖς λοιποῖς ἔθνεσιν ὡς πνεῦμα ἅγιον, ὑπομένειν
δὲ αὐτὸν καλεῖσθαι οἴῳ ἂν ὀνόματι καλεῖν βούλωνται οἱ ἄνθρωποι.
τοὺς δὲ προφήτας ἀπὸ τῶν κοσμοποιῶν ἀγγέλων ἐμπνευσθέντας εἰ- 7
10 ρηκέναι τὰς προφητείας· διὸ μὴ φροντίζειν αὐτῶν τοὺς εἰς τὸν Σίμωνα καὶ τὴν Ἑλένην πεπιστευκότας ἕως νῦν, πράσσειν τε ὅσα βούλονται ὡς ἐλευθέρους· κατὰ γὰρ τὴν αὐτοῦ χάριν σῴζεσθαι αὐτοὺς
φάσκουσι. μηδένα γὰρ εἶναι αἴτιον δίκης εἰ πράξει τις κακῶς· οὐ γάρ 8
ἐστι φύσει κακὸν ἀλλὰ θέσει. ἔθεντο γάρ, φησίν, οἱ ἄγγελοι οἱ τὸν
15 κόσμον ποιήσαντες ὅσα ἐβούλοντο, διὰ τῶν τοιούτων λόγων δουλοῦν
νομίζοντες τοὺς αὐτῶν ἀκούοντας. φθίσειν δὲ αὖθις λέγουσι τὸν
κόσμον ἐπὶ λυτρώσει τῶν ἰδίων ἀνθρώπων.

5—8 *Iren.* I 23, 1: docuit semetipsum esse, qui inter Iudaeos quidem quasi
filius apparuerit, in Samaria autem quasi pater descenderit, in reliquis vero gentibus quasi spiritus sanctus adventaverit. esse autem se sublimissimam virtutem,
hoc est eum qui sit super omnia pater (vgl. Hipp. S. 146, 7), et sustinere vocari
se quodcumque eum vocant homines — 9—17 *Iren.* 23, 3: prophetas autem a
mundi fabricatoribus angelis inspiratos dixisse prophetias, quapropter nec ulterius curarent eos hi qui in eum et in Helenam eius spem habeant, et ut
liberos agere quae velint; secundum enim ipsius gratiam salvari homines, sed
non secundum operas iustas. nec enim esse naturaliter operationes iustas,
sed ex accidenti, quemadmodum posuerunt qui mundum fecerunt angeli, per
huiusmodi praecepta in servitutem deducentes homines. quapropter et solvi
mundum et liberari eos qui sunt eius ab imperio eorum qui mundum fecerunt
repromisit.

3 αὐτὸν P   5 καὶ² > Bunsen I 352 (I 39), s. Iren. ob. zu S. 146,4, δεδοκηκέναι
καὶ ∾ Cruice   8 αὐτὸν P   βούλονται P, o² undeutlich   9 ὑπὸ We.   11 ⟨τοῦ⟩
νῦν Cruice, man erwartet ἀπὸ τοῦ νῦν (*ulterius* Iren.)   τε ὅσα Gö. (vgl. Iren.):
τὰ σὰ P   13 μηδένα Bunsen a. a. O. I 353 (I 41): μηδὲν P   εἰσπράξει P   τι
κακόν Bunsen   14 ἔστι ⟨τι⟩ Bunsen   κακός P, verb. Bunsen [Iren.]   16 φθίσειν
We.: φύσιν (φ nicht ganz kenntlich) P, vgl. Bunsen I 354 (I 41), λύσιν (dann τοῦ
κόσμου) Gö. (vgl. *solvi* Iren.)

10*

by means of his own recognition. For since the angels were managing the world badly because they desired supremacy, he said that he himself had come for the restoration of the world, changing his form and becoming assimilated to the principalities and powers and angels, so that he appeared as man though he was not man, and was thought to suffer in Judaea though he did not suffer, but he appeared to the Jews as son, but in Samaria as Father, and in the rest of the nations as Holy Spirit, but he submits to being called by whatever name men wish to call him.

The prophets spoke their prophecies under the inspiration of the angels who made the world; for this reason those who believe on Simon and Helen do not heed the prophets even now, and they act as they wish like free men; for they claim that they are saved by his grace. There is no reason for punishment if one acts wickedly; for it is not wicked by nature but by ordinance. For the angels who made the world ordained what they liked, believing that by means of such words they could enslave those who paid attention to them. And they say that the world will pass away again at the time of the redemption of their own men. /

1
148W
f. 67r

20. Οἱ οὖν τούτου μαθηταὶ μαγείας ἐπιτελοῦσι καὶ ἐπαοιδὰς
φίλτρα τε καὶ ἀγώγιμα καὶ τοὺς λεγομένους ὀνειροπόμπους δαίμονας
| ἐπιπέμπουσι πρὸς τὸ ταράσσειν οὓς βούλονται· ἀλλὰ καὶ παρέδρους
τοὺς λεγομένους ἀσκοῦσιν, εἰκόνα τε τοῦ Σίμωνος ἔχουσιν εἰς Διὸς
μορφὴν καὶ τῆς Ἑλένης ἐν μορφῇ Ἀθηνᾶς, καὶ ταύτας προσκυνοῦσι, 5

2 τὸν μὲν καλοῦντες κύριον, τὴν δὲ κυρίαν. εἰ δέ τις ὀνόματι καλέσει
παρ᾽ αὐτοῖς ἰδὼν τὰς εἰκόνας ἢ Σίμωνος ἢ Ἑλένης, ἀπόβλητος
γίνεται, ὡς ἀγνοῶν τὰ μυστήρια. οὗτος ὁ Σίμων πολλοὺς πλανῶν
ἐν τῇ Σαμαρείᾳ μαγείαις ὑπὸ τῶν ἀποστόλων ἠλέγχθη, καὶ ἐπάρατος
γενόμενος, καθὼς ἐν ταῖς Πράξεσι γέγραπται, ὕστερον ἀπευδοκήσας 10
ταῦτα ἐπεχείρησεν· ἕως καὶ τῆς Ῥώμης ἐπιδημήσας ἀντέπεσε τοῖς
ἀποστόλοις· πρὸς ὃν πολλὰ Πέτρος ἀντικατέστη μαγείαις πλα-

3 νῶντα πολλούς. οὗτος ἐπὶ τέλει ἐλθὼν ἔν τ . . . τῃ, ὑπὸ πλάτανον
καθεζόμενος ἐδίδασκε. καὶ δὴ λοιπὸν ἐγγὺς τοῦ ἐλέγχεσθαι γινόμενος
διὰ τὸ ἐγχρονίζειν, ἔφη, ὅτι εἰ χωσθείη ζῶν, ἀναστήσεται τῇ τρίτῃ 15
ἡμέρᾳ. καὶ δὴ τάφρον κελεύσας ὀρυγῆναι ὑπὸ τῶν μαθητῶν ἐκέλευσε
χωσθῆναι. οἱ μὲν οὖν τὸ προσταχθὲν ἐποίησαν, ὁ δὲ ἀπέμεινεν ἕως

4 νῦν· οὐ γὰρ ἦν ὁ Χριστός. οὗτος δὴ καὶ ὁ κατὰ τὸν Σίμωνα μῦθος,
ἀφ᾽ οὗ Οὐαλεντῖνος τὰς ἀφορμὰς λαβὼν ἄλλοις ὀνόμασι καλεῖ. ὁ γὰρ
Νοῦς καὶ ἡ Ἀλήθεια καὶ Λόγος καὶ Ζωὴ καὶ Ἄνθρωπος καὶ Ἐκκλη- 20
σία, οἱ Οὐαλεντίνου αἰῶνες, ὁμολογουμένως εἰσὶν αἱ Σίμωνος ἓξ ῥίζαι,
Νοῦς Ἐπίνοια Φωνὴ Ὄνομα Λογισμὸς καὶ Ἐνθύμησις. ἀλλ᾽ ἐπεὶ
ἱκανῶς ἡμῖν δοκεῖ ἐκτεθεῖσθαι τὴν Σίμωνος μυθοποιΐαν, ἴδωμεν τί
λέγει καὶ Οὐαλεντῖνος.

1 67v   21. | Ἔστι μὲν οὖν ἡ Οὐαλεντίνου αἵρεσις Πυθαγορικὴν ἔχουσα 25
καὶ Πλατωνικὴν τὴν ὑπόθεσιν. καὶ γὰρ Πλάτων ὅλως ἐν τῷ Τιμαίῳ

1—6 *Iren.*: igitur horum mystici sacerdotes libidinose quidem vivunt, magias
autem perficiunt, quemadmodum potest unusquisque eorum. exorcismis et incantationibus utuntur; amatoria quoque et agogima et qui dicuntur paredri (s.
zu S. 172, 15) et oniropompi et quaecumque sunt alia perierga apud eos studiose
exercentur. imaginem quoque Simonis habent factam ad figuram Iovis et Helenae
in figuram Minervae et has adorant . . . — 4—7 vgl. auch Eus. K. G. II 13, 6,
— 6 κύριον — κυρίαν] Bousset, Kyrios Christos S. 117 — 10 Act. 8, 20 ff, o. S. 135,5
Iren. 23, 1 — 13 ff singulärer Bericht über Simons Ende

1 μαγείαις P nach Miller, aber α² nur z. T. sichtbar, für ι kaum Platz
ἐπαοιδαῖς P, verb. Gö. vgl. Iren.   11 ταῦτα P   ἕως] + δὲ Gö.   τῇ Ῥώμῃ
wohl richtig Diels   13 τρίτῃ zieml. sicher P, τῇ Γίττῃ gut Hilg. S. 182   15 διὰ]
δὶς falsch als Text von P Miller   19 ⟨ταὐτὰ⟩ καλεῖ (vgl. S. 135, 1) We.   21 αἱ]
οἱ P   24 περὶ οὐαλεντίνου rot a. Rande   26 ὅλος P, ὅλον? We.

20. This man's disciples perform magic and spells and philtres and love-charms and they send out the daimones called dream-bringers to trouble whom they wish. And they exercise what are called familiar spirits, and they have an image of Simon in the form of Zeus and of Helen in the form of Athena, and they worship these, calling the one Lord and the other Lady. And if anyone, on seeing the images, calls either that of Simon or that of Helen by name, he becomes an outcast as being ignorant of the mysteries.

This man Simon led many astray by magic in Samaria and was refuted by the apostles, and became accursed, as it is written in Acts, and subsequently having despaired he put his hand to the same practices. Until he came to Rome and came into conflict with the Apostles; and Peter stood out against him when he was leading many astray with magic. Finally he came to (Gitta?) and sat down under a plane tree and taught. And at last when he was coming near to his refutation because of the long delay he said that if he was buried alive he would rise again on the third day. And indeed he ordered a grave to be dug and that he be buried in it by his disciples. They therefore did what was commanded, but he remained there to this day; for he was not the Christ. This then is the story told by Simon, and it is from this that Valentinus took his starting points and called them by different names. For Nous and Alêtheia and Logos and Zôe and Anthropos and Ecclesia, the aeons of Valentinus, are agreed to be the six roots of Simon, Nous, Epinoia, Phônê, Onoma, Logismos and Enthumêsis. But since it seems to us that we have sufficiently described the myths fabricated by Simon, let us see what Valentinus says too.

21. The heresy of Valentinus is one that has a Pythagorean and Platonic basis. For Plato modelled himself entirely on Pythagoras in the *Timaeus*. / And indeed Timaeus himself is

149W τὸν Πυθαγόραν ἀπεμάξατο· τοιγαροῦν καὶ ὁ Τίμαιος αὐτός ἐστιν
αὐτῷ Πυθαγόρειος ξένος. διὸ δοκεῖ ὀλίγα τῆς Πυθαγορείου καὶ Πλα-
τωνικῆς ὑπομνησθέντας ὑποθέσεως ἄρξασθαι καὶ τὰ Οὐαλεντίνου
λέγειν. εἰ γὰρ καὶ ἐν τοῖς πρότερον ὑφ᾽ ἡμῶν πεπονημένοις ἔγκειν- 2
5 ται καὶ τὰ Πυθαγόρᾳ καὶ Πλάτωνι δεδοκημένα, ἀλλά γε καὶ νῦν οὐκ
ἀλόγως ὑπομνησθήσομαι δι᾽ ἐπιτομῆς τὰ κορυφαιότατα τῶν αὐτοῖς ἀρε-
σκομένων, πρὸς τὸ εὐεπίγνωστα γενέσθαι τὰ Οὐαλεντίνῳ δόξαντα διὰ
τῆς ἐγγίονος παραθέσεως καὶ ὁμοίας συγκρίσεως, τῶν μὲν πάλαι ἀπ᾽ 3
Αἰγυπτίων ταῦτα παραλαβόντων καὶ εἰς Ἕλληνας μεταδιδαξάντων,
10 τοῦ δὲ παρὰ τούτων, ὅτι ⟨δὲ⟩ παρ᾽ αὐτῶν, διαψευσαμένου ἰδίαν τε
δόξαν συστῆσαι πεπειραμένου, * * * σπαράξαντα μὲν τὰ ἐκείνων ὀνόμασι καὶ ἀριθμοῖς, ἰδίως δὲ καλέσαντα καὶ μέτροις διορίσαντα, ὅπως
αἵρεσιν Ἑλληνικὴν ποικίλην μέν, ἀσύστατον δὲ καὶ οὐκ ἀνήκουσαν
Χριστῷ συστήσῃ.
15 22. Ἡ μὲν οὖν ἀρχὴ τῆς ὑποθέσεώς ἐστιν ἐν τῷ Τιμαίῳ τῷ 1
Πλάτωνι σοφία Αἰγυπτίων· ἐκεῖθεν γὰρ ὁ Σόλων τὴν ὅλην ὑπόθεσιν
περὶ τῆς κόσμου γενέσεως καὶ φθορᾶς παλαιῷ τινι λόγῳ καὶ προ-
φητικῷ, ὥς φησιν ὁ Πλάτων, τοὺς Ἕλληνας ἐδίδαξε, παῖδας νέους
ὄντας καὶ πρεσβύτερον | ἐπισταμένους μάθημα οὐδὲν θεολογούμενον. f.
20 ἵν᾽ οὖν παρακολουθήσωμεν τοῖς λόγοις, οἷς καταβέβληται Οὐαλεντῖνος, 2
προεκθήσομαι νῦν, τίνα ἐστὶν ἃ Πυθαγόρας ὁ Σάμιος μετὰ τῆς ὑμνου-
μένης ἐκείνης παρὰ τοῖς Ἕλλησι ⟨σι⟩γῆς φιλοσοφεῖ, εἶθ᾽ οὕτως ταῦτα,
ἃ ⟨παρὰ⟩ Πυθαγόρου λαβὼν καὶ Πλάτωνος Οὐαλεντῖνος σεμνολογῶν
ἀνατίθησι Χριστῷ καὶ πρὸ τοῦ Χριστοῦ τῷ πατρὶ τῶν ὅλων καὶ
25 Σιγῇ τῇ συνεζευγμένῃ τῷ πατρί.
23. Πυθαγόρας τοίνυν ἀρχὴν τῶν ὅλων ἀγέννητον ἀπεφήνατο 1
τὴν μονάδα, γεννητὴν δὲ τὴν δυάδα καὶ πάντας τοὺς ἄλλους ἀρι-
θμούς. καὶ τῆς μὲν δυάδος πατέρα φησὶν εἶναι τὴν μονάδα, πάντων
δὲ τῶν γεννωμένων μητέρα δυάδα, γεννητὴν γεννητῶν. καὶ Ζαράτας 2
30 ὁ Πυθαγόρου διδάσκαλος ἐκάλει τὸ μὲν ἓν πατέρα, τὰ δὲ δύο μητέρα.

4f s. I 2. 19; IV 51 — 15 Timaios 20 Eff — 18 Plato, Timaios 22 B
Ἕλληνες ἀεὶ παῖδές ἐστε κτλ. — 22 σιγῆς] vgl. S. 5, 11. 8, 14 — 26—S. 150, 6 vgl.
I 2,6—9. IV 51, 4—7 — 29f vgl. Plut. De animae procr. 2 S. 1012 E καὶ Z.

ὁ Πυθαγόρου διδάσκαλος ταύτην μὲν ἐκάλει τοῦ ἀριθμοῦ μητέρα, τὸ δ᾽ ἓν πατέρα

1 ἀπομάξατο P   2f Πλατωνικὴν corr. in Πλάτωνος P   8 ὁμοίων oder
ὁμοῦ We.   10 + δὲ Gö.   11 Lücke Gö., sonst müßte man mit Cruice die
3 Partic. in den Gen. setzen   παραλλάξαντα? Gö.   15 ⟨ἡ⟩ ἐν Miller   16 Πλάτωνος Miller   16 Σολομῶν P   17 γεννέσεως P, γεννήσεως Miller   22 σιγῆς Gö.:
γῆς P   23 ἃ παρὰ We., παρὰ Roeper Scott   24 Χριστοῦ] χριστῶ P (falsche
Angabe bei Miller)   29 γεννετὴν P

for Plato a Pythagorean stranger. Therefore it is best to begin to speak of the doctrines of Valentinus once we have reminded ourselves of a few points of the Pythagorean and Platonic hypothesis. For albeit the doctrines of Pythagoras and Plato are included in the accounts we worked on earlier, none the less not unreasonably I shall now mention the chief points of their theories in a summary, with the aim of making Valentinus' beliefs easier to understand by means of the closer proximity and greater similarity of the parallel comparison. Plato and Pythagoras derived these things from the Egyptians and taught them to the Greeks, and Valentinus derived them from the Greeks, that is from Plato and Pythagoras, but tried to pretend that he had set up a doctrine of his own ... pulling their ideas to pieces with names and numbers, but naming them in his own way and defining them with measurements, so that he contrived a Greek heresy that is complicated but also incoherent and not connected with Christ.

22. The starting point of the theory, therefore, is Egyptian wisdom in Plato's *Timaeus*. For it was from Egypt that Solon transmitted to the Greeks the whole theory about the coming-to-be and passing-away of the world in an ancient and prophetic account, as Plato says, the Greeks being young children and knowing no older theological learning. In order that we may follow the theories that Valentinus has issued I shall now explain beforehand what are the views that Pythagoras the Samian philosophised with that silence celebrated by the Greeks, and then these things which Valentinus took from Pythagoras and Plato and put into mystical language and applied to Christ and before Christ to the father of all things and to Silence who is coupled with the father.

22. Pythagoras declared that the ungenerated principle of all things was the monad, but the dyad was generated and all the other numbers. And the father of the dyad was the monad, and the mother of all the things that are generated was the dyad, generated mother of generated things. And Zaratas (Zoroaster), the teacher of Pythagoras, called the one father

150W γεγέννηται γὰρ ἐκ μὲν μονάδος δυὰς κατὰ τὸν Πυθαγόραν, καὶ ἔστιν
ἡ μὲν μονὰς ἄρρεν καὶ πρώτη, ἡ δὲ δυὰς θῆλυ. παρὰ τῆς δυάδος
δὲ πάλιν, ὡς ὁ Πυθαγόρας λέγει, ἡ τριὰς καὶ οἱ ἐφεξῆς ἀριθμοὶ μέχρι
3 τῶν δέκα. τοῦτον γὰρ οἶδε μόνον τέλειον ἀριθμὸν Πυθαγόρας τὸν
δέκα· τὸν γὰρ ἕνδεκα καὶ δώδεκα προσθήκην καὶ ἐπαναποδισμὸν τῆς   5
δεκάδος, οὐκ ἄλλου τινὸς ἀριθμοῦ γέννησιν [τὸ προστιθέμενον]. πάντα
τε σώματα στερεὰ ἐξ ἀσωμάτων γεννᾷ. τῶν τε γὰρ σωμάτων καὶ
ἀσωμάτων ὁμοῦ στοιχεῖον εἶναί φησι καὶ ἀρχὴν τὸ σημεῖον ὅ ἐστιν
ἀμερές· γίνεται δέ, φησίν, ἐκ σημείου γραμμή, καὶ ⟨ἐκ γραμμῆς ἐπι-
φάνεια⟩, ἐπιφάνεια δὲ ῥυεῖσα εἰς βάθος στερεὸν ὑφέστηκε, φησί, σῶμα.   10
f. 68ᵛ 4 ὅθεν καὶ ὅρκος τίς ἐστι τοῖς | Πυθαγορικοῖς ἡ τῶν τεσσάρων στοι-
χείων συμφωνία. ὀμνύουσι δ᾽ οὕτως·

νναὶ μὰ τὸν ἁμετέρᾳ κεφαλᾷ παραδόντα τετρακτύν,
πηγὴν ἀενάου φύσεως ⟨ῥιζώματ᾽⟩ ἔχουσαν.

ἔστι δὲ ἡ τετρακτὺς τῶν φυσικῶν καὶ στερεῶν σωμάτων ἀρχή, ὡς ἡ   15
5 μονὰς τῶν νοητῶν. ὅτι δὲ καὶ ἡ τετρακτὺς γεννᾷ, φησί, τὸν τέλειον
ἀριθμόν, ὡς ἐν τοῖς νοητοῖς ⟨ἡ μονάς⟩, τὸν δέκα, διδάσκουσιν οὕτως·
εἰ ἀρξάμενος ἀριθμεῖν λέγει τις ὅτι ἕν, καὶ ἐπιφέρει δύο, ἔπειτα
ὁμοίως τρία, ἔσονται ταῦτα ἕξ· πρὸς δὲ τούτοις ἔτι τέσσαρα, ἔσται
ὁμοίως τὸ πᾶν δέκα. τὸ γὰρ ἕν, δύο, τρία, τέσσαρα γίνεται δέκα, ὁ   20
τέλειος ἀριθμός. οὕτως, φησί, κατὰ πάντα ἐμιμήσατο ἡ τετρακτὺς
τὴν νοητὴν μονάδα, τέλειον ἀριθμὸν γεννῆσαι δυνηθεῖσαν.
1   24. Δύο οὖν κατὰ τὸν Πυθαγόραν εἰσὶ κόσμοι, εἷς μὲν νοητός,
ὃς ἔχει τὴν μονάδα ἀρχήν, εἷς δὲ αἰσθητός· τούτου δέ ἐστι τετρακτὺς
ἔχουσα ἰῶτα, τὴν »μίαν κεραίαν«, ἀριθμὸν τέλειον· καὶ ἔστι κατὰ   25
τοὺς Πυθαγορικοὺς τὸ ῑ, ἡ μία κεραία, πρώτη καὶ κυριωτάτη καὶ
τῶν νοητῶν ⟨καὶ τῶν αἰσθητῶν⟩ οὐσία νοητῶς καὶ αἰσθητῶς λαμ-
2 βανομένη· ⟨ἢ⟩ συμβεβηκότα γένη ἀσώματα ἐννέα, ἃ χωρὶς εἶναι τῆς οὐσίας οὐ δύναται, ποιὸν καὶ ποσὸν καὶ πρός τι καὶ ποῦ καὶ πότε καὶ
κεῖσθαι καὶ ἔχειν καὶ ποιεῖν καὶ πάσχειν. ἔστιν οὖν ἐννέα τὰ συμ-   30

6–10 vgl. IV 51, 2. 3 — 12 vgl. zu S. 6, 10 — 25 Matth. 5, 18; vgl.
Iren. I 3, 2 S. 26 H. — 26 ff über die Quelle (Archytas) s. Zeller III 2³ S. 103 f.
129, Comm. in Arist. VIII 558 f

2 θῆλυ ⟨καὶ δευτέρα⟩ Cruice   6 γέννησίν ⟨φησιν⟩ We.   τὸ προστιθέμενον
> We., Glosse zu προσθήκην: νομιστέον oder νομίζει μόνον Miller   7 τε¹] δὲ
Miller   9 f ⟨ ⟩ H: > P   13 ἁμάτερα κεφᾳ P   14 ἀεννάου P   17 ⟨ ⟩
Miller   20 δέκα² P (nicht δὲ καὶ)   24 τούτου Gö.: τοῦτο P   26 f καὶ τῶν
Roeper: ἡ τῶν P   27 ⟨ ⟩ We.   28 + ἢ Harvey Iren. I S. CXVII: + καὶ
Roeper   ⟨γὰρ⟩ γένη? We., ⟨δὲ⟩ γένη Petersen   γέννη P

and the two mother. / For the dyad was born from the monad according to Pythagoras and the monad is male and primary and the dyad female. And besides the dyad there is the triad and the numbers in sequence up to ten, as Pythagoras says. For Pythagoras knows of ten as the only perfect number; eleven and twelve are additions and repetitions of the decad, not the birth of another number. And he generates all three dimensional bodies from incorporeals; he says that the principle and element of both bodies and incorporeals alike is the point which is partless. From the point, he says, comes the line, and (from the line, plane), and plane run to depth establishes the solid body, he says. Hence the symphony of the four elements is also an oath for the Pythagoreans. They swear thus:

'Yes, by the one who transmits the tetraktys to our head,
the spring having the roots of ever-flowing nature.'

The tetraktys is the principle of natural and solid bodies, as the monad is of intelligible things. And they teach that the tetraktys generates the perfect number ten, as (the monad does) among the intelligibles, thus: if someone begins to count and says one, and adds two, and then similarly three, these will make six; add to these four, the whole will then similarly be ten. For one, two, three, and four make ten, the perfect number. Thus, it says, the tetraktys imitated the intelligible monad in all respects, being able to generate the perfect number.

24. There are, therefore, two worlds according to Pythagoras, one intelligible, which has the monad as principle, and one sensible; the principle of the latter is the tetraktys which has the iota, the 'single horn', the perfect number; and according to the Pythagoreans ten, the single horn, is the first and chief substance both of the intelligibles (and of the sensibles) apprehended intelligibly and sensibly. There are nine classes of incorporeal accidents which cannot exist without substance, quality, quantity, relation, place where, time when, position, state, acting and being acted upon. The categories accidental to substance are therefore nine, / and

151W βεβηκότα τῇ οὐσίᾳ, οἷς συναριθμουμένη ἔχει τὸν τέλειον ἀριθμόν,
τὸν ι̅. διόπερ διῃρημένου τοῦ παντός, ὡς εἴπομεν, εἰς νοητὸν καὶ |
αἰσθητὸν κόσμον, ἔχομεν καὶ ἡμεῖς ἀπὸ τοῦ νοητοῦ τὸν λόγον, ἵνα
τῷ λόγῳ τὴν τῶν νοητῶν καὶ ἀσωμάτων καὶ θείων ἐποπτεύωμεν
5 οὐσίαν· αἰσθήσεις δέ, φησίν, ἔχομεν πέντε, ὄσφρησιν, ὅρασιν, ἀκοήν,
γεῦσιν καὶ ἀφήν, ἐν οἷς τῶν αἰσθητῶν ἐρχόμεθα εἰς γνῶσιν· καὶ
οὕτω, φησίν, ἐστὶ διῃρημένος ⟨ὁ⟩ αἰσθητὸς ἀπὸ τοῦ νοητοῦ κόσμου.
καὶ ὅτι ἔχομεν γνώσεως ὄργανον πρὸς ἑκάτερον αὐτῶν, ἐντεῦθεν
κατανοῶμεν. οὐδέν, φησί, τῶν νοητῶν γνωστὸν ἡμῖν δύναται γενέ-
10 σθαι δι᾽ αἰσθήσεως· ἐκεῖνο γὰρ οὔτε ›ὀφθαλμὸς εἶδε οὔτε οὖς ἤκουσεν‹
οὔτ᾽ ἔγνω, φησί, τῶν ἄλλων αἰσθήσεων οἱαδητισοῦν. οὐδ᾽ αὖ πάλιν
τῷ λόγῳ εἰς γνῶσιν τῶν αἰσθητῶν οὐχ οἷόν τε ἐλθεῖν τινος, ἀλλὰ
δεῖ ὅτι λευκόν ἐστιν ἰδεῖν, καὶ γεύσασθαι ὅτι γλυκύ, καὶ ὅτι ᾠδικὸν
ἢ ἀπῳδικὸν ἀκούσαντας εἰδέναι, καὶ εἴ τι τῶν ὀσμῶν ἐστιν εὐῶδες
15 ἢ ἀηδές, ὀσφρήσεως ἔργον, οὐ λόγου. ὡσαύτως δὲ ἔχει καὶ τὰ τῆς
ἀφῆς· σκληρὸν γὰρ ἢ ἁπαλόν, ἢ θερμὸν ἢ ψυχρὸν οὐχ οἷόν τέ ἐστιν
ἀκούσαντα εἰδέναι, ἀλλὰ γὰρ τῶν τοιούτων ἐστὶ κρίσις ἢ ἀφή. τούτων οὕτως ὑφεστηκότων ἡ διακόσμησις τῶν γεγονότων καὶ γινομένων ἀριθμητικῶς γινομένη θεωρεῖται. ὃν γὰρ τρόπον ἀπὸ μονάδος
20 ἀρξάμενοι κατὰ προσθήκην μονάδων ἢ τριάδων καὶ τῶν ἑξῆς ἀθροι-
ζομένων ἀριθμῶν ἕν τι σύστημα ποιοῦμεν μέγιστον ἀριθμοῦ, εἶτα
πάλιν ἀπὸ τοῦ κατὰ τὴν σύνθεσιν ἀθροισθέντος ἀφαιρέσει τινὶ
καὶ ἀναποδισμῷ λύσιν τῶν συνεστώτων ἀριθμητικῶς ἐργαζόμεθα,
(25.) οὕτω φησὶ καὶ τὸν κόσμον ἀριθμητικῷ τινι καὶ μουσικῷ δεσμῷ |
25 δεδεμένον ἐπιτάσει καὶ ἀνέσει καὶ προσθήκῃ καὶ ἀφαιρέσει ἀεὶ καὶ
διὰ παντὸς ἀδιάφθορον φυλαχθῆναι. τοιγαροῦν καὶ περὶ τῆς διαμο-
νῆς τοῦ κόσμου ἀποφαίνονται τοιοῦτόν τινα τρόπον οἱ Πυθαγορικοί·

ἢ γὰρ καὶ πάρος ἦν καὶ ἔσσεται, οὐδέ ποτ᾽, οἴω,
τούτων ἀμφοτέρων κενεώσεται ἄσπετος αἰών.

10 I Kor. 2, 9 — 28 Empedokles Fr. 16 D., wiederholt VII 29, 10

1 συναριθμουμένη ἔχει Roeper: ἀριθμουμένη συνέχει P   2 τὸν ῑα P   4 ἐπι-
πτεύωμεν P   6 ἐν οἷς] αἷς We.   7 + ὁ Miller   13f ὅτι δίκαιον ἢ ἄδικον P,
verb. Gö.   15 λόγον, ⟨κρῖναι⟩ We.   20 μονάδων ⟨ἢ δυάδων⟩ Cruice   22 ἀναι-
ρέσει falsch als Text von P Miller   23 ἀναποδισμῷ Roeper: ἀναλογισμῷ P
26f διανομῆς Gö. (s. S. 152, 15)   28 ἢ Miller: ἦν P, εἰ H, ᾗ Nauck, Iam-
blichi De vita Pyth. S. 236 (so Emp.), s. zu VII 29, 10   ἦν καὶ P H: ἦν τε καὶ
Gö., ἔσκε καὶ Emp. nach Diels   ἔσται οὐδέπω τοίω P H, verb. Miller   29 κενεώσεται Roeper: κενώσεται H, καινὸς ἔσται P   ἄσπετος Miller: ἄσβεστος P H

substance counted in with them makes the perfect number, ten. The world is divided, as we said, into intelligible and sensible worlds, and we have our reason from the intelligible world, so that we can observe the substance of the intelligible and incorporeal and divine things with our reason. But we have five senses, it says, smell, sight, hearing, taste and touch, by which we come to knowledge of the sensible things. And in this way, he says, the sensible world is divided from the intelligible world. And we can tell that we have an organ of knowledge for each of them from the following. Nothing, it says, of the intelligible things can become known to us through perception. For that neither 'eye has seen nor ear heard' nor, it says, has any of the other senses known. Nor again is anyone able to come to knowledge of sensible things by reason, but one must see that it is white and taste that it is sweet and know whether it is tuneful or tuneless by hearing, and telling whether a smell is pleasant or unpleasant is the work of the sense of smell, not reason. It is the same with matters of touch; for one cannot know hard or soft or hot or cold by hearing, but the judgment of these sorts of things is the sense of touch. These things being established in this way there is a theory about the arrangement of the things that are and have been created coming about arithmetically; in the manner in which we construct one great system of number by starting from the monad and by addition of monads or triads and the numbers which are accumulated in order, and then again by subtraction from the number accumulated by combination and by reversing the process we bring about the dissolution of the constructed numbers arithmetically, (25) in this way he says that the cosmos is bound with a certain arithmetical and musical bond and is preserved indestructible for ever and throughout by tension and relaxation and addition and subtraction. And concerning the permanence of the world the Pythagoreans issue a statement in this sort of way:

'For indeed they were before and will be, nor ever I think, will the ceaseless age be devoid of these two.' /

2 τίνων δὲ τούτων; τοῦ νείκους καὶ τῆς φιλίας. ἀπεργάζεται δὲ αὐ-
152W τοῖς ἡ φιλία ἄφθαρτον, ἀίδιον τὸν κόσμον, ὡς ὑπονοοῦσιν — ἔστι γὰρ
ἡ οὐσία καὶ ὁ κόσμος ἕν —, τὸ δὲ νεῖκος διασπᾷ καὶ διαφέρει καὶ πολλὰ
3 πειρᾶται καταδιαιροῦν τὸν κόσμον ποιεῖν. ὥσπερ εἴ τις ἀριθμητικῶς
τὴν μυριάδα εἰς χιλιάδας καὶ ἑκατοντάδας καὶ δεκάδας, καὶ δραχμὰς
εἰς ὀβολοὺς καὶ κοδράντας μικροὺς κατακερματίσας τέμνει, οὕτω τὸ
νεῖκος τὴν οὐσίαν τοῦ κόσμου, φησί, τέμνει εἰς ζῷα, φυτά, μέταλλα
καὶ τὰ τούτοις παραπλήσια· καὶ ἔστι τῆς γενέσεως τῶν γινομένων
πάντων κατ᾽ αὐτοὺς δημιουργὸς τὸ νεῖκος, ἡ δ᾽ αὖ φιλία ἐπιτρο-
πεύουσα καὶ προνοουμένη τοῦ παντὸς ἵνα μένῃ καὶ εἰς τὸ ἓν ⟨τὰ⟩
διῃρημένα καὶ τοῦ παντὸς ἀπεσπασμένα συνάγουσα καὶ ἐξάγουσα τοῦ
4 βίου, συνάπτει καὶ προστίθησι τῷ παντί, ἵνα μένῃ καὶ ἔσται ἕν. οὐ
παύσεται οὖν οὔτε τὸ νεῖκος τὸν κόσμον διαιροῦν οὔτε ἡ φιλία τὰ
διῃρημένα τῷ κόσμῳ προσνέμουσα. ⟨τοι⟩αύτη τίς ἐστιν, ὡς ἔοικε,
κατὰ Πυθαγόραν ἡ τοῦ κόσμου διανομή. λέγει δὲ Πυθαγόρας εἶναι
ἀπορραγάδας τοῦ ἡλίου τοὺς ἀστέρας, καὶ τὰς ψυχὰς τῶν ζῴων ἀπὸ
τῶν ἄστρων φέρεσθαι· εἶναι δὲ αὐτὰς θνητὰς μέν, ὅταν ὦσιν ἐν τῷ
σώματι, οἱονεὶ ἐγκατορωρυγμένας ὡς ἐν τάφῳ, ἀνίστασθαι δὲ καὶ
f. 70r γίνεσθαι ἀθανάτους, ὅταν τῶν σωμάτων ἀπολυθῶμεν. ὅθεν ὁ
Πλάτων ἐρωτηθεὶς ὑπό τινος· τί ἐστι φιλοσοφία; ἔφη· χωρισμὸς
1 ψυχῆς ἀπὸ σώματος, (26.) Πυθαγόρου καὶ τούτου τῶν λόγων γενόμενος μαθητής, ἐν οἷς λέγει καὶ δι᾽ αἰνιγμάτων [καὶ τοιούτων

---

15 f u. S. 153, 10 f Plato, Timaios 41 D. διεῖλε ψυχὰς ἰσαρίθμους τοῖς ἄστροις
Zeller III 2³ S. 138¹; Cumont, Les religions orientales dans le paganisme romain²
p. 264. 398 f; Le mysticisme astral, Bull. de l'Acad. royale de Belgique 1909
S. 265 ff — 18 vgl. S. 93, 13 οἱονεὶ ἐν μνήματι καὶ τάφῳ ἐγκατωρυγμένον ἐν
τῷ σώματι. Philolaos Fr. 14 Diels ἁ ψυχὰ τῷ σώματι συνέζευκται καὶ καθάπερ ἐν σάματι τούτῳ τέθαπται. Orpheus Fr. 3 Diels — 19 ff Plato, Phaidon 64 C.
65 A ff

---

2 ⟨καὶ⟩ ἀίδιον We.   4 καταδιαιροῦν Cruice (s. Z. 13): καταδιαιροῦσα P
ὥσπερ ⟨οὖν⟩ We.   6 εἰς Roeper: καὶ P   6 f τὸν εἰκοστὴν P, verb. Roeper (Harvey
Iren. I S. XLV)   7 μετ᾽ ἄλλα P   10 + τὰ Miller   12 συνάπτει Gö.: συνάγει
P aus Z. 11   ἵνα μένῃ καὶ ἔσται ἕν We.: ἵνα μένῃ, καὶ ἔστιν ἕν P, > Diels (s.
Z. 10)   14 τοιαύτη Cruice vgl. S. 155, 15: αὕτη P   17 ὦσιν Miller: εἰσίν P
19 ἀπολυθῶσιν We.   21 Πυθαγόρου Roeper: πυθαγόρας οὖν P   καὶ > Cruice
τούτου τῶν We.: τούτων τῶν P, τοιούτων Cruice, s. zu Z. 22   22 ἐν οἷς]
σεμνῶς Diels (Z. 21 nach P)   22 f καὶ τοιούτων λόγων > Cruice (emendierende
Randnote zu Z. 21?)

But what are 'these two'? Strife and Love. For Love makes the cosmos imperishable and eternal, so they think – for substance and the cosmos are one – but Strife disperses and differentiates and tries to make the cosmos many by dividing it. As if someone divides ten thousand arithmetically into thousands and hundreds and tens, and chops up drachmas into obols and small quadrantes, so Strife, it says, cuts up the substance of the cosmos into animals, plants, minerals and such like. And according to them Strife is the 'creator of all the things that come into being, but Love is the one who acts as guardian and takes forethought for the whole that it should remain and brings together into one the things that have been divided and scattered from the whole, so that it may remain and be one. Neither Strife dividing the cosmos nor Love adding the divided parts to the cosmos will ever cease. Some such, so it seems, is the arrangement of the cosmos according to Pythagoras. And Pythagoras says that the stars are fragments of the sun, and that the souls of animals are brought down from the stars; and these souls are mortal when they are in the body, as if buried in a tomb, but they rise up and become immortal when we are released from our bodies. Hence Plato, asked once by someone 'What is philosophy?' replied: the separation of soul from body, (26) becoming a disciple of Pythagoras and his doctrines in which he says enigmatically: / 'If you are away

268   Rethinking Early Greek Philosophy

153W λόγων]· »ἐκ τῆς ἰδίης ἐὰν ἀποδημῇς, μὴ ἐπιστρέφου· εἰ δὲ μή, Ἐριν-
νύες Δίκης ἐπίκουροί σε μετελεύσονται«· ἰδίην καλῶν τὸ σῶμα,
Ἐριννύας δὲ τὰ πάθη. ἐὰν οὖν, φησίν, ἀποδημῇς, τουτέστιν ἐὰν 2
ἐξέρχῃ ἐκ τοῦ σώματος, μὴ αὐτοῦ ἀντιποιοῦ· ἐὰν δὲ ἀντιποιήσῃ,
5 πάλιν σε τὰ πάθη καθείρξουσιν εἰς σῶμα. εἶναι γὰρ οὗτοι τῶν
ψυχῶν μετενσωμάτωσιν νομίζουσιν, ὡς καὶ ὁ Ἐμπεδοκλῆς πυθαγορί-
ζων λέγει. δεῖ γάρ, φησί, τὰς φιληδόνους ψυχάς, ὡς ὁ Πλάτων 3
λέγει, ἐὰν ἐν ἀνθρώπου πάθει γενόμεναι μὴ φιλοσοφήσωσι, διὰ πάντων ζῴων ἐλθεῖν καὶ φυτῶν πάλιν εἰς ἀνθρώπινον σῶμα, καὶ ἐὰν
10 μὲν φιλοσοφήσῃ κατὰ τὸ αὐτὸ τρίς, εἰς τὴν τοῦ συννόμου ἄστρου
φύσιν ἀνελθεῖν, ἐὰν δὲ μὴ φιλοσοφήσῃ, πάλιν ἐπὶ τὰ αὐτά. δύνασθαι
οὖν φησί ποτε τὴν ψυχὴν καὶ θνητὴν γενέσθαι, ἐὰν ὑπὸ τῶν Ἐριν-
νύων κρατῆται, τουτέστι τῶν παθῶν, καὶ ἀθάνατον, ἐὰν τὰς Ἐριννῦς
ἐκφύγῃ, ἅ ἐστι πάθη.
15   27. Ἀλλ᾽ ἐπεὶ καὶ τὰ σκοτεινῶς ὑπὸ τοῦ Πυθαγόρου λεγόμενα 1
πρὸς τοὺς μαθητὰς δι᾽ ὑποσυμβόλων ἐνηρ⟨ξά⟩μεθα λέγειν, δοκεῖ καὶ
τῶν ἑτέρων ὑπομνησθῆναι διὰ τὸ καὶ τοὺς αἱρεσιάρχας τοιούτῳ τινὶ
τρόπῳ ἐπικεχειρηκέναι ὁμιλεῖν διὰ ὑποσυμβόλων, καὶ τοῦτο οὐκ ἰδίων,
ἀλλὰ Πυθαγορείων πλεονεκτήσαντας λόγων. διδάσκει οὖν ὁ Πυθα- 2
20 γόρας τοὺς μαθητὰς λέγων· »τὸν στρωματόδεσμον δῆσον«, ἐπεὶ οἱ
ὁδοιπορεῖν μέλλοντες εἰς δέρμα δεσμοῦσι τὰ ἱμάτια αὐτῶν | πρὸς f.
ἑτοιμασίαν τῆς ὁδοῦ, οὕτως ἑτοίμους εἶναι θέλων τοὺς μαθητάς, ὡς καθ᾽
ἑκάστην στιγμὴν τοῦ θανάτου ἐφεστηκέναι μέλλοντος, μηδὲν ἔχοντας
τῶν μαθη⟨μά⟩των ἐνδεές. διόπερ ἐξ ἀνάγκης ἅμα τῷ ἡμέραν γενέσθαι 3
25 ἐδίδασκε διακελεύεσθαι αὐτοῖς τοὺς Πυθαγορείους »δεσμεύειν τὸν
στρωματόδεσμον«, τουτέστιν ἑτοίμους εἶναι πρὸς θάνατον. »πῦρ

1 Iamblich Protr. 21 S. 107, 14. 114, 29 ff P ist. ἀποδημῶν τῆς οἰκείας μὴ
ἐπιστρέφου· Ἐρινύες γὰρ μετέρχονται (vgl. Heraklit Fr. 94 D.). — Ebenda S. 115, 9
θάνατος δὲ ὁ τῆς ψυχῆς χωρισμὸς ἀπὸ τοῦ σώματος (s. 152, 20 f). Die Deutungen
Iamblichs und Hippolyts gehen auf eine Quelle zurück; vgl. Porphyrios V. Pyth.
S. 39, 14. 15 N.; Diog. Laert. VIII 18; Plut. Numa 14 — 6 Empedokles] Fr. 117 ff D.,
vgl. Zeller III 2³ S. 138¹ — 7 Plato] Phaidros 248 Eff — 20 Diog. Laert. VIII 17
τὰ στρώματα ἀεὶ συνδεδεσμένα ἔχειν, vgl. Xenophon Cyropädie VIII 7, 2 —
26 f vgl. Porph. V. Pyth. 42; Iamblich Prot. 21 S. 112, 24 ff P.; vgl. Hölk, De acus-
matis Pythagoricis, Kiel 1894 p. 53

1 ἰδίας P, verb. Cruice nach Z. 2   13 κρατῆται aus κρατεῖται P   14 ⟨τὰ⟩
πάθη oder ἅ ἐστι πάθη > Diels   16 ἐνηρξάμεθα Gö.: ἐνήρμεθα P, ἐνήργμεθα
Göttling (Progr. Jena 1852) Roeper   18 οὐχ P   19 πλεονεκτήσαντες P, verb. Klost.
22 θέλειν P, verb. We. (θέλει Miller)   25 διακελεύεσθε αὐτοῖς P   26 ff f. 72 r (!)
oben a. R. πῦρ μαχαίρῃ — τὸν θυμούμενον — ἐρέθιζε. ἄσαρον(?) μὴ ὑπέρβαινε P

from your own home do not go back; otherwise the Erinyes, companions of Justice, will come after you.' By 'your own home' he refers to the body, and by the Erinyes he means the passions. If, therefore, you go away from home, he says, that is if you come out of the body, do not seek it again; but if you do seek it again the passions will shut you up again into the body. For the Pythagoreans believe in the reincarnation of souls, as also Empedocles does, Pythagorising. For it is necessary, it says, for pleasure-loving souls to go through all sorts of animals and plants and back into the body of a man, if when they are in the human condition they do not do philosophy, so Plato says, and if one does philosophy three times in succession one goes up to the nature of one's associated star, but if one does not do philosophy one comes back to the same things. Hence he says that the soul can sometimes be mortal if it is overcome by the Erinyes, that is the passions, and immortal if it escapes the Erinyes, who are the passions.

27. Given that we have started to relate the sayings of Pythagoras expressed in symbolic form to his disciples, it is a good idea to mention the rest as well because the heresiarchs also attempted to discourse in this kind of way by means of symbols, and this not with their own sayings but stealing Pythagorean ones. Pythagoras teaches his disciples saying 'Tie up your bedding', since those preparing to go on a journey tie up their clothes in a bag in readiness for the road, and he wishes his disciples to be ready in the same way, and not to have any lack of teachings, death being about to come upon them at every point. For this reason he taught the Pythagoreans that as soon as day began they must perforce command themselves to bind up their bedding, that is to be

154W μαχαίρῃ μὴ σκάλευε«, τὸν τεθυμωμένον ἄνθρωπον λέγων μὴ ἐρέθιζε·
4 πυρὶ γὰρ ἔοικεν ὁ θυμούμενος, μαχαίρᾳ δὲ λόγος. »σάρον μὴ ὑπέρβαινε«, μικροῦ πράγματος μὴ καταφρόνει. »φοίνικα ἐν οἰκίᾳ μὴ φύτευε«, φιλονεικίαν ἐν οἰκίᾳ μὴ κατασκεύαζε· μάχης γὰρ καὶ διαφορᾶς
ἐστιν ὁ φοῖνιξ σημεῖον. »ἀπὸ δίφρου μὴ ἔσθιε«, βάναυσον τέχνην μὴ
μεταχειρίζου, ἵνα μὴ δουλεύσῃς τῷ σώματι ὄντι φθαρτῷ, ἀλλὰ ποιοῦ
τὸν βίον ἀπὸ λόγων· ἐνέσται γάρ σοι καὶ τρέφειν τὸ σῶμα καὶ τὴν
5 ψυχὴν ποιεῖν κρείττονα. »ἀπὸ ὅλου ἄρτου μὴ ἀπόδακνε«· τὰ ὑπάρ-
χοντά σου μὴ μειοῦ, ἀλλὰ ἀπὸ τῆς προσόδου ζῆθι, φύλασσε δὲ τὴν
οὐσίαν ὡς ἄρτον ὁλόκληρον. »κυάμους μὴ ἔσθιε«, ἀρχὴν πόλεως
μὴ ἀποδέχου· κυάμοις γὰρ ἐκληροῦντο τὰς ἀρχὰς κατ᾽ ἐκεῖνον τὸν
χρόνον.
1 28. Ταῦτα μὲν οὖν καὶ τὰ τοιαῦτα οἱ Πυθαγόρειοι λέγουσιν, οὓς
μιμούμενοι οἱ αἱρετικοὶ μεγάλα νομίζονταί τισι λέγειν. δημιουργὸν
δὲ εἶναι τῶν γενομένων πάντων φησὶν ὁ Πυθαγόρειος λόγος τὸν
μέγαν γεωμέτρην καὶ ἀριθμητὴν ἥλιον καὶ ἐστηρίχθαι τοῦτον ἐν ὅλῳ
τῷ κόσμῳ, καθάπερ ἐν τοῖς σώμασι ψυχήν, ὥς φησιν ὁ Πλάτων.
2 πῦρ γάρ ἐστιν ἥλιος ⟨ὡς⟩ ψυχή, σῶμα δὲ γῆ. »χωρισθὲν δὲ πυρὸς
οὐδὲν ἄν ποτε ὁρατὸν γένοιτο οὐδὲ ἁπτὸν ἄνευ τινὸς στερεοῦ·

2 Plut. Aetia Romana 112 S. 290 E., Quaest. conviv. VIII, 7, 1 p. 727 C —
3 Plut. De Iside 10 S. 354 F. — 5 Plut. Aetia Rom. a. a. O., De Iside a. a. O.
— 8 Suid. s. v. Ἀναξίμανδρος: ἀπὸ ὁλοκλήρου ἄρτου μὴ ἐσθίειν — 10 ff Ps.
Plut. De educ. puerorum 17 p. 12 EF, Corssen Rh. M. LVII 259 — 16 u. S. 155, 2 f
vgl. Cumont in der zu Z. 18 citierten Schrift S. 459 ff. Eine genaue Parallele
kenne ich nicht — 18 vgl. Chaldäisches Orakel bei Proclus In Remp. II 220, 14 Kroll
τὸ ἡλιακὸν πῦρ κραδίης τόπῳ ἐστήριξεν (Kroll· De orac. Chald. S. 32), vgl.
Cumont, La théologie solaire, Mémoires présentés à l'Académie des inscriptions
et belles-lettres XII 458. 471 — 17 Plato] wo? Das Citat scheint erst aufs
Folgende zuzutreffen, s. die folgende Note — 18—S. 155, 2 Plato Timaios 31 B:
σωματοειδὲς δὲ δὴ καὶ ὁρατὸν ἁπτόν τε δεῖ τὸ γενόμενον εἶναι· χωρισθὲν δὲ πυρὸς
οὐδὲν ἄν ποτε ὁρατὸν γένοιτο οὐδὲ ἁπτὸν ἄνευ τινὸς στερεοῦ, στερεὸν δὲ οὐκ ἄνευ
γῆς. ὅθεν ἐκ πυρὸς καὶ γῆς τὸ τοῦ παντὸς ἀρχόμενος ξυνιστάναι σῶμα ὁ θεὸς
ἐποίει . . . 32 B οὕτω δὴ πυρός τε καὶ γῆς ὕδωρ ἀέρα τε ὁ θεὸς ἐν μέσῳ θείς . . .

1 μαχαίρᾳ Hölk a. a. O., vgl. S. 153, 1, u. vorige Note   2 μάχαιρα P
σάρον Roeper: ἄσαρον P   3 f f. 71ʳ oben a. R. φιλονικίαν μὴ κατασκεύαζε.
φοίνικα — φύτευε P   4 διαφθορᾶς P, verb. Roeper   7 τῶν βίων ἀπόλογον P
11 f ἐκείνων τῶν χρόνων P   15 γενομένων Gö.: λεγομένων P   17 ὡς γὰρ
Diels (Z. 18 γὰρ >)   18 + ὡς Roeper   δὲ γῇ Roeper: σελήνη P   χωρι-
σθέντων P

ready for death. 'Do not poke the fire / with a sword,' meaning do not provoke an angry man. For he likens the angry man to fire and speech to a sword. 'Do not step over a besom' – do not despise a small matter. 'Do not rear a phoenix in your own home' – do not foster rivalry in your home; for the phoenix is the sign of hostility and disagreement. 'Do not eat from a stool' – do not turn your hand to banausic skill, so that you may not be enslaved to the body which is perishable, but make your living from words. For it will be possible for you both to nourish your body and to make your soul better. 'Do not take a bite from a whole loaf' – do not diminish your capital but live off the income and preserve your property as a whole loaf. 'Do not eat beans' – do not accept office in the government. For they used beans for the elections to offices in those days.

28. These and similar things are what the Pythagoreans say, and imitating them the heretics are believed by some to say great things. And the Pythagorean theory says that the creator of all the things that come to be is the great geometer and mathematician the sun and that this is set in the whole cosmos like the soul in bodies, as Plato says. For the sun and soul are fire and the body is earth. 'But without fire nothing could ever become visible, nor tangible without some solid; /

155W   στερεὸν δὲ οὐκ ἄνευ γῆς. ὅθεν ἐκ πυρὸς καὶ γῆς ἀέρα τε | ὁ θεὸς f. ?
ἐν μέσῳ θέμενος‹ τὸ τοῦ παντὸς ἐδημιούργησε σῶμα.
ἀριθμεῖ δέ,
φησί, καὶ γεωμετρεῖ τὸν κόσμον ὁ ἥλιος τοιοῦτόν τινα τρόπον· ὁ 3
μὲν κόσμος ἐστὶν ὁ αἰσθητὸς εἷς, περὶ οὗ λέγομεν τὰ νῦν. διήρηκε
5 δ' αὐτὸν ἀριθμητικός τις ὢν καὶ γεωμέτρης εἰς μοίρας ιβ. καὶ ἔστι
ταῖς μοίραις ταύταις ὀνόματα· Κριός, Ταῦρος, Δίδυμοι, Καρκίνος,
Λέων, Παρθένος, Ζυγός, Σκορπίος, Τοξότης, Αἰγόκερως, Ὑδροχόος,
Ἰχθύες. πάλιν τῶν δώδεκα μοιρῶν ἑκάστην διαιρεῖ εἰς μοίρας τριά- 4
κοντα, αἵτινές εἰσιν ἡμέραι μηνός. πάλιν αὖ τῶν τριάκοντα μοιρῶν
10 ἑκάστην μοῖραν διαιρεῖ εἰς λεπτὰ ἑξήκοντα καὶ τῶν λεπτῶν λεπτὰ
καὶ ἔτι λεπτότερα. καὶ τοῦτο ἀεὶ ποιῶν καὶ μὴ παυόμενος, ἀλλ'
ἀθροίζων ἐκ τούτων ⟨τῶν⟩ μοιρῶν τῶν διῃρημένων καὶ ποιῶν ἐνιαυτόν, καὶ αὖθις ἀναλύων καὶ διαιρῶν τὸ συγκείμενον τὸν μέγαν ἐνιαυτὸν ἀπεργάζεται κόσμου.

*

1 ⟨ὕδωρ⟩ ἀέρα τε We., s. Zeugnisse   6 δίδυμος P   9 αὐτῶν τῶν P
10 ἑκάστων P   12 τοῦ τῶν P   + τῶν Gö.   13f ἐνιαυτὸν Roeper: ἀθάνατον P   14 κόσμου Roeper: κόσμον P, τοῦ κόσμου Diels

but there is no solid without earth; hence from fire and earth God set air in the middle' and created the body of the universe. But the sun, it says, makes the cosmos numerical and geometrical in this sort of way: the cosmos is the sensible unity about which we speak at present. But being a mathematician and geometer he divided it into twelve parts. And the names of these parts are: Aries, Taurus, Gemini, Cancer, Leo, Virgo, Libra, Scorpio, Sagittarius, Capricorn, Aquarius, Pisces. Then again he divides each of the twelve parts into thirty parts, which are the days of the month. Then again he divides each of the thirty parts into sixty minutes and divisions of these and yet smaller divisions. And always going on doing this and not ceasing, but gathering together and making a year out of these divided parts and then again dissolving and dividing up the composition, he completes the great year of the cosmos.

*

Book 7, chapter 14

191W　　14. Ἐπειδὴ οὖν ἐν ταῖς πρὸ ταύτης βίβλοις ἓξ ἐκτεθείμεθα τὰ
πρότερα, δοκεῖ νῦν τὰ Βασιλείδου μὴ σιωπᾶν ⟨ὄν⟩τα Ἀριστοτέλους
τοῦ Σταγειρίτου δόγματα, οὐ Χριστοῦ. ἀλλ᾽ εἰ καὶ πρότερον ἔκκειται
15 τὰ Ἀριστοτέλει δοκοῦντα, οὐδὲ νῦν ὀκνήσομεν προϋποθέσθαι ἐν συν-
τόμῳ, πρὸς τὸ τοὺς ἐντυγχάνοντας διὰ τῆς τούτων ἔγγιον ἀντιπαραθέσεως συνιδεῖν εὐκόλως τὰ ὑπὸ Βασιλείδου ὄντα Ἀριστοτελικὰ
σοφιστεύματα.
　　15. Ἀριστοτέλης μὲν οὖν τὴν οὐσίαν διαιρεῖ τριχῶς. ἔστι γὰρ 1
20 αὐτῆς τὸ μέν τι γένος, τὸ δέ τι εἶδος, ὡς ἐκεῖνος λέγει, τὸ δέ τι
ἄτομον· ἄτομον δὲ οὐ διὰ σμικρότητα σώματος, ἀλλὰ φύσει τομὴν
ἀναδέξασθαι μηδ᾽ ἡντιναοῦν δυνάμενον. τὸ δὲ γένος ἐστὶν οἱονεὶ 2
σωρός τις ἐκ πολλῶν καὶ διαφόρων καταμεμιγμένος σπερμάτων, |
ἀφ᾽ οὗ γένους οἱονεί τινος σωροῦ πάντα τὰ τῶν γεγονότων εἴδη f.
25 διακέκριται. καὶ ἔστι τὸ γένος (ἓν) ὂν πᾶσι τοῖς γεγενημένοις ἀρκοῦν.
ἵνα δὲ σαφὲς ἔσται τὸ λεγόμενον, δείξω διὰ τὸν παραδείγματος, δι᾽
οὗ ἐπὶ τὴν ὅλην τοῦ Περιπάτου θεωρίαν ἀναδραμεῖν ἔσται.
　　16. Λέγομεν εἶναι ζῷον ἁπλῶς, οὐχὶ τὶ ζῷον. ἔστι δὲ τοῦτο τὸ 1
ζῷον οὐ βοῦς, οὐχ ἵππος, οὐκ ἄνθρωπος, οὐ θεός, οὐκ ἄλλο τι τῶν

---

14 s. I 20 — 21 ἄτομον] Arist. Kategorien 2. 5 S. 1b 6. 3a 35

12 προταύταις P　　13 ὄντα Gö.: τὰ P　　16 τούτων ἔγγιον (oder ἐγγίονος?
We.) Gö.: τῶν ἔγγιον ὧν P, τῶν ἐγγιζόντων Miller　　17 ὑπὸ >? We.　　21 τὸ
μὴν P　　22 οἱονεὶ P　　24 γένους > Diels　　οἱονεὶ P　　25 διακέκριται Roeper:
διάκεινται P　　ἓν ὂν Cruice (vgl. S. 193, 6), o und Gravis des voraufgehenden
Wortes sichtbar: θεὸς ὂν P nach Miller, αἴτιον Gö., πρῶτον Baur, Theol.
Jahrb. XV 1856 S. 147　　26 διὰ τοῦ P

Book 7, chapter 14.

Given that we have expounded the earlier things in the preceding six books, now is the time to break our silence on the doctrines of Basileides which are doctrines belonging to Aristotle the Stagirite, not to Christ. But although the doctrines of Aristotle have been set forth earlier, nevertheless we shall not hesitate to give a preliminary summary now, so that the readers may easily see that the sophistries put out by Basileides are Aristotelian ones, by means of the closer comparative juxtaposition.

15. Aristotle divides substance into three. One part of it is *genos*, one part is *eidos*, as he says, and one part is the individual; 'indivisible' (*atomon*) not due to smallness of body, but not being capable of undergoing any division by nature. But the genus is as it were a heap mixed up of many different seeds, and from this genus all the species of things that come to be are separated off as if from a heap. And the genus is one thing, sufficing for all the things that have come to be. But to make it clear I shall illustrate it with an example, by means of which it will be possible to proceed to the entire philosophy of the Peripatos.

16. We say that there is such a thing as animal straightforwardly, not any particular animal. This animal is not ox, not horse, not man, not god, not any other of those /

192W ὁ τιδήποτε ἔστι δηλοῦν, ἀλλὰ ἁπλῶς ζῷον. ἀπὸ τούτου τοῦ ζῴου
2 αἱ πάντων τῶν κατὰ μέρος ζῴων ἰδέαι τὴν ὑπόστασιν ἔχουσι. καὶ
ἔστιν ὑπόστασις τοῖς ζῴοις τοῖς γεγενημένοις ἐν εἴδεσι τοῦτο τὸ
ἀνείδεον ζῷον καὶ τῶν γεγενημένων οὐδέν. ἔστι γὰρ ἄνθρωπος
ζῷον ἀπ᾽ ἐκείνου τοῦ ζῴου λαμβάνον τὴν ἀρχήν, καὶ ζῷον ἵππος
ἀπ᾽ ἐκείνου τοῦ ζῴου λαμβάνον τὴν ἀρχήν. ὁ ἵππος καὶ βοῦς καὶ
κύων καὶ τῶν ἄλλων ζῴων ἕκαστον ἀπὸ τοῦ ζῴου τοῦ ἁπλοῦ λαμβάνει τὴν ἀρχήν, ὅ ἐστι τούτων οὐδὲ ἕν. (17.) εἰ δὲ οὐκ ἔστι τούτων οὐδὲ ἕν ἐκεῖνο τὸ ζῷον, ἐξ οὐκ ὄντων γέγονεν ἡ τῶν γεγενημένων κατὰ Ἀριστοτέλην ὑπόστασις· ⟨καὶ⟩ γὰρ τὸ ζῷον, ὅθεν ταῦτα
ἐλήφθη ⟨τὰ⟩ κατὰ μέρος, ἐστὶν οὐδὲ ἕν· οὐδὲ ἓν [οὐδὲ ἐν] δὲ ὂν γέγονε
τῶν ὄντων μία τις ἀρχή. τίς δὲ ὁ ταύτην καταβεβλημένος τὴν οὐσίαν τῶν γεγονότων ὕστερον ἀρχήν, ἐπὶ τὸν οἰκεῖον ἐρχόμενοι τούτων λόγον ἐροῦμεν.
1 18. Ἐπειδὴ ⟨δέ⟩ ἐστιν ἡ οὐσία τριχῇ ⟨διῃρημένη⟩, ὡς ἔφην, γένος,
εἶδος, ἄτομον, καὶ ἐθέμεθα τὸ γένος εἶναι ζῷον, τὸν δὲ ἄνθρωπον
εἶδος τῶν πολλῶν ζῴων ἤδη κεχωρισμένον, [ἔτι] συγκεχυμένον δὲ
ὅμως ἔτι καὶ μήπω μεμορφωμένον εἰς εἶδος οὐσίας ὑποστατῆς, ὀνόματι μορφώσας τὸν ἀπὸ τοῦ γένους ληφθέντα ἄνθρωπον ὀνομάζω
Σωκράτην ἢ Διογένην ἤ τι τῶν πολλῶν ὀνομάτων ἕν, καὶ ἐπειδὰν
ὀνόματι καταλάβω τὸν ἄνθρωπον εἶδος γένους γεγενημένον, ἄτομον
2 καλῶ τὴν τοιαύτην οὐσίαν. ἐτμήθη γὰρ τὸ μὲν γένος εἰς εἶδος, τὸ
δὲ εἶδος εἰς ἄτομον, τὸ δὲ ἄτομον, ἐπειδὰν γένηται ὀνόματι κατειλημ-
f. 87ʳ μένον, οὐχ οἷον τμηθῆναι κατὰ φύσιν εἰς ἄλλο τι, | ὡς ἐτέμομεν τῶν
προλελεγμένων ἕκαστον. ταύτην Ἀριστοτέλης πρώτως καὶ μάλιστα
καὶ κυριώτατα (οὐσίαν καλεῖ) μήτε καθ᾽ ὑποκειμένου τινὸς λεγομένην

17 ff Seneca Ep. 58, 16 quod generaliter est, tamquam homo generalis, sub
oculos non venit, sed specialis venit ut Cicero et Cato. Vgl. § 12 — 25 Ari-
stoteles] Kategorien 5 S. 2a 11 οὐσία δέ ἐστιν ἡ κυριώτατά τε καὶ πρώτως καὶ
μάλιστα λεγομένη, ἢ μήτε καθ᾽ ὑποκειμένου τινὸς λέγεται μήτ᾽ ἐν ὑποκειμένῳ
τινί ἐστιν

3 ἔστιν ὑπόστασις Gö.: ἔστι πᾶσις P   ἴδεσι P   4 ἀνίδεον P   5 λαμβάνων P   6 λαμβάνων P   10 + καὶ Gö.   11 + τὰ We.   [οὐδὲ ἐν] δὲ ὂν Gö.:
οὐδὲ ἐνδέον P   12 f τὴν οὐσίαν > Cruice   οὖσαν Klost.   13 f τούτων λόγον
(vgl. VII 22, 16) We.: τοιοῦτον λόγον P, τοιούτων λόγον Gö., λόγον Cruice
15 + δέ Gö.   + διῃρημένη Gö.   17 ἔτι > Miller   18 ὑποστατικῆς Gö.
19 ὀνομάζω We.: ὀνομάζων P   20 καὶ > Roeper   24 οἷόν ⟨τε⟩ Miller
25 πρώτην P, s. S. 193, 21f   26 κυριωτάτην P   ( ) Miller

that it is possible to identify in any way whatsoever, but simply animal. From this animal all the forms of the particular animals have their subsistence. And this formless animal, which is none of the things that have come to be, is the hypostasis for the animals which have come to be in the species. For man is an animal taking his origin from that animal, and horse is an animal taking its origin from that animal. Horse and ox and dog and each of the other animals takes its origin from the simple animal, which itself is not a single one of these. (17) But if that animal is not a single one of these, then the subsistence of the things that have come to be comes from non-existents, according to Aristotle. For the animal from which these particular animals are taken is not a single thing; but being not a single thing it became a single principle for the things that are. But who it is who lays down the substance as the origin of the things which come to be later, we shall say when we come to the proper account of these things.

18. Since substance is divided into three, as I said, genus, species and individual, and we posited that the genus was animal, and man a species already separated out from the many animals but still a collection and not yet shaped into a form of real substance, when I give shape to the man that is taken from the genus with a name and call it Socrates or Diogenes or one of the many names, and when I pick out by name the species man that has come from the genus, then I call that substance the individual. For the genus was divided into species and the species into individual, but the individual once it has become distinguished by name, cannot in accordance with nature, be divided into anything else, as we divided each of the aforesaid things. Aristotle calls this primarily, most of all and most properly substance, that which is neither said of a substrate / nor in a substrate. He uses the

193W μήτε ἐν ὑποκειμένῳ οὖσαν. καθ᾽ ὑποκειμένου λέγει οἱονεὶ τὸ γένος, 3
ὅπερ ἔφην ζῷον κατὰ πάντων τῶν κατὰ μέρος ὑποκειμένων ζῴων,
οἱονεὶ βοός, ἵππου καὶ τῶν ἐφεξῆς, κοινῷ ὀνόματι λεγόμενον.
ἀληθὲς γάρ ἐστιν εἰπεῖν, ὅτι ζῷον ἄνθρωπός ἐστι καὶ ζῷον ἵππος καὶ ζῷόν
5 ἐστι βοῦς καὶ τῶν ἄλλων ἕκαστον· τοῦτ᾽ ἔστι τὸ καθ᾽ ὑποκειμένου,
τὸ ἕν ὂν κατὰ πολλῶν καὶ διαφόρων τοῖς εἴδεσι δυνάμενον ὁμοίως
λέγεσθαι. οὐδὲν γὰρ διαφέρει ἵππος ἀνθρώπου ἢ ζῷον οὐδὲ βοῦς· 4
ὄρος γὰρ ὁ τοῦ ζῴου πᾶσιν ἁρμόζει τοῖς ζῴοις ὁμοίως λεγόμενος.
τί γάρ ἐστι ζῷον ἂν ὁριζώμεθα, πάντα τὰ ζῷα κοινὸς καταλήψεται
10 ὄρος. ζῷον γάρ ἐστιν οὐσία ἔμψυχος, αἰσθητική· τοῦτο βοῦς, ἄνθρωπος, ἵππος, τῶν ἄλλων ἕκαστον. ἐν ὑποκειμένῳ δέ, φησίν, ἐστίν, 5
»ὃ ἔν τινι μὴ ὡς μέρος ὑπάρχον ἀδύνατον χωρὶς εἶναι τοῦ ἐν ᾧ ἐστι«,
⟨ὃ ἐστι⟩ τῶν συμβεβηκότων ἕκαστον τῇ οὐσίᾳ, ὃ καλεῖται ποιότης,
καθ᾽ ὃ ποιοί τινες λεγόμεθα, οἷον λευκοί, γλαυκοί, μέλανες, δίκαιοι,
15 ἄδικοι, σώφρονες καὶ τὰ τούτων παραπλήσια. τούτων δὲ ἕν αὐτὸ
καθ᾽ αὑτὸ ἀδύνατόν ἐστι γενέσθαι, ἀλλὰ δεῖ ἔν τινι εἶναι. εἰ δὲ
οὔτε τὸ ζῷον, ὃ κατὰ πάντων λέγω τῶν καθ᾽ ἕκαστα ζῴων, οὔτε
⟨τὰ⟩ συμβεβηκότα, ἃ ἐν πᾶσιν οἷς συμβέβηκεν εὑρίσκεται, δυνατὸν
αὐτὰ καθ᾽ αὑτὰ γενέσθαι, ἐκ τούτων δὲ συμπληροῦται τὰ ἄτομα, ⟨ἐκ⟩
20 τῶν οὐκ ὄντων καθέστηκεν ἡ τριχῇ διηρημένη οὐσία οὐκ ἐξ ἄλλων
συνεστῶσα. πρώτως ἄρα καὶ κυριώτατα καὶ μάλιστα λεγομένη οὐσία
⟨εἰ⟩ ἐκ τούτων ὑπάρχει, ἐξ οὐκ ὄντων κατὰ τὸν Ἀριστοτέλην ἐστίν.
19. Ἀλλὰ περὶ μὲν τῆς οὐσίας ἀρκέσει τὰ λεγόμενα νῦν. οὐ
μόνον δὲ ἡ οὐσία καλεῖται [τὸ] γένος, εἶδος, ἄτομον. ἀλλὰ καὶ ὕλη

---

1 ff. 7 ff vgl. Arist. a. a. O. 5 S. 2a 20 ff, aber ähnlicher *Sen. Ep. 58, 9:*
homo species est, ut Aristoteles ait, equus species est, canis species est. ergo
commune aliquod quaerendum est his omnibus vinculum, quod illa complectatur
et sub se habeat. hoc quid est? animal. ergo genus esse coepit horum omnium,
quae modo rettuli, hominis equi canis, animal — **12** wörtliches Citat aus Kat.
S. 1a 24. 25 — **13 f** Kat. S. 8b 25 ποιότητα δὲ λέγω καθ᾽ ἣν ποιοί τινες εἶναι
λέγονται vgl. Gronau a. a. O. S. 23 — **14** vgl. S. 24, 7f — **21** vgl. S. 192, 25 f

1 ⟨δὲ⟩ λέγει Gö. οἷον εἰ P **2** ἔφην Roeper: ἔφη P **3** κοινῶν P
λεγομένων P **3f** ἀληθῶς γάρ ἐστιν We. **5** τὸ Miller: τοῦ P **6** ἴδεσι P
7 οὐδὲν Gö.: οὐδὲ P οὐδὲ] ὁ δὲ P **8** ⟨τὸ⟩ πᾶσιν Miller (dann ἁρμόζον
We.) ἁρμόζει Roeper: ἁρμόζειν P λεγόμενος Roeper: λεγόμενον P **10** τοῦτο]
οἷον? Miller, τουτέστι We. **12** ὑπάρχων P **13** + ὃ ἐστι Roeper **16** ἀδύνατόν Miller: τῷ δυνατὸν P **18** + τὰ Gö. **19** + ἐκ Gö. **20** καθέστηκεν
Gö.: καὶ ἔστιν P, ἔστιν Miller τριχῇ P **21** πρώτη P, ⟨ἡ⟩ πρώτως Pasquali
κυριωτάτη P **22** + εἰ Roeper **24** τὸ > Miller

term 'of a substrate' for the genus, for example, which I said was animal said of all the particular animals as substrates, such as ox, horse and so on, using a common name. For it is true to say that man is an animal and ox is an animal and each of the others. This is what is 'said of a substrate', what is one thing but able to be said similarly of many things differing in their species. For, *qua* animal, horse differs not at all from man, and nor does ox; the definition of animal fits all the animals when used in the same sense. For if we define what animal is, the definition will encompass all animals alike. For animal is an ensouled being that is perceptive; ox, man, horse, and each of the others is this. 'In a substrate', on the other hand, is, he says, 'that which subsists in something not as a part, and which is incapable of being separate from that in which it is', that is each of the things accidental to substance – this is called quality, in accordance with which we are said to be such and such, for example white, grey, black, just, unjust, sober and things like that. It is impossible for one of these to exist by itself but it must be in something. But if neither the animal, which I say of all the individual animals, nor the accidents, which are found in all the things to which they happen to belong, is capable of coming to be by itself, but the individuals are made up of these, then the three-fold substance has come to be composed not of other things but of non-existents. Clearly what is primarily and most properly and most of all called substance, if it consists of these things, consists of non-existents according to Aristotle.

19. About substance enough has been said. However substance is not only said to be genus, species and the individual, but also matter / and form and privation. But it

194W καὶ εἶδος καὶ στέρησις. διαφέρει δὲ οὐδὲν ἐν τούτοις μενούσης τῆς
τομῆς. τοιαύτης δὲ οὔσης τῆς οὐσίας ἔστιν ἡ τοῦ κόσμου διαταγὴ
f. 87ᵛ 2 γεγενημένη κατ᾽ αὐτὸν | τοιοῦτόν τινα τρόπον. ὁ κόσμος ἐστὶ κατὰ
Ἀριστοτέλην διῃρημένος εἰς μέρη πλείονα καὶ (διαφέροντα· καὶ) ἔστι
τοῦ κόσμου μέρος τοῦθ᾽ ὅπερ ἐστὶν ἀπὸ τῆς γῆς μέχρι τῆς σελήνης,
ἀπρονόητον, ἀκυβέρνητον, ἀρκούμενον μόνῃ τῇ φύσει τῇ ἑαυτοῦ, τὸ
δὲ μετὰ τὴν σελήνην ἐν πάσῃ τάξει καὶ προνοίᾳ καὶ κυβερνήσει
3 τεταγμένον μέχρι τῆς ἐπιφανείας τοῦ οὐρανοῦ· ἡ δὲ ἐπιφάνεια,
πέμπτη τις οὖσα οὐσία, φυσικῶν ἀπηλλαγμένη στοιχείων πάντων,
ἀφ᾽ ὧν ὁ κόσμος τὴν σύστασιν ἔχει· καὶ ἔστιν αὕτη τις ἡ πέμπτη
κατὰ τὸν Ἀριστοτέλην οὐσία οἱονεὶ οὐσία τις ὑπερκόσμιος. καὶ γέγονεν αὐτῷ κατὰ τὴν διαίρεσιν τοῦ κόσμου καὶ ὁ τῆς φιλοσοφίας
4 διῃρημένος λόγος. Φυσικὴ γάρ τις ἀκρόασις αὐτῷ γέγονεν, ἐν ᾗ
πεπόνηται περὶ τῶν φύσει καὶ οὐ προνοίᾳ διοικουμένων ἀπὸ τῆς
γῆς μέχρι τῆς σελήνης πραγμάτων. γέγονε δὲ αὐτῷ καὶ Μετὰ τὰ
φυσικὰ περὶ τῶν μετὰ σελήνην ἰδίᾳ τις ἄλλη οὕτως ἐπιγραφομένη
πραγματεία λόγων· γέγονε δὲ αὐτῷ περὶ πέμπτης οὐσίας ἴδιος λόγος,
ὅς ἐστιν αὐτῷ θεολογούμενος. τοιαύτη τις καὶ ἡ διαίρεσις τῶν ὅλων,
5 ὡς τύπῳ περιλαβεῖν, ⟨καὶ τῆς⟩ κατὰ Ἀριστοτέλην φιλοσοφίας. ὁ δὲ
Περὶ ψυχῆς αὐτῷ λόγος ἐστὶν ἀσαφής. ἐν τρισὶ γὰρ συγγράμμασιν
ὅλοις οὐκ ἔστιν εἰπεῖν σαφῶς ὅ τι φρονεῖ περὶ ψυχῆς Ἀριστοτέλης.
ὃν γὰρ ἀποδίδωσι τῆς ψυχῆς ὅρον ἔστιν εἰπεῖν ῥᾴδιον, τὸ δὲ ὑπὸ
6 ὅρου δεδηλωμένον ἐστὶ δυσεύρετον. ἔστι γάρ, φησί, ψυχὴ φυσικοῦ

3—8 vgl. Zeller II 2³ S. 434ff, aber der Gegensatz himmlischer und sublunarer
Region nach Art des Poseidonios gefaßt (s. zu S. 106, 1 Wendland, Philos Schrift über
die Vorsehung S. 68¹; Doxographi S. 592, 11. 12; Π. κόσμου 6; Möller, Kosmol.
S 357) — 9. 17 o. S. 24, 17, Arist. Gener. anim. II 3 S. 736 b 30: (Äther) ἕτερον σῶμα
καὶ θειότερον τῶν καλουμένων στοιχείων Zeller II 2³ S. 437f. Philo De somn. I § 21
We. πέμπτον κυκλοφορικὸν σῶμα, μηδενὸς τῶν τεττάρων στοιχείων μετέχον, vgl.
Pasquali, Gött. Nachr. 1910 S. 201. 206 ff; Capelle, Neue Jahrb. XV 537 —
15 f über den Titel s. W. Jäger, Studien zur Entstehungsgeschichte der Metaphysik
des Arist. S. 177 ff — 17 der Titel sonst nicht bezeugt — 23 f Aristoteles Περὶ
ψυχῆς II 1 S. 412a 19 ff, über ἐντελέχεια s. Wendland, S. A. B. 1897 S. 1077

---

1 ⟨οὐ⟩ διαφέρει Roeper   οὐδὲν Gö.: οὐδὲ P   ⟨καὶ⟩ ἐν Cruice   4 διάφορα καὶ
Miller (διαφέροντα We., weil 12 Buchst. fehlen)   8 τεταγμένον (oder τεταγμένῃ)
Miller: τεταγμένη P   ἀνθρώπου, a. R. οὐρανοῦ P   9 οὖσα >? We.   14 πε-
πόνηται Gö.: πεποίηται P   19 + καὶ τῆς Roeper   φιλοσοφίας Roeper, vgl.
Z. 12: φιλοσοφῆσαι P   22 ἦν P   ὂν   23 ⟨τοῦ⟩ ὅρον Klost.

makes no difference when the division is between these. Such is substance, and the arrangement of the cosmos has come about in the following manner on his view. The cosmos is, according to Aristotle, divided into several different parts; and this part which extends from the earth as far as the moon is without providence or control and self-sufficient in its own nature alone, but the part beyond the moon is arranged in order and with providence and governance as far as the outer surface of the heaven. But the outer surface is a fifth element and free from all the natural elements from which the world is constructed. And this fifth substance is as it were a *huperkosmic* substance according to Aristotle.

In accordance with the division of the cosmos Aristotle's philosophical theory has a similar division. For there are his *Physics* in which he works on matters governed by nature, not providence, from the earth to the moon; and there are his *Metaphysics* about things beyond the moon – a different special study of arguments which goes under this title: and he has a special work about the fifth substance which is his theology. Such is the division both of the universe and of philosophy on Aristotle's view, put into a schematic form. But his treatise *De anima* is unclear: in three whole books it is impossible to say clearly what Aristotle thinks about the soul. The definition that he gives is easy to recite, but the meaning conveyed by the definition is hard to discover. The soul is, he says, / 'the

195W σώματος ὀργανικοῦ ἐντελέχεια, ἢ τίς ποτέ ἐστι, λόγων ⟨πάνυ πολλῶν⟩ δεῖται καὶ μεγάλης ζητήσεως. ὁ δὲ θεός, ὁ πάντων τούτων τῶν ὄντων καλῶν αἴτιος, οὗτος τῆς ψυχῆς ἐστι [πάνυ πολλῶν] καὶ μακροτέρῳ λόγῳ θεωροῦντι γνωσθῆναι χαλεπώτερος. ὁ δὲ ὅρος, ὃν Ἀρι-
5 στοτέλης ἀποδίδωσι περὶ τοῦ θεοῦ, χαλεπὸς μὲν οὐκ ἔστι γνωσθῆναι, νοηθῆναι δέ ἐστιν ἀμήχανος. »νόησις« γάρ, φησίν, »ἔστι νοήσεως«, ὅπερ ἔστι | παντάπασιν οὐκ ὄν. ὁ δὲ κόσμος ἄφθαρτος, ἀΐδιος κατὰ Ἀριστοτέλην ἐστίν· οὐδὲν γὰρ ἔχει πλημμελὲς ἐν αὐτῷ, προνοίᾳ καὶ φύσει κυβερνώμενος. καταβέβληται δὲ Ἀριστοτέλης οὐ μόνον περὶ
10 φύσεως καὶ κόσμου καὶ προνοίας καὶ θεοῦ λόγους, ἀλλὰ γὰρ γέγονεν αὐτῷ καὶ πραγματεία λόγων τις ἠθικῶν, ἐπιγράφει δὲ ταῦτα Ἠθικὰ βιβλία, δι᾽ ὧν σπουδαῖον ἐκ φαύλου τὸ τῶν ἀκροωμένων ἦθος ἐργάζεται.

Ἐὰν ⟨οὖν⟩ ὁ Βασιλείδης εὑρεθῇ μὴ τῇ δυνάμει μόνῃ ἀλλὰ καὶ
15 τοῖς λόγοις αὐτοῖς καὶ τοῖς ὀνόμασι τὰ τοῦ Ἀριστοτέλους δόγματα εἰς τὸν εὐαγγελικὸν καὶ σωτήριον ἡμῶν λόγον μεθαρμοζόμενος, τί λείψει ἢ τὰ ἀλλότρια ἀποδόντας ἐπιδεικνύναι τοῖς τούτου μαθηταῖς, ὅτι ἐθνικοὺς ὄντας αὐτοὺς Χριστὸς οὐδὲν ὠφελήσει;
20. Βασιλείδης τοίνυν καὶ Ἰσίδωρος, ὁ Βασιλείδου παῖς γνήσιος
20 καὶ μαθητής, φησὶν εἰρηκέναι Ματθίαν αὐτοῖς λόγους ἀποκρύφους, οὓς ἤκουσε παρὰ τοῦ σωτῆρος κατ᾽ ἰδίαν διδαχθείς. ἴδωμεν οὖν πῶς καταφανῶς Βασιλείδης ὁμοῦ καὶ Ἰσίδωρος καὶ πᾶς ὁ τούτων χορὸς οὐχ ἁπλῶς καταψεύδεται μόνου Ματθίου, ἀλλὰ γὰρ καὶ τοῦ σωτῆρος αὐτοῦ. ἦν, φησίν, ὅτε ἦν οὐδέν, ἀλλ᾽ οὐδὲ τὸ οὐδὲν ἦν τι
25 τῶν ὄντων, ἀλλὰ ψιλῶς καὶ ἀνυπονοήτως δίχα παντὸς σοφίσματος ἦν ὅλως οὐδὲ ἕν. ὅταν δὲ λέγω, φησί, τὸ ἦν, οὐχ ὅτι ἦν λέγω, ἀλλ᾽ ἵνα σημάνω τοῦτο ὅπερ βούλομαι δεῖξαι, λέγω, φησίν, ὅτι ἦν ὅλως

6 Met. XII 9 S. 1074b, 33ff αὐτὸν ἄρα νοεῖ, εἴπερ ἐστὶ τὸ κράτιστον, καὶ ἔστιν ἡ νόησις νοήσεως νόησις, Zeller S. 365ff — 18 Gal. 5, 2 — 19 Cap. 20—27 ediert von Bunsen, Analecta Ante-Nicaena, London 1854, I 57ff mit Beiträgen von Bernays — 20ff Matthias] s. Klostermann, Apokrypha II² S. 14 — 24 über den Anfang ἦν, ὅτε ἦν οὐδέν s. Norden, Agnostos Theos S. 370ff; Clem. Homil. VI 3 ἦν ποτε ὅτε οὐδὲν ἦν πλὴν χάος, oben zu S. 156, 8

1 ἥτις P   λέγων P   + πάνυ πολλῶν aus Z. 3 Roeper   3 πάνυ πολλῶν > Roeper   7 ⟨καὶ⟩ ἀΐδιος? We.   8 αὐτῶ P   11 ἐπίγραφε (so) P   14 + οὖν Miller   17 λήψει P   ἀλλότρια ⟨ᾧ προσήκει⟩ Cruice   ἐπιδεικνῦν αὐτοῖς P, verb. Miller   19 Titel βασιλείδης P   20 φασὶν Miller   23 Ματθαίου P 24 τότε P   26 λέγω¹ Jacobi, Basilidis philosophi gnostici sententiae, 1852 S. 4: λέγῃ P

13*

actuality of a natural organic body', but what on earth this is
is a matter requiring much argument and a major inquiry.
But god, the cause of all these good things – he is even more
difficult to understand than the soul even to one who studies
an even longer treatise. The definition that Aristotle gives
concerning god is, on the one hand, not difficult to get to know
but it is by no means conceivable. For he says he is 'thought of
thought', which is entirely non-existent.

The cosmos is imperishable and eternal according to
Aristotle. For it has nothing faulty in it, being directed by
providence and nature. And Aristotle published treatises not
only about nature and the cosmos and providence and god,
but he also had a study of ethical arguments – the title of these
is the books of *Ethics* – by means of which he changed his
pupils' characters from bad to good.

If, therefore, Basileides is discovered adapting the doctrines
of Aristotle to the saving word of the Gospel, not merely in
effect but in the actual words and names, what will remain to
be done except restore the other man's property and
demonstrate to this man's disciples that they are gentiles and
hence Christ will be of no help to them?

20. Basileides, then, and Isidorus the illegitimate son and
disciple of Basileides, say that Matthias communicated to
them secret doctrines which he heard in private teaching from
the saviour. Let us see then how blatantly Basileides and
Isidorus and all their crew together tell lies about not merely
Matthias alone but also the saviour himself.

There once was when there was nothing, he says, but even
the nothing was not any of the things that are, but plainly and
ingenuously without any sophism there was absolutely not a
single thing. But, he says, when I say 'was' I do not mean that
it *was*, but in order to indicate what I want to demonstrate, I
mean, he says, that there was absolutely / nothing at all. For

3 οὐδέν. ἔστι γάρ, φησίν, ἐκεῖνο οὐχ ἁπλῶς ἄρρητον, ⟨ὃ⟩ ὀνομάζεται·
196W ἄρρητον γοῦν αὐτὸ καλοῦμεν, ἐκεῖνο δὲ οὐδὲ ἄρρητον· καὶ γὰρ τὸ
οὐδ᾽ ἄρρητον οὐκ ἄρρητον ὀνομάζεται, ἀλλὰ ἔστι, φησίν, ὑπεράνω
4 παντὸς ὀνόματος ὀνομαζομένου. οὐδὲ γὰρ τῷ κόσμῳ, φησίν, ἐξαρκεῖ
f. 88ᵛ τὰ ὀνόματα, οὕτως ἐστὶ πολυσχιδής, ἀλλὰ ἐπι|λέλοιπε· καὶ οὐ δέχο-
μαι, φησί, κατὰ πάντων εὑρεῖν κυρίως ὀνόματα, ἀλλὰ δεῖ τῇ διανοίᾳ
† αὐτοῖς ὀνόματα τῶν ὀνομαζομένων τὰς ἰδιότητας ἀρρήτως ἐκλαμ-
βάνειν. ἡ γὰρ ὁμωνυμία ταραχὴν ἐμπεποίηκε καὶ πλάνην τῶν πραγ-
5 μάτων τοῖς ἀκροωμένοις. τοῦτο πρῶτον σφετέρισμα καὶ κλέμμα τοῦ
Περιπάτου λαβόντες ἀπατῶσι τὴν ἄνοιαν τῶν συναγελαζομένων ἅμα
αὐτοῖς· πολλαῖς γὰρ γενεαῖς Ἀριστοτέλης Βασιλείδου γεγενημένος
πρότερος τὸν περὶ τῶν ὁμωνύμων ἐν ταῖς Κατηγορίαις καταβέβληται
λόγον, ὃν ὡς ἴδιον οὗτοι καὶ καινόν τινα καὶ τῶν Ματθίου λόγων
κρυφίων τινὰ † ἐνδιασαφοῦσιν.

1 21. Ἐπεὶ ⟨οὖν⟩ οὐδὲν ⟨ἦν⟩, οὐχ ὕλη, οὐκ οὐσία, οὐκ ἀνούσιον,
οὐχ ἁπλοῦν, οὐ σύνθετον, οὐκ † ἀνόητον, οὐκ ἀναίσθητον, οὐκ ἄνθρωπος, οὐκ ἄγγελος, οὐ θεός, οὐδὲ ὅλως τι τῶν ὀνομαζομένων ἢ δι᾽
αἰσθήσεως λαμβανομένων ἢ νοητῶν πραγμάτων, ἀλλ᾽ οὕτω καὶ ἔτι
λεπτομερεστέρως πάντων ἁπλῶς περιγεγραμμένων, ⟨ὁ⟩ οὐκ ὢν θεός,
ὃν Ἀριστοτέλης καλεῖ νόησιν νοήσεως, οὗτοι δὲ οὐκ ὄντα, ἀνοήτως,
ἀναισθήτως, ἀβούλως, ἀπροαιρέτως, ἀπαθῶς, ἀνεπιθυμήτως κόσμον
2 ἠθέλησε ποιῆσαι. τὸ δὲ ἠθέλησε λέγω, φησί, σημασίας χάριν, ἀθε-

---

3f vgl. Ephes. 1, 21 — 5f vgl. Vahlen zu Arist. Poetik S. 1447b 9 —
12 Kat. 1 S. 1a, 1ff — 19—S. 197, 16 vgl. X 14, 1 — 20 s. zu S. 195, 6

1 + 8 Bernays (oder ἔτι st. ἔστι We.) 2 αὐτὸ] τὸ ὄν? Gö., αὐτὸν τὸν ἄρχοντα
Uhlhorn, Das basilidianische System, Gött. 1855 S. 6 3 οὐδ᾽ Bernays: οὐκ P, ὄν
Möller, Kosmol. S. 345 4 οὐδὲ Gö.: οὐδὲν P · 5f οὐκ ἐνδέχεται Roeper 6 δεῖ
Bernays, Uhlhorn S. 7: δὴ P 7 αὐτῇ ἄνευ (oder χωρὶς) ὀνομάτων Roeper, οὐ τοῖς
ὀνόμασι Bernays (so P nach Cruice), ἐκ τῶν αὐτῶν ὀνομάτων Gö. 8 ὁμωνημία P
ἐκπεποίηκε P 12 πρότερος Gö.: πρῶτος P 13f τινα ἐκ τῶν — λόγων κρυφίων τινῶν δ. Bunsen, Hipp. and his age I 368 (I 65) 14 κρυφίον P εἶναι δ. We.,
ἕνα δ. Gö., ὄντα δ. Preuschen, Antilegomena² S. 14 15 + οὖν Gö. + ἦν
Bernays, Jacobi S. 5 ὕλη] Gruppe, Griech. Mythol. S. 1624¹ vermutet den Aus-
fall des Gegensatzes von ὕλη 16 οὐκ ἀσύνθετον P, verb. Miller οὐ νοητόν,
οὐκ αἰσθητόν Jacobi a. a. O. S. 5 wohl mit Recht, ⟨οὐ νοητόν, οὐκ αἰσθητόν⟩,
οὐκ ἀνόητον, οὐκ ἀναίσθητον Diels nach Uhlhorn a. a. O. S. 7 19 λεπτομερεστέρως Gö. (λεπτομεροτέρως Bernays): λεπτομερῶς P, λεπτοτέρως Uhlhorn
+ ὁ Roeper 20 οὗτος Miller 21 ⟨τὸν⟩ κόσμον Cruice, doch s. H

that nothing, he says, is not merely unspeakable, since the unspeakable has a name – we call it unspeakable – but that nothing is not unspeakable either. And what is not unspeakable either is not named unspeakable but is, he says, over and above every name that is named. Nor indeed, he says, are there even enough names for the cosmos, because it is divided into such a multitude of parts, but they fall short. And I cannot, he says, find proper names for all things but it is necessary to understand with the intellect ... unspeakably the characteristics of the things named. For the homonymy of things had caused difficulty and error to the disciples. Making this first appropriation and theft from the Peripatos they deceive the foolish minds of those who gather round them. For Aristotle, who lived many generations before Basileides, laid down the doctrine concerning homonyms in the *Categories*, but these men put it out as a new exclusive doctrine, one of the secret doctrines of Matthias.

21. Therefore when there was nothing, not matter, not substance, not without substance, not simple, not compound, not unthinkable, not imperceptible, not man, not angel, not god, not any one of the things that are named or grasped by sense or conceived at all, but with everything circumscribed in this way and even more minutely, the non-existent god (whom Aristotle calls 'thought of thought', but these men call non-existent) without conception, without perception, without will or choice or passion and without desire wished to make the world. I say 'wished', he says, merely for the sake of signifying / – without wish, without conception, without

197W λήτως καὶ ἀνοήτως καὶ ἀναισθήτως· κόσμον δὲ οὐ τὸν κατὰ πλάτος
καὶ διαίρεσιν γεγενημένον ὕστερον καὶ διεστῶτα, ἀλλὰ γὰρ σπέρμα
κόσμου. τὸ δὲ σπέρμα τοῦ κόσμου πάντα εἶχεν ἐν ἑαυτῷ, ὡς ὁ τοῦ 3
σινάπεως κόκκος ἐν ἐλαχίστῳ συλλαβὼν ἔχει πάντα ὁμοῦ, τὰς ῥίζας,
5 τὸ πρέμνον, τοὺς κλάδους, τὰ φύλλα τὰ ἀνεξαρίθμητα, σπέρματα τῶν
κόκκων (τὰ ἀπ)ὸ τοῦ φυτοῦ γεννώμενα, σπέρματα πάλιν ἄλλων καὶ
ἄλλων πολλάκις φυτῶν κεχυμένα. οὕτως ⟨ὁ⟩ οὐκ ὢν θεὸς ἐποίησε 4
κόσμον οὐκ ὄντα | ἐξ οὐκ ὄντων, καταβαλόμενος καὶ ὑποστήσας f.
σπέρμα τι ἓν ἔχον πᾶσαν ἐν ἑαυτῷ τὴν τοῦ κόσμου πανσπερμίαν.
10 ἵνα δὲ καταφανέστερον ποιήσω τοῦτο ὅπερ ἐκεῖνοι λέγουσι· καθάπερ 5
ᾠὸν ὄρνιθος εὐποικίλου τινὸς καὶ πολυχρωμάτου, οἱονεὶ τοῦ ταῶνος
ἢ ἄλλου τινὸς ἔτι μᾶλλον πολυμόρφου καὶ πολυχρωμάτου, ἓν ὂν
ὅμως ἔχει ἐν ἑαυτῷ πολλὰς οὐσιῶν πολυμόρφων καὶ πολυχρωμάτων
καὶ πολυσυστάτων ἰδέας, οὕτως ἔχει τὸ καταβληθέν, φησίν, ὑπὸ τοῦ
15 οὐκ ὄντος θεοῦ οὐκ ὂν σπέρμα ⟨πανσπερμίαν⟩ τοῦ κόσμου πολύμορφον
ὁμοῦ καὶ πολυούσιον.
22. Πάντα οὖν, ὅσα ἔστιν εἰπεῖν καὶ ἔτι μὴ εὑρόντα παραλιπεῖν, 1
ὅσα τῷ μέλλοντι κόσμῳ γενέσθαι ἀπὸ τοῦ σπέρματος ἔμελλεν ἁρμόζειν ἀναγκαίως καιροῖς ἰδίοις κατὰ προσθήκην αὐξανομένῳ ὑπὸ
20 τηλικούτου καὶ τοιούτου θεοῦ, ὁποῖον οὐκ εἰπεῖν οὐ⟨δὲ⟩ νοήσει δυ-
νατὴ γέγονε χωρῆσαι ἡ κτίσις, [καὶ] ἐνυπῆρχε τεθησαυρισμένα τῷ
σπέρματι, καθάπερ νεογενεῖ παιδίῳ ὀδόντας ὕστερον ὁρῶμεν καὶ
πατρικὴν προσγενέσθαι οὐσίαν καὶ φρένας καὶ ὅσα παραυξανομένῳ

3 f Mark. 4, 31, o. S. 98, 25 — 5 vgl. VI 9, 9 — 9. 15 πανσπερμίαν] s.
Wortindex zu Diels' Vorsokr. (Demokrit) — 10—16 vgl. [Clemens] Homil. VI 3
S. 74, 18. 19. 5 S. 75, 8ff Lag. — 17f vgl. zu S. 116, 20

4 πάντα Gö.: πάσας P   5 ἀνεξαρίθμητα, εἶτα τὸν καρπὸν καὶ τὰ ἀπὸ
Roeper   σπέρματα Diels: μετὰ P, > Gö.   5f τὸν κόκκον P, verb. Gö.   6 τὰ ἀπὸ
Miller, ἀπὸ Gö., aber es fehlen 4 Buchst.   7 κεκρυμμένα Bernays, κεχυμένων Gö.
+ ὁ Roeper   8 ⟨τὸν⟩ κόσμον Cruice   ὄντα Jacobi S. 6: ὢν P   καταβαλλό-
μενος P   9 σπέρματι P   11 ὠιὸν P   εὐποικίλου Gö.: ἐκ ποικίλου P, ἐκ-
ποικιλλομένου Bernays   13 ὅμως Miller (s. Register): οὕτως P, ὄντως Gö.
15 ⟨ ⟩ Uhlhorn S. 11   18 ὅσα > Bernays bei Bunsen I 369 (1 66)   γενήσεσθαι Roeper   18f ἁρμόζει? Miller   19 ἀναγκαίως καιροῖς ἰδίοις Miller (Bernays) vgl. S. 206, 21: ἀναγκαίοις καιροῖς ἰδίους P, ἀναγκαίοις καιροῖς ἰδίως Gö.
αὐξανομένῳ We.: αὐξανομένου ὡς P: αὐξανομένῳ ὡς Bernays, αὐξανόμενα Gö.
20 οὐ νοῆσαι P, verb. Bernays   21 καὶ > Gö., ἀεὶ Bernays   23 προσγενέσθαι
οὐσίαν (προσγίνεσθαι Bernays) Gö.: προσγένεσιν οὐσίας P   παραυξανομένου P

perception. But the world – not the one that subsequently came to be with dimension and division, but rather the seed of the world. The seed of the world had everything within itself, just as the mustard seed contains everything together gathered into the smallest space, the roots, the trunk, the branches, leaves innumerable, germs of the seeds borne by the plant, further germs brought forth by other and yet other plants many times again. Thus the non-existent god made a non-existent world of non-existent things, setting down and hypostasising a single seed that has within itself the all-seed of the cosmos in its entirety. But let me make what they say clearer: like the egg of a variegated and multicoloured bird, such as a peacock or some other even more multiform and multicoloured one, it is one thing and yet it has within itself many 'forms' of polymorphous and multicoloured and complex things; this is what the thing deposited, he says, by the non-existent god was like, the non-existent seed of the world, polymorphous and multifarious all together.

22. All things, then, as many as it is possible to say and again to pass over without discovering, as many as were to be fixed in their own times, by necessity, the cosmos which was to come to be from the seed, increased by such a god by addition – such a god as the creation could neither express nor encompass in thought – these things were stored away in the seed, just as we see the teeth of a newborn infant later on, and his inherited character and wits and everything / which he did

2 ἐκ νέου κατὰ μικρὸν ἀνθρώπῳ ἃ μὴ πρότερον ἦν γίνεται. ἐπεὶ δὲ
198W ἦν ἄπορον εἰπεῖν προβολήν τινα τοῦ μὴ ὄντος θεοῦ γεγονέναι τὸ
οὐκ ὄν — φεύγει γὰρ πάνυ καὶ δέδοικε τὰς κατὰ προβολὴν τῶν γεγονότων οὐσίας ὁ Βασιλείδης —, ποίας γὰρ προβολῆς χρεία ἢ ποίας
ὕλης ὑπόθεσις, ἵνα κόσμον θεὸς ἐργάσηται, καθάπερ ὁ ἀράχνης τὰ   5
μηρύματα ἢ θνητὸς ἄνθρωπος χαλκὸν ἢ ξύλον ἤ τι τῶν τῆς ὕλης
3 μερῶν ἐργαζόμενος λαμβάνει; ἀλλὰ »εἶπε«, φησί, »καὶ ἐγένετο«, καὶ
τοῦτό ἐστιν, ὡς λέγουσιν οἱ ἄνδρες οὗτοι, τὸ λεχθὲν ὑπὸ Μωσέως·
»γενηθήτω φῶς, καὶ ἐγένετο φῶς«. πόθεν, φησί, γέγονε τὸ φῶς;
ἐξ οὐδενός· οὐ γὰρ γέγραπται, φησί, πόθεν, ἀλλ' αὐτὸ μόνον ἐκ τῆς 10
φωνῆς τοῦ λέγοντος· ὁ δὲ λέγων, φησίν, οὐκ ἦν, οὐδὲ τὸ γενόμενον
f. 89 v 4 ἦν. γέγονε, φησίν, ἐξ οὐκ ὄντων | τὸ σπέρμα τοῦ κόσμου, ὁ λόγος
ὁ λεχθεὶς »γενηθήτω φῶς«, καὶ τοῦτο, φησίν, ἔστι τὸ λεγόμενον ἐν
τοῖς εὐαγγελίοις »ἦν τὸ φῶς τὸ ἀληθινόν, ὃ φωτίζει πάντα ἄνθρω-
5 πον ἐρχόμενον εἰς τὸν κόσμον«. λαμβάνει τὰς ἀρχὰς ἀπὸ τοῦ σπέρ- 15
ματος ἐκείνου καὶ φωτίζεται. τοῦτό ἐστι τὸ σπέρμα, ὃ ἔχει ἐν ἑαυτῷ
πᾶσαν τὴν πανσπερμίαν, ὅ φησιν Ἀριστοτέλης γένος εἶναι εἰς ἀπεί-
ρους τεμνόμενον ἰδέας, ὡς τέμνομεν ἀπὸ τοῦ ζῴου βοῦν, ἵππον,
6 ἄνθρωπον, ὅπερ ἐστὶν οὐκ ὄν. ὑποκειμένου τοίνυν τοῦ κοσμικοῦ
σπέρματος, ἐκεῖνοι λέγουσιν· ὅ τι ἂν λέγω, φησίν, μετὰ ταῦτα γεγο- 20
νέναι, μὴ ἐπιζήτει πόθεν. εἶχε γὰρ πάντα τὰ σπέρματα ἐν ἑαυτῷ
τεθησαυρισμένα καὶ κατακείμενα, οἷον οὐκ ὄν⟨τα⟩ ὑπό τε τοῦ οὐ⟨κ
7 ὄν⟩τος θεοῦ γενέσθαι προβεβουλευμένα. ἴδωμεν οὖν, τί λέγουσι πρῶτον ἢ τί δεύτερον ἢ τί τρίτον τὸ ἀπὸ τοῦ σπέρματος τοῦ κοσμικοῦ
γεγενημένον. ἦν, φησίν, ἐν αὐτῷ τῷ σπέρματι υἱότης τριμερής, κατὰ 25
πάντα τῷ οὐκ ὄντι θεῷ ὁμοούσιος, γεννητὴ ἐξ οὐκ ὄντων. ταύτης
τῆς υἱότητος τῆς τριχῇ διῃρημένης τὸ μέν τι ἦν λεπτομερές, τὸ δὲ
8 ⟨παχυμερές, τὸ δὲ⟩ ἀποκαθάρσεως δεόμενον. τὸ μὲν οὖν λεπτομερὲς
εὐθέως πρῶτον ἅμα τῷ γενέσθαι τοῦ σπέρματος τὴν πρώτην κατα-
βολὴν ὑπὸ τοῦ ⟨οὐκ⟩ ὄντος διέσφυξε καὶ ἀνῆλθε καὶ ἀνέδραμε κάτω- 30
θεν ἄνω, ποιητικῷ τινι χρησάμενον τάχει

7 vgl. Psal. 32, 9. 148, 5 — 9 Gen. 1, 3 — 14 Joh. 1, 9 — 16—19 vgl.
S. 197, 9 — 21—23 vgl. X 14, 2 Anf. — 25—S. 199, 10 vgl. X 14, 2—4 —
30 διέσφυξε vgl. S. 97, 26

1 ἐπεί] ἔτι? We.   2 τὸ (so) P: τι als Text von P falsch Miller   4 ποία² We.
5 ὑλικῆς ὑποθέσεως Bernays   8 ὡς Gö.: δ P   11 τὸ λεγόμενον Roeper
12f λόγος ἐλεχθεὶς P   20 ἐκεῖνοι λέγουσιν > Cruice   22 οὐκ ὄντα H Gö.:
οὐκ ὄν P   24 τὸ Gö.: δ P   25 αὐτῷ Uhlhorn S. 17: ἑαυτῶ P   26 θεο-
μοούσιος P, verb. nach H   γεννητὴ H: γενητὴ P   28 ⟨ ⟩ H Bernays, Uhlhorn
S. 17   30 + οὐκ H Uhlhorn S. 18   31 χρησάμενος P

not have before but comes to him little by little as he grows
from being a youth into a man. Since it was impossible to say
that the non-existent had been a projection of the non-existent
god – for Basileides avoids beings that are by projection from
things that have come to be, and is very much afraid of them –
for what sort of projection is needed, or what sort of matter
must we assume, in order that god should make the world like
a spider makes webs or a mortal man takes bronze or wood or
one of the parts of matter to make something? But, it says, 'he
spoke and it was done' and this corresponds to the saying of
Moses, so these men say, 'Let there be light, and there was
light.' Whence, it says, came the light? From nothing. For it is
not written whence it came, it says, but just that, from the
voice of the one speaking; but, it says, the one speaking was
not, nor was that which came to be. Out of things that were
not, it says, came the seed of the world, the word spoken 'Let
there be light,' and this, it says, is that which is said in the
Gospels 'That was the true light which lighteth every man that
cometh into the world'. He takes his origins from that seed
and is lit. This is the seed, which has within itself the entire
all-seed, which Aristotle says is the genus divided up into
unlimited species, in the way in which we divide ox, horse and
man off from animal, which itself is non-existent. Hence
having the cosmic seed underlying they say: Whatever I say
came after these things, it says, do not enquire whence it
came. For it had all the seeds stored away and buried within
itself, like non-existents premeditated to come into being by
the non-existent god.

Let us see, then, what they say was first and what second
and what third to come into being from the cosmic seed.
There was, it says, in that seed, a tripartite sonship, in every
respect consubstantial with the non-existent god, begotten
from non-existents. Of this thrice-divided sonship one part was
of fine particles, one of dense particles and one requiring
purification. The fine-particled one readily pulsed and arose
and shot up from below at once as soon as the seed was first
deposited by the non-existent, and it employed a certain poetic
swiftness /

199W

ὡσεὶ πτερὸν ἠὲ νόημα,

καὶ ἐγένετο, φησί, πρὸς τὸν οὐκ ὄντα· ἐκείνου γὰρ δι' ὑπερβολὴν
κάλλους καὶ ὡραιότητος πᾶσα φύσις ὀρέγεται, ἄλλη δὲ ἄλλως. ἡ δὲ 9
παχυμερεστέρα ἔτι μένουσα ἐν τῷ σπέρματι, μιμητική τις οὖσα, ἀνα-
5 δραμεῖν μὲν οὐκ ἠδυνήθη· πολὺ γὰρ ἐνδεεστέρα τῆς λεπτομερείας, ἧς
εἶχεν ἡ δι' αὐτῆς νιότης ἀναδραμοῦσα, ἀπελείπετο. ἐπτέρωσεν οὖν 10
αὐτὴν ἡ νιότης ἡ πα|χυμερεστέρα τοιούτῳ τινὶ πτερῷ, ὁποίῳ διδάσκα- f. 9
λος ὢν Πλάτων Ἀριστοτέλους ἐν Φαίδρῳ τὴν ψυχὴν πτεροῖ, καὶ
καλεῖ τὸ τοιοῦτο Βασιλείδης οὐ πτερόν, ἀλλὰ πνεῦμα ἅγιον, ὃ εὐεργε-
10 τεῖ ἡ νιότης ἐνδυσαμένη καὶ εὐεργετεῖται. εὐεργετεῖ μέν, ὅτι καθάπερ 11
ὄρνιθος πτερὸν αὐτὸ κατ' αὐτὸ τοῦ ὄρνιθος ἀπηλλαγμένον οὐκ ἂν
γένοιτό ποτε ὑψηλὸν οὐδὲ μετάρσιον, οὐδ' αὖ ὄρνις ἀπολελυμένος
τοῦ πτεροῦ οὐκ ἄν ποτε γένοιτο ὑψηλὸς οὐδὲ μετάρσιος· τοιοῦτόν
τινα τὸν λόγον ἔσχεν ἡ νιότης πρὸς τὸ πνεῦμα τὸ ἅγιον καὶ τὸ
15 πνεῦμα πρὸς τὴν νιότητα. ἀναφερομένη γὰρ ὑπὸ τοῦ πνεύματος ἡ 12
νιότης ὡς ὑπὸ πτεροῦ ἀναφέρει τὸ πτερόν, τουτέστι τὸ πνεῦμα, καὶ
πλησίον γενομένη τῆς λεπτομεροῦς νιότητος καὶ τοῦ θεοῦ τοῦ οὐκ
ὄντος καὶ δημιουργήσαντος ἐξ οὐκ ὄντων, ἔχειν μὲν αὐτὸ μετ' αὐτῆς
οὐκ ἠδύνατο· ἦν γὰρ οὐχ ὁμοούσιον οὐδὲ φύσιν εἶχε μετὰ τῆς νιότη-
20 τος· ἀλλὰ ὥσπερ ἐστὶ παρὰ φύσιν καὶ ὀλέθριος τοῖς ἰχθύσιν ἀὴρ 13
καθαρὸς καὶ ξηρός, οὕτω τῷ πνεύματι τῷ ἁγίῳ ἦν παρὰ φύσιν
ἐκεῖνο τὸ ἀρρήτων ἀρρητότερον καὶ πάντων ἀνώτερον ὀνομάτων
τοῦ οὐκ ὄντος ὁμοῦ θεοῦ χωρίον καὶ τῆς νιότητος. κατέλιπεν οὖν
αὐτὸ πλησίον ⟨ἡ⟩ νιότης ἐκείνου τοῦ μακαρίου καὶ νοηθῆναι μὴ
25 δυναμένου [μὴ] μηδὲ χαρακτηρισθῆναί τινι λόγῳ χωρίου, οὐ παντά-
πασιν ἔρημον οὐδὲ ἀπηλλαγμένον τῆς νιότητος· ἀλλὰ γὰρ ὥσπερ εἰς 14
ἄγγος ἐμβληθὲν μύρον εὐωδέστατον εἰ καὶ ὅτι μάλιστα ἐπιμελῶς
ἐκκενωθείη, ὅμως ὀσμή τις ἔτι μένει τοῦ μύρου καὶ καταλείπεται,

---

1 η 36 — 2f s. zu S. 81, 7. 98, 15f — 8 Φαίδρῳ] S. 246 Aff — 20 vgl.
Heraklit Fr. 61 D. — 26ff vgl. V 19, 3ff

1 ἢ ἐνόημα P   5 λεπτομερίας P   6 ἡ δι' αὐτῆς ἀναδραμοῦσα Uhlhorn
S. 18   δι'] πρὸ Jacobi S. 7   αὐτῆς P   ἀναδραμοῦσα, ⟨ἀναδραμοῦσα δὲ⟩
Bernays   7 αὐτὴν P   8 ὢν Gö.: ὦ P, ὁ Miller   Φαίδρῳ Gö: φαίδωνι P
10 ἐβεργετεῖται P   11 καθ᾽ αὐτὸ Miller   12 man erwartet ⟨εὐεργετεῖται δὲ
ὅτι⟩ οὐδ᾽ αὖ We.   15 ὑπὸ] Jacobi S. 8: ἀπὸ P   17f οὐκ ὄντος Jacobi: οἰ-
κοῦντος P   19 οὐχ] οὐκ P   οὐδὲ Jacobi S. 8: οὖσ δὲ P   μετὰ] αὐτῆς Bunsen
22 ἀρρήτων Jacobi S. 8: ἄρρητον P   23 θεοχωρίον P   24 ἡ νιότης Bernays:
νιότητος P   27 μῦρον P

'like a bird or a thought'

and came to be, it says, with the non-existent. For due to his exceeding beauty and loveliness all nature yearned for him in different ways. But the more densely particled one still remained in the seed – it was inclined to imitate, yet it was unable to go up, for it severely lacked the fine-particled nature possessed by the sonship that shot up of its own accord, and hence it was left behind. Therefore the more densely particled sonship equipped itself with a wing – a wing such as Aristotle's teacher Plato equipped the soul with in the *Phaedrus* – and Basileides calls this thing not a wing but the holy spirit, and when the sonship puts it on it does it a service and has a service done to it. It does it a service in that just as a bird's wing by itself and separated from the bird could not get up into the air or on high, nor again would a bird which had lost its wing get up into the air or on high – this is the sort of relationship that the sonship had to the holy spirit and the spirit to the sonship. For the sonship in being raised up by the spirit as if by a wing raises up the wing, that is the spirit; and when it came close to the fine-particled sonship and the non-existent god who created out of non-existents, it could not keep the spirit with it; for the spirit was not consubstantial nor of like nature with the sonship; but just as pure dry air is contrary to nature and deadly to fishes so for the holy spirit that region of the non-existent god and the sonship, more unspeakable than unspeakables and above all names, was contrary to nature. Therefore the sonship left it near that blessed region that cannot be conceived nor characterised in any word, not entirely deserted or deprived of the sonship – but like sweet-smelling unguent put into a vessel, even if it is emptied out with the utmost care, nevertheless a smell of the unguent stays and is still left / even when the vessel has been emptied,

200W κἂν ἦ κεχωρισμένον τοῦ ἀγγείου, καὶ μύρου ὀσμὴν τὸ ἀγγεῖον ⟨ἔχει⟩
εἰ καὶ μὴ μύρον, οὕτως τὸ πνεῦμα τὸ ἅγιον μεμένηκε τῆς υἱότητος
ἄμοιρον καὶ ἀπηλλαγμένον, ἔχει δὲ ἐν ἑαυτῷ μύρου παραπλησίως

f. 90v 15 τὴν δύναμιν, ⟨τῆς υἱότητος τὴν⟩ ὀσμήν· | καὶ τοῦτό ἐστι τὸ λεγόμενον
›ὡς μύρον ἐπὶ κεφαλῆς τὸ καταβαῖνον ἐπὶ τὸν πώγωνα τὸν Ἀαρών‹, 5
ἡ ἀπὸ τοῦ πνεύματος τοῦ ἁγίου φερομένη ὀσμὴ ἄνωθεν κάτω μέχρι
τῆς ἀμορφίας καὶ τοῦ διαστήματος τοῦ καθ᾽ ἡμᾶς· ὅθεν ἤρξατο
ἀνελθεῖν ἡ υἱότης οἱονεὶ ἐπὶ πτερύγων ἀετοῦ, φησί, καὶ τῶν μετα-
16 φρένων ἐνεχθεῖσα. σπεύδει γάρ, φησί, πάντα κάτωθεν ἄνω, ἀπὸ τῶν
χειρόνων ἐπὶ τὰ κρείττονα· οὐδὲν δὲ οὕτως † ἀνόητόν ἐστι τῶν ⟨ἐν⟩ 10
τοῖς κρείττοσιν, ἵνα μὴ κατέλθῃ κάτω. ἡ δὲ τρίτη υἱότης, φησίν,
ἡ ἀποκαθάρσεως δεομένη μεμένηκεν ⟨ἐν⟩ τῷ μεγάλῳ τῆς πανσπερμίας
σωρῷ εὐεργετοῦσα καὶ εὐεργετουμένη. τίνα δὲ τὸν τρόπον εὐεργετεῖται καὶ εὐεργετεῖ, ὕστερον ἐροῦμεν κατὰ τὸν οἰκεῖον αὐτοῦ γενόμενοι λόγον. 15

1   23. Ἐπεὶ οὖν γέγονε πρώτη καὶ δευτέρα ἀναδρομὴ τῆς υἱότητος
καὶ μεμένηκεν αὐτοῦ τὸ πνεῦμα τὸ ἅγιον τὸν εἰρημένον τρόπον,
στερέωμα τῶν ὑπερκοσμίων καὶ τοῦ κόσμου μεταξὺ τεταγμένον —
2 διῄρηται γὰρ ὑπὸ Βασιλείδου τὰ ὄντα εἰς δύο τὰς προσεχεῖς καὶ
πρώτας διαιρέσεις, καὶ καλεῖται κατ᾽ αὐτὸν τὸ μέν τι κόσμος, τὸ δέ 20
τι ὑπερκόσμια, τὸ δὲ μεταξὺ τοῦ κόσμου καὶ τῶν ὑπερκοσμίων μεθόριον πνεῦμα τοῦτο, ὅπερ ἐστὶ καὶ ἅγιον καὶ τῆς υἱότητος ἔχει μένου-
3 σαν ἐν ἑαυτῷ τὴν ὀσμήν· — ὄντος οὖν τοῦ στερεώματος, ὅ ἐστιν
ὑπεράνω τοῦ οὐρανοῦ, διέσφυξε καὶ ἐγεννήθη ἀπὸ τοῦ κοσμικοῦ
σπέρματος καὶ τῆς πανσπερμίας τοῦ σωροῦ ὁ μέγας ἄρχων, ἡ κεφαλὴ 25
τοῦ κόσμου, κάλλος τι καὶ μέγεθος καὶ δύναμις λαληθῆναι μὴ δυνα-
μένη. ἀρρήτων γάρ, φησίν, ἐστὶν ἀρρητότερος καὶ δυνατῶν δυνατώτερος καὶ σοφῶν σοφώτερος καὶ ὅ τι ἂν εἴπῃς πάντων τῶν καλῶν
4 κρείττων. οὗτος γεννηθεὶς ἐπῆρεν ἑαυτὸν καὶ μετεώρισε καὶ ἠνέ-

---

5 Psal. 132, 2 (ἐπὶ πώγωνα, τὸν πώγωνα τὸν Ἀαρὼν) — 8f Deut. 32, 11;
Exod. 19, 4 — 11—13 vgl. X 14, 5 Anf. — 14 s. C. 25f — 18 vgl. Gen. 1, 7 —
18—S. 201, 16 vgl. X 14, 5—7 — 24 διέσφυξε] s. zu S. 198, 30

1 + ἔχει Bernays (ἔχει st. εἰ Miller)   2 μύρον P   4 ⟨ ⟩ Uhlhorn S. 20
(+ τὴν Diels vgl. Z. 22f)   5 τὸν² P (nicht τοῦ)   10 ἀκοινώνητον We., ἀκίνη-
τον Bunsen I 369 (I 66)   + ἐν Miller   11 μὴ > Miller   12 μεμένηκεν ἐν H
Möller S. 354: μεμένηκε P, ἐμμεμένηκε Roeper   18 στερέωμα τῶν Gö.: στερεω-
μένων P, στερεωμάτων Miller   21f μενθόριον P   23 ὄντος] ἐντὸς Bernays
24 ἐγενήθη P   26 λαληθῆναι Bernays (H): λυθῆναι P   27 ἄρρητον P   28 παντὸς τοῦ καλοῦ We.   29 καὶ¹ steht in P   29f ἐνεχθεὶς Uhlhorn S. 22, um ἔστη
halten zu können

and the vessel has a smell of unguent even if not unguent, in this way the holy spirit remained parted from the sonship and deprived of it, but had within itself an effect much like that of the unguent, the smell of the sonship. And this is the saying:

> 'It is like the ointment on the head that ran down upon the beard of Aaron',

the smell carried down from above from the holy spirit, down to the formlessness and the expanse where we are. It was from here that the sonship began to ascend as it were on an eagle's wings, it says, and borne upon its back. For everything strives upward from below, it says, from the worse to the better. But nothing among the better things is so (unintelligible) that it does not come down below.

But the third sonship, it says, the one requiring purification, remained in the great heap of the all-seed doing services and having services done to it. But in what manner it has services done to it and does services we shall say later when we come to the proper account of it.

23. When the first and second ascent of the sonship had occurred, and its holy spirit remained in the said manner as the firmament fixed between the cosmos and the *huperkosmia* – things are divided by Basileides into two primary and proximate divisions, the one called cosmos and the other *huperkosmia*, and the boundary between the cosmos and the *huperkosmia* is this spirit, which is both holy and has the smell of the sonship remaining in it – when the firmament which is above the heaven was in existence, there pulsed and was born from the cosmic seed and from the heap of the all-seed the great archon, the head of the cosmos, a beauty and a magnitude and a power that cannot be spoken. For he is more unspeakable than unspeakables, it says, and more powerful than the powerful and wiser than the wise and better than all fine things you might say. Once born he mutilated himself and rose up and was borne up / as far as the firmament; but

201W χθη | ὅλος ἄνω μέχρι τοῦ στερεώματος, [ἔστη] τῆς δὲ ἀναδρομῆς καὶ f.
τοῦ ὑψώματος τὸ στερέωμα τέλος εἶναι νομίσας καὶ μηδὲ εἶναι μετὰ
ταῦτα ὅλως μηδὲν [εἶναι] ἐπινοήσας, ἐγένετο μὲν ὑποκειμένων πάντων, ὅσα ἦν λοιπὸν κοσμικά, σοφώτερος, δυνατώτερος, ἐκπρεπέστερος,
5 φωτεινότερος, πᾶν ὅ τι ἂν εἴπῃς καλὸν διαφέρον χωρὶς μόνης τῆς
ὑπολελειμμένης υἱότητος ἔτι ἐν τῇ πανσπερμίᾳ· ἠγνόει γὰρ ὅτι ἐστὶν
αὐτοῦ σοφωτέρα καὶ δυνατωτέρα καὶ κρείττων. νομίσας οὖν αὐτὸς 5
εἶναι κύριος καὶ δεσπότης καὶ σοφὸς ἀρχιτέκτων τρέπεται εἰς τὴν
καθ᾽ ἕκαστα κτίσιν τοῦ κόσμου. καὶ πρῶτον μὲν ἠξίωσε μὴ εἶναι
10 μόνος, ἀλλὰ ἐποίησεν ἑαυτῷ καὶ ἐγέννησεν ἐκ τῶν ὑποκειμένων υἱὸν
ἑαυτοῦ πολὺ κρείττονα καὶ σοφώτερον. ταῦτα γὰρ ἦν πάντα προ- 6
βεβουλευμένος ὁ οὐκ ὢν θεός, ὅτε τὴν πανσπερμίαν κατέβαλεν. ἰδὼν
οὖν τὸν υἱὸν ἐθαύμασε καὶ ἠγάπησε καὶ κατεπλάγη· τοιοῦτον γάρ τι
κάλλος ἐφαίνετο υἱοῦ τῷ μεγάλῳ ἄρχοντι· καὶ ἐκάθισεν αὐτὸν ἐκ
15 δεξιῶν ὁ ἄρχων. αὕτη ἐστὶν ἡ κατ᾽ αὐτοὺς ὀγδοὰς λεγομένη, ὅπου 7
ἐστὶν ὁ μέγας ἄρχων καθήμενος. πᾶσαν οὖν τὴν ἐπουράνιον κτίσιν,
τουτέστι τὴν αἰθέριον, αὐτὸς εἰργάσατο ὁ δημιουργὸς ὁ μέγας σοφός·
ἐνήργει δὲ αὐτῷ καὶ ὑπετίθετο ὁ υἱὸς ὁ τούτου γενόμενος, ὢν αὐτοῦ
τοῦ δημιουργοῦ πολὺ σοφώτερος.
20 24. Αὕτη ἐστὶν ἡ κατὰ Ἀριστοτέλην σώματος φυσικοῦ ὀργανικοῦ 1
ἐντελέχεια, ψυχὴ ἐνεργοῦσα τῷ σώματι, ἧς δίχα τὸ σῶμα ἐργάζεσθαι
οὐδὲν δύναται, μεῖζον καὶ ἐπιφανέστερον καὶ δυνατώτερον καὶ σοφώτερον τοῦ σώματος. ὃν λόγον οὖν Ἀριστοτέλης ἀποδέδωκε περὶ τῆς
ψυχῆς καὶ τοῦ σώματος πρότερος, Βασιλείδης περὶ τοῦ μεγάλου
25 ἄρχοντος καὶ τοῦ κατ᾽ αὐτὸν υἱοῦ διασαφεῖ. τόν τε γὰρ υἱὸν ὁ ἄρχων 2
κατὰ Βασιλείδην γεγέννηκεν, τήν τε ψυχὴν ἔργον καὶ ἀποτέλεσμά
[ὥς] φησιν εἶναι ὁ Ἀριστοτέλης, φυσικοῦ σώματος ὀργανικοῦ ἐντελέ-

8 I Kor. 3, 10 ὡς σοφὸς ἀρχιτέκτων — 13 Mark. 1, 11? — 14 vgl. Psal.
109, 1 (Mark. 12, 36) — 20 f. 27 vgl. S. 194, 23 f

1 ἔστη > Miller, ἔστη δέ, τῆς ἀναδρομῆς Bunsen   2 μηδὲ] μηδὲν (nicht
μηδὲ) P   3 μηδὲν] μηδὲ (nicht μηδὲν) P   εἶναι > Miller, Uhlhorn S. 22 tilgt
vorher μηδὲ εἶναι, vgl. S. 203, 6. μηδὲ εἶναι Z. 3 wohl Correctur des μηδὲν εἶναι
Z. 2, bei Eintragung dieser Dublette fiel das μηδέν   5 παντός — καλοῦ We.
5 f μονῆς τῆς ὑπολελυμμένης P   6 f ἐστὶν αὐτοῦ Miller: ἔστι νῦν τοῦ P   7 σο-
φώτερα καὶ δυνατώτερα P   8 καὶ] ὡς Klost.   10 υἱῶν P   12 κατεβάλετο?
We.   14 ἐφαίνετο Bunsen: ἐγένετο P, ἐγένετο τῷ υἱῷ τοῦ μεγάλου ἄρχοντος
Jacobi S. 21   15 αὐτοὺς Gö.: αὐτοῦ P, αὐτὸν Miller   17 ⟨ὁ⟩ σοφὸς oder μέγα
We.   22 μεῖζόν ⟨τι⟩ Cruice   22 f σωφότερον P   23 τοῦ σώματος Gö.: τῆς
ψυχῆς P   26 γεγένηκεν P   τῆς τε ψυχῆς Bunsen   27 ὥς > Bunsen

thinking that the firmament was the end of his rise and of the height and that there was absolutely nothing beyond it, he was become wiser, more powerful, more honourable and more brilliant, and everything exceedingly fine that you might say, compared with the things lying below that remained cosmic, save only the sonship that was still left behind in the all-seed. For he was not aware that it was wiser and more powerful and better than him. Therefore believing that he was lord and master and the wise architect he turned to the detailed creation of the world. And first he thought good that he should not be alone and made for himself and begat a son from the things below, a son much better and wiser than himself. For all these things had the non-existent god predetermined when he deposited the all-seed.

When he saw his son he was filled with wonder and love and astonishment, such was the beauty of the son as it appeared to the great archon. And the archon set him at his right hand. This is what they call the ogdoad, where the great archon sits. And he himself, the great wise creator, worked the whole of the heavenly creation, that is that of *aithêr*. But subject to him and acting for him was his created son, who was much wiser than the creator himself.

24. This is Aristotle's actuality of a physical organic body, the soul acting on the body, without which the body cannot function at all, itself greater and more honourable and more powerful and wiser than the body. It is, therefore, the definition that Aristotle gave of soul and body at an earlier date, that Basileides expounds in connection with the great archon and his so-called son. For according to Basileides the archon begat the son, and Aristotle says that the soul is the work and finished product, the actuality of a physical organic body. / Therefore just as the actuality controls the body, so

f. 91ᵛ χειαν. ὡς οὖν | ἡ ἐντελέχεια διοικεῖ τὸ σῶμα, οὕτως ὁ υἱὸς διοικε‹
202W **3** κατὰ Βασιλείδην τὸν ἀρρήτων ἀρρητότερον θεόν. πάντα οὖν ἐστ‹
πρόνοούμενα καὶ διοικούμενα ὑπὸ τῆς ἐντελεχείας τοῦ ἄρχοντος τοῦ
μεγάλου τὰ αἰθέρια, ἅτινα μέχρι σελήνης ἐστίν· ἐκεῖθεν γὰρ ἀὴ
αἰθέρος διακρίνεται. κεκοσμημένων οὖν πάντων τῶν αἰθερίων πάλι‹
ἀπὸ τῆς πανσπερμίας ἄλλος ἄρχων ἀνέβη, μείζων μὲν[τοι] πάντω‹
τῶν ὑποκειμένων χωρὶς μέντοι τῆς καταλελειμμένης νίότητος, πολ‹
δὲ ὑποδεέστερος τοῦ πρώτου ἄρχοντος. ἔστι δὲ καὶ οὗτος ἄρρητο
4 ὑπ᾿ αὐτῶν λεγόμενος. καὶ καλεῖται ὁ τόπος οὗτος ἑβδομάς, κα
πάντων τῶν ὑποκειμένων οὗτός ἐστι διοικητὴς καὶ δημιουργός
ποιήσας καὶ αὐτὸς ἑαυτῷ υἱὸν ἐκ τῆς πανσπερμίας [καὶ αὐτὸς] ἑαυτο
φρονιμώτερον καὶ σοφώτερον, παραπλησίως τοῖς ἐπὶ τοῦ πρώτο
5 λελεγμένοις. τὸ δὲ ἐν τῷ διαστήματι τούτῳ ὁ σωρὸς αὐτός ἐστι‹
φησί, καὶ ἡ πανσπερμία, καὶ γίνεται κατὰ φύσιν τὰ γινόμενα ὡ
φθάσαν⟨τα⟩ τεχθῆναι ὑπὸ τοῦ τὰ μέλλοντα λέγεσθαι ὅτε δεῖ καὶ οἷ
δεῖ καὶ· ὡς δεῖ λελογισμένου. καὶ τούτων ἐστὶν ἐπιστάτης ἢ φροι
τιστὴς ἢ δημιουργὸς οὐδείς· ἀρκεῖ γὰρ αὐτοῖς ὁ λογισμὸς ἐκεῖνο‹
⟨ὃν⟩ ὁ οὐκ ὢν ὅτε ἐποίει ἐλογίζετο.
1 25. Ἐπεὶ οὖν τετέλεσται κατ᾿ αὐτοὺς ὁ κόσμος ὅλος καὶ τὰ ὑπε‹
κόσμια καὶ ἔστιν ἐνδεὲς οὐδέν, λείπεται δὲ ἐν τῇ πανσπερμίᾳ ἡ νιότη
ἡ τρίτη, ἡ καταλελειμμένη εὐεργετεῖν καὶ εὐεργετεῖσθαι ἐν τῷ σπέ‹
ματι, καὶ ἔδει τὴν ὑπολελειμμένην νιότητα ἀποκαλυφθῆναι καὶ ἀπ‹
κατασταθῆναι ἄνω ἐκεῖ ὑπὲρ τὸ μεθόριον πνεῦμα πρὸς τὴν νιότητ
τὴν λεπτομερῆ καὶ μιμητικὴν καὶ τὸν οὐκ ὄντα, ὡς γέγραπται, φησ‹
›καὶ ἡ κτίσις αὐτὴ συστενάζει καὶ συνωδίνει τὴν ἀποκάλυψιν τῶ‹
2 υἱῶν τοῦ θεοῦ ἐκδεχομένη‹. υἱοὶ δέ, φησίν, ἐσμὲν ἡμεῖς οἱ πνε‹

6—13 vgl. X 14, 8 — 25. S. 203, 17. 18ff Röm. 8, 19 ἡ γὰρ ἀποκαραδοκ‹
τῆς κτίσεως τὴν ἀποκάλυψιν τῶν υἱῶν τοῦ θεοῦ ἀπεκδέχεται 22 οἴδαμεν γὰρ ὃ
πᾶσα ἡ κτίσις συστενάζει καὶ συνωδίνει ἄχρι τοῦ νῦν — 26—S. 203, 3 vgl. X 14, ‹

3 ἐντελεχείας Gö.: μεγάλης P, μεγαλειότητος Miller   **5** αἰθέρος Gö.: αἰθ‹
ρίος P   κεκοσμιμένων P   **6** τοι > H Bernays   **8** καὶ οὗτος ἄρρητος] οὔτ‹
καὶ ὁ ῥητός Bunsen   **11** καὶ αὐτὸς > Cruice, καὶ αὐτὸν Miller   **14f** ὡς φαʋ‹
ἄν τ. Usener, Weihnachtsfest² S. 139   **15** φθάσαντα Uhlhorn: φθάσαν P, ἔφθα
Bunsen   φθάσαν ἐλέχθη ὑπὸ — γενήσεσθαι Roeper   λεχθῆναι Scott   λέγεσθ‹
γίνεσθαι Bunsen, γενέσθαι Üsener a. a. O.   δεῖ καὶ οἷα Bernays (vgl. Jacobi S. 2‹
δικαιοῖ ἆ P   **16** λελογισμένου Bunsen: λελογισμένῳ P   **18** + ὃν Jacobi S. ‹
ὁτὲ P   **20** δὲ] δὴ Miller   **21** ἐβεργετεῖσθαι P   **22** καὶ ἔδει Gö.: καὶ δὴ
καὶ δεῖ Bunsen, s. Register δεῖν   **25** συνστενάζει P

the son, according to Basileides, controls the god more unspeakable than unspeakables. All the aetherial things, therefore, are forethought and controlled by the actuality of the great archon, that is all things as far as the moon; for it is from there that aether is divided from air. When all the aetherial things had been set in order another archon arose from the all-seed again, greater than all the things lying below except the sonship that was left behind, but yet far inferior to the first archon. And this one is also called unspeakable by them. And this region is called the hebdomad, and this is the governor and creator of all the things lying below, and he also makes for himself a son from the all-seed who is more intelligent and wiser than himself, much like what was said about the first one. But what is in this area here is the heap itself, it says, and the all-seed, and the things that come to be come into being in accordance with nature, as if each succeeded in being brought forth by the one who has calculated the things that are to be selected at the proper time, of the proper sort and in the proper way. And these things have neither supervisor nor caretaker nor creator; for that calculation which the non-existent worked out when he made them is sufficient for them.

25. When the entire cosmos is finished, and the *huperkosmia*, and nothing is lacking, according to them, but the third sonship is left in the all-seed – the sonship left behind to do services and have services done to it in the seed – and the sonship left behind needed to be revealed and re-established above, up there with the fine-particled sonship and the imitative and the non-existent beyond the boundary spirit, then as it is written, it says, 'and the creation itself groans and travails awaiting the revelation of the Sons of God.' We, the *pneumatikoi*, it says, we are the sons, / left behind here to

203W μ̓ατικοί, ἐνθάδε καταλελειμμένοι διακοσμῆσαι καὶ διατυπῶσαι καὶ
διορθώσασθαι καὶ τελει|ῶσαι τὰς ψυχὰς κάτω φύσιν ἐχούσας μένειν f
ἐν τούτῳ τῷ διαστήματι. »μέχρι μὲν οὖν Μωσέως ἀπὸ Ἀδὰμ ἐβασίλευσεν ἡ ἁμαρτία«, καθὼς γέγραπται· ἐβασίλευσε γὰρ ὁ μέγας ἄρχων ·
5 ὁ ἔχων τὸ τέλος αὐτοῦ μέχρι στερεώματος, νομίζων αὐτὸς εἶναι θεὸς
μόνος καὶ ὑπὲρ αὐτὸν εἶναι μηδέν· πάντα γὰρ ἦν φυλασσόμενα ἀπο-
κρύφῳ σιωπῇ. τοῦτο, φησίν, ἐστὶ τὸ μυστήριον, ὃ ταῖς προτέραις
γενεαῖς οὐκ ἐγνωρίσθη, ἀλλὰ ἦν ἐν ἐκείνοις τοῖς χρόνοις βασιλεὺς καὶ
κύριος, ὡς ἐδόκει, τῶν ὅλων ὁ μέγας ἄρχων, ἡ ὀγδοάς· ἦν δὲ καὶ
10 τούτου τοῦ διαστήματος βασιλεὺς καὶ κύριος ἡ ἑβδομάς, καὶ ἔστιν ἡ
μὲν ὀγδοὰς ἄρρητος, ῥητὸν δὲ ἡ ἑβδομάς. οὗτός ἐστι, φησίν, ὁ τῆς
ἑβδομάδος ἄρχων ὁ λαλήσας τῷ Μωϋσῇ καὶ εἰπών· »ἐγὼ ὁ θεὸς
Ἀβραὰμ καὶ Ἰσαὰκ καὶ Ἰακώβ, καὶ τὸ ὄνομα τοῦ θεοῦ οὐκ ἐδήλωσα
αὐτοῖς« — οὕτως γὰρ θέλουσι γεγράφθαι —, τουτέστι τοῦ ἀρρήτου
15 τῆς ὀγδοάδος ἄρχοντος θεοῦ. πάντες οὖν οἱ προφῆται οἱ πρὸ τοῦ
σωτῆρος, φησίν, ἐκεῖθεν ἐλάλησαν. ἐπεὶ οὖν ἔδει ἀποκαλυφθῆναι,
φησίν, ἡμᾶς τὰ τέκνα τοῦ θεοῦ, περὶ ὧν ἐστέναξε, φησίν, ἡ κτίσις
καὶ ὤδινεν ἀπεκδεχομένη τὴν ἀποκάλυψιν, ἦλθε τὸ εὐαγγέλιον
εἰς τὸν κόσμον καὶ διῆλθε διὰ πάσης ἀρχῆς καὶ ἐξουσίας ⟨καὶ⟩ κυριό-
20 τητος ⟨καὶ⟩ παντὸς ὀνόματος ὀνομαζομένου· ἦλθε δὲ ὄντως, καί⟨τοι⟩
οὐδὲν κατῆλθεν ἄνωθεν οὐδὲ ἐξέστη ἡ μακαρία υἱότης ἐκείνου τοῦ
ἀπερινοήτου καὶ μακαρίου οὐκ ὄντος θεοῦ. ἀλλὰ γὰρ καθάπερ ὁ
νάφθας ὁ Ἰνδικὸ ὀφθεὶς μόνον ἀπὸ πάνυ πολλοῦ διαστήματος
συνάπτει πῦρ, οὕτω κάτωθεν ἀπὸ τῆς ἀμορφίας τοῦ σωροῦ διήκουσιν
25 αἱ δυνάμεις μέχρις ἄνω τῆς υἱότητος. ἅπτει μὲν γὰρ καὶ λαμβάνει
τὰ νοήματα κατὰ τὸν νάφθαν τὸν Ἰνδικόν, οἷον ἄφθας τις ὢν ὁ
τοῦ μεγάλου τῆς ὀγδοάδος ἄρχοντος υἱὸς ἀπὸ τῆς μετὰ τὸ μεθόριον
μακαρίας υἱότητος. ἡ γὰρ ἐν μέσῳ τοῦ ἁγίου πνεύματος ἐν τῷ
μεθορίῳ τῆς υἱότητος δύναμις ῥέοντα καὶ φερόμενα τὰ νοήματα τῆς
30 υἱότητος μεταδίδωσι τῷ υἱῷ τοῦ μεγάλου ἄρχοντος.

---

3 Röm. 5, 13. 14 ἄχρι γὰρ νόμου ἁμαρτία ἦν ἐν κόσμῳ .... ἀλλ᾽ ἐβασίλευσεν
ὁ θάνατος ἀπὸ Ἀδὰμ μέχρι Μωυσέως — 5f Deut. 32, 39; Jes. 45, 5 — 7f vgl.
Ephes. 3, 3—5; Kol. 1, 26. 27 — 12 Exod. 6, 2. 3, vgl. VI 36, 2 — 15f Hebr.
1, 1 und Matth. 11, 13? — 16—18 Röm. 8, 19. 22, vgl. VI 35, 2 — 19f vgl.
Ephes. 1, 21 — 23 vgl. zu S. 115, 18—22 — 28f Ephes. 1, 21

1 ⟨πρὸς τὸ⟩ διακοσμῆσαι Cruice, vgl. S. 207, 26. 208, 3, doch s. 202, 21
2 κάτω Gö.: κατὰ P, τὰς Bunsen   19 + καὶ Miller   20 + καὶ Bunsen
ὄντως Uhlhorn S. 29: οὕτως P   καίτοι Uhlhorn: καὶ P, καίπερ Gö.   23 ἄψας P
24 διήκησιν P   25 ἄνω μέχρις Jacobi S. 28   26 νάφθαν Miller: ἄφθαν P
ἄφθας Gö.: ἄφθας P, νάφθας Miller   29 φερόμενον P

arrange and order and correct and perfect the souls below that have a nature such as to remain in this region. 'From Adam until Moses sin reigned', as it is written. For the great archon reigned, the one who has his limit as far as the firmament and thinks that he is the only god and that there is nothing above him. For all things were guarded in hidden silence. This, it says, is the mystery which was not revealed to previous generations, but in those times the great archon, the ogdoad, was king and lord of all, so he thought. And of this region here the hebdomad was king and lord, and the ogdoad is unspeakable but the hebdomad is speakable. This is the archon of the hebdomad, it says, who spoke to Moses and said 'I am the god of Abraham and Isaac and Jacob, and I did not reveal the name of God to them' – this is how they like it to be written – that is the name of the unspeakable god, archon of the ogdoad.

All the prophets who came before the saviour, it says, spoke from that place. Therefore when the time came for us, the children of god, it says, to be revealed, concerning whom the creation groaned, it says, and travailed awaiting the revelation, then the gospel came to the world and spread through every governance and power and dominion and every name that is named. And it really came, although nothing came down from above nor did the blessed sonship depart from that inconceivable and blessed non-existent god. But just like the Indian naphtha kindles fire when it is merely looked upon from a very great distance, so the powers reached from down below from the formlessness of the heap right up to the sonship. For the son of the great archon of the ogdoad lights and takes up the thoughts from the blessed sonship beyond the boundary like the Indian naphtha, as if he was something catching fire. For the power of the sonship within the midst of the holy spirit in the boundary transmits to the son of the great archon the thoughts of the sonship which flow and move. /

1   26. Ἦλθεν οὖν τὸ εὐαγγέλιον πρῶτον ἀπὸ τῆς υἰότητος, φησίν,
204W διὰ τοῦ παρακαθημένου τῷ ἄρχοντι υἰοῦ [τὸ] πρὸς τὸν ἄρχοντα, καὶ
f. 92ᵛ ἔμαθεν ὁ | ἄρχων, ὅτι οὐκ ἦν θεὸς τῶν ὅλων, ἀλλ᾽ ἦν γεννητὸς καὶ
ἔχων αὐτοῦ ὑπεράνω ⟨τὸν⟩ τοῦ ἀρρήτου καὶ ⟨ἀ⟩κατονομάστου οὐκ
ὄντος καὶ τῆς υἰότητος κατακείμενον θησαυρόν, καὶ ἐπέστρεψε καὶ 5
2 ἐφοβήθη, συνιεὶς ἐν οἵᾳ ἦν ἀγνοίᾳ. τοῦτό ἐστι, φησίν, τὸ εἰρημένον·
»ἀρχὴ σοφίας φόβος κυρίου«. ἤρξατο γὰρ σοφίζεσθαι κατηχούμενος
ὑπὸ τοῦ παρακαθημένου Χριστοῦ, διδασκόμενος τίς ἐστιν ὁ οὐκ ὤν,
τίς ἡ υἰότης, τί τὸ ἅγιον πνεῦμα, τίς ἡ τῶν ὅλων κατασκευή, ποῦ
3 ταῦτα ἀποκατασταθήσεται· αὕτη ἐστὶν ἡ σοφία ⟨ἡ⟩ ἐν μυστηρίῳ λεγο- 10
μένη, περὶ ἧς, φησίν, ἡ γραφὴ λέγει· »οὐκ ἐν διδακτοῖς ἀνθρωπίνης
σοφίας λόγοις, ἀλλ᾽ ἐν διδακτοῖς πνεύματος«. κατηχηθεὶς οὖν,
φησίν, ὁ ἄρχων καὶ διδαχθεὶς καὶ φοβηθεὶς ἐξωμολογήσατο περὶ
4 ἁμαρτίας, ἧς ἐποίησε μεγαλύνων ἑαυτόν. τοῦτό ἐστι, φησί, τὸ εἰρη-
μένον· »τὴν ἁμαρτίαν μου ἐγνώρισα, καὶ τὴν ἀνομίαν μου ἐγὼ γι- 15
νώσκω, ὑπὲρ ταύτης ἐξομολογήσομαι εἰς τὸν αἰῶνα«. ἐπεὶ οὖν
κατήχητο μὲν ὁ μέγας ἄρχων, κατήχητο δὲ καὶ δεδίδακτο πᾶσα ἡ
τῆς ὀγδοάδος κτίσις καὶ ἐγνωρίσθη τοῖς ἐπουρανίοις τὸ μυστήριον,
ἔδει λοιπὸν καὶ ἐπὶ τὴν ἑβδομάδα ἐλθεῖν τὸ εὐαγγέλιον, ἵνα καὶ ὁ
τῆς ἑβδομάδος παραπλησίως ἄρχων διδαχθῇ καὶ εὐαγγελισθήσεται. 20
5 ἐπέλαμψεν ⟨οὖν⟩ ὁ υἰὸς τοῦ μεγάλου ἄρχοντος τῷ υἰῷ τοῦ ἄρχοντος
τῆς ἑβδομάδος τὸ φῶς, ὃ εἶχεν ἅψας αὐτὸς ἄνωθεν ἀπὸ τῆς υἰότητος,
καὶ ἐφωτίσθη ὁ υἰὸς τοῦ ἄρχοντος τῆς ἑβδομάδος, καὶ εὐηγγελίσατο
τὸ εὐαγγέλιον τῷ ἄρχοντι τῆς ἑβδομάδος, καὶ ὁμοίως κατὰ τὸν
6 πρῶτον λόγον καὶ αὐτὸς ἐφοβήθη καὶ ἐξωμολογήσατο. ἐπεὶ οὖν καὶ 25
τὰ ἐν τῇ ἑβδομάδι πάντα πεφώτιστο καὶ διήγγελτο τὸ εὐαγγέλιον
αὐτοῖς — κτίσεις γάρ εἰσι κατ᾽ αὐτὰ τὰ διαστήματα [καὶ] κατ᾽ αὐτοὺς

1—7 Clemens Stróm. II 35, 5. 36, 1 S. 131, 28 ff St. ὅθεν »ἀρχὴ σοφίας φόβος
θεοῦ« θείως λέλεκται. ἐνταῦθα οἱ ἀμφὶ Βασιλείδην τοῦτο ἐξηγούμενοι τὸ ῥητὸν
αὐτόν φασιν Ἄρχοντα ἐπακούσαντα τὴν φάσιν τοῦ διακονουμένου πνεύματος ἐκ-
πλαγῆναι τῷ τε ἀκούσματι καὶ τῷ θεάματι παρ᾽ ἐλπίδας εὐηγγελισμένον, καὶ τὴν
ἔκπληξιν φόβον κληθῆναι — 7 Psal. 110, 10; Prov. 1, 7. 9, 10, vgl. VI 32, 7 —
11 I Kor. 2, 13 — 15 Psal. 31, 5 frei wiedergegeben — 18 vgl. Ephes. 3, 9f

2 τὸ > Jacobi S. 29   4 ἔχων ὑπεράνω ἑαυτοῦ τὸν τοῦ Roeper   αὐτοῦ
Gö.: τὸν P, > Uhlhorn S. 29   ὑπὲρ ἄνω P   + τὸν Uhlhorn   κατονομάστου P
9 ἡ² Miller: ὁ P   ποῦ] πῶς? Bunsen   10 + ἡ Cruice   13 ἐξομολογήσατο P
19 εὐδομάδα P   21 + οὖν Gö.   22 εὐδομάδος P, so auch im Folgenden
ἅψας P   αὐτὸς Miller: αὐτοὺς P   25 ἐξομολογήσατο P   27 κατὰ τὰ Cruice
καὶ > Miller, καὶ κατ᾽ αὐτοὺς ⟨τοὺς τόπους τῶν ἀρχόντων⟩ Uhlhorn S. 25

26. The gospel came first, it says, from the sonship via the son who sits beside the archon to the archon, and the archon learnt that he was not god of all things but that he was created and had lying above him the treasure store of the unspeakable and unnamed non-existent one and of the sonship, and he repented and was afraid, realising what ignorance he was in. This, it says, is the saying 'The fear of the Lord is the beginning of wisdom'. For he began to become wise, catechised by the Christ who sat beside him, and he was taught who the non-existent is, who the sonship is, what the holy spirit, the construction of the universe, and where these things are to achieve restoration. This is the wisdom spoken in a mystery, concerning which, it says, scripture speaks: 'not in words taught by human wisdom, but in those taught by the spirit.' The archon, it says, was catechised and taught and was afraid and confessed his sin which he had committed in magnifying himself. This, it says, is the saying 'I acknowledged my sin and I know my iniquity and I will confess this for ever'.

When the great archon had been instructed, therefore, and also the whole creation of the ogdoad had been instructed and taught and the mystery had been explained to the heavenly beings, then it was necessary that the gospel should come to the hebdomad next, so that the archon of the hebdomad also should likewise be taught and evangelised. The son of the great archon, therefore, shone upon the son of the archon of the hebdomad the light which he had himself lit from above from the sonship, and the son of the archon of the hebdomad was enlightened and the gospel was brought to the archon of the hebdomad, and just as in the first account he too was afraid and confessed.

When all the things in the hebdomad had also been enlightened and the gospel had been delivered to them – for there are, on their view, infinite creations / and principalities

205W ἄ|πειροι καὶ ἀρχαὶ καὶ δυνάμεις καὶ ἐξουσίαι, περὶ ὧν μακρός ἐστι f.
κατ' αὐτοὺς πάνυ λόγος λεγόμενος διὰ πολλῶν, ἔνθα καὶ τριακοσίους
ἑξήκοντα πέντε οὐρανοὺς φάσκουσι, καὶ τὸν μέγαν ἄρχοντα αὐτῶν
εἶναι τὸν Ἀβρασὰξ διὰ τὸ περιέχειν τὸ ὄνομα αὐτοῦ ψῆφον τξε, ὡς
5 δὴ τοῦ ὀνόματος τὴν ψῆφον περιέχειν πάντα, καὶ διὰ τοῦτο τὸν
ἐνιαυτὸν τοσαύταις ἡμέραις συνεστάναι —· ἀλλ' ἐπεί, φησίν, ταῦθ' 7
οὕτως ἐγένετο, ἔδει λοιπὸν καὶ τὴν ἀμορφίαν καθ' ἡμᾶς φωτισθῆναι
καὶ τῇ υἱότητι τῇ ἐν τῇ ἀμορφίᾳ καταλελειμμένῃ οἱονεὶ ἐκτρώματι
ἀποκαλυφθῆναι τὸ μυστήριον, ὃ ταῖς προτέραις γενεαῖς οὐκ ἐγνωρίσθη,
10 καθὼς γέγραπται, φησίν· »κατὰ ἀποκάλυψιν ἐγνωρίσθη μοι τὸ μυστήριον«, καί »ἤκουσα ἄρρητα ῥήματα, ἃ οὐκ ἐξὸν ἀνθρώπῳ εἰπεῖν«.
κατῆλθεν ⟨οὖν⟩ ἀπὸ τῆς ἑβδομάδος τὸ φῶς, τὸ κατελθὸν ἀπὸ τῆς 8
ὀγδοάδος ἄνωθεν τῷ υἱῷ τῆς ἑβδομάδος, ἐπὶ τὸν Ἰησοῦν τὸν υἱὸν
τῆς Μαρίας, καὶ ἐφωτίσθη συνεξαφθεὶς τῷ φωτὶ τῷ λάμψαντι εἰς
15 αὐτόν. τοῦτό ἐστι, φησί, τὸ εἰρημένον »πνεῦμα ἅγιον ἐπελεύσεται 9
ἐπὶ σέ«, τὸ ἀπὸ τῆς υἱότητος διὰ τοῦ μεθορίου πνεύματος ἐπὶ τὴν
ὀγδοάδα καὶ τὴν ἑβδομάδα διελθὸν μέχρι τῆς Μαρίας, »καὶ δύναμις
ὑψίστου ἐπισκιάσει σοι«, ἡ δύναμις τῆς κρίσεως ἀπὸ τῆς ἀκρωρείας
ἄνωθεν ⟨διὰ⟩ τοῦ δημιουργοῦ μέχρι τῆς κτίσεως, ὅ ἐστι τοῦ υἱοῦ.
20 μέχρι δὲ ἐκείνου φησὶ συνεστηκέναι τὸν κόσμον οὕτως, μέχρις οὗ
πᾶσα ἡ υἱότης ἡ καταλελειμμένη εἰς τὸ εὐεργετεῖν τὰς ψυχὰς ἐν
ἀμορφίᾳ καὶ εὐεργετεῖσθαι διαμορφουμένη κατακολουθήσῃ τῷ Ἰησοῦ
καὶ ἀναδράμῃ καὶ ἔλθῃ ἀποκαθαρισθεῖσα· καὶ γίνεται λεπτομερεστάτη,
ὡς δύνασθαι δι' αὐτῆς ἀναδραμεῖν ὥσπερ ἡ πρώτη. πᾶσαν γὰρ ἔχει
25 τὴν δύναμιν συνεστηριγμένην φυσικῶς τῷ φωτὶ τῷ λάμψαντι ἄνωθεν κάτω.
27. Ὅταν οὖν ἔλθῃ, φησί, πᾶσα υἱότης καὶ ἔσται ὑπὲρ τὸ μεθό-
ριον, | τὸ πνεῦμα, τότε ἐλεηθήσεται ἡ κτίσις· στένει γὰρ μέχρι τοῦ
νῦν καὶ βασανίζεται καὶ μένει τὴν ἀποκάλυψιν τῶν υἱῶν τοῦ θεοῦ,

---

4f vgl. Irenaeus I 24, 3. 5. 7 S. 199ff H.; Epiphanius XXIV 7; Tertullian Adv.
haer. I S. 214, 18ff Kr.; Theodoret I 4 S. 349 C Migne; Dieterich, Abraxas S. 46
— **9** Ephes. 3, 5, vgl. S. 203, 7 — **10** Ephes. 3, 3 — **11** II Kor. 12, 4 ἤκουσεν
ἄρρητα ῥήματα, ἃ οὐκ ἐξὸν ἀνθρώπῳ λαλῆσαι — **12—18** vgl. X 14, 9 — **15** Luk.
1, 35 — **20—23** vgl. X 14, 10 Anf. — **28f** Röm. 8, 19. 22, vgl. S. 202, 25. 203, 18

4f ὥστε τοῦ Gö.   **5** τοῦτο Gö.: τούτων P, τοῦτον Bunsen   **7** ⟨τὴν⟩ καθ'
Roeper   **12** + οὖν Gö.   **18** ἐπισκειάσει P   χρίσεως? Gö., ὀγδοάδος Roeper,
doch s. S. 207, 12. 30   ⟨ἡ⟩ ἀπὸ Cruice   **19** + διὰ Gö.   **20** μέχρι σου P
23 γένηται Usener S. 139   **24** αὐτῆς P

and powers and authorities in these regions, concerning which a very lengthy account is given by them in great detail, in which they say there are three hundred and sixty-five heavens, and the great archon of these is Habrasax on account of the fact that his name incorporates the number 365, so that the number of his name incorporates all things, and for this reason the year is composed of that many days – but when, it says, these things had come to pass in this way, then it was necessary that the formlessness in our region should be enlightened next and that the mystery should be revealed to the sonship that was left behind in the formlessness like an abortion, the mystery which was not revealed to previous generations, as it is written, it says: 'The mystery was made known to me by revelation' and 'I heard unspeakable words which it is not possible for man to utter'.

The light that had come down from the ogdoad above to the son of the hebdomad now came down from the hebdomad onto Jesus the son of Mary, and he was enlightened, catching light from the light that was shining upon him. This, it says, is the saying 'the holy spirit will come upon thee' that is what comes through from the sonship, through the boundary spirit to the ogdoad and hebdomad as far as Mary, 'and the power of the most high shall overshadow thee' – the power of judgment from the height above down to the creation of the demiurge, that is of the son. Until that time, it says, the world was set up in this way, until the time when all the sonship that is left behind to do services to the souls in formlessness and to have services done to it is transformed and has followed Jesus and ascended and gone up once purified. And it becomes most fine-particled, so that it is capable of ascending by itself like the first one. For it has all the power firmly fixed by nature from the light shining down from above.

27. When, therefore, all the sonship has gone up and is above the boundary, the spirit, then the creation will be granted mercy. For until now it groans and is tortured and waits for the revelation of the sons of god, / so that all the men of the

206W ἵνα πάντες ἀνέλθωσιν ἐντεῦθεν οἱ τῆς νιότητος ἄνθρωποι· ἐπειδὰν
⟨οὖν⟩ γένηται τοῦτο, ἐπάξει, φησίν, ὁ θεὸς ἐπὶ τὸν κόσμον ὅλον τὴν
μεγάλην ἄγνοιαν, ἵνα μένῃ πάντα κατὰ φύσιν καὶ μηδὲν μηδενὸς τῶν
2 παρὰ φύσιν ἐπιθυ⟨μήσῃ⟩. ἀλλὰ γὰρ πᾶσαι αἱ ψυχαὶ τούτου τοῦ διαστήματος, ὅσαι φύσιν ἔχουσιν ἐν τούτῳ ἀθάνατοι διαμένειν μόνῳ,   5
μενοῦσιν οὐδὲν ἐπιστάμεναι τούτου τοῦ διαστήματος διάφορον οὐ⟨δὲ⟩
βέλτιον, οὐδὲ ἀκοή τις ἔσται τῶν ὑπερκειμένων ἐν τοῖς ὑποκειμένοις
οὐδὲ γνῶσις, ἵνα μὴ τῶν ἀδυνάτων αἱ ὑποκείμεναι ψυχαὶ ὀρεγόμεναι
βασανίζωνται, καθάπερ ἰχθὺς ἐπιθυμήσας ἐν τοῖς ὄρεσι μετὰ τῶν
προβάτων νέμεσθαι· ἐγένετο ⟨γὰρ⟩ ἄν, φησίν, αὐτοῖς ἡ τοιαύτη ἐπι-   10
3 θυμία φθορά. ἔστιν οὖν, φησίν, ἄφθαρτα πάντα τὰ κατὰ χώραν
μένοντα, φθαρτὰ δέ, ἐὰν ἐκ τῶν κατὰ φύσιν ὑπερπηδᾶν καὶ ὑπερ-
βαίνειν βούλοιντο. οὕτως οὐδὲν ὁ ἄρχων τῆς ἑβδομάδος γνώσεται
τῶν ὑπερκειμένων· καταλήψεται γὰρ καὶ τοῦτον ἡ μεγάλη ἄγνοια,
ἵνα ἀποστῇ ἀπ' αὐτοῦ ›λύπη καὶ ὀδύνη καὶ στεναγμός‹· ἐπιθυμήσει   15
4 γὰρ οὐδενὸς τῶν ἀδυνάτων οὐδὲ λυπηθήσεται. καταλήψεται δὲ
ὁμοίως καὶ τὸν μέγαν ἄρχοντα τῆς ὀγδοάδος ἡ ἄγνοια αὕτη καὶ πάσας
τὰς ὑποκειμένας αὐτῷ κτίσεις παραπλησίως, ἵνα μηδὲν κατὰ μηδὲν
ὀρέγηται τῶν παρὰ φύσιν τινὸς μηδὲ ὀδυνῆται· καὶ οὕτως ἡ ἀποκατάστασις ἔσται πάντων κατὰ φύσιν τεθεμελιωμένων μὲν ἐν τῷ   20
σπέρματι τῶν ὅλων ἐν ἀρχῇ, ἀποκαταστα θησομένων δὲ καιροῖς ἰδίοις.
f. 94r 5 ὅτι δέ, φησίν, ἕκαστον | ἰδίους ἔχει καιρούς, ἱκανὸς ὁ σωτὴρ λέγων·
›οὔπω ἥκει ἡ ὥρα μου‹, καὶ οἱ μάγοι τὸν ἀστέρα τεθεαμένοι· ἦν
γάρ, φησί, καὶ αὐτὸς ὑπὸ γένεσιν ἀστέρων καὶ ὥραν ἀποκαταστάσεως
6 ἐν τῷ μεγάλῳ προλελογισμένος σωρῷ. οὗτός ἐστιν ὁ κατ' αὐτοὺς   25
νενοημένος ἔσω ἄνθρωπος πνευματικὸς ἐν τῷ ψυχικῷ — ὅ ἐστιν
νίοτης ἐνταῦθα ἀπολιποῦσα τὴν ψυχήν, οὐ θνητὴν ἀλλὰ αὐτοῦ μέ-
νουσαν κατὰ φύσιν, ἥπερ ἄνω λέλοιπεν ἡ πρώτη νίοτης τὸ ἅγιον

---

15 Jes. 35, 10. 51, 11 — 21 vgl. I Tim. 6, 15 — 23 Joh. 2, 4 — Matth.
2, 1. 2 — 26 ἔσω ἄνθρωπος] s. zu S. 163, 11

2 + οὖν Gö. ἐπαύξει P   3 μένῃ Bernays, Uhlhorn S. 33: μὴ P, ἢ Miller
4 ἐπιθυ (Ende der Zeile) ἀλλά P   6 μενοῦσιν Bunsen Roeper: μένουσιν P
εἰστάμεναι P   διάφορα B   οὐδὲ Bunsen Scott: οὐ P, οὐ γὰρ Roeper   7 ἀπο-
κειμένοις P   9 βασανίζονται P   10 + γὰρ Miller   13 βούληται? We.
οὐδὲν Miller: οὐδὲ P (Roeper, dann γνώσεταί τι)   18 κατὰ μηδένα P   19 παρὰ
Miller: κατὰ P   ὀδύνηται P, ὀδυνᾶται? We.   21 ἀποκαταστα θησομένων Roeper:
ἀποκαταστα μένων P   καιροῖς] καιρὸς P   22 ἱκανὸς Miller: ἱκανῶς P, ἱκανῶς
μαρτυρεῖ Gö., μάρτυς ἱκανὸς Bunsen   24 ἐπὶ γένεσιν δι' ἀστέρων Bunsen
ὥραν Usener, Weihnachtsfest² S. 139: ὡρῶν P   28 ἥπερ Gö.: καίπερ P
λέλυπεν P

sonship may ascend from it. When this comes to pass, god, it says, will bring upon the whole world a great ignorance, so that all things may remain in accordance with nature and nothing desires anything contrary to nature. For all the souls of this region which have a nature to remain immortal in this region alone remain knowing nothing different from this region nor any better, and there will be neither hearing nor knowledge of the things above among the things below, so that the souls that are below shall not be tortured by yearning for things that are impossible, like a fish desiring to graze on the mountains with the sheep. For such a desire, it says, would be the destruction of them. Therefore, it says, all the things that remain in their place are unperishing, but they are perishable if they wish to leap over and transgress the bounds of what is in accordance with nature.

Thus the archon of the hebdomad will know nothing of things that lie above; for the great ignorance will comprehend him also, so that 'sorrow and pain and grief' may depart from him; for he will not desire nor grieve for any of the impossible things. This ignorance will also overtake the great archon of the ogdoad and all the creations under him likewise, so that nothing may yearn for any of the things that are contrary to nature, nor grieve for it. And in this way there shall be a restoration of all the things rooted in accordance with nature in the seed of the universe in the beginning but restored in their proper times. That each has his proper times, it says, is sufficiently clear when the saviour says 'Mine hour is not yet come', and the magi watching the star. For he himself was also predetermined and subject to the creation of stars and the hour of restoration in the great seed.

This is the inner spiritual man within the psychic man, on their conception of it, that is the sonship leaving the soul behind here, not mortal but remaining here in accordance with nature, just as the first sonship left the holy spirit above /

207W πνεῦμα τὸ μεθόριον ἐν οἰκείῳ τόπῳ —, ἰδίαν τότε περιβεβλημένος
ψυχήν.
Ἵνα δὲ μηδὲν τῶν κατ᾽ αὐτοὺς παραλείπωμεν, ὅσα καὶ περὶ 7
εὐαγγελίου λέγουσιν ἐκθήσομαι. εὐαγγέλιόν ἐστι κατ᾽ αὐτοὺς ἡ τῶν
5 ὑπερκοσμίων γνῶσις, ὡς δεδήλωται, ἣν ὁ μέγας ἄρχων οὐκ ἠπίστατο.
ὡς οὖν ἐδηλώθη αὐτῷ, ὅτι καὶ τὸ πνεῦμα ἅγιόν ἐστι, τουτέστι τὸ
μεθόριον, καὶ ἡ υἱότης καὶ θεὸς ὁ τούτων αἴτιος πάντων ὁ οὐκ ὤν,
ἐχάρη ἐπὶ τοῖς λεχθεῖσι καὶ ἠγαλλιάσατο· τοῦτ᾽ ἔστι κατ᾽ αὐτοὺς τὸ
εὐαγγέλιον. ὁ δὲ Ἰησοῦς γεγένηται κατ᾽ αὐτοὺς ὡς προειρήκαμεν· 8
10 γεγενημένης δὲ τῆς γενέσεως τῆς προδεδηλωμένης γέγονε πάντα
ὁμοίως κατ᾽ αὐτοὺς τὰ περὶ τοῦ σωτῆρος, ὡς ἐν τοῖς εὐαγγελίοις
γέγραπται. γέγονε δὲ ταῦτα, φησίν, ἵνα ἀπαρχὴ τῆς φυλοκρινήσεως
γένηται τῶν συγκεχυμένων ὁ Ἰησοῦς. ἐπεὶ γάρ ἐστιν ὁ κόσμος διῃρη- 9
μένος εἰς ὀγδοάδα, ἥτις ἐστὶν ἡ κεφαλὴ τοῦ παντὸς κόσμου — κεφαλὴ
15 δὲ τοῦ παντὸς κόσμου ὁ μέγας ἄρχων —, καὶ εἰς ἑβδομάδα, ἥτις
ἐστὶν †ἡ κεφαλὴ τῆς ἑβδομάδος, ὁ δημιουργὸς τῶν ὑποκειμένων, καὶ
εἰς τοῦτο τὸ διάστημα τὸ καθ᾽ ἡμᾶς, ὅπου ἐστὶν ἡ ἀμορφία, | ἀναγ- f.
καῖον ἦν τὰ συγκεχυμένα φυλοκρινηθῆναι διὰ τῆς τοῦ Ἰησοῦ διαιρέ-
σεως. ἔπαθεν οὖν τοῦτο ὅπερ ἦν αὐτοῦ σωματικὸν μέρος, ὃ ἦν τῆς 10
20 ἀμορφίας, καὶ ἀπεκατέστη εἰς τὴν ἀμορφίαν· ἀνέστη δὲ τοῦτο ὅπερ
ἦν ψυχικὸν αὐτοῦ μέρος, ὅπερ ἦν τῆς ἑβδομάδος, καὶ ἀπεκατέστη εἰς
τὴν ἑβδομάδα· ἀνέστησε δὲ τοῦτο ὅπερ ἦν τῆς ἀκρωρείας οἰκεῖον
τοῦ μεγάλου ἄρχοντος καὶ ἔμεινε παρὰ τὸν ἄρχοντα τὸν μέγαν·
ἀνήνεγκε δὲ μέχρις ἄνω τοῦτο ὅπερ ἦν τοῦ μεθορίου πνεύματος καὶ
25 ἔμεινεν ἐν τῷ μεθορίῳ πνεύματι· ἀπεκαθάρθη δὲ ἡ υἱότης ἡ τρίτη 11
δι᾽ αὐτοῦ, ἡ ἐγκαταλελειμμένη πρὸς τὸ εὐεργετεῖν καὶ εὐεργετεῖσθαι,
καὶ ἀνῆλθε πρὸς τὴν μακαρίαν υἱότητα διὰ πάντων τούτων διελ-
θοῦσα. ὅλη γὰρ αὐτῶν ἡ ὑπόθεσις σύγχυσις οἱονεὶ πανσπερμίας καὶ
φυλοκρίνησις καὶ ἀποκατάστασις τῶν συγκεχυμένων εἰς τὰ οἰκεῖα.
30 τῆς οὖν φυλοκρινήσεως ἀπαρχὴ γέγονεν ὁ Ἰησοῦς, καὶ τὸ πάθος οὐκ 1

8 Matth. 5, 12 χαίρετε καὶ ἀγαλλιᾶσθε (LXX) — 12 Clemens Strom. II 36, 1
S. 132, 4 St. σοφίας φυλοκρινητικῆς 38, 2 S. 133, 12 — 28 vgl. Basilides bei
Clemens Strom. II 112 S. 174, 8 St. — 29 vgl. Basilides a. a. O. II 36, 1 S. 132, 4. 5 St.
σοφίας φυλοκρινητικῆς τε καὶ διακριτικῆς καὶ τελεωτικῆς καὶ ἀποκαταστατικῆς

3 αὐτοὺς (nicht αὐτοῦ) P   8 ἠγαλλιάσατο P   12 ἀπαρχὴ Scott, Uhlhorn
S. 31: ἀπ᾽ ἀρχῆς P   φυλοκρίνης ἕως P   14 κεφαλὴ δὲ — 15 κόσμου > Bunsen
δὲ τῆς ὀγδοάδος ὁ? Gö.   15 f ἑβδομάδα, κεφαλὴ δὲ τῆς Gö.   16 ἡ κεφαλὴ τῆς
ἑβδομάδος > Bunsen   18 συνγεχυμένα P   φυλοκριθῆναι P   20 ἀνέστησε?
Jacobi S. 36   28 σύγχησις P

as the boundary in its proper place – the spiritual man which at that time had put on its own individual soul.

But so that I do not leave out any of their views, I shall explain what they say about the gospel too. The gospel, according to them, is the knowledge of hypercosmic things as has been shown, which the great archon did not know. Therefore when it was made clear to him that there is also the holy spirit, that is the boundary, and the sonship, and the god who is cause of all these things, the non-existent, he rejoiced at what was said and exulted; this is the 'good news' according to them. But Jesus was born as we have already said; once the birth that had been foreshown had occurred then all the things concerning the saviour happened likewise, according to them, as it is written in the gospels. These things came to pass, it says, that Jesus might become the first fruit of the segregation of the things that had been heaped together. For since the cosmos is divided into ogdoad, which is the head of the whole cosmos – but the head of the whole cosmos is the great archon – and into hebdomad, which is the head of the hebdomad, the creator of the things below, and into this region where we are, where the formlessness is, it was necessary that the things that were heaped together should be segregated by means of Jesus' division. Therefore this which was the bodily part of him suffered – this was of the formlessness and was restored to the formlessness; but that which properly belonged to the height of the great archon rose again and remained with the great archon; and that which was of the boundary spirit was carried up above and remained in the boundary spirit. And the third sonship, the one left behind to do services and have services done to it, was purified through Jesus and went up to the blessed sonship, passing through all these things. For their whole theory is one of confusion, as in the case of the all-seed, and segregation and restoration of the things that had been in confusion to their proper places. Therefore Jesus became the first fruit of the segregation, and his suffering / was merely for the sake of the

208W ἄλλου τινὸς χάριν γέγονεν ⟨ἢ⟩ ὑπὲρ τοῦ φυλοκρινηθῆναι τὰ συγκεχυμένα. τούτῳ γὰρ τῷ τρόπῳ φησὶν ὅλην τὴν υἱότητα τὴν κατα-
λελειμμένην εἰς τὴν ἀμορφίαν πρὸς τὸ εὐεργετεῖν καὶ εὐεργετεῖσθαι
13 δεῖν φυλοκρινηθῆναι, ᾧ τρόπῳ καὶ ὁ Ἰησοῦς πεφυλοκρίνηται. ταῦτα
μὲν οὖν ἐστιν ἃ καὶ Βασιλείδης μυθεύει σχολάσας κατὰ τὴν Αἴγυπτον,
καὶ παρ᾽ αὐτῶν τὴν τοσαύτην σοφίαν διδαχθεὶς ἐκαρποφόρησε τοι-
ούτους καρπούς.

*

1 ἢ ὑπὲρ Cruice : ὑπὸ P, ἢ Jacobi S. 36, Roeper, ἢ ὑπὸ Miller   2 f κατα-
λελεγμένην P   4 δεῖν φυλοκρινηθῆναι Gö.: διαφυλοκριθῆναι P ͺ   5 κατὰ τὸν
Περίπατον Bernays

segregation of the things in confusion and for no other cause. For the whole of the sonship left behind in the formlessness to do services and have services done to it, it says, must be segregated in the manner in which Jesus also was segregated.

These are the myths that Basileides tells from his schooling in Egyptian wisdom, and having learnt such wisdom from them he bears this sort of fruit.

*

1   29. Μαρκίων δὲ ὁ Ποντικὸς πολὺ τούτων μανικώτερος, τὰ πολλὰ
210W τῶν πλειόνων παραπεμψάμενος ἐπὶ τὸ ἀναιδέστερον ὁρμήσας δύο
ἀρχὰς τοῦ παντὸς ὑπέθετο, ἀγαθόν τινα λέγων καὶ τὸν ἕτερον πονη-
ρόν· καὶ αὐτὸς δὲ νομίζων καινόν τι παρεισαγαγεῖν σχολὴν ἐσκεύασεν
2 ἀπονοίας γέμουσαν καὶ κυνικοῦ βίου, ὧν τις μάχιμος. οὗτος νομίζων
λήσεσθαι τοὺς πολλούς, ὅτι μὴ Χριστοῦ τυγχάνοι μαθητὴς ἀλλ᾽
Ἐμπεδοκλέους πολὺ αὐτοῦ προγενεστέρου τυγχάνοντος, ταὐτὰ ὁρίσας
3 ἐδογμάτισε δύο εἶναι τὰ τοῦ παντὸς αἴτια, νεῖκος καὶ φιλίαν. τί γὰρ
φησιν ὁ Ἐμπεδοκλῆς περὶ τῆς τοῦ κόσμου διαγωγῆς εἰ καὶ προείπο-
μεν, ἀλλά γε καὶ νῦν πρὸς τὸ ἀντιπαραθεῖναι τῇ τοῦ κλεψιλόγου
4 αἱρέσει οὐ σιωπήσομαι. οὗτός φησιν εἶναι τὰ πάντα στοιχεῖα, ἐξ ὧν
ὁ κόσμος συνέστηκε καὶ ἔστιν, ἕξ, δύο μὲν ὑλικά, γῆν καὶ ὕδωρ, δύο
δὲ ὄργανα, οἷς τὰ ὑλικὰ κοσμεῖται καὶ μεταβάλλεται, πῦρ καὶ ἀέρα,
δύο δὲ τὰ ἐργαζόμενα τοῖς ὀργάνοις τὴν ὕλην καὶ δημιουργοῦντα,
νεῖκος καὶ φιλίαν, λέγων ὧδέ πως·

τέσσαρα τῶν πάντων ῥιζώματα πρῶτον ἄκουε·
Ζεὺς ⟨ἀργὴς⟩ Ἥρη τε φερέσβιος ἠδὲ Ἀϊδωνεύς
Νῆστίς τε ἣ δακρύοις τέγγει κρούνωμα βρότειον.

6 f vgl. Filastrius C. 44, 1 S. 23, 10—12 M.; Tert. Adv. haer. 6 S. 222, 18—20 Kr.;
Theodoret I 24 S. 373 BC; s. Lipsius, Zur Quellenkritik des Ep. 197 ff — 13 f προεί-
πομεν] S. 9, 3—15 — 15 f Simplicius Phys. S. 25. 26 (Vorsokr. 1³ S. 204): ὥστε
καὶ ἓξ εἶναι κατ᾽ αὐτὸν ἀρχάς, Sext. Adv. math. VII 317 (= Hipp. X 7, 4), Doxographi S. 93² — 20 Empedokles Fr. 6 Diels, vgl. unten X 7, 3

5 Titel περὶ μαρ-
κίωνος rot P   7 λέγων ⟨θεὸν⟩ Miller, vgl. S. 224, 1   9 γέμουσα P   μανικός?
Gö., μάχλος Miller   οὗτος Miller: ὅτι P   11 αὐτοῦ Cruice: αὐτῷ P   ταῦτα P
20 τῶν P H: γὰρ Emp.   21 ἀργὴς Emp.: ἀὴρ H, > P   ἢ δὲ P   22 τε We.
(θ᾽ Emp.): γε P, δὲ H   κρούνωμα βρότειον Emp.: κρουνῷ μαβρόντιον H, κρουνῷ
μακρόγιον P

29. Marcion of Pontus was much more mad than these (Basileides and Satornilus); dismissing the many things of popular opinion he progressed to the more shocking view in positing two principles of the universe, and saying that one is good and the other evil. He thought that he had introduced something new and therefore set up a school that was full of foolishness and the dog's life of the Cynics, for he was a pugnacious character. He thought it would pass unnoticed by the majority that he was not a disciple of Christ but of Empedocles who lived long before him, and he made the same divisions as him and taught that the causes of everything were two, strife and love. Although we have already mentioned what Empedocles says about the history of the cosmos earlier, nevertheless for the sake of making a comparative juxta-position with the heresy of the theory-stealer I shall not remain silent now.

Empedocles says that all the elements, of which the world is constituted and has its being, are six – two material ones, earth and water; two instrumental ones, by which the material ones are ordered and changed, fire and air; and two that work the material by means of the instruments and create, Strife and Love· he speaks thus:

'First hear that there are four roots of all things:
Bright Zeus, Life-bringing Hera, Aidoneus
and Nestis who wets the mortal stream with tears.' /

211W Ζεύς ἐστι τὸ πῦρ, Ἥρη δὲ φερέσβιος ἡ γῆ ἡ φέρουσα τοὺς πρὸς τὸν
βίον καρπούς, Ἀϊδωνεὺς δὲ ὁ ἀήρ, ὅτι πάντα δι' αὐτοῦ βλέποντες
μόνον αὐτὸν οὐ καθορῶμεν, Νῆστις δὲ τὸ ὕδωρ· μόνον γὰρ τοῦτο
ὄχημα τροφῆς αἴτιον γινόμενον πᾶσι τοῖς τρεφομένοις, αὐτὸ καθ'
5 αὑτὸ τρέφειν οὐ δυνάμενον τὰ τρεφόμενα. εἰ γὰρ ἔτρεφε, φησίν,
οὐκ ἄν ποτε λιμῷ κατελή|φθη τὰ ζῷα, ὕδατος ἐν τῷ κόσμῳ πλεονά-
ζοντος ἀεί. διὰ τοῦτο Νῆστιν καλεῖ τὸ ὕδωρ, ὅτι τροφῆς αἴτιον
γινόμενον τρέφειν οὐκ εὐτονεῖ τὰ τρεφόμενα. ταῦτα μὲν οὖν ἐστιν
ὡς τύπῳ περιλαβεῖν τοῦ κόσμου τὰ συνέχοντα τὴν ὅλην ὑπόθεσιν·
10 ὕδωρ καὶ γῆ, ἐξ ὧν τὰ γινόμενα, πῦρ καὶ πνεῦμα, τὰ ὄργανα καὶ τὰ
δραστήρια, νεῖκος δὲ καὶ φιλία, τὰ δημιουργοῦντα τεχνικῶς. καὶ ἡ
μὲν φιλία εἰρήνη τίς ἐστι καὶ ὁμόνοια καὶ στοργὴ ἕνα τέλειον κατηρτισμένον εἶναι προαιρουμένη τὸν κόσμον, τὸ δὲ νεῖκος ἀεὶ διασπᾷ
τὸν ἕνα καὶ κατακερματίζει ἢ ἀπεργάζεται ἐξ ἑνὸς πολλά. ἔστι μὲν
15 οὖν τὸ μὲν νεῖκος αἴτιον τῆς κτίσεως πάσης, ὅ φησιν »οὐλόμενον«
εἶναι, τουτέστιν ὀλέθριον· μέλει γὰρ αὐτῷ, ὅπως διὰ παντὸς αἰῶνος
ἡ κτίσις αὕτη συνεστήκῃ· καὶ ἔστι πάντων τῶν γεγονότων τῆς
γενέσεως δημιουργὸς καὶ ποιητὴς τὸ νεῖκος τὸ ὀλέθριον, τῆς δὲ ἐκ
τοῦ κόσμου τῶν γεγονότων ἐξαγωγῆς καὶ μεταβολῆς καὶ εἰς τὸ ἕν
20 ἀποκαταστάσεως ἡ φιλία· περὶ ὧν ὁ Ἐμπεδοκλῆς ὅτι ἐστὶν ἀθάνατ
δύο καὶ ἀγένητα καὶ ἀρχὴν τοῦ γενέσθαι μηδέποτε εἰληφότα, ἄλλα
λέγει τοιοῦτόν τινα τρόπον·

> ἢ γὰρ καὶ πάρος ἦν καὶ ἔσσεται, οὐδέ ποτ', οἴω,
> τούτων ἀμφοτέρων κενεώσεται ἄσπετος αἰών.

25 τίνων τούτων; τοῦ νείκους καὶ τῆς φιλίας· οὐ γὰρ ἤρξαντο γενέσθαι, ἀλλὰ προῆσαν καὶ ἔσονται ἀεὶ διὰ τὴν ἀγεννησίαν φθορὰν

1—3 vgl. Diog. Laert. VIII 76 (Vorsokr. I³ 199, 1ff) und etwas abweichend
[Plut.] De plac. I 3, 20 (Doxogr. S. 287) u. Stob. Ecl. I 10, 11b S. 121, 10—14 W.
Über die Verzweigung der Überlieferung Diels, Poet. philos. fr. S. 108. Diels ver-
mutet Vorsokr. S. 206, 4 Plutarchs Schrift über Emp. als Quelle — 15 vgl.
Fr. 17, 19 D., unten Hipp. X 7, 5 — 23 Empedokles Fr. 16 D., vgl. VI 25, 1

2 βλέποτες P   4 αἴτιον > Kranz bei Diels, Vorsokr. I³ 206, 7   4f καθ'
αὐτὸ P   12f κατειρτισμένον P, ⟨καὶ⟩ κατηρτισμένον Miller   17 αὐτὴ P, αὐτὴ
Gö.   συνέστηκε P   19 τὸ ἕν Cruice und Sauppe (bei Gö.): τὸν ἕνα P   20 ⟨φη-
σιν⟩ ὅτι Cruice   21 ἀγέννητα Gö., vgl. S. 214, 23   ἄλλα Kranz bei Diels Vor-
sokr.³ I 229, 5: ἀλλὰ P, > (oder Lücke) Miller, ἅμα früher Diels   23 ἢ Miller:
εἰ P, s. zu S. 151, 28. Daß H. ἢ schrieb, folgt wohl aus Z. 26   ἦν καὶ] s. zu
S. 151, 28   ἔσται P H   οὐδέπω τοίω P, s. H   24 κενώσεται P, s. H   ἄσβεστος P H   25 ἤρξατο P

Zeus is the fire and Life-bringing Hera is the earth which
brings forth the fruits for life, Aidoneus is the air because we
look at everything through it but it alone we do not see, and
Nestis is the water. For this alone is the vehicle which becomes
the cause of nourishment to all things that are nourished, but
in itself it cannot nourish them. For if it did nourish, it says,
living things would never be overcome by hunger, since there
is always plenty of water in the world. For this reason he calls
the water Nestis, fasting, because it becomes the cause of
nourishment but does not have power to nourish the things
that are nourished. These are the chief points that hold
together the whole theory of the cosmos, to sum it up
schematically: water and earth – the constituents of the things
made; fire and breath – the instruments and efficient causes;
Strife and Love – the things that create by craftsmanship.

Love is a certain peace and unanimity and affection which
prefers the world to be one, perfect and restored, but Strife is
always dispersing the one and chopping it up and making many
instead of one. Therefore Strife is cause of all creation and he
says it is '*oulomenon*', that is destructive; for it is Strife's concern
that this creation should stand firm through all ages; and
destructive Strife is creator and maker of the coming-to-be of
the created things, but Love of their leading-out from the
world and transformation and restoration to the one. About
these Empedocles says that they are two immortals and
uncreated and that they never had an origin of their coming to
birth – in this sort of way:

'For indeed they were before and will be, nor ever, I think,
will the ceaseless age be devoid of these two.'

What are 'these two'? Strife and Love. For they did not begin
to come into being, but pre-existed and will be always,
incapable of admitting death because of their uncreatedness.

314 Rethinking Early Greek Philosophy

212W ὑπομεῖναι μὴ δυνάμενα· τὸ δὲ πῦρ ⟨καὶ τὸ ὕδωρ⟩ καὶ ἡ γῆ καὶ ὁ
11 ἀὴρ θνήσκοντα καὶ ἀναβιοῦντα. ὅταν μὲν γὰρ ἀποθάνῃ [ταῦ]τὰ ὑπὸ
τοῦ νείκους γινόμενα, παραλαμβάνουσα αὐτὰ ἡ φιλία προσάγει καὶ
προστίθησι καὶ προσοικειοῖ τῷ παντί, ἵνα μένῃ τὸ πᾶν ἕν, ὑπὸ τῆς
f. 96ᵛ 12 φιλίας ἀεὶ διακοσμούμενον | μονοτρόπως καὶ μονοειδῶς. ὅταν δὲ ἡ
φιλία ἐκ πολλῶν ποιήσῃ τὸ ἓν καὶ τὰ διεσπασμένα προσοικειώσῃ τῷ
ἑνί, πάλιν τὸ νεῖκος ἀπὸ τοῦ ἑνὸς ἀποσπᾷ καὶ ποιεῖ πολλά, τουτέστι
πῦρ, ὕδωρ, γῆν, ἀέρα, τὰ ἐκ τούτων γεννώμενα ζῷα καὶ φυτὰ καὶ
13 ὅσα μέρη τοῦ κόσμου κατανοοῦμεν. καὶ περὶ μὲν τῆς τοῦ κόσμου
ἰδέας, ὁποία τίς ἐστιν ὑπὸ τῆς φιλίας κοσμουμένη, λέγει τοιοῦτόν
τινα τρόπον·

οὐ γὰρ ἀπὸ νώτοιο δύο κλάδοι ἀίσσονται,
οὐ πόδες, οὐ θοὰ γούνατ᾽, οὐ μήδεα γεννήεντα,
ἀλλὰ σφαῖρος ἔην καὶ † ἴσος ἐστὶν αὐτῷ.

14 τοιοῦτόν τι καὶ κάλλιστον εἶδος τοῦ κόσμου ἡ φιλία ἐκ πολλῶν ἓν
ἀπεργάζεται· τὸ δὲ νεῖκος, τὸ τῆς τῶν κατὰ μέρος διακοσμήσεως
αἴτιον, ἐξ ἑνὸς ἐκείνου ἀποσπᾷ καὶ ἀπεργάζεται πολλά. καὶ τοῦτό
ἐστιν ὃ λέγει περὶ τῆς ἑαυτοῦ γεννήσεως ὁ Ἐμπεδοκλῆς·

τῶν καὶ ἐγὼ ⟨νῦν⟩ εἰμι φυγὰς θεόθεν καὶ ἀλήτης,

τουτέστι θεὸν καλῶν τὸ ἓν καὶ τὴν ἐκείνου ἑνότητα, ἐν ᾧ ἦν πρὶν
ὑπὸ τοῦ νείκους ἀποσπασθῆναι καὶ γενέσθαι ἐν τοῖς πολλοῖς τούτοις
15 τοῖς κατὰ τὴν τοῦ νείκους διακόσμησιν· »νείκεϊ« γάρ φησι »μαι⟨νο-
μένῳ πίσυνος«, νεῖκος μαι⟩νόμενον καὶ τετα⟨ρα⟩γμένον καὶ ἄστα-
τον τὸν δημιουργὸν τοῦδε τοῦ κόσμου ὁ Ἐμπεδοκλῆς ἀποκαλῶν. αὕτη
γάρ ἐστιν ἡ καταδίκη καὶ ἀνάγκη τῶν ψυχῶν, ὧν ἀποσπᾷ τὸ νεῖκος
ἀπὸ τοῦ ἑνὸς καὶ δημιουργεῖ καὶ ἐργάζεται, λέγων τοιοῦτόν τινα
τρόπον·

12 Empedokles Fr. 29 D. (= Fr. 134, 2–4) — 19. 22 Empedokles Fr. 115,
13. 14 D. Plotin Enn. IV 8, 1 (Vorsokr. I³ S. 266) hat dieselbe Folge der Verse
wie Hipp. Z. 19 u. S. 213, 1

1 ⟨ ⟩ Gö. 2 θνήσκουσι καὶ ἀναβιοῦσι Sauppe τὰ We.: ταῦτα P 5 διὰ
κοσμομούμενον P 6 ποιήσει P προσοικειώσῃ Roeper: προσοικονομήσει P,
προσοικονομήσῃ Miller 8 ⟨καὶ⟩ τὰ ἐκ Sauppe 10 κοσμομουμένη P λέγει
zweimal P 12 νότοιο P ἀίσονται P 13 γοῦν(α) Emp. Fr. 134 γεννήεντα Sauppe: γενήεντα P, λαχνήεντα Emp. Fr. 134 14 ⟨πάντοθεν⟩ ἴσος ἑαυτῷ
(vgl. Hesiod Theog. 126) Schneidewin Philol. VI 161, πάντ᾽ ἴσος ἐστὶν ἑαυτῷ Miller
16 τῶν > Sauppe 19 νῦν Emp. bei Plut.: > P 20 τουτέστι > We. 22 νείκη P
22f ⟨ ⟩ Gö. 23 καὶ¹ > Gö. τεταγμένον P 24 τοῦδε Roeper: τὸ δὲ P
26 λέγων] ὃ λέγει Sauppe

/But fire and water and earth and air are things that die and
come to life again. For when the things created by Strife die
Love gathers them and takes them and adds them to the all
and adapts them to it, so that the all should remain one,
always arranged in a single manner and a single form by Love.
But when Love has made one instead of many and has adapted
the scattered things to the one, then Strife scatters them again
from the one and makes many, that is fire, water, earth, air
and the animals and plants created out of these and all the
parts of the cosmos that we perceive. And concerning the form
of the cosmos – what it is like when arranged under Love, he
speaks in this way:

> 'For two branches do not project from the back
> nor feet, nor nimble knees, nor begetting genitals,
> but it was a sphere and (is equal to itself).'

Such a form, the most beautiful form of the cosmos, Love
produces, one out of many. But Strife, the cause of the cosmic
ordering of the individual things, scatters them from that one
and produces many.

And this is what Empedocles says about his own birth:

> 'And I am now one of these, a fugitive from god and a
> wanderer',

that is using the term 'god' for the one and its unity in which
he was before he was torn away by Strife and was born among
these many things that are in the cosmic ordering of Strife;

> 'Relying on raving Strife'

Empedocles says, calling the creator of this world 'raving
Strife' and disordered and unstable. For this is the punishment
and torture of the souls which Strife tears from the one and
creates and manufactures – he speaks in this sort of way: /

ὅς κε ἐπίορκον ἁμαρτήσας ἐπομώσει,   1(
δαίμονες οἵτε μακραίωνος λελάχασι βίοιο,
δαίμονας τὰς ψυχὰς λέγων μακραίωνας, ὅτι εἰσὶν ἀθάνατοι καὶ
μακροὺς ζῶσιν αἰῶνας·
5   τρὶς μὲν μυρίας ὥρας ἀπὸ μακάρων ἀλάλησθαι,   1
μάκαρας καλῶν τοὺς συνηγμένους ὑπὸ τῆς φιλίας ἀπὸ τῶν πολλῶν
εἰς τὴν ἑνότητα | τοῦ κόσμου τοῦ νοητοῦ. τούτους οὖν φησιν ἀλά- f.
λησθαι καὶ
        φυομένους παντοῖα διὰ χρόνου εἴδεα θνητῶν,
10   ἀργαλέας βιότοιο μεταλλάσσοντα κελεύθους.
Ἀργαλέας κελεύθους φησὶν εἶναι τῶν ψυχῶν τὰς εἰς τὰ σώματα
μεταβολὰς καὶ μετακοσμήσεις. τοῦτ᾽ ἐστὶν ὃ λέγει·   1
        ἀργαλέας βιότοιο μεταλλάσσοντα κελεύθους·
μεταλλάσσουσι γὰρ αἱ ψυχαὶ σῶμα ἐκ σώματος, ὑπὸ τοῦ νείκους
15 μεταβαλλόμεναι καὶ κολαζόμεναι καὶ οὐκ ἐώμεναι μένειν εἰς τὸ ἕν·
ἀλλὰ κολάζεσθαι ἐν πάσαις κολάσεσιν ὑπὸ τοῦ νείκους τὰς ψυχὰς
μεταβαλλομένας σῶμα ἐκ σώματος.
        αἰθέριόν γε, φησί, μένος ψυχὰς πόντονδε διώκει,   1
        πόντος δ᾽ ἐς χθονὸς οὖδας ἀπέπτυσε, γαῖα δ᾽ ἐς αὐγὰς
20   ἠελίου φαέθοντος, ὁ δ᾽ αἰθέρος ἔμβαλε δίναις·
        ἄλλος δ᾽ ἐξ ἄλλου δέχεται, στυγέουσι δὲ πάντες.
αὕτη ἐστὶν ἡ κόλασις ἣν κολάζει ὁ δημιουργός, καθάπερ χαλκεύς τις 2
μετακοσμῶν σίδηρον καὶ ἐκ πυρὸς εἰς ὕδωρ μεταβάπτων· πῦρ γάρ
ἐστιν ὁ αἰθήρ, ὅθεν εἰς πόντον μεταβάλλει τὰς ψυχὰς ὁ δημιουργός,
52 χθὼν δὲ ἡ γῆ· ὅθεν φησίν· ἐξ ὕδατος εἰς γῆν, ἐκ γῆς δὲ εἰς τὸν ἀέρα.
τοῦτ᾽ ἐστὶν ὃ λέγει·

1 Empedokles Fr. 115, 4. 5 D. (⟨Νείκεἴ θ᾽⟩ ὅς κ(ε) ἐπίορκον κτλ.) — 5. 9.
10. 18 ebenda V. 6—9 — 18 ebenda V. 9—12

1 κε Emp.: καὶ P   ἐπομόσσῃ Emp.   2 δαίμονες οἵτε Plut. und Hippolyts
Paraphrase Z. 3: δαιμόνιοί τε P   Nach Z. 3 las Hipp. μακραίωνες wie Plut.
(Klost.)   βίοις P   3 μακρεῶνας P   5 μὲν] μιν   Emp. bei Plut.
ὥρας P   ἀλάλησθε P   6 μακαρίας P   ὑπὸ Gö.: ἀπὸ P   9 χρόνου Bergk:
χρόνον P   ἴδεα P   11 εἰς τὰ steht in P   12 μετὰ κοσμίσεις P   18 γε P:
μὲν γάρ σφε Emp. bei Plut., ψυχὰς > Plut.   18. 19 ποντονδέ ἐχθονὸς (spiritus
ausgestr.) διώκει· πόντοσδε ε .(Loch) χθονὸσ οὖδασ P, verb. nach Plut.   19 γέα
δ᾽ εἰς P   22 ἣν aus ἦν P

'Someone who foreswears himself, breaking his oath,
the *daimones* who are blessed with a long life,'

calling the souls 'long-lived *daimones*' because they are
immortal and live for long ages:

'Wander thirty thousand seasons far from the place of the
blessed',

'the blessed' refers to the ones gathered together by Love from
the many into the unity of the intelligible cosmos. These he
says 'wander' and

'they are born as all forms of mortal creatures in the course of
time, creatures who change, traversing the rugged paths of life'.

'The rugged paths' he says are the transfers of the souls into
the bodies and their rearrangements. This is what he says:

'Creatures who change, traversing the rugged paths of life.'

For the souls 'change' from body to body, thrown about and
chastised by Strife and not allowed to remain with the one;
but the souls are chastised by Strife with every sort of
punishment and thrown from body to body.

'The fury of *aithêr*', he says, 'drives the souls to the deep, the
deep spits them out onto the ground, earth to the rays of the
brilliant sun, and the sun casts them into the whirlwinds of
aithêr; one receives them from another, but all of them hate.'

This is the punishment which the creator inflicts, like a smith
reshaping iron and taking it out of the fire and dipping it into
water; for the *aithêr* is fire, from which the creator throws the
souls into the sea, and the earth is the ground. Hence he says –
from water to earth and from earth to the air. This is what he
says: /

21
214W

γαῖα δ' ἐς αὐγὰς
ἠελίου φαέθοντος, ὁ δ' αἰθέρος ἔμβαλε δίναις·
ἄλλος ⟨δ'⟩ ἐξ ἄλλου δέχεται, στυγέουσι δὲ πάντες.

μισουμένας οὖν τὰς ψυχὰς καὶ βασανιζομένας καὶ κολαζομένας ἐν
τῷδε τῷ κόσμῳ κατὰ τὸν Ἐμπεδοκλέα συνάγει ἡ φιλία, ἀγαθή τις   5
οὖσα καὶ κατοικτείρουσα τὸν στεναγμὸν αὐτῶν καὶ τὴν ἄτακτον καὶ
πονηρὰν τοῦ νείκους τοῦ μαινομένου κατασκευὴν καὶ ἐξάγειν κατ'
ὀλίγον ἐκ τοῦ κόσμου καὶ προσοικειοῦν τῷ ἑνὶ σπεύδουσα καὶ κοπιῶσα.
22 ὅπως τὰ πάντα εἰς τὴν ἑνότητα καταντήσῃ ὑπ' αὐτῆς ἀγόμενα. διὰ
τὴν τοιαύτην οὖν τοῦ ὀλεθρίου νείκους διακόσμησιν τοῦδε τοῦ μεμε-   10
f. 97ᵛ ρισμένου κόσμου πάντων ἐμψύχων ὁ Ἐμπεδοκλῆς | τοὺς ἑαυτοῦ μα-
θητὰς ἀπέχεσθαι παρακαλεῖ· εἶναι γάρ φησι τὰ σώματα τῶν ζῴων
τὰ ἐσθιόμενα ψυχῶν κεκολασμένων οἰκητήρια· καὶ ἐγκρατεῖς εἶναι
τοὺς τῶν τοιούτων λόγων ἀκροωμένους τῆς πρὸς γυναῖκα ὁμιλίας
διδάσκει, ἵνα μὴ συνεργάζωνται καὶ συνεπιλαμβάνωνται τῶν ἔργων.   15
ὧν δημιουργεῖ τὸ νεῖκος, τὸ τῆς φιλίας ἔργον λύον ἀεὶ καὶ διασπῶν.
23 τοῦτον εἶναί φησιν ὁ Ἐμπεδοκλῆς νόμον μέγιστον τῆς τοῦ παντὸς
διοικήσεως, λέγων ὧδέ πως·

ἔστιν ἀνάγκης χρῆμα, θεῶν ψήφισμα παλαιόν,
ἀίδιον, πλατέεσσι κατεσφρηγισμένον ὅρκοις,   20

ἀνάγκην καλῶν τὴν ἐξ ἑνὸς εἰς πολλὰ κατὰ τὸ νεῖκος καὶ ἐκ πολλῶν
εἰς ἓν κατὰ τὴν φιλίαν μεταβολήν· θεοὺς δέ, ὡς ἔφην, τέσσαρας μὲν
θνητούς, πῦρ, ὕδωρ, γῆν, ἀέρα, δύο δὲ ἀθανάτους, ἀγενήτους, πολε-
24 μίους ἑαυτοῖς διὰ παντός, τὸ νεῖκος καὶ τὴν φιλίαν· καὶ τὸ μὲν νεῖκος ἀδικεῖν διὰ παντὸς καὶ πλεονεκτεῖν καὶ ἀποσπᾶν τὰ τῆς φιλίας   25
καὶ ἑαυτῷ προσνέμειν, τὴν δὲ φιλίαν ἀεὶ καὶ διὰ παντός, ἀγαθήν
τινα οὖσαν καὶ τῆς ἑνότητος ἐπιμελουμένην, τὰ ἀπεσπασμένα τοῦ
παντὸς καὶ βεβασανισμένα καὶ κεκολασμένα ἐν τῇ κτίσει ὑπὸ τοῦ
25 δημιουργοῦ ἀνακαλεῖσθαι καὶ προσάγειν καὶ ἓν ποιεῖν. τοιαύτη τις
ἡ κατὰ τὸν Ἐμπεδοκλέα ἡμῖν ἡ τοῦ κόσμου γένεσις καὶ φθορὰ καὶ   30
σύστασις ἐξ ἀγαθοῦ καὶ κακοῦ συνεστῶσα φιλοσοφεῖται. εἶναι δέ

---

7 s. S. 212, 23 — 19 Empedokles a. a. O. V. 1. 2

1 εἰς P   2 ὅδ' αἰθέρος ἔμβαλλε P   3 δ' > P   7 κατὰ σκευὴν P
9 ἀγόμενα so P   11 πάντων ⟨τῶν⟩ We., πάντως Klost.   14 τοὺς so P   14f ὁμι-
λήσας διδάσκειν P   15 συνεργάζονται καὶ συνεπιλαμβάνονται P   19 ἔστιν]
ἔστι τι P   ἀνάγκη (nicht ἀνάγκης) P   20 πλατέεσι κατεσφραγισμένον ὅρκοις P
23 ἀγεννήτους P   29 ἓν ποιεῖν Gö.: ἐμποιεῖν P, ἐνοποιεῖν Miller   30 ἡ¹ > We.

'earth to the rays of the brilliant sun, and the sun casts them into the whirlwinds of *aithêr*; one receives them from another, but all of them hate.'

The souls are, therefore, hated and tortured and punished in this world according to Empedocles, but Love brings them together. She is a good thing and pities their misery and the bad disorderly set-up of 'raving strife', and she is keen to bring them out of the world little by little and adapt them to the one and she strives to bring it about that everything be brought out by her and return to the unity.

Because of this cosmic-ordering of this divided world by destructive Strife Empedocles instructs his disciples to abstain from all living creatures. For he says the bodies of the animals which are eaten are the dwellings of souls undergoing punishment. And he teaches those who study these theories to be abstemious with regard to sexual intercourse with women, so that they should not aid and contribute towards the works which Strife creates, always dissolving and scattering the work of Love.

This, Empedocles says, is the greatest law of the cosmic order; he speaks like this:

'There is an oracle of necessity, the ancient decree of the gods eternal, sealed down with broad oaths.'

He terms 'necessity' the change from one to many under Strife and from many to one under Love. 'The gods', as I said, are four mortal ones, fire, water, earth, air and two immortal, ingenerate, hostile to each other in everything, Strife and Love. And Strife commits injustice in everything and is greedy and tears away the things belonging to Love and takes them for itself, but Love, being a good thing and caring for the unity, always and in everything recalls the things that are torn away from the all and tortured and punished by the creator in the world, and leads them forth and makes them one. Such is the origin of our world according to Empedocles, and its decease, and its composition made up of good and evil. /

215W   φησι καὶ νοητὴν τρίτην τινὰ δύναμιν, ἥν καὶ ἐκ τούτων ἐπινοεῖσθαι
δύνασθαι, λέγων ὧδέ πως·

    εἰ γὰρ καὶ ἐν σφαδινῇσιν ὑπὸ πραπίδεσσιν ἐρείσας   26
    εὐμενέως καθαρῇσιν ἐποπτεύεις μελέτῃσιν,
5   ταῦτα δέ σοι μάλα πάντα δι᾽ αἰῶνος παρέσονται,
    ἄλλα τε πόλλ᾽ ἀπὸ τῶνδε κτ .. ηται· αὐτὰ γὰρ αὔξει
    ταῦτ᾽ εἰς ἦθος ἕκαστον, ὅπη φύσις ἐστὶν | ἑκάστῳ.   f. 9ᵛ
    εἰ δὲ σύ γ᾽ ἀλλοίων ἐπορέξεαι οἷα κατ᾽ ἄνδρας
    μυρία δειλὰ πέλονται ἅ τ᾽ ἀμβλύνουσι μέριμναι,
10   ἦ σ᾽ ἄφαρ ἐκλείψουσι περιπλομένοιο χρόνοιο
    σφῶν αὐτῶν ποθέοντα φίλην ἐπὶ γένναν ἱκέσθαι·
    πάντα γὰρ ἴσθι φρόνησιν ἔχειν καὶ νώματος αἶσαν.

30. Ἐπειδὰν οὖν Μαρκίων ἢ τῶν ἐκείνου κυνῶν τις ὑλακτῇ κατὰ 1
τοῦ δημιουργοῦ, τοὺς ἐκ τῆς ἀντιπαραθέσεως ἀγαθοῦ καὶ κακοῦ προ-
15 φέρων λόγους, δεῖ αὐτοῖς λέγειν, ὅτι τούτους οὔτε Παῦλος ὁ ἀπόστο-
λος οὔτε Μάρκος ὁ κολοβοδάκτυλος ἀνήγγειλαν — τούτων γὰρ οὐδὲν
ἐν τῷ ⟨κατὰ⟩ Μάρκον εὐαγγελίῳ γέγραπται —, ἀλλὰ Ἐμπεδοκλῆς
Μέτωνος Ἀκραγαντίνος, ὃν συλαγωγῶν μέχρι νῦν λανθάνειν ὑπελάμ-
βανε τὴν διαταγὴν πάσης τῆς κατ᾽ αὐτὸν αἱρέσεως ἀπὸ τῆς Σικελίας
20 εἰς τοὺς εὐαγγελικοὺς λόγους μεταφέρων αὐταῖς λέξεσι. φέρε γάρ, 2
ὦ Μαρκίων, καθάπερ τὴν ἀντιπαράθεσιν πεποίηκας ἀγαθοῦ καὶ κακοῦ, ἀντιπαραθῶ κἀγὼ σήμερον κατακολουθῶν τοῖς σοῖς, ὡς ὑπο-

7 Empedokles Fr. 110 D., der letzte V. auch bei Sext., sonst nur bei Hipp.
überliefert. Ich gebe im Apparat nur die von Diels aufgenommenen Emendationen,
meist von Schn(eidewin) Philol. VI 166 — 14. 21 Anspielung auf Marcions Anti-
thesen — 16 κολοβοδάκτυλος] alte Vorrede zu Marcus (s. Zahn, Einleitung II²
S. 211f; s. auch Zahn, Gesch. des neutest. Kanons I S. 621): amputasse sibi post
fidem pollicem dicitur, ut sacerdotio reprobus haberetur (Corssen T. U. XV 1
S. 10, 10)

    1 καὶ νοητὴν Miller: καινὸν τὴν P   3 κέν σφ᾽ ἀδινῇσιν Schn. Emp. σφαδίνη-
σιν P   4 ἐποπτεύσῃς Schn. Emp. 5 δὲ] τε Schn. δέ τοι μάλα Diels nach β 306
μᾶλλα P   6 τῶνδεκτ . ηται P (κτ(η . η)ται exesis partim litteris η P nach
Diels): τῶνδ᾽ ἐκτήσεαι (oder τῶν κεκτήσεαι Meineke, Z. f. Altertumswiss. X 376)
Diels   ἄξει und Z. 7 ἔθνος Heidel, Proceedings of American Acad. XLVIII
S. 426ff   7 ἦθος Miller: ἔθος P   8 σὺ τἀλλ᾽ οἷων ἐπιρέξεις P, verb. Schn.
9 δεῖλα Schn.: δῆλα P ἅ τ᾽ Diels: τά τ᾽ P μερίμνας Schn. 10 ἦ σ᾽ Meineke,
Z. für Altertumswiss. X 376: σῆς P περιπλομένοις P 11 γένναν P 12 γνωμα-
τοσισον P, verb. nach Sext. Schn.   14 κακοῦ Gö.: καλοῦ P 16 οὐδὲν] οὐδὲ P
17 + κατὰ Miller   18 Μέτωνος Miller: μιῶνος P

But he says that there is also a third intelligible power,[1] which it is possible to invent from these things, saying thus:

> 'If you take these things to heart and fix them into your bosom
> and study them favourably with pure thought,
> these will remain with you in their entirety for all time,
> and many other things from these … For these increase themselves
> each to its character, whatever is the nature of each.
> But if you seek after other things such as exist among men
> in myriads and worthless, and blunted by cares,
> they will be gone from you as time goes round,
> yearning to return to their own place of origin.
> For you must know that all things have understanding and a share of intelligence.'

30. When Marcion, therefore, or one of his dogs barks at the creator, producing the arguments from the contrast of good and evil, we should say to them that these arguments were not reported either by Paul the apostle or by stump-fingered Mark – none of these is written in the Gospel according to Mark – but by Empedocles of Acragas, the son of Meton. Up till now Marcion thought he had succeeded in stealing from Empedocles unnoticed and adapting the structure of his entire heresy to the gospel accounts from Sicily in the very same words.

Come, Marcion, just as you make a comparative juxtaposition of good and evil, so today, following your doctrines as you understand, / I will myself make such a

---

[1] See above, pp. 129-30.

216W λαμβάνεις, δόγμασι. δημιουργὸν φῇς εἶναι τοῦ κόσμου πονηρόν· εἶτα
οὐκ ἐγκαλύπτῃ τοὺς Ἐμπεδοκλέους λόγους τὴν ἐκκλησίαν κατηχῶν;
3 ἀγαθὸν φῇς εἶναι θεὸν καταλύοντα τὰ τοῦ δημιουργοῦ ποιήματα·
εἶτ᾽ οὐ καταφανῶς τὴν Ἐμπεδοκλέους φιλίαν εὐαγγελίζῃ τοῖς ἀκροωμένοις τὸν ἀγαθόν; κωλύεις γαμεῖν, τεκνοῦν, ἀπέχεσθαι βρωμάτων,   5
ὧν ὁ θεὸς ἔκτισεν εἰς μετάληψιν τοῖς πιστοῖς καὶ ἐπεγνωκόσι τὴν
4 ἀλήθειαν· τοὺς Ἐμπεδοκλέους λανθάνεις διδάσκων Καθαρμούς. ἐπό-
μενος γὰρ ὡς ἀληθῶς κατὰ πάντα τούτῳ τὰ βρώματα παραιτεῖσθαι
τοὺς ἑαυτοῦ μαθητὰς διδάσκεις, ἵνα μὴ φάγωσι σῶμά τι λείψανον
f. 98ᵛ ψυχῆς ὑπὸ τοῦ δημιουργοῦ | κεκολασμένης· λύεις τοὺς ὑπὸ τοῦ θεοῦ 10
συνηρμοσμένους γάμους τοῖς Ἐμπεδοκλέους ἀκολουθῶν δόγμασιν, ἵνα
σοι φυλαχθῇ τὸ τῆς φιλίας ἔργον ἓν ἀδιαίρετον. διαιρεῖ γὰρ ὁ γάμος
κατὰ Ἐμπεδοκλέα τὸ ἓν καὶ ποιεῖ πολλά, καθὼς ἀπεδείξαμεν.
1   31. Ἡ μὲν οὖν πρώτη καὶ καθαριωτάτη Μαρκίωνος αἵρεσις, ἐξ
ἀγαθοῦ καὶ κακοῦ τὴν σύστασιν ἔχουσα, Ἐμπεδοκλέους ἡμῖν εἶναι 15
πεφανέρωται· ἐπεὶ δὲ ἐν τοῖς καθ᾽ ἡμᾶς χρόνοις νῦν καινότερόν τι
ἐπεχείρησε Μαρκιωνιστής τις Πρέπων Ἀσσύριος, πρὸς (Β)αρδησιάνην
τὸν Ἀρμένιον ἐγγράφως ποιήσασθαι λόγους περὶ τῆς αἱρέσεως, οὐδὲ
2 τοῦτο σιωπήσομαι. τρίτην φάσκων [δίκαιον εἶναι ἀρχὴν καὶ μέσην
ἀγαθοῦ καὶ κακοῦ τεταγμένην, οὐδ᾽ οὕτως δὴ ὁ Πρέπων τὰς Ἐμπε- 20
3 δοκλέους διαφυγεῖν ἴσχυσε δόξας. κόσμον γάρ φησιν εἶναι ὁ Ἐμπεδοκλῆς τὸν ὑπὸ τοῦ νείκους διοικούμενον τοῦ πονηροῦ καὶ ἕτερον
νοητὸν τὸν ὑπὸ τῆς φιλίας, καὶ εἶναι ταύτας τὰς διαφερούσας ἀρχὰς
δύο ἀγαθοῦ καὶ κακοῦ, μέσον δὲ εἶναι τῶν διαφόρων ἀρχῶν δίκαιον
λόγον, καθ᾽ ὃν συγκρίνεται τὰ διῃρημένα ὑπὸ τοῦ νείκους καὶ προσ- 25
4 αρμόζεται κατὰ τὴν φιλίαν τῷ ἑνί. τοῦτον δὲ αὐτὸν τὸν δίκαιον
λόγον τὸν τῇ φιλίᾳ συναγωνιζόμενον Μοῦσαν ὁ Ἐμπεδοκλῆς προσα-
γορεύων, καὶ αὐτὸς αὐτῷ συναγωνίζεσθαι παρακαλεῖ, λέγων ὧδέ πως·

3 vgl. Hilgenfeld S. 528 Anm. 869 — 5 f᛫I Tim. 4, 3 κωλυόντων γαμεῖν,
ἀπέχεσθαι βρωμάτων, ἃ ὁ θεὸς .... ἔκτισεν εἰς μετάληψιν μετὰ εὐχαριστίας τοῖς
πιστοῖς—ἀλήθειαν, vgl. Hilgenfeld S. 529 Anm. 874 — 7 Καθαρμούς] aber Hipp.
hat vorher nur Περὶ φύσεως benutzt, nicht die Καθαρμοί — 17 Über den
Streit des B. mit den Marcioniten s. Eusebius KG IV 30, 1 (Epiph. LVI 1); Zahn,
Forschungen I 378 ff

2 ἐγκαταλύπτῃ P   4 εἶ τοῦ P   εὐαγγελήζῃ P   9 ἕδρανον? We.   10 καὶ
κολασμένης P   14 αἵρεσις P   16 ἐπὶ P   κενώτερόν P   17 μαρκίων, νῆστίς τις P, verb. Bunsen I 370 (I 68)   ἀσύριος P   Βαρδησιάνης schreibt auch
Epiph. LVI   18 ποιήσας Scott, ποιησάμενος We.   20 οὕτως Gö: οὗτος P
δὴ Miller: δὲ P   τῆς — 21 δόξης P, verb. Gö.   27 συναγονιζόμενον P   28 αὐτῷ P

juxtaposition. You say the creator of the world is wicked; well then are you not concealing the fact that you are teaching the church the doctrines of Empedocles? You say that the god who undoes the things made by the creator is good; well then are you not blatantly evangelising Empedocles' Love to those who hear about the good god? You issue prohibitions on marriage and procreation and on abstention from foods which God created for the partaking of the faithful and those who know the truth; you are teaching the purifications of Empedocles unobserved. The truth is that, following him in everything, you teach your disciples to reject the foods, so that they shall not eat a body which is the remains of a soul punished by the creator. You dissolve the marriages joined by God, following the doctrines of Empedocles, so that the work of love may be preserved for you one and undivided. For marriage divides the one according to Empedocles and makes many, as we have shown.

31. The first and purest heresy of Marcion, which has a structure of good and evil, has been shown to belong to Empedocles. But now in our own times a Marcionite named Prepon the Assyrian has ventured an innovation and written that he has held discussions about the heresy with Bardesianes the Armenian, and I shall not be silent on this either. When he says there is a third just principle located midway between good and evil, Prepon still does not manage to escape Empedocles' views even in this way. For Empedocles says there is the cosmos that is governed by Strife the evil one, and another intelligible one governed by Love, and that these are the two different principles of good and evil, but between the different principles there is a just *logos*, according to which the things divided by Strife are combined and joined to the one in accordance with Love. This just *logos* which fights along with Love is called Muse by Empedocles, and he calls upon it to fight along with him, saying thus: /

εἰ γὰρ ἐφημερίων ἕνεκεν τινός, ἄμβροτε Μοῦσα,
ἡμετέρας μελέτας † διὰ φροντίδος ἐλθεῖν,
εὐχομένῳ νῦν αὖτε παρίστασο, Καλλιόπεια,
ἀμφὶ θεῶν μακάρων ἀγαθὸν λόγον ἐμφαίνοντι.

5 τούτοις κατακολουθῶν Μαρκίων τὴν γένεσιν τοῦ σωτῆρος ἡμῶν 5
παντάπασι παρῃτήσατο, ἄτοπον εἶναι νομίζων ὑπὸ τὸ πλάσμα | τοῦ f.
ὀλεθριωτάτου νείκους γεγονέναι τὸν λόγον τὸν τῇ φιλίᾳ συναγωνιζόμενον, τουτέστι τῷ ἀγαθῷ, ἀλλὰ χωρὶς γενέσεως »ἔτει πεντεκαι-
δεκάτῳ τῆς ἡγεμονίας Τιβερίου Καίσαρος« κατεληλυθότα αὐτὸν ἄνω-
10 θεν, μέσον ὄντα κακοῦ καὶ ἀγαθοῦ, διδάσκειν »ἐν ταῖς συναγωγαῖς«.
εἰ γὰρ μεσότης ἐστίν, ἀπήλλακται, φησί, πάσης τῆς τοῦ κακοῦ 6
φύσεως· κακὸς δ᾽ ἐστίν, ὡς λέγει, ὁ δημιουργὸς καὶ τούτου τὰ ποιή-
ματα. διὰ τοῦτο ἀγέννητος κατῆλθεν ὁ Ἰησοῦς, φησίν, ἵνα ᾖ πάσης
ἀπηλλαγμένος κακίας. ἀπήλλακται δέ, φησί, καὶ τῆς τοῦ ἀγαθοῦ
15 φύσεως, ἵνα ᾖ μεσότης, ὥς φησιν ὁ Παῦλος καὶ ὡς αὐτὸς ὁμολογεῖ·
»τί με λέγετε ἀγαθόν; εἷς ἐστιν ἀγαθός«. ταῦτα μὲν οὖν τὰ Μαρ- 7
κίωνι δόξαντα, δι᾽ ὧν ἐπλάνησε πολλοὺς τοῖς Ἐμπεδοκλέους λόγοις
χρησάμενος καὶ τὴν ὑπ᾽ ἐκείνου ἐφηυρημένην φιλοσοφίαν ἰδίᾳ δόξῃ
μετάγων αἵρεσιν ἄθεον συνεστήσατο· ἣν ἱκανῶς ἠλέγχθαι ὑφ᾽ ἡμῶν 8
20 νομίζω μηθέν τε καταλελεῖφθαι, ὧν κλεψιλογήσαντες παρ᾽ Ἑλλήνων τοὺς Χριστοῦ μαθητὰς ἐπηρεάζουσιν, ὡς τούτων αὐτοῖς γενο-
μένους διδασκάλους. ἀλλ᾽ ἐπεὶ καὶ τὰ τούτου ἱκανῶς ἡμῖν δοκεῖ
ἐκτεθεῖσθαι, ἴδωμεν τί λέγει Καρποκράτης.

1 Fr. 131 D. — 5—9 vgl. Filastrius C. 45, 4 S. 24, 5—7 M. (vgl. C. 44, 2);
Theodoret I 24 S. 376 A Migne; Tert. Adv. haer. 6 S. 222, 21—25 Kr. (Kerdon);
Hilgenfeld S. 528 Anm. 870 — 6—10 Über den Eingang des Evangeliums Marcions s. Zahn, Gesch. des neutest. Kanons II 455 f — 8 Luk. 3, 1 — 9 vgl. Iren.
I 27, 2 S. 216 f H. — 10 Luk. 4, 15. — 15 Paulus] Röm. 8, 3 τὸν ἑαυτοῦ υἱὸν πέμψας
ἐν ὁμοιώματι σαρκὸς ἁμαρτίας? Das Pauluscitat muß wie das folgende Citat
sich auf τῆς τοῦ ἀγαθοῦ φύσεως beziehen; also kann Gal. 3, 19 oder I Tim. 2, 5
nicht gemeint sein. — 16 Mark. 10, 18; Luk. 18, 19; Matth. 19, 17 s. zu S. 84, 20
und Epiph. LXII Schol. 50

*

1 εἰκάραι φημερίων P   2 μελέτας ⟨μέλε τοι⟩ Diels   3 εὐχομένων P,
verb. Schn. Philol VI 167   4 μακαρίων P   7 ὀλεθριωτάτου Klost.: ὀλεθρίου τὰ
τοῦ P, ὀλεθρίου τούτου Miller   7 f συναγονιζόμενον P   8 γεννήσεως? Usener,
Weihnachtsfest² S. 93²²   8 f ἔτη πέντε καὶ δεκάτω P   9 τηβερίου P   11 μεσότης P:
μέσος τις Gö., μεσίτης nach Gal. 3, 19 Bunsen   13 ἀγένητος P   15 ἡ μεσότης P:
ἢ μέσος τις Gö., ἢ μεσίτης Bunsen Roeper   16 εἷς] εἰ P   19 ἤλεγχεν P   23 ⟨καὶ⟩
Καρποκράτης Gö.

'If for the sake of one of the mortals, divine Muse,
it might be that our cares come to thy mind,
now stand again beside him who prays to thee, Calliopeia,
that he may present a good *logos* about the blessed gods.'

Following these things Marcion denies the birth of our saviour altogether, considering it absurd that the *Logos* that fights along with Love, that is the good, should have been born under the fashioning of most destructive Strife, but he came down from above without birth 'in the fifteenth year of the reign of Tiberius Caesar', being intermediate between good and bad, to teach 'in the synagogues'. For if he is a mean he is free from all evil nature. But the creator is evil, so he says, and the things made by him. For this reason Jesus came down unbegotten, he says, so that he should be free of all evil. But he is free also of the nature of the good, he says, so that he may be a mean, as Paul says and he himself agrees: 'Why do you call me good? There is but one good.'

These, therefore, are the opinions of Marcion, by which he leads many astray, using the words of Empedocles and by adapting the philosophy invented by Empedocles to his own view he has set up a godless heresy. This heresy I consider to have been adequately refuted by us, and nothing left out – none of the things which they got by theory-stealing from the Greeks, but which they claim were taught to them by Christ's disciples, thus maligning the disciples of Christ. But since we consider this man's views have been adequately explained, let us see what Carpocrates says.

*

Book 9, chapter 7

1
240W
f. 110ʳ

7. | Γεγένηταί τις ὀνόματι Νοητός, τῷ γένει Σμυρναῖος. οὗτος εἰσηγήσατο αἵρεσιν ἐκ τῶν Ἡρακλείτου δογμάτων· οὗ διάκονος καὶ μαθητὴς γίνεται Ἐπίγονός τις τοὔνομα, ὃς τῇ Ῥώμῃ ἐπιδημήσας ἐπέσπειρε τὴν ἄθεον γνώμην. ᾧ μαθητεύσας Κλεομένης, καὶ βίῳ καὶ τρόπῳ ἀλλότριος τῆς ἐκκλησίας, ἐκράτυνε τὸ δόγμα, κατ᾽ ἐκεῖνο 2 καιροῦ Ζεφυρίνου διέπειν νομίζοντος τὴν ἐκκλησίαν, ἀνδρὸς ἰδιώτου 2 καὶ αἰσχροκερδοῦς· ⟨ὃς⟩ τῷ κέρδει προσφερομένῳ πειθόμενος συνεχώρει τοῖς προσιοῦσι τῷ Κλεομένει μαθητεύεσθαι καὶ αὐτὸς ὑποσυρόμενος τῷ χρόνῳ ἐπὶ τὰ αὐτὰ ὥρμητο, συμβούλου καὶ συναγωνιστοῦ τῶν κακῶν ὄντος αὐτῷ Καλλίστου, οὗ τὸν βίον καὶ τὴν ἐφευρεθεῖσαν 2 3 αἵρεσιν μετ᾽ οὐ πολὺ ἐκθήσομαι. τούτων κατὰ διαδοχὴν διέμεινε τὸ διδασκαλεῖον κρατυνόμενον καὶ ἐπαῦξον διὰ τὸ συναίρεσθαι αὐτοῖς τὸν Ζεφυρῖνον καὶ τὸν Κάλλιστον, καίτοι ἡμῶν μηδέποτε συγχωρησάντων, ἀλλὰ πλειστάκις ἀντικαθεστώτων πρὸς αὐτοὺς καὶ

16—20 vgl. X 27, 1 —
16 Hippolyt G. Noetos S. 43, 11 L. τὸ μὲν γένος ἦν Σμυρναῖος — 26 ἐκθήσομαι] C. 11 ff

18 τῇ ῥώμην
                    ᵛ
P   22 + δς Miller   23 κλεομένη P   24 ὡρμᾶτο Wordsworth   συμβόλου P
27 συναιρεῖσθαι P, verb. Wordsworth   29 ἀντικαθεστότων P

Book 9, *chapter 7*

There was a man by name of Noetus, a Smyrnaean by race. He introduced a heresy derived from the doctrines of Heraclitus. A man called Epigonus became his minister and disciple, and he visited Rome and spread abroad the godless idea. Cleomenes studied under him – a man alien to the church both in life and character – and strengthened the doctrine, at that point of time when Zephyrinus, an ignorant man and shamefully greedy, was, by custom, running the church. Zephyrinus was persuaded by the offer of a bribe to comply with those going to study under Cleomenes, and he himself was beguiled in time and embarked upon the same things, with Callistus as his adviser and accomplice in the evil things. The life of Callistus and the heresy invented by him I shall explain in a little while.

The school set up by these men continued by succession, strengthened and enlarged due to the fact that Zephyrinus and Callistus had joined their heresy, although we never agreed but frequently stood out in opposition to them and / refuted

241W διελεγξάντων καὶ ἄκοντας βιασαμένων τὴν ἀλήθειαν ὁμολογεῖν· οἳ
πρὸς μὲν ὥραν αἰδούμενοι καὶ ὑπὸ τῆς ἀληθείας συναγόμενοι ὡμο-
λόγουν, μετ᾽ οὐ πολὺ δὲ ἐπὶ τὸν αὐτὸν βόρβορον ἀνεκυλίοντο.

8. Ἀλλ᾽ ἐπεὶ τῆς γενεαλογίας αὐτῶν τὴν διαδοχὴν ἐπεδείξαμεν, **1**
5 δοκεῖ λοιπὸν καὶ τῶν δογμάτων τὴν κακοδιδασκαλίαν ἐκθέσθαι,
⟨καὶ⟩ πρότερον τὰ Ἡρακλείτῳ τῷ σκοτεινῷ δόξαντα παρατεθεμένους,
ἔπει⟨τα⟩ καὶ τὰ τούτων μέρη Ἡράκλειτεια ὄντα φανερῶσαι, ἃ
τυχὸν[τες] οἱ νῦν προστάται τῆς αἱρέσεως | οὐκ ἴσασιν ὄντα τοῦ **⁂**
σκοτεινοῦ, νομίζοντες εἶναι Χριστοῦ. οἷς εἰ ἐνέτυχον, κἂν οὕτω **⁂**
10 δυσωπηθέντες παύσονται τῆς ἀθέου δυσφημίας. ἀλλ᾽ εἰ καὶ πρότερον
ἔκκειται ὑφ᾽ ἡμῶν ἐν τοῖς Φιλοσοφουμένοις ἡ δόξα Ἡρακλείτου, ἀλλά
γε δοκεῖ προσαντιπαραχθῆναι καὶ νῦν, ὅπως διὰ τοῦ ἐγγίονος ἐλέγχου
φανερῶς διδαχθῶσιν οἱ τούτου, νομίζοντες Χριστοῦ εἶναι μαθηταί,·
οὐκ ὄντες, ἀλλὰ τοῦ σκοτεινοῦ.
15 9. Ἡράκλειτος μὲν οὖν φησιν εἶναι τὸ πᾶν διαιρετὸν ἀδιαίρετον,
γενητὸν ἀγένητον, θνητὸν ἀθάνατον, λόγον αἰῶνα, πατέρα υἱόν,
θεὸν δίκαιον. »οὐκ ἐμοῦ ἀλλὰ τοῦ λόγου ἀκούσαντας ὁμολογεῖν
σοφόν ἐστιν, ἓν πάντα εἶναι«, ὁ Ἡράκλειτός φησι· καὶ ὅτι τοῦτο οὐκ **⁂**
ἴσασιν πάντες οὐδὲ ὁμολογοῦσιν, ἐπιμέμφεται ὧδέ πως· ᾽οὐ ξυνιᾶσιν
20 ὅκως διαφερόμενον ἑωυτῷ ὁμολογέει· παλίντροπος ἁρμονίη ὅκως
περ τόξου καὶ λύρης.« ὅτι δὲ λόγος ἐστὶν ἀεὶ τὸ πᾶν καὶ διὰ παντὸς
ὤν, οὕτως λέγει· »τοῦ δὲ λόγου τοῦδ᾽ ἐόντος ἀεὶ ἀξύνετοι γίνονται
ἄνθρωποι καὶ πρόσθεν ἢ ἀκοῦσαι καὶ ἀκούσαντες τὸ πρῶτον· γινο-

---

3 II Petr. 2, 22, vgl. Wendland S. A. B. 1898 S. 794 — 11 I 4 — 15—17 vgl.
Heraklit Fr. 67 D. — **17** den Gegensatz θεὸν δίκαιον kann H. gebildet haben
aus der gnostischen Antithese (Marcion) — Heraklit Fr. 50 D., s. auch Heidel,
Proceedings of the American Academy of Arts and Sciences XLVIII S. 704 —
19 Heraklit Fr. 51 D. — 22 Heraklit Fr. 1 D.

1 διελλεγξάντων P　2 συναναγκαζόμενοι We.　**6** + καὶ Sauppe　7 ἔπειτα
Miller: ἐπεὶ P　μέρη >? Gö.　**8** τυχὸν Cruice: τυχόντες P　εἴσασιν P　10 παύ-
σαιντό τι Wordsworth (oder ἐπαύσαντ᾽ ἄν), παύσαιντ᾽ ἄν Diels　11 φιλοσοφομένους
(so) P　12 προσαντιπαραχθῆναι Gö.: πρὸς ἀνπαραχθῆναι P　ἀγγίονος ἐλλέγχου P
13 τούτου] τοιοῦτοι Sauppe, τούτους Klost.　**13f** μαθηταί, οὐκ ὄντες Sauppe: μαθητάς, οὐκ ὄντας P　15 ⟨ἓν⟩ φησιν Bernays, doch s. Heidel　16 λόγον ⟨ἄλογον,
χρόνον⟩ αἰῶνα Diels Vorsokr. I³ S. 87　πατέρα υἱόν christlicher Zusatz　17 δίκαιον
⟨ἄδικον⟩ Diels　λόγου Bernays: δόγμ̅τ̅ P　18 ἐν P　εἶναι Miller: εἰδέναι P,
>? Heidel (Glosse von ὁμολογεῖν)　19 εἴσασιν P　20 ὁμολογεῖν P　22 ὧν
P, αἰῶνος Bernays　τοῦ δέοντος P　ἀξύνετοι Heraklit bei Sext.: ξετοὶ P
23 ἀκούσαντας P　23f γινόμενον P

them and forced them against their will to confess the truth.
For the time being they were ashamed and were brought to
agreement by the truth, but in a little while they rolled back to
their old mud-bath.

8. Now that we have indicated the sequence of their
genealogical succession, the next thing to do is to set forth the
evil teaching of their doctrines: first we must set the opinions of
Heraclitus alongside and then reveal the parts of their
doctrines that are Heraclitean and which the present leaders of
the heresy do not know belong to Heraclitus the obscure,
when they chance upon them, believing them to be Christ's.
But if they happened to read these Heraclitean doctrines they
would even thus likely be put to shame and give up their
godless blasphemy. But although Heraclitus' view was set out
by us earlier, in the *Philosophoumena*, nevertheless it is as well to
set it alongside for comparison now also, so that this man's
disciples, who think they are Christ's disciples when they are
not, but rather disciples of Heraclitus the obscure, may be
taught obviously by means of the closer refutation.

9. Heraclitus says that the all is divisible, indivisible,
created, uncreated, mortal, immortal, *logos*, *aeon*, father, son,
god, just.

> 'Listening not to me but to the *logos* wise it is to agree that one
> thing is all things/all things are one thing,'

Heraclitus says. And he complains that all men do not know
this nor agree, like this:

> 'They do not understand how in differing from itself it agrees
> with itself: a back-turning construction like that of the bow
> and lyre.'

But he says that the all is always *logos*, and being through
everything, thus:

242W μένων γὰρ πάντων κατὰ τὸν λόγον τόνδε ἀπείροισιν ἐοίκασι, πειρώ-
μενοι καὶ ἐπέων καὶ ἔργων τοιουτέων, ὁποῖα ἐγὼ διηγεῦμαι, διαιρέων
4 κατὰ φύσιν καὶ φράζων ὅπως ἔχει.« ὅτι δέ ἐστι παῖς τὸ πᾶν καὶ
δι' αἰῶνος αἰώνιος βασιλεὺς τῶν ὅλων οὕτως λέγει· »αἰὼν παῖς
ἐστι παίζων, πεττεύων· παιδὸς ἡ βασιληίη.« ὅτι δέ ἐστιν ὁ πατὴρ
πάντων τῶν γεγονότων γενητὸς ἀγένητος, κτίσις δημιουργός, ἐκείνου
λέγοντος ἀκούομεν· »πόλεμος πάντων μὲν πατήρ ἐστι, πάντων δὲ
βασιλεύς, καὶ τοὺς μὲν θεοὺς ἔδειξε τοὺς δὲ ἀνθρώπους, τοὺς μὲν |
f. 111ʳ 5 δούλους ἐποίησε τοὺς δὲ ἐλευθέρους«. ὅτι δέ ἐστιν * * * »ἁρμονίη
ὅκως περ τόξου καὶ λύρης.« ὅτι δὲ (ὁ θεὸς) ἀφανὴς [ὁ] ἀόρατος
ἄγνωστος ἀνθρώποις, ἐν τούτοις λέγει· »ἁρμονίη ἀφανὴς φανερῆς
κρείττων·« ἐπαινεῖ καὶ προθαυμάζει πρὸ τοῦ γινωσκομένου τὸ
ἄγνωστον αὐτοῦ καὶ ἀόρατον τῆς δυνάμεως. ὅτι δέ ἐστιν ὁρατὸς
ἀνθρώποις καὶ οὐκ ἀνεξεύρετος, ἐν τούτοις λέγει· »ὅσων ὄψις, ἀκοή,
μάθησις, ταῦτα ἐγὼ προτιμέω«, φησί, τουτέστι τὰ ὁρατὰ τῶν
ἀοράτων. * * * ἀπὸ τῶν τοιούτων αὐτοῦ λόγων κατανοεῖν ῥᾴδιον·
6 »ἐξηπάτηνται«, φησίν, »οἱ ἄνθρωποι πρὸς τὴν γνῶσιν τῶν φανερῶν
παραπλησίως Ὁμήρῳ, ὃς ἐγένετο τῶν Ἑλλήνων σοφώτερος πάντων.
ἐκεῖνόν τε γὰρ παῖδες φθεῖρας κατακτείνοντες ἐξηπάτησαν εἰπόντες·
ὅσα εἴδομεν καὶ [κατ]ελάβομεν, ταῦτα ἀπολείπομεν, ὅσα δὲ οὔτε
εἴδομεν οὔτ' ἐλάβομεν ταῦτα φέρομεν.«
1   10. Οὕτως Ἡράκλειτος ἐν ἴσῃ μοίρᾳ τίθεται καὶ τιμᾷ τὰ ἐμφανῆ
τοῖς ἀφανέσιν, ὡς ἕν τι τὸ ἐμφανὲς καὶ τὸ ἀφανὲς ὁμολογουμένως
ὑπάρχον. »ἔστι γάρ«, φησίν, »ἁρμονίη ἀφανὴς φανερῆς κρείττων«,
καὶ »ὅσων ὄψις, ἀκοή, μάθησις« — τουτέστι τὰ ὄργανα —, »ταῦτα«,
2 φησίν, »ἐγὼ προτιμέω«, οὐ τὰ ἀφανῆ προτιμήσας. τοιγαροῦν οὐδὲ
σκότος οὐδὲ φῶς, οὐδὲ πονηρὸν οὐδὲ ἀγαθὸν ἕτερόν φησιν εἶναι ὁ
Ἡράκλειτος, ἀλλὰ ἓν καὶ τὸ αὐτό. ἐπιτιμᾷ γοῦν Ἡσιόδῳ, ὅτι ἡμέραν

---

4 Heraklit Fr. 52 D. — 7 Heraklit Fr. 53 D. — 9 Heraklit Fr. 51 —
11 Heraklit Fr. 54 D. — 13f Röm. 1, 19. 20? — 14 Heraklit Fr. 55 D —
17 Heraklit Fr. 56 D. — 24—26 = 11. 14. 15

1 ἄπειροι εἰσὶν P, verb. Wordsworth   2 ὁκοίων Her.   διήγευμαι διερέων P
3 ὅκως Her.   5 ὁ ⟨πόλεμος⟩ oder τίς δέ ἐστιν Miller   6 γενητὸς Bernays:
γενητῶν P   7 ἀκούομεν Miller   9 Lücke Miller, etwa ἁρμονία, ἐν τούτοις
λέγει We.   10 ὁ θσ We.: 3 Lettern unlesbar P, ἔστιν Miller   ὁ < We.
12 ⟨ἐν οἷς⟩ ἐπαινεῖ Diels   14 ἂν ἐξευρετὸς P   ὅσον P   16 Lücke Miller,
etwa ταὐτὸ δὲ καὶ We.   20 ἐλάβομεν Bernays: κατελάβομεν P   ἀπελίπομεν
Cruice   24 ἔστι Miller: τίς P, τί Bernays   ἁρμονίη Wordsworth vgl. Z. 11:
ἁρμονία ἡ P   26 οὐ] ὁ Wordsworth   26. 27 οὔτε viermal Sauppe

'Of this thing which is always the *logos* men are always uncomprehending both before they hear and after they hear for the first time; for while all things / come to be according to this *logos* they resemble those with no experience of them, although they experience both words and facts of the very sort I am describing, as I divide according to nature and say what is the case.'

That the all is a child and eternal king of all things to eternity he says thus:

'Eternity is a child playing at draughts; the kingdom is the kingdom of a child.'

That the father of all things created is created and uncreated, creation and creator we hear him saying:

'War is father of all and king of all, and he reveals some as gods and some men, makes some slaves and others free.'

But that (it) is ...[2] 'a harmonia like that of the bow and lyre'. But that (god) is invisible, unseen, unknown to men he says in the following words:

'The invisible harmonia is better than the visible';

he praises and extols the unknown part of it and the unseen part of its power more highly than the known part. But that it is visible to men and not impossible to discover he says in the following words:

'Things of which there is sight, hearing, learning, these things I honour more',

he says, that is honouring the visible more than the invisible ... from such words of his it is easy to understand.

'Men are deceived,' he says, 'with regard to knowledge of evident things like Homer, who was wisest of all the Greeks. For boys who were killing lice deceived him by saying: the things that we see and grasp we leave behind, but the things that we neither see nor grasp, these we take away.'

10. Thus Heraclitus places the visible things in the same rank as the invisible things and honours them equally, on the grounds that the visible and the invisible are undoubtedly one thing. For, he says,

[2] See pp. 160-1.

243W καὶ νύκτα οἶδεν· ἡμέρα γάρ, φησί, καὶ νὺξ ἔστιν ἕν, λέγων ὧδέ πως·
»διδάσκαλος δὲ πλείστων Ἡσίοδος· τοῦτον ἐπίστανται πλεῖστα εἰδέναι,
ὅστις ἡμέρην καὶ εὐφρόνην οὐκ ἐγίνωσκεν· ἔστι γὰρ ἕν«. καὶ ἀγαθὸν 3
καὶ κακόν· »οἱ γοῦν ἰατροί«, φησὶν ὁ Ἡράκλειτος, »τέμνοντες,
5 καίοντες, πάντῃ βασανίζοντες κακῶς τοὺς ἀρρωστοῦντας, | ἐπαιτέον- f. 1
ται μηδὲν ἄξιοι μισθὸν λαμβάνειν παρὰ τῶν ἀρρωστούντων, ταὐτὰ
ἐργαζόμενοι, τὰ ἀγαθὰ καὶ τὰς νόσους.« καὶ εὐθὺ δέ, φησί, καὶ 4
στρεβλὸν τὸ αὐτό ἐστι. »γναφείῳ«, φησίν, »ὁδὸς εὐθεῖα καὶ σκολιή«
— ἡ τοῦ ὀργάνου τοῦ καλουμένου κοχλίου ἐν τῷ γναφείῳ περιστροφὴ
10 εὐθεῖα καὶ σκολιή· ἄνω γὰρ ὁμοῦ καὶ κύκλῳ περιέρχεται — »μία
ἐστί«, φησί, »καὶ ἡ αὐτή.« καὶ τὸ ἄνω καὶ τὸ κάτω ἕν ἐστι καὶ τὸ
αὐτό· »ὁδὸς ἄνω κάτω μία καὶ ωὐτή«. καὶ τὸ μιαρόν φησιν καὶ τὸ 5
καθαρὸν ἕν καὶ ταὐτὸν εἶναι, καὶ τὸ πότιμον καὶ τὸ ἄποτον ἕν καὶ
τὸ αὐτὸ εἶναι· »θάλασσα«, φησίν, »ὕδωρ καθαρώτατον καὶ μιαρώτα-
15 τον, ἰχθύσι μὲν πότιμον καὶ σωτήριον, ἀνθρώποις δὲ ἄποτον καὶ
ὀλέθριον.« λέγει δὲ ὁμολογουμένως τὸ ἀθάνατον εἶναι θνητὸν καὶ 6
τὸ θνητὸν ἀθάνατον διὰ τῶν τοιούτων λόγων· »ἀθάνατοι θνητοί,
θνητοὶ ἀθάνατοι, ζῶντες τὸν ἐκείνων θάνατον, τὸν δὲ ἐκείνων βίον
τεθνεῶτες.« λέγει δὲ καὶ σαρκὸς ἀνάστασιν ταύτης ⟨τῆς⟩ φανερᾶς
20 ἐν ᾗ γεγενήμεθα, καὶ τὸν θεὸν οἶδε ταύτης τῆς ἀναστάσεως αἴτιον
οὕτως λέγων· »ἔνθα δ᾽ ἐόντι ἐπανίστασθαι καὶ φύλακας γίνεσθαι
ἐγερτὶ ζώντων καὶ νεκρῶν«. λέγει δὲ καὶ τοῦ κόσμου κρίσιν καὶ 7
πάντων τῶν ἐν αὐτῷ διὰ πυρὸς γίνεσθαι λέγων οὕτως· »τὰ δὲ
πάντα οἰακίζει κεραυνός«, τουτέστι κατευθύνει, κεραυνὸν τὸ πῦρ
25 λέγων τὸ αἰώνιον. λέγει δὲ καὶ φρόνιμον τοῦτο εἶναι τὸ πῦρ καὶ
τῆς διοικήσεως τῶν ὅλων αἴτιον· καλεῖ δὲ αὐτὸ »χρησμοσύνην καὶ
κόρον«· χρησμοσύνη δέ ἐστιν ἡ διακόσμησις κατ᾽ αὐτόν, ἡ δὲ ἐκπύρωσις

---

2 Heraklit Fr. 57 D. — 4 Heraklit Fr. 58 D. — 8 Heraklit Fr. 59 D. —
12 Heraklit Fr. 60 D. — 14 Heraklit Fr. 61 D. — 16 Heraklit Fr. 63 D. —
19—21. 22. 23 Martin, TU XXXIX 4 S. 115ff vergleicht mehrere Stellen des
Commodian — 23 Heraklit Fr. 64 D. — 24f vgl. Matth. 25, 41 — 26 Heraklit
Fr. 65 D.

1 ⟨οὐκ⟩ οἶδεν? Gö.   3 εὐφρόνην Miller: εὐφροσύνην P   5f ἐπαιτῶνται
μηδὲν ἄξιον μισθω≡ P, verb. Bernays   6 ταῦτα P   8 γναφείῳ Bernays: γρα-
φέων P, γναφέων Gö.   9 γραφείῳ P   10 περιέρχεται Roeper: περιέχεται P,
περιέλχεται Bernays   12 μίη Gö.   ωὐτὴ P   19 + τῆς Diels, Vorsokr. I³ 90
φανερῶς Zeller, Philos. der Griechen I⁵ S. 712³   21 ἐνθάδ᾽ ἐόντας Bernays in
Bunsen Analecta I 367, ἔνθα διὰ θεόν τε Bernays in der Epist. crit. (= Ges. Abh.
I 324)   22 ἐγερτιζόντων P, verb. Bernays   26 καλεῖς P

16*

'The invisible harmonia is better than the visible'

and 'things of which there is sight, hearing, learning' – that is the faculties – 'these things,' he says, 'I honour more', not honouring the invisible more. Therefore Heraclitus says that neither darkness nor light, neither evil nor good are any different, but one and the same. He downgrades Hesiod because he knows day / and night. For day and night are one, he says, speaking in this way:

> 'Teacher of many Hesiod, they understand that he knew many things, he who did not know day and night; for they are one.'

And good and bad:

> 'The doctors', says Heraclitus, 'cut, burn, torture the weak badly in every way, and beg for money though they do not deserve to take a fee from the weak, when they produce the same effects, good things and diseases.'

And straight, he says, and crooked are the same.

> 'For the fuller's shop,' he says, 'the straight and twisted way'

– the rotation of the instrument called *kochlias* in the fuller's shop is straight and twisted; for it goes up and round and round at the same time –

> 'is one and the same', he says.

And up and down are one and the same:

> 'The road up and down is one and the same.'

And the impure and the pure are one and the same and the drinkable and the undrinkable are one and the same:

> 'The sea,' he says, 'is water most pure and most impure; for fishes it is drinkable and healthy, but for men undrinkable and deadly.'

But he says, undeniably, that the immortal is mortal and the mortal immortal, in words such as these:

> 'Immortals mortals, mortals immortals, living the death of those but dying the life of those.'

And he speaks of the resurrection of the flesh – of this visible

334   *Rethinking Early Greek Philosophy*

244W κόρος· »πάντα γάρ«, φησί, »τὸ πῦρ ἐπελθὸν κρινεῖ καὶ καταλήψεται.«
  8 ἐν δὲ τούτῳ τῷ κεφαλαίῳ πάντα ὁμοῦ τὸν ἴδιον νοῦν ἐξέθετο, ἅμα
f. 112ʳ δὲ καὶ τὸν τῆς Νοητοῦ αἱρέσεως, ⟨ὃν⟩ δι᾽ ὀλίγων ἐπέδειξα | οὐκ
  ὄντα Χριστοῦ ἀλλὰ Ἡρακλείτου μαθητήν. τὸν γὰρ ποιητὸν κόσμον
  αὐτὸν δημιουργὸν καὶ ποιητὴν ἑαυτοῦ γινόμενον οὕτω λέγει· »ὁ θεὸς 5
  ἡμέρη εὐφρόνη, χειμὼν θέρος, πόλεμος εἰρήνη, κόρος λιμός« —
  τἀναντία ἅπαντα· οὗτος ὁ νοῦς· — »ἀλλοιοῦται δὲ ὄκωσπερ ⟨πῦρ⟩
  9 ὁκόταν συμμιγῇ θυώμασιν, ὀνομάζεται καθ᾽ ἡδονὴν ἑκάστου.« φανερὸν
  δὲ πᾶσι τοὺς ⟨ἀ⟩νοήτους Νοητοῦ διαδόχους καὶ τῆς αἱρέσεως προ-
  στάτας, εἰ καὶ Ἡρακλείτου λέγοιεν ἑαυτοὺς μὴ γεγονέναι ἀκροατάς, 10
  ἀλλά γε τὰ Νοητῷ δόξαντα αἱρουμένους ἀναφανδὸν ταὐτὰ ὁμολογεῖν.
  λέγουσι γὰρ οὕτως· ἕνα καὶ τὸν αὐτὸν θεὸν εἶναι πάντων δημιουργὸν
  καὶ πατέρα, εὐδοκήσαντα δὲ πεφηνέναι τοῖς ἀρχῆθεν δικαίοις ὄντα
  10 ἀόρατον· ὅτε μὲν γὰρ οὐχ ὁρᾶται ἦν ἀόρατος, ⟨ὅτε δὲ ὁρᾶται ὁρατός⟩,
  ἀχώρητος δὲ ὅτε μὴ χωρεῖσθαι θέλει, χωρητὸς δὲ ὅτε χωρεῖται· 15
  οὕτως κατὰ τὸν αὐτὸν λόγον ἀκράτητος καὶ κρατητός, ἀγένητος
  ⟨καὶ γενητός⟩, ἀθάνατος καὶ θνητός. πῶς οὐχ Ἡρακλείτου οἱ
  τοιοῦτοι δειχθήσονται μαθηταί, ⟨εἰ καὶ⟩ μὴ τῇδε τῇ λέξει διαφθάσας
  ἐφιλοσόφησεν ὁ σκοτεινός; ὅτι δὲ καὶ τὸν αὐτὸν υἱὸν εἶναι λέγει καὶ
  11 πατέρα οὐδεὶς ἀγνοεῖ. λέγει δὲ οὕτως· ὅτε μὲν οὖν μὴ ⟨γε⟩γένητο 20
  ὁ πατήρ, δικαίως πατὴρ προσηγόρευτο· ὅτε δὲ ηὐδόκησε γένεσιν
  ὑπομεῖναι, γενηθεὶς ὁ υἱὸς ἐγένετο αὐτὸς ἑαυτοῦ, οὐχ ἑτέρου. οὕτως
  γὰρ δοκεῖ μοναρχίαν συνιστᾶν, ἓν καὶ τὸ αὐτὸ φάσκων ὑπάρχειν

---

1 Heraklit Fr. 66 D. — 3 f vgl. S. 241, 9. 13 f — 5 Heraklit Fr. 67 D. vgl. V
21, 2. 3 — 12–S. 245, 2 vgl. X 27, 1 E. 1

3 + ὃν Gö. ἐπέδειξε Bernays   4 ποιητὸν Bernays: πρῶτον P   6 εὐφράνθη P
7 Heidel, Proceedings of the Am. Acad. XLVIII S. 707 f schreibt ὠντός und findet
auch in der Parenthese Worte Heraklits (*opposites quite, but the sens is the same*)
+ πῦρ Diels, + μύρον Heidel S. 704 ff   8 ὁπόταν P   9 νοητοὺς P, verb. Bernays
(Filastrius C. 53 *insensati cuiusdam nomine Noeti*)   10 λέγοιεν Miller: λέγοισαν
P   λέγοις ἂν αὐτοὺς Bernays   11 τά] τῶ P   ταῦτα P   13 πεφηκέναι P
14 ἦν] ἐστὶν Cruice   ⟨ ⟩ Gö., vgl. H   16 καὶ κρατητός Bernays (κρατητός
Wordsworth): ἀκράτητος P, > Miller   ἀγέννητος Gö.   17 ⟨ ⟩ Bernays (+ γεν-
νητός Wordsworth)   ⟨οὖν⟩ οὐχ We.   18 εἰ καὶ μὴ τῇδε τῇ λέξει We.: μὴ τῇ δὲ τῇ
λέξει P, μὴ αὐτῇ τῇ λέξει als Frage Miller   ἰδίᾳ δὲ φθάσας We.   20 γέ-
νητο P   21 προσηγορεύετο Wordsworth   22 γεννηθεὶς Gö.   ὁ > oder ὁ ⟨πα-
τήρ⟩ We.

flesh in which we were born, and he knows of god as the cause
of this resurrection, saying thus:

> 'When he was here in this world they rose up against him and
> set themselves as guards (wakefully)[3] of the living and the
> dead.'

But he also says that a judgment of the world and of all the
things in it occurs by fire, saying thus:

> 'Thunderbolt steers all things,'

that is corrects, meaning by thunderbolt the eternal fire. And
he says this fire is intelligent and the cause of the cosmic
arrangement of things; but he calls it 'need and satiety': need
is the arranging of the cosmos, according to him, and the
ekpurôsis is / satiety. 'For fire, attending to all things in turn,'
he says, 'will judge them and grasp them.'

In this chapter all things together have set forth Heraclitus'
own idea, and at the same time also that of the heresy of
Noetus, (whom) I have briefly demonstrated to be a disciple
not of Christ but of Heraclitus.[4] For he says the made world
has itself become creator and maker of itself, thus:

> 'God is day, night, winter, summer, war, peace, satiety, hunger'
> – all the opposites, that is the idea – 'but it changes like (fire),
> when it is mixed with spices, is named according to the savour
> of each.'

But it is clear to all that the unintelligent successors of
Noetus and the leaders of the heresy, even if they say that they
have not been students of Heraclitus, nevertheless in adhering
to the doctrines of Noetus plainly confess the same things. For
they speak as follows: that one and the same god is the creator
of all things and father, but he was pleased to appear to the just
men of old as being invisible. For when he was not seen he was
invisible, (but when seen, visible), unconfined when he does
not wish to be confined, but confinable when he is confined;
and thus by the same reasoning he is unmasterable and
mastered, uncreated and created, immortal and mortal. How
can such men be shown to be not the disciples of Heraclitus,
even though Heraclitus did not anticipate these very words in
his philosophy? But that he (Noetus) also says that son and

[3] See pp. 173-6.
[4] See p. 180.

245W πατέρα καὶ υἱὸν καλούμενον, οὐχ ἕτερον ἐξ ἑτέρου, ἀλλ᾽ αὐτὸν ἐξ
ἑαυτοῦ, ὀνόματι μὲν πατέρα καὶ υἱὸν καλούμενον κατὰ χρόνων τροπήν,
ἕνα δὲ εἶναι τοῦτον τὸν φανέντα καὶ γένεσιν ἐκ παρθένου ὑπομείναντα
καὶ ἐν ἀνθρώποις ἄνθρωπον ἀναστραφέντα, υἱὸν μὲν ἑαυτὸν τοῖς
5 ὁρῶσιν ὁμολογοῦντα διὰ τὴν γενομένην γένεσιν, πατέρα δὲ εἶναι | καὶ f. 1
τοῖς χωροῦσιν μὴ ἀποκρύψαντα. τοῦτον πάθει ξύλου προσπαγέντα 12
καὶ ἑαυτῷ τὸ πνεῦμα παραδόντα, ἀποθανόντα καὶ μὴ ἀποθανόντα
καὶ ἑαυτὸν τῇ τρίτῃ ἡμέρᾳ ἀναστήσαντα, τὸν ἐν μνημείῳ ταφέντα
καὶ λόγχῃ τρωθέντα καὶ ἥλοις καταπαγέντα, τοῦτον τὸν τῶν
10 ὅλων θεὸν καὶ πατέρα εἶναι λέγει Κλεομένης καὶ ὁ τούτου χορός,
Ἡρακλείτειον σκότος ἐπεισάγοντες πολλοῖς.

11. Ταύτην τὴν αἵρεσιν ἐκράτυνε Κάλλιστος, ἀνὴρ ἐν κακίᾳ 1
πανοῦργος καὶ ποικίλος πρὸς πλάνην, θηρώμενος τὸν τῆς ἐπισκοπῆς
θρόνον. τὸν Ζεφυρῖνον, ἄνδρα ἰδιώτην καὶ ἀγράμματον καὶ ἄπειρον
15 τῶν ἐκκλησιαστικῶν ὅρων, ὃν πείθων δόμασι καὶ ἀπαιτήσεσιν ἀπειρη-
μέναις ἦγεν εἰς ὃ ⟨ἐ⟩βούλετο, ὄντα δωρολήπτην καὶ φιλάργυρον,
ἔπειθεν ἀεὶ στάσεις ἐμβαλεῖν ἀνὰ μέσον τῶν ἀδελφῶν, αὐτὸς τὰ
ἀμφότερα μέρη ὕστερον κερκωπείοις λόγοις πρὸς ἑαυτοῦ φιλίαν
κατασκευάζων, καὶ τοῖς μὲν ἀλήθειαν [λέγων ὅμοια] φρονοῦσι ποτὲ
20 κατ᾽ ἰδίαν ⟨λέγων⟩ τὰ ὅμοια φρονεῖν ἠπάτα, πάλιν δ᾽ αὖ τοῖς τὰ
Σαβελλίου ὁμοίως· ὃν καὶ αὐτὸν ἐξέστησε δυνάμενος κατορθοῦν. ἐν 2
γὰρ τῷ ὑφ᾽ ἡμῶν παραινεῖσθαι οὐκ ἐσκληρύνετο, ἡνίκα δὲ σὺν τῷ
Καλλίστῳ ἐμόναζεν, ὑπ᾽ αὐτοῦ ἀνεσείετο πρὸς τὸ δόγμα τὸ Κλεομέ-
νους ῥέπειν φάσκοντος τὰ ὅμοια φρονεῖν. ὁ δὲ τότε μὲν τὴν
25 πανουργίαν αὐτοῦ οὐκ ἐνόει, αὖθις δὲ ἔγνω, ὡς διηγήσομαι μετ᾽ οὐ

---

1 ff vgl. G. Noetos; besonders S. 43, 13 Lag. τὸν Χριστὸν αὐτὸν. εἶναι τὸν
πατέρα καὶ αὐτὸν τὸν πατέρα γεγεννῆσθαι καὶ πεπονθέναι καὶ ἀποτεθνηκέναι
44, 24. 25. 45, 6 αὐτός ἐστι Χριστὸς ὁ πατήρ, αὐτὸς υἱός, αὐτὸς ἐγεννήθη, αὐτὸς
ἔπαθεν, αὐτὸς ἑαυτὸν ἤγειρεν. 48, 23. 56, 1 οὐ γὰρ κατὰ φαντασίαν ἢ τροπήν,
ἀλλ᾽ ἀληθῶς γενόμενος ἄνθρωπος. Filastrius C. 53 Tert. Adv. haer. 8 S. 226, 1—6 Kr.
— 14 Act. 4, 13 ἄνθρωποι ἀγράμματοί εἰσιν καὶ ἰδιῶται — 25 διηγήσομαι]
S. 248, 18

4 ἀναστρεφέντα P   6 τοῦτον ⟨τὸν⟩ We.   παθεῖν ξύλῳ Wordsworth   13 θη-
ρόμενος P   14 τὸν ⟨γὰρ⟩ oder δὲ Gö., ⟨οὗτος⟩ τὸν Roeper   15 δόμασι Gö.:
δόγμασι P, δωρήμασι Bernays   ἀπαντήσεσιν Bernays, ἀπατήσεσιν We.   16 βού-
λετο P   17 ἀναμέσων P   18 κερκώποις P   ἑαυτοὺς P   19 λέγων ὅμοια
> Bunsen, Hipp. I, 393 (I 98), Correctur zum folgenden τὰ ὅμοια   20 καθ᾽ ἡδίαν
P, verb. Miller (vielleicht schrieb H. καθ᾽ ἰδίαν)   + λέγων Miller, hinter φρονεῖν Bunsen   αὐτοῖς P   21 δυνάμενος Miller: δυνάμενον P   24 ῥαπεῖν P

father are the same is a fact of which no one is ignorant. He speaks as follows: When, therefore, the father had not been born, he was justly termed 'father'; but when it pleased him to undergo birth, in being born he became his own son, not the son of another. For in this way he thinks he can construct a monarchy, saying that one and the same thing exists, / called father and son, not one person from another, but the same person from himself, called by the name of father or son in the course of time, and that this is one person who appeared and underwent birth from a virgin, and went about among men as man, confessing to those who saw him that he was son because of the birth that occurred, but not concealing from able minds the fact that he was father. This is he who was nailed to the passion of the cross and committed his spirit to himself, who died and did not die and raised himself on the third day, who was buried in the tomb and pierced with a lance and fastened with nails, this is the god and father of all things, says Cleomenes and his chorus, bringing Heraclitean darkness upon many.

11. This heresy was strengthened by Callistus, a man unscrupulous in wickedness and cunning with regard to error, who was fishing for the episcopal throne. He led on Zephyrinus, who was a foolish man and illiterate and inexperienced in church doctrines, and persuaded him to do what he wanted by means of unending gifts and obligations – he was readily bribed and a lover of money; he persuaded him to keep on instigating disputes in the midst of the brethren, and subsequently he himself brought both parties into friendship with him by cunning arguments, and he deceived the ones who thought the truth by telling them in private that he thought the same, and similarly again with those who held Sabellian doctrines. And Sabellius himself he drove into heresy, while having the power to set him right. For when he was being advised by us he had not hardened his heart, but when he spent time alone with Callistus he was shaken into inclining towards the doctrine of Cleomenes by Callistus saying that he thought the same. But at that time he did not recognise Callistus' wickedness, but later he realised, as I shall explain in a little while. /

3 πολύ. αὐτὸν δὲ τὸν Ζεφυρῖνον προάγων δημοσίᾳ ἔπειθε λέγειν·
246W ἐγὼ οἶδα ἕνα θεὸν Χριστὸν Ἰησοῦν, καὶ πλὴν αὐτοῦ ἕτερον οὐδένα
γενητὸν καὶ παθητόν· ποτὲ δὲ λέγων· οὐχ ὁ πατὴρ ἀπέθανεν, ἀλλὰ
f. 113ʳ ὁ υἱός, οὕτως ἄπαυστον τὴν στάσιν ἐν τῷ λαῷ διετήρησεν· | οὗ τὰ
νοήματα γνόντες ἡμεῖς οὐ συνεχωροῦμεν, ἐλέγχοντες καὶ ἀντικαθι- 5
στάμενοι ὑπὲρ τῆς ἀληθείας· ὃς εἰς ἀπόνοιαν χωρῶν διὰ τὸ πάντας
αὐτοῦ τῇ ὑποκρίσει συντρέχειν, ἡμᾶς δὲ οὔ, ἀπεκάλει ἡμᾶς διθέους,
4 ἐξεμῶν παρὰ βίαν τὸν ἐνδομυχοῦντα αὐτῷ ἰόν. τούτου τὸν βίον
δοκεῖ ἡμῖν ἀγαπητὸν ἐκθέσθαι, ἐπεὶ κατὰ τὸν αὐτὸν χρόνον ἡμῖν
ἐγεγόνει, ὅπως διὰ τοῦ φανῆναι τοῦ τοιούτου τὴν ἀναστροφὴν 10
εὐεπίγνωστος καὶ φανερὰ τοῖς νοῦν ἔχουσιν εὐθὺς γένηται ἡ διὰ
τούτου ἐπικεχειρημένη αἵρεσις. οὗτος ἐμαρτύρησεν ἐπὶ Φουσκιανοῦ
ἐπάρχου ὄντος Ῥώμης· ὁ δὲ τρόπος τῆς αὐτοῦ μαρτυρίας τοιόσδε ἦν·
1 12. Οἰκέτης ἐτύγχανε Καρποφόρου τινὸς ἀνδρὸς πιστοῦ ὄντος
ἐκ τῆς Καίσαρος οἰκίας. τούτῳ ὁ Καρποφόρος, ἅτε δὴ ὡς πιστῷ, 15
χρῆμα οὐκ ὀλίγον κατεπίστευσεν, ἐπαγγειλαμένῳ κέρδος προσοίσειν
ἐκ πραγματείας τραπεζιτικῆς· ὃς λαβὼν τράπεζαν ἐπεχείρησεν ἐν τῇ
λεγομένῃ πισκινῇ πουπλικῇ, ᾧ οὐκ ὀλίγαι παραθῆκαι τῷ χρόνῳ
ἐπιστεύθησαν ὑπὸ χηρῶν καὶ ἀδελφῶν προσχήματι τοῦ Καρποφόρου·
ὁ δὲ ἐξαφανίσας τὰ πάντα ἠπόρει. οὗ ταῦτα πράξαντος, οὐκ ἔλιπεν 20
2 ὃς ἀπαγγείλῃ τῷ Καρποφόρῳ· ὁ δὲ ἔφη ἀπαιτήσειν λόγους παρ'
αὐτοῦ. ταῦτα συνιδὼν ὁ Κάλλιστος καὶ τὸν παρὰ τοῦ δεσπότου
κίνδυνον ὑφορώμενος, ἀπέδρα τὴν φυγὴν κατὰ θάλασσαν ποιούμενος·
ὃς εὑρὼν πλοῖον ἐν τῷ Πόρτῳ ἕτοιμον πρὸς ἀναγωγήν, ὅπου ἐτύγχανε πλέον ἀνέβη πλευσόμενος. ἀλλ' οὐδὲ οὕτως λαθεῖν δεδύνηται· 25
f. 113ᵛ 3 οὐ γὰρ ἔλιπεν ὃς ἀπαγγείλῃ τῷ Καρποφόρῳ τὸ γεγε|νημένον. ὁ δὲ
ἐπιστὰς ·κατὰ τὸν λιμένα ἐπειρᾶτο ἐπὶ τὸ πλοῖον ὁρμᾶν κατὰ ⟨τὰ⟩
μεμηνυμένα· τοῦτο δὲ ἦν ἑστὸς ἐν μέσῳ τῷ λιμένι. τοῦ δὲ πορθμέως
βραδύνοντος, ἰδὼν πόρρωθεν ὁ Κάλλιστος τὸν δεσπότην, ὢν ἐν τῷ
πλοίῳ καὶ γνοὺς ἑαυτὸν συνειλῆφθαι, ἠφείδησε τοῦ ζῆν, καὶ ἔσχατα 30
4 ταῦτα λογισάμενος ἔρριψεν ἑαυτὸν εἰς τὴν θάλασσαν. οἱ δὲ ναῦται
καταπηδήσαντες εἰς τὰ σκάφη ἄκοντα αὐτὸν ἀνείλοντο, τῶν [δὲ]

---

5 ἐλλέγχοντες P   8 παραβίαν P   ἐνδομοιχοῦντα P   11 φανερά We.
(vgl. X 8): ταχεῖα P   τάχα und εὐήθης Wordsworth bei Bunsen   12 ἐπικε·
χειρημέναι P   16 ἐπαγγειλαμένῳ Wordsworth: ἐπαγγειλάμενος P   18 πισκίνῃ
Sauppe   τῷ ⟨τότε⟩ Cruice   20 ἐξαφανήσας P   ἔλειπεν P   21 ἀπαιτήσειν
We.: ἀπαιτεῖν P, ἀπαιτεῖν ἂν Wordsworth   24 ὅποι Roeper   25 πλέον Wordsworth Roeper: πλέων P   27 + τὰ Wordsworth   29 πόρροθεν P   30 συνη-
λεῖφθαι P, verb. Wordsworth   32 δὲ > Sauppe, δὴ Klost.

Callistus led Zephyrinus on and in public persuaded him to say: I know one God Jesus Christ, and apart from him no other that is subject to birth and suffering. And at another time he said: It was not the Father who died but the Son, and in this way he maintained the dispute among the people ceaselessly. Knowing his opinions we did not go along with him, but refuted him and stood out against him on behalf of the truth. But he proceeded to go mad because of the fact that everyone flocked to his show (though we did not), and called us ditheists, spewing out by force the poison lurking within him.

It seems a suitable thing if we now expound the life of Callistus, since he lived in the same period as us, so that by means of the revelation of such a man's behaviour the heresy undertaken with his aid may at once become recognisable and obvious to those who have sense. He became a martyr under Fuscianus, then Praefectus of Rome; but the manner of his martyrdom was as follows:

12. It so happened that Callistus was the household slave of a man named Carpophorus, a man of the faith who was from the household of Caesar. Carpophorus entrusted not a small sum of money to Callistus, as if he were a man of faith, telling him to bring back the profit from a banking enterprise. Callistus took the money and set to work on a bank in the place called the piscina publica, and in time not a few deposits were entrusted to him on the good repute of Carpophorus by widows and brethren. But he lost all the money and was left penniless, nor was there any difficulty in finding someone to inform Carpophorus of what he had done. Carpophorus said he would demand accounts from him. Perceiving these things and suspecting danger from his master Callistus ran away, reckoning on flight by sea. He found a ship at Portus ready to sail and embarked to sail wherever it happened to be going. But he could not escape notice even in this way; for there was no difficulty in finding someone to inform Carpophorus of what had happened. When he heard he tried to hasten to the ship in the harbour according to the informer's reports; but the ship was anchored in the middle of the harbour. Since the ferryman went rather slowly Callistus saw his master from afar off, and because he was in the ship and knew he would be caught, he became reckless with life and reckoning that this

247W ἀπὸ τῆς γῆς μεγάλα βοώντων· καὶ οὕτως τῷ δεσπότῃ παραδοθεὶς
ἐπανήχθη εἰς τὴν Ῥώμην, ὃν ὁ δεσπότης εἰς πίστρινον κατέθετο.
χρόνου δὲ διελθόντος, ὡς συμβαίνει γίνεσθαι, προσελθόντες ἀδελφοὶ 5
παρεκάλουν τὸν Καρποφόρον, ὅπως ἐξαγάγῃ τῆς κολάσεως τὸν
5 δραπέτην, φάσκοντες αὐτὸν ὁμολογεῖν ἔχειν παρά τισι χρῆμα ἀποκεί-
μενον. ὁ δὲ Καρποφόρος, ὡς εὐλαβής, τοῦ μὲν ἰδίου ἔλεγεν ἀφειδεῖν, 6
τῶν δὲ παραθηκῶν φροντίζειν — πολλοὶ γὰρ αὐτῷ ἀπεκλαίοντο
λέγοντες, ὅτι τῷ αὐτοῦ προσχήματι ἐπίστευσαν τῷ Καλλίστῳ, ἃ
πεπιστεύκεισαν — καὶ πεισθεὶς ἐκέλευσεν ἐξαγαγεῖν αὐτόν. ὁ δὲ 7
10 μηδὲν ἔχων ἀποδιδόναι καὶ πάλιν ἀποδιδράσκειν μὴ δυνάμενος διὰ
τὸ φρουρεῖσθαι, τέχνην θανάτου ἐπενόησε καὶ σαββάτῳ σκηψάμενος
ἀπιέναι ὡς ἐπὶ χρεώστας ὥρμησεν ἐπὶ τὴν συναγωγὴν τῶν Ἰουδαίων
συνηγμένων καὶ στὰς κατεστασίαζεν αὐτῶν. οἱ δὲ καταστασιασθέντες
ὑπ' αὐτοῦ, ἐνυβρίσαντες αὐτὸν καὶ πληγὰς ἐμφορήσαντες ἔσυρον ἐπὶ
15 τὸν Φουσκιανὸν ἔπαρχον ὄντα τῆς πόλεως. ἀπεκρίναντο δὲ τάδε· 8
Ῥωμαῖοι συνεχώρησαν ἡμῖν τοὺς πατρῴους νόμους δημοσίᾳ ἀνα-
γινώσκειν, οὗτος δὲ ἐπεισελθὼν | ἐκώλυε καταστασιάζων ἡμῶν, f.
φάσκων εἶναι Χριστιανός. τοῦ δὲ Φουσκιανοῦ πρὸ βήματος τυγχάνοντος καὶ τοῖς ὑπὸ Ἰουδαίων λεγομένοις κατὰ τοῦ Καλλίστου ἀγανα-
20 κτοῦντος, οὐκ ἔλιπεν ὁ ἀπαγγείλας τῷ Καρποφόρῳ τὰ πρασσόμενα.
ὁ δὲ σπεύσας ἐπὶ τὸ βῆμα τοῦ ἐπάρχου ἐβόα· δέομαι, κύριε Φουσκιανέ, 9
μὴ σὺ αὐτῷ πίστευε, οὐ γάρ ἐστι Χριστιανός, ἀφορμὴν δὲ ζητεῖ
θανάτου χρήματά μου πολλὰ ἀφανίσας, ὡς ἀποδείξω. τῶν δὲ Ἰουδαίων ὑποβολὴν τοῦτο νομισάντων, ὡς ζητοῦντος τοῦ Καρποφόρου
25 ταύτῃ τῇ προφάσει ἐξελέσθαι αὐτόν, μᾶλλον ἐπιφθόνως κατεβόων
τοῦ ἐπάρχου. ὁ δὲ κινηθεὶς ὑπ' αὐτῶν, μαστιγώσας αὐτὸν ἔδωκεν
εἰς μέταλλον Σαρδονίας. μετὰ χρόνον δὲ ἑτέρων ἐκεῖ ὄντων μαρτύρων, 1
θελήσασα ἡ Μαρκία ἔργον τι ἀγαθὸν ἐργάσασθαι, οὖσα φιλόθεος
παλλακὴ Κομόδου, προσκαλεσαμένη τὸν μακάριον Οὐίκτορα, ὄντα
30 ἐπίσκοπον τῆς ἐκκλησίας κατ' ἐκεῖνο καιροῦ, ἐπηρώτα, τίνες εἶεν ἐν
Σαρδονίᾳ μάρτυρες. ὁ δὲ πάντων ἀναδοὺς τὰ ὀνόματα, τὸ τοῦ
Καλλίστου οὐκ ἔδωκεν, εἰδὼς τὰ ⟨τε⟩τολμημένα παρ' αὐτοῦ. τυχοῦσα
οὖν τῆς ἀξιώσεως ἡ Μαρκία παρὰ τοῦ Κομόδου, δίδωσι τὴν ἀπολύ-
σιμον ἐπιστολὴν Ὑακίνθῳ τινὶ σπάδοντι πρεσβυτέρῳ, ὃς λαβὼν

1 οὕτως Bunsen: οὗτος P   2 πιστρῖνον Sauppe   8 τῶ αὐτῶ P   11 φθο-
ρεῖσθαι P   σκεψάμενος P   13 ἐπιστὰς? Gö.   18 φοσκιανοῦ P, doch s.
Z. 15. 21 und S. 246, 12   20 ἐπαγγείλας P   22 σὺ αὐτῷ Miller: ἑαυτῶ P
29 παλακὴ P   Κομμόδου? Gö.   32 τολμημένα P   33f ἀπολυσίμην P,
verb. Gö.

was the end cast himself into the sea. But the sailors leapt into
the boats and dragged him out against his will, while others /
shouted loudly from the land; and so he was handed over to
his master and taken back to Rome and his master placed him
in the mill. But as time went on, as it happens, some brethren
came to Carpophorus and urged him to release the runaway
from his punishment, saying that he had admitted to having
some money lodged away with certain people. Carpophorus,
readily taken in, said he did not care about his own money but
was concerned about the deposits – for many had complained
to him saying that it was on his good repute that they had
entrusted what they had entrusted to Callistus – and he was
persuaded and ordered that he be taken out. But Callistus had
nothing to pay back and was unable to run away again
because he was being watched, so he thought up a scheme for
death and one Saturday pretending that he was going out to
find debtors he set out to the synagogue where the Jews were
assembled, and stood up and stirred up trouble among them.
And they, stirred up by him, insulted him and beat him up and
dragged him to Fuscianus who was prefect of the city. And
they made the following defence: 'The Romans permitted us to
read our inherited laws in public, but this man came in and
prevented us, and stirred up trouble for us, saying he was a
Christian.' But Fuscianus happened to be at his tribunal and
was annoyed at what the Jews said against Callistus, nor was
there any difficulty in finding someone to report what had
been done to Carpophorus. Carpophorus hastened to the
tribunal of the Prefect and shouted: 'I beg you, my lord
Fuscianus, do not believe him, for he is not a Christian but is
looking for a means of death having lost a lot of my money, as
I shall demonstrate.' But the Jews thought this was a trick and
that Carpophorus was seeking to get him released on this
excuse, and they shouted at the Prefect all the more angrily.
Stirred by them he whipped him and sent him to the mine in
Sardinia. There were other martyrs there and after a while
Marcia, the concubine of Commodus, who was a god-loving
woman and who wanted to do a good deed, summoned the
blessed Victor, who was bishop of the church at that time, and
asked him who there might be in Sardinia in the way of
martyrs. He gave her the names of all of them but he did not

248W διέπλευσεν εἰς τὴν Σαρδονίαν, καὶ ἀποδοὺς τῷ κατ᾽ ἐκεῖνο καιροῦ
τῆς χώρας ἐπιτροπεύοντι ἀπέλυσε τοὺς μάρτυρας πλὴν τοῦ Καλ-
12 λίστου. ὁ δὲ γονυπετῶν καὶ δακρύων ἱκέτευε καὶ αὐτὸς τυχεῖν
ἀπολύσεως. δυσωπηθεὶς οὖν ὁ Ὑάκινθος ἀξιοῖ τὸν ἐπίτροπον,
φάσκων θρέψας εἶναι Μαρκίας, τασσόμενος αὐτῷ τὸ ἀκίνδυνον· ὁ δὲ
13 πεισθεὶς ἀπέλυσε καὶ τὸν Κάλλιστον. οὗ παραγενομένου ὁ Οὐίκτωρ
f. 114ᵛ πάνυ ἤχθετο ἐπὶ τῷ γεγο|νότι, ἀλλ᾽ ἐπεὶ εὔσπλαγχνος ἦν, ἡσύχασε·
φυλασσόμενος δὲ τὸν ὑπὸ πολλῶν ὄνειδον — οὐ γὰρ ἦν μακρὰν τὰ ὑπ᾽
αὐτοῦ τετολμημένα —, ἔτι δὲ καὶ τοῦ Καρποφόρου ἀντιπίπτοντος,
πέμπει αὐτὸν καταμένειν ἐν Ἀνθείῳ, ὁρίσας αὐτῷ μηνιαῖόν τι εἰς
14 τροφάς. μεθ᾽ οὗ κοίμησιν Ζεφυρῖνος συναράμενον αὐτὸν σχὼν πρὸς
τὴν κατάστασιν τοῦ κλήρου, ἐτίμησε τῷ ἰδίῳ κακῷ, καὶ τοῦτον
μεταγαγὼν ἀπὸ τοῦ Ἀνθείου εἰς τὸ κοιμητήριον κατέστησεν. ᾧ ἀεὶ
συνὼν καί, καθὼς φθάσας προεῖπον, ὑποκρίσει αὐτὸν θεραπεύων,
ἐξηφάνισε μήτε κρῖναι τὰ λεγόμενα δυνάμενον μήτε νοοῦντα τὴν τοῦ
15 Καλλίστου ἐπιβουλήν, πάντα αὐτῷ πρὸς ἃ ἤδετο ὁμιλοῦντος. οὕτω
μετὰ τὴν τοῦ Ζεφυρίνου τελευτὴν νομίζων τετυχηκέναι οὗ ἐθηρᾶτο,
τὸν Σαβέλλιον ἀπέωσεν ὡς μὴ φρονοῦντα ὀρθῶς, δεδοικὼς ἐμὲ καὶ
νομίζων οὕτω δύνασθαι ἀποτρίψασθαι τὴν πρὸς τὰς ἐκκλησίας
κατηγορίαν, ὡς μὴ ἀλλοτρίως φρονῶν. ἦν οὖν γόης καὶ πανοῦργος
16 καὶ ἐπὶ χρόνῳ συνήρπασε πολλούς. ἔχων δὲ καὶ τὸν ἰὸν ἐγκείμενον
ἐν τῇ καρδίᾳ καὶ εὐθέως μηδὲν φρονῶν, ἅμα δὲ καὶ αἰδούμενος τὰ
ἀληθῆ λέγειν, διὰ τὸ δημοσίᾳ ἡμῖν ὀνειδίζοντα εἰπεῖν Δίθεοί ἐστε,
ἀλλὰ καὶ διὰ τὸ ὑπὸ τοῦ Σαβελλίου συχνῶς κατηγορεῖσθαι ὡς παρα-
βάντα τὴν πρώτην πίστιν, ἐφεῦρεν αἵρεσιν τοιάνδε, λέγων τὸν λόγον
αὐτὸν εἶναι υἱόν, αὐτὸν καὶ πατέρα ὀνόματι μὲν καλούμενον, ἓν δὲ
17 ὂν τὸ πνεῦμα ἀδιαίρετον· οὐκ ἄλλο εἶναι πατέρα, ἄλλο δὲ υἱόν, ἓν
δὲ καὶ τὸ αὐτὸ ὑπάρχειν· καὶ τὰ πάντα γέμειν τοῦ θείου πνεύματος,
τά τε ἄνω καὶ κάτω· καὶ εἶναι τὸ ἐν τῇ παρθένῳ σαρκωθὲν πνεῦμα
οὐχ ἕτερον παρὰ τὸν πατέρα, ἀλλὰ ἓν καὶ τὸ αὐτό. καὶ τοῦτο εἶναι

---

17 vgl. S. 245, 13f — 23 Hippolyt G. Noetos S. 52, 28 τί οὖν φήσειεν ἄν τις,
Δύο λέγεις υἱούς; *Tert. Adv. Prax.* 13 S. 246, 28 Kr. duo dii praedicantur 19 S. 262, 22.
263, 1; 8 S. 238, 27 und öfter — 25—S. 249, 12 vgl. X 27, 3. 4

4 ἐπίτροπον ⟨ἀπολύειν⟩ Bunsen I 392 (I 96)   8 τὸ — ὄνειδος? Gö.   10 Ἀν-
τίῳ Miller   10f εἰς τροφὰς We.: ἐκτροφὰς aus ἐκτροφῆς? P (Circumflex aus-
radiert), ἐκτροφῆς Gö.   11 κύμησιν P   12 καταστασιασιν Sauppe, κατάσχεσιν
Wordsworth   15 ἐξεφάνισε P   21 χρόνον? We.   24f παραβάντος P, verb.
Wordsworth   26 καλούμενον ⟨ἄλλο⟩ Wordsworth   27 ὄντα πνεῦμα Bunsen
I 387 (I 86)   οὐκ ἄλο P   28 γεμεῖν P

give her Callistus' name because he knew the things he had committed. Marcia succeeded in her request to Commodus and gave the letter of release to a man named Hyacinthus, a eunuch presbyter, who took it and / sailed to Sardinia where he gave it to the procurator of the country at the time and released the martyrs, except for Callistus. But Callistus got on his knees and wept and implored that he too might have his release. Hyacinthus was put out and asked the procurator, saying that he was reared by Marcia and granting him a no-risk guarantee. The procurator was persuaded and released Callistus as well.

When Callistus arrived Victor was much vexed at what had happened, but since he was a compassionate men he held his peace. But he took precautions against the widespread censure – for it was not very long since the deeds had been committed by Callistus – and Carpophorus was still raising objections as well, and he sent him to stay at Antheios, granting him a monthly allowance for maintenance. After Victor's death Zephyrinus had him helping him towards achieving his election and honoured him for his own evil, and bringing him back from Antheios placed him in charge of the cemetery. Callistus associated with Zephyrinus constantly, and as I have already said, he did service for Zephyrinus with hypocrisy and brought him to ruin since he was incapable of judging what was said nor did he recognise Callistus' intention, and Callistus consorted with him in all things as much as he liked.

Thus after the death of Zephyrinus Callistus thought he had achieved what he had aimed for, and expelled Sabellius as one who did not think aright, fearing me and thinking that in this way he would be able to rub off the charge against him in the eyes of the churches that he was one who thought no differently from Sabellius. He was, therefore, a cheat and an evil-doer, and in the course of time he carried many away with him. But he had the poison lying in his heart and never had a straight thought, but at the same time he was reluctant to speak the truth on account of having reproached us in public saying 'You are Ditheists', but also because he had frequently been accused by Sabellius of transgressing the first item of the faith. Hence he devised a heresy of the following sort: he said the *Logos* is himself a son, and is himself called by the name

344   *Rethinking Early Greek Philosophy*

249W τὸ εἰρημένον· »οὐ πιστεύεις ὅτι ἐγὼ ἐν τῷ πατρὶ καὶ ὁ πατὴρ ἐν
ἐμοί;« τὸ μὲν γὰρ βλεπόμενον, ὅπερ ἐστὶν ἄνθρωπος, τοῦτο εἶναι 18
τὸν υἱόν, τὸ δὲ ἐν τῷ υἱῷ χωρηθὲν πνεῦμα τοῦτο εἶναι τὸν πατέρα·
οὐ γάρ, φησίν, ἐρῶ | δύο θεούς, πατέρα καὶ υἱόν, ἀλλ᾽ ἕνα. ὁ γὰρ f. 11
5 ἐν αὐτῷ γενόμενος πατὴρ προσλαβόμενος τὴν σάρκα ἐθεοποίησεν
ἑνώσας ἑαυτῷ καὶ ἐποίησεν ἕν, ὡς καλεῖσθαι πατέρα καὶ υἱὸν ἕνα
θεόν, καὶ τοῦτο ἓν ὂν πρόσωπον μὴ δύνασθαι εἶναι δύο, καὶ οὕτως
τὸν πατέρα συμπεπονθέναι τῷ υἱῷ· οὐ γὰρ θέλει λέγειν τὸν πατέρα 19
πεπονθέναι καὶ ἓν εἶναι πρόσωπον, ⟨ἀλλ᾽⟩ ἐκφυγεῖν τὴν εἰς τὸν πα-
10 τέρα βλασφημίαν ὁ ἀνόητος καὶ ποικίλος, ὁ ἄνω κάτω σχεδιάζων
βλασφημίας, ἵνα μόνον κατὰ τῆς ἀληθείας λέγειν δοκῇ, ποτὲ μὲν εἰς
τὸ Σαβελλίου δόγμα ἐμπίπτων, ποτὲ δὲ εἰς τὸ Θεοδότου οὐκ αἰδεῖται.
τοιαῦτα ὁ γόης τολμήσας συνεστήσατο διδασκαλεῖον κατὰ τῆς ἐκκλη- 20
σίας οὕτως διδάξας, καὶ πρῶτος τὰ πρὸς τὰς ἡδονὰς τοῖς ἀνθρώποις
15 συγχωρεῖν ἐπενόησε, λέγων πᾶσιν ὑπ᾽ αὐτοῦ ἀφίεσθαι ἁμαρτίας.
ὁ γὰρ παρ᾽ ἑτέρῳ τινὶ συναγόμενος καὶ λεγόμενος Χριστιανὸς εἴ τι
ἂν ἁμάρτῃ, φασίν, οὐ λογίζεται αὐτῷ ἡ ἁμαρτία, εἰ προσδράμοι τῇ
τοῦ Καλλίστου σχολῇ. οὗ τῷ ὅρῳ ἀρεσκόμενοι πολλοὶ συνείδησιν 21
πεπληγότες ἅμα τε καὶ ὑπὸ πολλῶν αἱρέσεων ἀποβληθέντες, τινὲς
20 δὲ καὶ ἐπὶ καταγνώσει ἔκβλητοι τῆς ἐκκλησίας ὑφ᾽ ἡμῶν γενόμενοι,
προσχωρήσαντες αὐτοῖς ἐπλήθυναν τὸ διδασκαλεῖον αὐτοῦ. οὗτος
ἐδογμάτισεν ὅπως εἰ ἐπίσκοπος ἁμάρτοι τι, εἰ καὶ πρὸς θάνατον, μὴ
δεῖν κατατίθεσθαι. ἐπὶ τούτου ἤρξαντο ἐπίσκοποι καὶ πρεσβύτεροι 22
καὶ διάκονοι δίγαμοι καὶ τρίγαμοι καθίστασθαι εἰς κλήρους· εἰ δὲ
25 καί τις ἐν κλήρῳ ὢν γαμοίη, μένειν τὸν τοιοῦτον ἐν τῷ κλήρῳ ὡς

---

1 Joh. 14, 11 πιστεύετέ μοι ὅτι ἐγὼ κτλ. vgl. Tert. Adv. Praxeam 20 S. 263,
10 Kr. — 8—10 *Tert. Adv. Praxeam 29 S. 286, 4ff Kr.* ergo nec compassus est
pater filio. scilicet directam blasphemiam in patrem veriti diminui eam hoc modo
sperant, si filius quidem patitur, pater vero compatitur . . . . times dicere pas-
sibilem, quem dicis compassibilem — 13—S. 251, 7 vgl. E. Rolffs, Das Indulgenz-
Edict des römischen Bischofs Kallist, T. U. XI 3, Lpz. 1893 — 22 πρὸς θάνατον]
vgl. I Joh. 5, 16

8 συνπεπονθέναι P θέλων? We. 9 Lücke Miller, + ἀλλ᾽ We., οὕτω πως
ἐλπίζων Bunsen, ὥστε Volkmar S. 125⁷, ὡς Gö. ἐκφυγὸν Cruice 10 ὁ²] ὃς
Gö., wohl richtig σκεδάζων Scott Bunsen 12 X 27, 4 Noetos statt Sabellios
genannt 15 συγχαρεῖν P 16f ὃ τι ἄν? Miller 18 ⟨τὴν⟩ συνείδησιν
E. Schwartz, Schriften der Wiss. Ges. in Straßburg, 7. Heft S. 10 20 ἔκκλη-
τοι P 21 αὐτῷ We. 22 ἐδογμάτισέν πως (ὄντως Diels) We. Daß H. hier
nicht genau citiert, ist schon öfter betont worden (Rolffs S. 137) 23 δέῃ Pasquali
25 ὢν γνώμῃ P

Father, but the spirit is one, indivisible; it is not the case that the Father is one thing, the Son another, but they exist as one and the same; and all things are full of the divine spirit, both things above and things below; and the spirit incarnated in the Virgin is not different from the Father, but one and the same. And he says that this is /what is said: 'Do you not believe that I am in the Father and the Father in me?' For that which is seen, which is man, that is the son, but the spirit contained within the son, that is the Father; for, he says, I do not speak of two gods, Father and Son, but one. For the Father was born in him and by taking on flesh deified it, uniting it to himself, and made one thing, so that one god should be called Father and Son, and being one 'person' this cannot be two, and in this way the Father suffered in sympathy with the Son; for he does not want to say that the Father suffered and is one 'person', but he wants to avoid blasphemy against the Father, the foolish and artful man, inventor of blasphemy above and below, and simply so that he should appear to speak in accordance with the truth, he is not ashamed to fall at one time into the teaching of Sabellius and at another into that of Theodotus.

Such things did this cheat venture to do, and he set up a school in opposition to the church teaching in this way, and he first thought to allow men the things that made for pleasures, saying that sins were remitted for all by him. Someone who is admitted and called a Christian in someone else's church, if he commits a sin at all, they say, it is not reckoned to him as a sin if he comes over to the school of Callistus. Many of those who were struck down with guilt, and had also been thrown out by many sects as well, were much pleased at his decree, and some had been expelled from the church by us on grounds of moral censure – these went over to them and filled his school.

Callistus declared that if a bishop should commit a sin, even a mortal sin, he need not resign. On this account bishops and priests and deacons began to be appointed to office who were bigamous and trigamous. And if someone should marry while in clerical office, such a man might stay in office as if / he had

346   Rethinking Early Greek Philosophy

250W μὴ ἡμαρτηκότα, ἐπὶ τούτῳ φάσκων εἰρῆσθαι τὸ ὑπὸ τοῦ ἀποστόλου
ῥηθέν· »σὺ τίς εἶ ὁ κρίνων ἀλλότριον οἰκέτην;« ἀλλὰ καὶ παραβολὴν
f. 115ᵛ τῶν ζι|ζανίων πρὸς τοῦτο ἔφη λέγεσθαι· »ἄφετε τὰ ζιζάνια συναύξειν
23 τῷ σίτῳ«, τουτέστιν ἐν τῇ ἐκκλησίᾳ τοὺς ἁμαρτάνοντας. ἀλλὰ καὶ
τὴν κιβωτὸν τοῦ Νῶε εἰς ὁμοίωμα ἐκκλησίας ἔφη γεγονέναι, ἐν ᾗ 5
καὶ κύνες καὶ λύκοι καὶ κόρακες καὶ πάντα τὰ καθαρὰ καὶ ἀκάθαρτα,
οὕτω φάσκων δεῖν εἶναι ἐν ἐκκλησίᾳ ὁμοίως, καὶ ὅσα πρὸς τοῦτο
δυνατὸς ἦν συνάγειν οὕτως ἡρμήνευσεν· οὗ οἱ ἀκροαταὶ ἡσθέντες
τοῖς δόγμασι διαμένουσιν ἐμπαίζοντες ἑαυτοῖς τε καὶ πολλοῖς, ὧν
24 τῷ διδασκαλείῳ συρρέουσιν ὄχλοι. διὸ καὶ πληθύνονται, γαυριώμενοι 10
ἐπὶ ὄχλοις διὰ τὰς ἡδονάς, ἃς οὐ συνεχώρησεν ὁ Χριστός· οὗ κατα-
φρονήσαντες οὐδέν· ἁμαρτεῖν κωλύουσι, φάσκοντες αὐτὸν ἀφιέναι
τοῖς εὐδοκοῦσι. καὶ γὰρ καὶ γυναιξὶν ἐπέτρεψεν, εἰ ἄνανδροι εἶεν
καὶ ἡλικίᾳ γέ τι καίοιντο αἱ ἐν ἀξίᾳ, εἰ ἑαυτῶν ἀξίαν [ἢν] μὴ βούλοιντο
καθαιρεῖν διὰ τοῦ[το] νομίμως γαμηθῆναι, ἔχειν ἕνα ὃν ἂν αἱρήσων- 15
ται σύγκοιτον, εἴτε οἰκέτην εἴτε ἐλεύθερον, καὶ τοῦτον κρίνειν ἀντὶ
25 ἀνδρὸς μὴ νόμῳ γεγαμημένην. ἔνθεν ἤρξαντο ἐπιχειρεῖν πισταὶ λεγό-
μεναι ἀτοκίας φαρμάκοις καὶ περιδεσμεῖσθαι πρὸς τὸ τὰ συλλαμβα-
νόμενα καταβάλλειν, διὰ τὸ μήτε ἐκ δούλου βούλεσθαι ἔχειν τέκνον
μήτε ἐξ εὐτελοῦς διὰ τὴν συγγένειαν καὶ ὑπέρογκον οὐσίαν. ὁρᾶτε 20
εἰς ὅσην ἀσέβειαν ἐχώρησεν ὁ ἄνομος μοιχείαν καὶ φόνον ἐν τῷ
αὐτῷ διδάσκων· καὶ ἐπὶ τούτοις τοῖς τολμήμασιν ἑαυτ(οὺ)ς οἱ
ἀπηρυθριασμένοι καθολικὴν ἐκκλησίαν ἀποκαλεῖν ἐπιχειροῦσι, καί

2 Röm. 14, 4 u. vgl. Tert. De pud. 2 S. 222, 16 — 3 Matth. 13, 29. 30 οὔ,
μήποτε συλλέγοντες τὰ ζιζάνια ἐκριζώσητε ἅμα αὐτοῖς τὸν σῖτον· ἄφετε συναυ-
ξάνεσθαι ἀμφότερα ἕως τοῦ θερισμοῦ — 5f Gen. 6, 19ff, vgl. Rolffs S. 68³

3 τοῦτο Miller: τούτῳ P   9 ἐμπέζοντες P   10 τῷ διδασκαλείων P
12 οὐδὲν P, οὐδένα Bunsen Hipp. I 394 (I 99)   αὐτὸν Miller: αὐτῷ P, αὐτοὺς
Bunsen I 395, αὐτοὶ Cruice   14 ἡλικίᾳ γέ τι καίοιντο αἱ ἐν ἀξίᾳ We.: ἡλικία τε
τε καίοντα ἐναξία P, ἡλικίᾳ καίοιντο αἱ ἐν ἀξίᾳ Miller, ἡλικίᾳ γε ἐκκαίοιντο
ἀναξίᾳ Gö., ἡλικίᾳ τινὸς καίοιντο ἀναξίου τῆς ἑαυτῶν ἀξίας, ἣν Roeper, s. auch
Neumann, Hipp. von Rom I, Lpz. 1902 S. 128 und Der römische Staat und die
Kirche, Lpz. 1890 S. 202; d'Alès, La théologie de St. Hippolyte, Paris 1906 p. 56f
εἰ We.: ἡ P, ἢ Miller   ἢν > Gö.: viell. εἰ τὴν ἑαυτῶν ἀξίαν μὴ We.   15 τοῦ
Neumann: τοῦτο P, τὸ Gö.   ἔχειν Gö.: ἔχει P   17 ἤρξατο P   18 ἀτοκίας
We.: ἀτοκία P, ἀτοκίοις Bunsen Gö.   φαρμάκοις καὶ περιδεσμεῖσθαι Gö. (ebenso
Bunsen, aber καὶ ⟨τῷ⟩): περιδ. καὶ φαρμ. P, ἐπ' ἀτοκίᾳ περιδεσμεῖσθαι (amuletis)
καὶ φαρμακεύεσθαι Roeper   20 οὖσαν? We.   22 τολμήσασιν P   23 ἀπερυ-
θριασμένοι P

not sinned, so Callistus said claiming that the saying of the Apostle 'Who are you to judge another man's slave?' was spoken with regard to this matter. And he also said that the parable of the tares was told with respect to this: 'Leave the tares to grow with the corn', that is leave the sinners in the church. And he also said that Noah's ark was made to be an analogy of the church – in the ark there were dogs and wolves and ravens and all the clean and unclean animals, and so he said there should be in the church similarly, and anything that he was able to adapt to this meaning he interpreted in this way. His followers, pleased with his teachings, continue to delude themselves and many others, and crowds pour into their school. Hence they grow in numbers and exult in their crowds because of the pleasures which Christ did not allow; but they despise Christ and forbid nobody to sin, saying that he forgives those who find favour with him. And indeed he permitted to women that if those who were women of dignity and of age and who were unmarried burned with some desire, if they did not wish to lower their dignity by being legally married, they could have one man whom they chose, either slave or free, as bedfellow, and consider him to be a substitute for a husband, although she was not married by law. Hence so-called faithful women began to try contraceptive drugs, and to bind themselves round in the hope of aborting what they had conceived, because they did not want to have a child by a slave or a humble man on account of the family ties and their huge property. Look what a pitch of impiety this lawless man has come to, in teaching adultery and murder in one go. And in addition to these outrages these shameful people try to call themselves the catholic church, and / some people, thinking

251W τινες νομίζοντες εὖ πράττειν συντρέχουσιν αὐτοῖς. ἐπὶ τούτου 2θ
πρώτως τετ(όλμ)ηται δεύτερον | αὐτοῖς βάπτισμα. ταῦτα μὲν οὖν ὁ f.
θαυμασιώτατος Κάλλιστος συνεστήσατο, οὗ διαμένει τὸ διδασκαλεῖον
φυλάσσον τὰ ἔθη καὶ τὴν παράδοσιν, μὴ διακρῖνον, τίσιν δεῖ
5 κοινωνεῖν, πᾶσιν ἀκρίτως προσφέρον τὴν κοινωνίαν· ἀφ᾽ οὗ καὶ
τὴν τοῦ ὀνόματος μετέσχον ἐπίκλησιν καλεῖσθαι διὰ τὸν πρωτο-
στατήσαντα τῶν τοιούτων ἔργων Κάλλιστον Καλλιστιανοί.

*

2 über die zweite Taufe s. d'Alès, La théologie de St. Hippolyte, Paris 1906
S. 59 ff — 3 διδασκαλεῖον] vgl. G. Noetos 1 S. 44, 2 L.

1 αὐτοῖς] τούτοις Roeper   2 βάπτησμα P   5 πᾶσι δ᾽ ἀκρίτως Miller
προσφέρων P   7 Ende Raum gelassen für Überschrift

they are doing the right thing, join them. In addition to this they have undergone a second baptism first of all.

These are the things that that most amazing man Callistus set up, and his school continues to maintain the customs and the tradition, making no distinction as to whom one should associate with, but offering association to all indiscriminately; it is from Callistus that the school takes its name so as to be called Callistians because of Callistus the founder of these things.

*

Book 10, chapter 6

265W   6. Συμπεριλαβόντες τοίνυν τὰ πάντων τῶν παρ᾽ Ἕλλησι σοφῶν 1
δόγματα ἐν τέσσαρσι βιβλίοις, τὰ δὲ τοῖς αἱρεσιάρχαις ἐν πέντε, νῦν
τὸν περὶ ἀληθείας λόγον ἐν ᾱ ἐπιδείξομεν, ἀνακεφαλαιούμενοι πρῶτον
τὰ πᾶσι δεδοκημένα. οἱ μὲν γὰρ τῶν Ἑλλήνων δογματισταὶ τὴν
25 φιλοσοφίαν τριχῇ διελόντες οὕτως ἐφιλοσόφησαν, οἱ μὲν φυσικήν,
οἱ δὲ ἠθικήν, οἱ δὲ διαλεκτικὴν προσαγορεύσαντες. καὶ οἱ μὲν τὴν 2
φυσικὴν οὗτοι γεγένηνται, οὕτως δὲ διηγήσαντο· οἱ μὲν ἐξ ἑνὸς τὰ

27—S. 268, 2
wörtlich aus Sext. Emp. Adv. phys. II 310—318. Über die Vorlage des Sextus
und ihre Entstellung bei Sextus s. Diels, Doxographi S. 91 ff

22 βιβλοις P
τῶν αἱρεσιάρχων Cruice   αἱρεσιάρχαις ⟨δεδοκημένα⟩ Miller, doch s. S. 268, S
23 ἐν ᾱ Bernays: ἕνα P, ἑνὶ Miller   27 ἑνὸς] + ἐγέννησαν Sext.

Book 10, chapter 6

Having gathered together in four books the doctrines of all who are wise among the Greeks, and in five books the opinions of the heresiarchs, we shall now expound an account of the truth in one book, summarising first the opinions of all.

The Greek dogmatists divided philosophy into three parts and did their philosophy in this way, some calling it natural philosophy, some ethics and some dialectic. And these were the ones who did natural philosophy, and they discoursed in the following way: some say that all things are from one thing, /

266W πάντα, οἱ δὲ ἐκ πλειόνων· καὶ τῶν ἐξ ἑνὸς οἱ μὲν ἐξ ἀποίου, οἱ δὲ
ἐκ [τοῦ] ποιοῦ· καὶ τῶν ἐκ ποιοῦ οἱ μὲν ἐκ πυρός, οἱ δὲ ἐξ ἀέρος,
3 οἱ δὲ ἐξ ὕδατος, ἄλλοι δὲ ἐκ γῆς· καὶ τῶν ἐκ πλειόνων οἱ μὲν ἐξ
ἀριθμητῶν, ⟨οἱ δὲ ἐξ ἀπείρων· καὶ τῶν ἐξ ἀριθμητῶν⟩ οἱ μὲν ἐκ
δυ(ο)ῖν, οἱ δὲ ἐκ τεσσάρων, οἱ δὲ ἐκ ε, οἱ δὲ ἐκ ς· καὶ τῶν ἐξ ἀπείρων
f. 125ʳ οἱ μὲν | ἐξ ὁμοίων τοῖς γεννωμένοις, οἱ δὲ ἐξ ἀνομοίων· καὶ πρὸς
4 τούτοις οἱ μὲν ἐξ (ἀπα)θῶν, οἱ δὲ ἐκ παθητῶν. ⟨ἐξ⟩ ἀποίου μὲν οὖν
καὶ ἑνὸς σώματος τὴν τῶν ὅλων συνεστήσαντο γένεσιν οἱ Στωϊκοί.
ἀρχὴ γὰρ τῶν ὅλων κατ᾽ αὐτούς ἐστιν ἡ ἄποιος ὕλη καὶ δι᾽ ὅλων
τρεπτή· μεταβαλλούσης δὲ αὐτῆς γίνεται πῦρ, ἀήρ, ὕδωρ, γῆ. ἐξ ἑνὸς
δὲ καὶ ποιοῦ γεγενῆσθαι τὰ πάντα θέλουσιν οἵ τε περὶ τὸν Ἵππασον
καὶ Ἀναξίμανδρον καὶ Θαλῆ τὸν Μιλήσιον· ⟨ὧν⟩ Ἵππασος μὲν ὁ
Μεταπόντιος καὶ Ἡράκλειτος ὁ Ἐφέσιος ἐκ πυρὸς ἀπεφήναντο τὴν
γένεσιν, Ἀναξίμανδρος δὲ ἐξ ἀέρος, Θαλῆς δὲ ἐξ ὕδατος, Ξενοφάνης
δὲ ἐκ γῆς. »ἐκ γῆς γάρ, φησί, πάντα ἐστί, καὶ εἰς τὴν γῆν πάντα
τελευτᾷ.«
1 7. Ἐκ πλειόνων δὲ καὶ ἀριθμητῶν, δυεῖν μέν, γῆς τε καὶ ὕδατος,
τὰ ὅλα συνεστηκέναι φησὶ ὁ ποιητὴς Ὅμηρος, ὁτὲ μὲν λέγων·

Ὠκεανόν τε θεῶν γένεσιν καὶ μητέρα Τηθύν,

ποτὲ δέ·

ἀλλ᾽ ὑμεῖς ⟨μὲν⟩ πάντες ὕδωρ καὶ γαῖα γένοισθε.

2 συμφέρεσθαι δ᾽ αὐτῷ δοκεῖ καὶ ὁ Κολοφώνιος Ξενοφάνης· φησὶ γάρ·
πάντες ⟨γὰρ⟩ γαίης ⟨τε⟩ καὶ ὕδατος ἐκγενόμεσθα.

15 f Xenophanes Fr. 27 D. ἐκ γαίης γὰρ πάντα καὶ εἰς γῆν πάντα τελευτᾷ
(so auch Sext.) — **19** Ξ 201 — **21** H 99 — **23** Xenophanes Fr. 33 D.

2 τοῦ > Sext. Gö.   ἐξ < Hdschr. Sext.   **3** ἐξ¹ < Hdschr. Sext.   **4** ⟨ ⟩
Sext. Miller   **5** δύο Sext.   ἐκ πέντε, οἱ δὲ ἐξ ἓξ Sext.   **6** γεννωμένοις
Sext.: γενομένοις P   **6 f** πρὸς τούτοις P: τούτων Sext. Gö.   **7** παθητῶν
Sext. Gö.: παθητικῶν P   + ἐξ Sext. Gö.   **8** ὑπεστήσαντο Sext.   **9** τῶν
ὄντων Sext.   **10** τρεπτή Sext.: τρέπει P   δὲ αὐτῆς] τε ταύτης Sext.   γίνεται
τὰ τέσσαρα στοιχεῖα, πῦρ καὶ ἀήρ, ὕδωρ καὶ γῆ Sext.   **11** τε Sext.: δὲ P
12 Ἀναξίμανδρον schon Sext. (Ἀναξιμένη Meineke)   + ὧν Gö. (Θαλῆ, ὧν
Ἵππασος καὶ Sext.)   **13** καὶ] + κατά τινας Sext.   ἀπεφήναντο] ἀπέλιπον
Sext.   **14** Ἀναξίμανδρος schon Sext. (Ἀναξιμένης Meineke)   **15** δὲ] + κατ
ἐνίους Sext.   τὴν > Gö.   **17** ἀριθμητῶν Sext.: ἀριθμῶν P   δυοῖν Sext
18 τὰ — φησὶ > Sext.   **19** Τηθύν] τιθέν P   **20** ὁτὲ Sext.   **21** + μὲν Miller
22 συμφερὲς P ·   δοκεῖ] + κατ᾽ ἐνίους Sext.   **23** ergänzt von Miller nach
Sext.   ἐγενόμεθα P

and some say from more than one; and of those who say from one thing, some say from something without quality, some from something with quality; and of those who say from something with quality, some say from fire, some from air, some from water and some from earth; and of those who say from more than one thing some say from a finite number, some from an infinite number; and of those who say from an infinite number, some say from things similar to the things produced, some say from things dissimilar; and in addition to these some say from impassible things, some from passible things.

From one body without quality, therefore, the Stoics established the creation of all things. For the principle of all things according to them is the unqualified matter which changes through all things; this alters to become fire, air, water, earth. From one thing with quality Hippasus and his school like to have all things come into being, and Anaximander, and Thales of Miletus; Hippasus of Metapontum and Heraclitus of Ephesus declare that genesis is from fire, but Anaximander from air, Thales from water, Xenophanes from earth. 'For from earth,' he says, 'are all things, and unto earth do all things have their ending.'

7. From many and finite: from two, earth and water, the poet Homer says all things were composed: at one time he says

'Oceanus the origin of gods and mother Tethys',

and at another time:

'But would that you all would become water and earth.'

Xenophanes of Colophon seems to agree with Homer; he says:

'For we all came into being out of earth and water', /

267W ἐκ γῆς δὲ καὶ αἰθέρος Εὐριπίδης, ὡς πάρεστιν ἐπιγνῶναι ἐκ τοῦ
λέγειν αὐτόν·

αἰθέρα καὶ γαῖαν πάντων γενέτειραν ἀείδω.

ἐκ τεσσάρων δὲ Ἐμπεδοκλῆς, οὕτως λέγων·

5   τέσσαρα τῶν πάντων ῥιζώματα πρῶτον ἄκουε·
Ζεὺς ἀήρ, Ἥρη τε φερέσβιος, ἠδ' Ἀϊδωνεύς,
Νῆστις δὲ ἣ δακρύοις τέγγει κρούνωμα βρότειον.

ἐκ πέντε δὲ Ὄκελλος ὁ Λευκανὸς καὶ Ἀριστοτέλης· συμπαρέλαβον
γὰρ τοῖς τέσσαρσι στοιχείοις τὸ πέμπτον καὶ κυκλοφορητικὸν | σῶμα,
10 ἐξ οὗ λέγουσιν εἶναι τὰ οὐράνια. ἐκ δὲ τῶν ϛ τὴν τῶν πάντων
ὑπέθεντο γένεσιν οἱ περὶ τὸν Ἐμπεδοκλέα. ἐν οἷς μὲν γὰρ λέγει·
τέσσαρα τῶν πάντων ῥιζώματα πρῶτον ἄκουε,
ἐκ τεσσάρων ποιεῖ τὴν γένεσιν· ὅταν δὲ προσθῇ·

νεῖκός τ' οὐλόμενον δίχα τῶν, ἀτάλαντον ἁπάντη,
15   καὶ φιλία μετὰ τοῖσιν, ἴση μῆκός τε πλάτος τε,

ἓξ [καὶ] παραδίδωσι τὰς τῶν ὅλων ἀρχάς, δ᾽ μὲν ὑλικάς, γῆν, ὕδωρ,
πῦρ, ἀέρα, δύο δὲ τὰς δραστηρίους, φιλίαν καὶ νεῖκος. ἐξ ἀπείρων
δὲ ἐδογμάτισαν τὴν τῶν πάντων γένεσιν οἱ περὶ Ἀναξαγόραν τὸν
Κλαζομένιον καὶ Δημόκριτον καὶ Ἐπίκουρον καὶ ἄλλοι παμπληθεῖς,
20 ὧν ἐκ μέρους πρότερον ἐμνήσθημεν. ἀλλ' ὁ μὲν Ἀναξαγόρας ἐξ
ὁμοίων τοῖς γεννωμένοις, οἱ δὲ περὶ τὸν Δημόκριτον καὶ Ἐπίκουρον
ἐξ ἀνομοίων τε καὶ ἀπαθῶν, τουτέστιν ἐκ τῶν ἀτόμων, οἱ δὲ περὶ
τὸν Ποντικὸν Ἡρακλείδην καὶ Ἀσκληπιάδην ἐξ ἀνομοίων ⟨μέν⟩, πα-

---

3 Euripides Fr. 1023 Nauck, vgl. Diels, Doxographi S. 92[1] — 5 Empedokles
Fr. 6 D. vgl. S. 210, 20 (= H) — 8 Ocellus Lucanus De universo C. 2 — 12 s.
zu Z. 5 — 14 Empedokles Fr. 17, 19. 20 D. — 20 ἐμνήσθημεν] s. I 8. 13. 22

1 αἰθέρος Sext. Gö.: ἀέρος P   4 δὲ] + ὁ Sext.   οὕτως λέγων ≻ Sext.
5 τῶν P H: γὰρ Sext. (Emp.)   6 ἀήρ P: ≻ H, ἀργὴς Sext.   ἥρη P   7 δὲ P:
γε H, ϑ' Sext. (Emp.)   ἢ δακρύοις H Sext.: ἠδακτοῖς P   τέγγει H Sext.: σπονδε
P (σπένδει? Miller)   κρούνωμα βρότειον Sext.: κρουνῶ μαβρόντιον P, κρουνῶ
μακρόγιον H   8 ὁ κη.γλος λευκανός P (vor λευκ. dicker Punkt, vielleicht ο)
9 πέμπτον] ε̄ P   10 ἐξ οὗ Sext. Gö.: καὶ P   τῶν² ≻ Sext.   12 δ̄ Miller:
δὲ P, τέσσαρα Sext.   πρῶτον ἄκουε Sext., vgl. zu Z. 5   14 διχάζων ἀταλλάττον
P, verb. nach Sext. Miller   15 φιλίη Sext. Miller   τοῖσιν Sext.: οἶσιν P
16 καὶ ≻ Sext. Gö.   ὄντων Sext.   τέσσαρας μὲν τὰς ὑλικάς Sext.   17 ἀέρα
πῦρ Sext.   18 δ' ἐδόξασαν Sext.   πάντων P: πραγμάτων Sext.   20 ὧν
— ἐμνήσθημεν ≻ Sext.   22 τουτέστι τῶν Sext.   23 + μὲν Sext. Gö.

but Euripides says from earth and *aithêr*, as one can tell from the fact that he says:

> '*Aithêr* and earth I hymn, as mother of all things.'

From four things, Empedocles, who speaks as follows:

> 'First hear that there are four roots of all things:
> Zeus the air, Life-bringing Hera, Aidoneus,
> and Nestis who wets the mortal stream with tears.'

From five things Ocellus of Lucania and Aristotle; for they counted in with the four elements the fifth body with circular motion out of which things in the heavens are made. But from six things Empedocles and his school posited the genesis of all things. For in the verses in which he says:

> 'First hear that there are four roots of all things'

he makes genesis to be from four things; but when he adds

> 'And destructive Strife apart from them, alike in every part
> and Love among them, equal in length and breadth',

he gives the principles of the universe as six, four material ones, earth, water, fire, air, and two efficient ones, Love and Strife.

From an infinite number of things, Anaxagoras of Clazomenae and his school taught the genesis of all things, and Democritus and Epicurus and a great many others, whom we have recorded in detail earlier. But Anaxagoras had genesis from things similar to the things that have come into being, but Democritus and Epicurus and their followers had it from things dissimilar and impassible, that is from the atoms, but Heraclides Ponticus and Asclepiades had genesis from

268W θητῶν δέ, καθάπερ τῶν ἀνάρμων ὄγκων, οἱ δὲ περὶ τὸν Πλάτωνα
7 ἐκ τριῶν· εἶναι ταῦτα λέγουσι θεὸν καὶ ὕλην καὶ παράδειγμα. τὴν
δὲ ὕλην μερίζει εἰς τέσσαρας ἀρχάς, πῦρ, ὕδωρ, γῆν, ἀέρα· θεὸν δὲ
τὸν ταύτης εἶναι δημιουργόν, τὸ δὲ παράδειγμα νοῦν.

*

1—4 aus S. 19, 4—20, 4 —

1 ἀνάρμων Sext. Gö.: ἀνάρχων P   2 ⟨καὶ⟩ εἶναι Cruice

things dissimilar but passible, / like the 'unjointed particles'; but Plato and his school have genesis from three things: they say these are god and matter and paradigm. But he divides matter into four principles, fire, water, earth, air; god is the demiurge of this and the paradigm is mind.

*

Appendix D
Greek texts of passages discussed in translation

Maximus of Tyre   41.4   (p.481)

ζῆι πῦρ τὸν γῆς θάνατον καὶ ἀὴρ τὸν πυρὸς θάνατον, ὕδωρ ζῆι τὸν ἀέρος θάνατον, γῆ τὸν ὕδατος.

Plutarch De E   18.392C

πυρὸς θάνατος ἀέρι γένεσις, καὶ ἀέρος θάνατος ὕδατι γένεσις.

Marcus Aurelius 4.46

ὅτι γῆς θάνατος ὕδωρ γενέσθαι καὶ ὕδατος θάνατος ἀέρα γενέσθαι καὶ ἀέρος πῦρ καὶ ἔμπαλιν.

Clement Stromateis   6.17.2   (II. 435.25)

ψυχῆισιν θάνατος ὕδωρ γενέσθαι, ὕδατι δὲ θάνατος γῆν γενέσθαι, ἐκ γῆς δὲ ὕδωρ γίνεται, ἐξ ὕδατος δὲ ψυχή.

Clement Stromateis   6.17.1   (Orpheus fr.226 K)

ἔστιν ὕδωρ ψυχῆ, θάνατος δ'ὑδάτεσσιν ἀμοιβή,
ἐκ δὲ ὕδατος μέν γαῖα, τὸ δ'ἐκ γαίας πάλιν ὕδωρ·
ἐκ τοῦ δὴ ψυχὴ ὅλον αἰθέρα ἀλλάσσουσα.

Aristotle Categories   1a 24-5

ἐν ὑποκειμένῳ δὲ λέγω ὃ ἔν τινι μὴ ὡς μέρος ὑπάρχον ἀδύνατον χωρὶς εἶναι τοῦ ἐν ᾧ ἐστίν.

Aristotle De anima 2,   412b 4-5

εἰ δή τι κοινὸν ἐπὶ πάσης ψυχῆς δεῖ λέγειν, εἴη ἂν ἐντελέχεια ἡ πρώτη σώματος φυσικοῦ ὀργανικοῦ.

Aristotle Metaphysics Λ 1074b 33-4

αὑτὸν ἄρα νοεῖ, εἴπερ ἐστὶ τὸ κράτιστον, καὶ ἔστιν ἡ νόησις νοήσεως
νόησις.

Aristotle Metaphysics Z.16, 1040b 5

φανερὸν δὲ ὅτι καὶ τῶν δοκουσῶν εἶναι οὐσιῶν αἱ πλεῖσται δυνάμεις
εἰσί, τά τε μόρια τῶν ζῴων (οὐθὲν γὰρ κεχωρισμένον αὐτων ἐστίν·
ὅταν δὲ χωρισθῇ καὶ τότε ὄντα ὡς ὕλη πάντα) καὶ γῆ καὶ πῦρ καὶ
ἀήρ· οὐδὲν γὰρ αὐτῶν ἕν ἐστιν, ἀλλ᾽ οἷον σωρός, πρὶν ἢ πεφθῇ καὶ
γένηταί τι ἐξ αὐτῶν ἕν.

Aristotle Categories 2a 11

οὐσία δέ ἐστιν ἡ κυριώτατά τε καὶ πρώτως καὶ μάλιστα λεγομένη, ἡ
μήτε καθ᾽ ὑποκειμένου τινος λέγεται μήτ᾽ ἐν ὑποκειμένῳ τινί ἐστιν.

Maximus of Tyre 29.4

καὶ ἐν Λιβύῃ ἀνὴρ Λίβυς, Ψάφων ὄνομα, ἐραστὴς εὐδαιμονίας οὐ
ταπεινῆς, μὰ Δία, οὐδε τῆς περιθεούσης ταύτης, ἀλλὰ ἤθελεν γὰρ
θεὸς εἶναι δοκεῖν· ξυλλαβὼν οὖν τῶν ᾠδικῶν ὀρνίθων πολλούς,
ἐδίδασκεν ᾄδειν τοὺς ὄρνιθας· ᾽Μέγας θεὸς Ψάφων᾽· καὶ ἠφίει
αὖθις ἐπὶ τὰ ὄρη. οἱ δὲ οἱ αὐτοί τε ᾖδον, καὶ οἱ ἄλλοι ὄρνιθες
ἐθιζόμενοι τῇ φωνῇ. Λίβυες δὲ θείαν νομίσαντες εἶναι τὴν φήμην,
ἔθυον Ψάφωνι, καὶ ἦν αὐτοῖς θεὸς ὑπὸ ὀρνίθων κεχειροτονημένος.

Aelian Varia Historia 14.30

῎Αννων ὁ καρχηδόνιος ὑπὸ τρυφῆς ἐν τοῖς ἀνθρώπων ὅροις οὐκ ἠξίου
διαμένειν, ἀλλ᾽ ἐπενόει φήμας ὑπὲρ ἑαυτοῦ κατασπείρεσθαι κρείττονας
ἢ κατὰ τὴν φύσιν, ἥνπερ οὖν ἔλαχεν. ὄρνιθας γάρ τοι τῶν ᾠδικῶν
παμπόλλους πριάμενος ἔτρεφεν ἐν σκότῳ αὐτούς, ἐν διδάσκων μάθημα
λέγειν· ᾽θεός ἐστιν ῎Αννων᾽. ἐπεὶ δὲ ἐκεῖνοι μίαν φωνὴν ταύτην
ἀκούοντες ἐγκρατεῖς ταύτης ἐγένοντο, ἄλλον ἄλλοσε διαφῆκεν,
οἰόμενος διαρρεῦσαι τῶν ὀρνίθων τὸ ὑπὲρ ἑαυτοῦ μέλος. οἱ δὲ τὸ
πτερὸν ἀπολύσαντες ἅπαξ καὶ ἐλευθερίας λαβόμενοι καὶ εἰς ἤθη τὰ
σύντροφα αὐτοῖς ἐλθόντες, τὰ οἰκεῖα ᾖδον καὶ τὰ ὀρνίθων ἐμουσούργ-
ουν, μακρὰ χαίρειν εἰπόντες ῎Αννωνι καὶ μαθήμασι τοῖς ἐν τῇ
δουλείᾳ.

Scholion to Dio Chrysostom <u>Orat.</u> 1. 14

ὁποῖον ἱστορεῖται καὶ περὶ τοῦ Λιβύων βασιλέως ᾿Αψεφᾶ διὰ τῶν
ψιττάκων μεμηχανῆσθαι, ἱπταμένων καὶ κελαδούντων ᾿Αψεφᾶς θεός
ἐστιν᾿.

αὐτὰρ ἐπὴν νοῦσον τελέσει μέγαν εἰς ἐνιαυτόν,
800 ἄλλος δ᾿ ἐξ ἄλλου δέχεται χαλεπώτερος ἆθλος᾿
εἰνάετες δὲ θεῶν ἀπαμείρεται αἰὲν ἐόντων,
οὐδέ ποτ᾿ ἐς βουλὴν ἐπιμίσγεται οὐδ᾿ ἐπὶ δαῖτας
ἐννέα πάντ᾿ ἔτεα᾿ δεκάτῳ δ᾿ ἐπιμίσγεται αὖτις
εἴρας ἐς ἀθανάτων οἵ᾿ Ὀλύμπια δώματ᾿ ἔχουσι.
805 τοῖον ἄρ᾿ ὅρκον ἔθεντο θεοὶ Στυγὸς ἄφθιτον ὕδωρ

Empedocles B 136 (Sextus Empiricus <u>Adv. Math.</u> 9.129)

οὐ παύσεσθε φόνοιο δυσηχέος; οὐκ ἐσορᾶτε
ἀλλήλους δάπτοντες ἀκηδείηισι νόοιο;

Empedocles B 137 (Sextus Empiricus <u>Adv.</u> Math. 9.129)

μορφὴν δ᾿ ἀλλάξαντα πατὴρ φίλον υἱὸν ἀείρας
σφάζει ἐπευχόμενος μέγα νήπιος᾿ οἱ δ᾿ ἀπορεῦνται
λισσόμενον θύοντες᾿ ὁ δ᾿ αὖ νήκουστος ὁμοκλέων
σφάξας ἐν μεγάροισι κακὴν ἀλεγύνατο δαῖτα.
ὣς δ᾿ αὔτως πάτερ᾿ υἱὸς ἑλὼν καὶ μητέρα παῖδες
θυμὸν ἀπορραίσαντε φίλας κατὰ σάρκας ἔδουσιν.

Empedocles B 145 (Clement <u>Protr.</u> 2.27)

τοιγάρτοι χαλεπῆισιν ἀλύοντες κακότησιν
οὔποτε δειλαίων ἀχέων λωφήσετε θυμόν.

Empedocles B 15 (Plutarch <u>Adv. Col.</u> 12, 1113D)

οὐκ ἂν ἀνὴρ τοιαῦτα σοφὸς φρεσὶ μαντεύσαιτο,
ὡς ὄφρα μέν τε βιῶσι, τὸ δὴ βίοτον καλέουσι
τόφρα μὲν οὖν εἰσίν, καί σφιν πάρα δειλὰ καὶ ἐσθλά,
πρὶν δὲ πάγεν τε βροτοὶ καὶ ἐπεὶ λύθεν, οὐδὲν ἄρ᾿ εἰσιν.

Empedocles B 4 (Clement <u>Stromateis</u> 5.18)

ἀλλὰ κακοῖς μὲν κάρτα μέλει κρατέουσιν ἀπιστεῖν᾿
ὡς δὲ παρ᾿ ἡμετέρης κέλεται πιστώματα Μούσης,

γνῶθι διασσηθέντος ἐνί σπλάγχνοισι λόγοιο.

Empedocles B 115 (as reconstructed in Diels Kranz 31 B 115)

ἔστιν Ἀνάγκης χρῆμα, θεῶν ψήφισμα παλαιόν,
ἀίδιον, πλατέεσσι κατεσφρηγισμένον ὅρκοις·
εὖτέ τις ἀμπλακίηισι φόνωι φίλα γυῖα μιήνηι,
νείκεΐ θ' ὅς κ(ε) ἐπίορκον ἁμαρτήσας ἐπομόσσηι,
5 δαίμονες οἵτε μακραίωνος λελάχασι βίοιο,
τρίς μιν μυρίας ὥρας ἀπό μακάρων ἀλάλησθαι,
φυομένους παντοῖα διά χρόνου εἴδεα θνητῶν
ἀργαλέας βιότοιο μεταλλάσσοντα κελεύθους.
αἰθέριον μέν γάρ σφε μένος πόντονδε διώκει,
10 πόντος δ'ἐς χθονός οὖδας ἀπέπτυσε, γαῖα δ'ἐς αὐγάς
ἠελίου φαέθοντος, ὁ δ'αἰθέρος ἔμβαλε δίναις·
ἄλλος δ'ἐξ ἄλλου δέχεται, στυγέουσι δέ πάντες.
τῶν καί ἐγώ νῦν εἰμι, φυγάς θεόθεν καί ἀλήτης,
νείκεΐ μαινομένωι πίσυνος.

4 νείκεΐ θ' Diels
6 μιν Plut.: μέν Hipp.

Hesiod Theogony 782 805

ὁππότ'ἔρις καί νεῖκος ἐν ἀθανάτοισιν ὄρηται,
καί ρ' ὅστις ψεύδηται Ὀλύμπια δώματ' ἐχόντων,
Ζεύς δέ τε Ἶριν ἔπεμψε θεῶν μέγαν ὅρκον ἐνεῖκαι
785 τηλόθεν ἐν χρυσέῃ προχόῳ πολυώνυμον ὕδωρ,
ψυχρόν, ὅ τ' ἐκ πέτρης καταλείβεται ἠλιβάτοιο
ὑψηλῆς· πολλόν δέ ὑπό χθονός εὐρυοδείης
ἐξ ἱεροῦ ποταμοῖο ῥέει διά νύκτα μέλαιναν·
Ὠκεανοῖο κέρας, δεκάτη δ' ἐπί μοῖρα δέδασται·
790 ἐννέα μέν περί γῆν τε καί εὐρέα νῶτα θαλάσσης
δίνης ἀργυρέης εἱλιγμένος εἰς ἅλα πίπτει,
ἡ δέ μί' ἐκ πέτρης προρέει, μέγα πῆμα θεοῖσιν.
ὅς κεν τήν ἐπίορκον ἀπολλείψας ἐπομόσση
ἀθανάτων οἵ' ἔχουσι κάρη νιφόεντος Ὀλύμπου,
795 κεῖται νήυτμος τετελεσμένον εἰς ἐνιαυτόν·
οὐδέ ποτ' ἀμβροσίης καί νέκταρος ἔρχεται ἄσσον
βρώσιος, ἀλλά τε κεῖται ἀνάπνευστος καί ἄναυδος
στρωτοῖς ἐν λεχέεσσι, κακόν δ' ἐπι κῶμα καλύπτει.

Bibliography

This bibliography is restricted to those works to which reference has been made in the book, as a key to the abbreviations used there. It makes no claim to represent all the works that are relevant to this study.

Albritton, R. (1957) 'Forms of particular substances in Aristotle's Metaphysics', *Journal of Philosophy* 54 (1957), 699-708
Allen, R.E. and Furley, D.J. (edd.) (1975) *Studies in Presocratic Philosophy* vol. 2, London
Anton, J.P. and Kustas, G.L. (ed) (1971) *Essays in Greek Philosophy*, New York
Barnes, J. (1979) *The Presocratic Philosophers*, 2 vols. London
Bianchi, U. (ed.) (1967) *Le origini dello gnosticismo*: Messena colloquium, Leiden
Bianchi, U. (1967b) 'Marcion: théologien biblique ou docteur gnostique?', *Vigiliae Christianae* 21 (1967) 141-149
Bidez, J. (1896) 'Observations sur quelques fragments d'Empédocle et de Parmenide', *AGP* 9 n.F.2 190-207, 298-309
Bignone, E. (1916) *Empedocle*, Turin
Blackman, E.C. (1948) *Marcion and his Influence*, London
Bollack, J. (1965-9) *Empédocle*, 4 vols. Paris
Bollack, J. and Wismann, H. (1972) *Héraclite ou la séparation*, Paris
Brenk, F.E. (1977) *In Mist Apparelled*, Leiden
Bunsen, C.J. (1852) *Hippolytus and his Age*, London (2nd ed. 1854)
Cherniss, H. (1935) *Aristotle's Criticism of Presocratic Philosophy*, Baltimore
Darcus, S.M. (1977) 'Daimon parallels the Holy Phren in Empedocles', *Phronesis* 22 (1977) 175-190
Detienne, M. (1959) 'Le "demonologie" d'Empédocle', *REF* 72 (1959) 1-17
Detienne, M. (1963) *La Notion de DAIMON dans le Pythagorisme ancien*, Paris
Detienne, M. (1967) *Les Maîtres de vérité dans la grèce archaique*, Paris
Diels, H. (1879) *Doxographi Graeci*, Berlin
Diels, H. (1898a) 'Uber die Gedichte des Empedokles', *Sitzungsberi-

chte der Kgl. Pr. Akademie der Wissenschaften zu Berlin 1898, 396-415, = Diels, H. *Kleine Schriften* ed. Burkert, 127-146

Diels, H. (1898b) 'Symbola Empedoclea', *Mélanges Henri-Weil*, Paris

Diels, H. and Kranz. W. (1951) *Die Fragmente der Vorsokratiker*, 6th edition, reprinted many times

Duncker, L. and Schneidewin, F.G. (1859) *S. Hippolyti ep. et mart. Refutationis omnium haeresium librorum decem quae supersunt*, Gottingae

Düring, I (1957) *Aristotle in the Ancient Briographical Tradition*, Göteborg

Evans, E (1972) *Tertullian Adversus Marcionem*, ed. and transl. Oxford

Faye, E. de (1925) *Gnostiques et gnosticisme*, 2nd ed. Paris

Flesseman-van Leer, E. (1953) *Tradition and Scripture in the Early Church*, Assen

Frickel, J. (1967) 'Die Apophasis Megale, eine Grundschrift der Gnosis?', in Bianchi (1967) 197-202

Frickel, J. (1968) *Die Apophasis Megale in Hippolyts Refutatio VI 9-18*, Orientalia Christiana Analecta

Furley, D.J. and Allen, R.E. (ed.) (1970) *Studies in Presocratic Philosophy*, vol. 1. London

Gager, J.G. (1972) 'Marcion and philosophy', *Vigiliae Christianae* 26 (1972) 53-59

Girard, R (1972/7) *Violence and the Sacred*, translated by Patrick Gregory, Johns Hopkins U.P. 1977

Gordon, R. (1979) Review of Girard (1977) in *Comparative Criticism: a yearbook* 1, ed. E. Shaffer, 279-310

Grant, R.M. (1946) *Second Century Christianity*, London (2nd ed. 1957)

Grant, R.M. (1959) 'Gnostic origins and the Basileidians of Irenaeus', *Vigiliae Christianae* 13 (1959) 121-125

Griffiths, J. Gwyn (1970) *Plutarch's De Iside et Osiride*, University of Wales Press

Guthrie, W.K.C. (1957) 'Aristotle as an historian of philosophy', *JHS* 77 (1957) 35-41

Guthrie, W.K.C. (1965) *A History of Greek Philosophy* vol. 2, Cambridge

Guthrie, W.K.C. (1981) *A History of Greek Philosophy* vol. 6, Cambridge

Hahm, D.E. (1982) 'The fifth element in Aristotle's De Philosophia: a criticial re-examination', *JHS* 102 (1982) 60-74

Harnack. A. von (1924) *Marcion: das Evangelium vom fremden Gott*, Leipzig²

Harvey, W.W. (ed.) (1857) *Sancti Irenaei Libros quinque adversus haereses*, Cambridge

Helmbold, W.C. and O'Neil, E.N. *Plutarch's Quotations*, Philol.

monogr. of Am. Phil. Assoc. 19, 1959

Hershbell, J.P. (1971) 'Plutarch as a source for Empedokles re-examined', *AJP* 92 (1971) 156-184

Hershbell, J.P. (1973) 'Hippolytus' *Elenchos* as a source for Empedokles reexamined', *Phronesis* 18 (1973) 97-114, 187-203

Horton, R. (1967) 'African traditional thought and Western science', *Africa* 37 (1967) 50-71, 155-187. Repr. (abbr.) in B.R. Wilson (ed.) *Rationality* (Oxford, 1970) 131-171

Hughes, G.J. (1979) 'Universals as potential substances: the interpretation of Metaphysics Z13' in *Notes on Zeta* (Burnyeat et al.) Oxford.

Hunger, H (1967) 'Palimpsest-Fragmente aus Herodians *Katholikê Prosôdia*', *Jahrbuch der Österreichischen Byz. Gesellschaft* 16 (1967) 1-33

Hussey, E. (1982) 'Epistemology and meaning in Heraclitus', in *Language and Logos* ed. M. Schofield and M. Nussbaum, 33-59

Janacek, K. (1959) 'Hippolytus and Sextus Empiricus', *Eunomia* (*Listy Filologické suppl.*) 1959, 19-21

Janacek, K. (1979) 'Das Wort *skeptikos* in Philons Schriften', *Listy Filologické* 101 (1979) 65-68

Janacek, K. (1980) 'Ainesidemos und Sextos Empeirikos', *Eirene* 17 (1980) 5-16

Kahn, C.H. (1960) 'Religion and natural philosophy in Empedocles' doctrine of the soul', *AGPh* 42 (1960) 3-35. Repr. Anton and Kustas (1971) and Mourelatos (1974)

Kahn, C.H. (1979) *The Art and Thought of Heraclitus*, Cambridge

Kienle, W. Von (1961) *Die Berichte über die Sukzessionen der Philosophen*, Berlin

Kingsley, P. (1979) *On the Teaching of Empedocles.* Unpublished dissertation Cambridge (M. Litt.) 1979

Kirk, G.S. (1950) 'The Michigan Alcidamas-Papyrus: Heraclitus fr. 56D; the riddle of the lice', *CQ* 44 (1950) 149-167

Kirk, G.S. (1954) *Heraclitus, the Cosmic Fragments*, Cambridge

Kirk, G.S. and Raven, J. (1957) *The Presocratic Philosophers*, Cambridge

Kirk, G.S., Raven, J., Schofield, M. (1983) *The Presocratic Philosophers* (second edition), Cambridge

Koschorke, K. (1975) *Hippolyts Ketzerbekämpfung und Polemik gegen die Gnostiker.* Wiesbaden.

Kranz, W. (1958) '*Palintropos harmoniê*', *Rh.Mus.* 101 (1958) 250-254

Leach, E. (1964) 'Anthropological aspects of language: animal categories and verbal abuse' in Lenneberg, *New Directions in the Study of Language*, 23-63

Lebreton, J. (1946) *The History of the Primitive Church* vol.3, London

Lesher, J.H. (1972) 'Aristotle on form, substance and universals: a dilemma', *Phronesis* 16 (1972) 169-178

Lloyd, G.E.R. (1966) *Polarity and Analogy*, Cambridge

Lloyd, G.E.R. (1979) *Magic, Reason and Experience*, Cambridge

Loi, V. et al. (1977) *Ricerche su Ippolito*, Rome

Long, A.A. (1966) 'Thinking and sense-perception in Empedocles: mysticism or materialism?', *CQ* 16 (1966) 256-276

Long, H.S. (1949) 'The unity of Empedocles' thought', *AJP* 70 (1949) 142-158

McDiarmid, J.B. (1953) 'Theophrastus on the Presocratic causes', *HSCP* 61 (1953) 85-156. Repr. (abbr.) in Furley and Allen (1970) vol. 1

Marcovich, M. (1959) 'On Heraclitus fr. 66DK', Paper to *3rd Int. Congress of Class. Studies*, Mérida 1959, 1-11

Marcovich, M. (1966) 'Hippolytus and Heraclitus', *Studia Patristica* (Berlin) 7 (1966) (Texte and Untersuchungen 92) 255ff.

Marcovich, M. (1967) *Heraclitus: editio major*, Merida, Venezuela

Martin, H. (jr) (1969a) 'Plutarch's citation of Empedocles at *Amatorius* 756D', *GRBS* 10 (1969) 57-70

Martin, H. (jr) (1969b) '*Amatorius* 756E-F: Plutarch's citation of Parmenides and Hesiod', *AJP* 90 (1969) 183-200

Mejer, J. (1978) *Diogenes Laertius and his Hellenistic background*, Hermes Einzelschriften 40

Mourelatos, A.P.D. (ed.) (1974) *The Presocratics*, New York

Nautin, P. (1947) *Hippolyte et Josipe*, Paris

Nautin, P. (1949) *Hippolyte contre les hérésies. Fragment*, Paris

O'Brien, D. (1969) *Empedocles' Cosmic Cycle*, Cambridge

O'Brien, D. (1981) *Pour interpréter Empédocle*, Paris-Leiden

Osborne, C.J. (1983) 'Archimedes on the dimensions of the cosmos', *Isis* 74 (1983) 234-242

Owen, G.E.L. (1958) 'Zeno and the mathematicians', *PAS* 1957-8, 199-222

Owen, G.E.L. (1978/9) 'Particular and general', *PAS* 79 (1978-9) 1-21

Prier, R.A. (1976) *Archaic Logic: symbol and structure in Heraclitus, Parmenides and Empedocles*, The Hague, 1976

Ramnoux, C. (1959) *Héraclite ou l'homme entre les choses et les mots*, Paris

Ramnoux, C. (1961/9) 'Commentaire a la réfutation des hérésies' in Ramnoux (1970) 67-121 (Repr. from *Revue Philosophique* 1961-2 and 1967-9)

Ramnoux, C. (1970) *Etudes Présocratiques*, Paris

Reinhardt, K. (1916) *Parmenides und die Geschichte der griechiscen*

Philosophie, Bonn. (repr. 1959)

Reinhardt, K. (1942) 'Heraklits Lehre vom Feuer', *Hermes* 77 (1942) 1-27

Salles-Dabadie, J.M. (1969), *Recherches sur Simon le Mage: I L'Apophasis Megale*, Cahiers de la Revue Biblique 10

Salmon, G. (1885) 'The cross references in the *Philosophoumena*', *Hermathena* 2 (1885) 389-402

Schofield, M. and Nussbaum, M.C. (1982) (edd.) *Language and Logos*, Cambridge

Skydsgaard, J.E. (1968) *Varro the Scholar*, Copenhagen

Stadter, P. (1965) *Plutarch's Historical Methods, an analysis of Mulierum Virtutes*, Harvard

Stead, G.C. (1976) 'Rhetorical method in Athanasius', *Vigiliae Christianae* 30 (1976) 121-137

Sturz, F.W. (1805) *Empedocles Agrigentinus*, Leipzig

Van der Ben, N. (1975) *The Proem of Empedocles' Peri Physios*, Amsterdam

Vlastos, G. (1955) 'On Heraclitus', *AJP* 76 (1955) 337-368

Wendland, P. (ed.) (1916) *Hippolytus Refutatio Omnium Haeresium*, Leipzig

West, M.L. (1966) *Hesiod, Theogony*, Oxford

Wright, M.R. (1981) *Empedocles: the extant fragments*, Yale

Woods, M.J. (1967) 'Problems in Metaphysics Z chapter 13' in *Aristotle* ed. J.M.E. Moravcsik, Garden City

Zeitlin, F.I. 'The motif of the corrupted sacrifice in Aeschylus' *Oresteia*', *TAPhA* 96 (1965) 463-508; postscript *TAPhA* 97 (1966) 645-653

Zuntz, G. (1965) 'De Empedoclis librorum numero coniectura', *Mnemosyne* 4.18 (1965) 365

Zuntz, G. (1971) *Persephone*, Oxford

Glossary and index of Greek and Latin terms

Page references are to the first occurrence of the *word*, or to pages on which the meaning is discussed. In appropriate cases the translations given in this glossary appear as index entries in the General index, where references to discussions of the *concept* in question are given.

Index locorum

General index

References in **bold** type locate the main discussions of the topic in question. References in *italics* are to Appendix C (Hippolytus, *Refutation*); these page references are to the facing translation. Index entries for Appendix C are given only for the names of Greek thinkers and heretics.

378 *General index*

Basileides, 35, 36, 48, 50-1, 52-8, 62-3, 67
Marcion, 85, 97-108, 119, 128-9, 146
Valentinus, 69, 77, 111
God
  in philosophers: Aristotle, 39, 49, 50, 55, 62, 64-5; Empedocles (the one), 114; Heraclitus, 144, 159n.80, supposed contrast with 'just', 141, 145, 146, identified with world, 142, 147n.43, 158-9
  in heretics: Basileides, 50, 53-4, 55, 57, 62; Marcion (the stranger-god), 100, 103, 107, 146; Noetus (unity of), 135-6, 144, 149n.49, 153, passibility of, 138, 159n.81, mortality of, 169, 176, responsible for resurrection, 137-8, 173-7; Simon Magus, 69, 70
  see also creator; Old Testament god
gods, 115, 117, 125, 127, 158; *see also* religion, conventional
good, 58n.46, 62
  relation to 'just', 101-2, 105, 108
  in Marcion, 100-8
  in Empedocles (defined by Strife), 119-22
  in Heraclitus, 164-7
gospel, 53, 102, 106

harmony, 148, 150, 151, 160-1
Harnack, A. von, 100-6 *passim*
Helen (companion of Simon Magus), 71, 73-83, 217
Helen of Troy, 71, 75, 80, 83
hell, 107, 164
Heraclitus, 2, 3, 5-7, 37n.3, 85, **132-82**, 183, 184, 188, 190, 194-5, 207, 208n.18, 209, 221, *235, 327-49, 353*
  reading Heraclitus, 23-4, 142-3, 183
  Sceptical interpretation, 133-4
  Stoic interpretation, 172
  Hippolytus' interpretation: sources 132-4, 149n.51, lack of material, 170-3; relation to Monarchianism, 134-9, 140-2, 143-81 *passim*; unity of opposites, 132, 133, 143-69, 181, 184, and all things, 156, 173; contradiction, 133; values, 135, 169, 172, 182; judgment, 172-3; fire, 170-2, 221; resurrection, 177-8; epistemology, 132-3, 160-3, 165n.93,

169, 172-3
heresies, 14, 15, 69, 140, 170
  Gnostic, 16, 68, 81, 101, 111, 141, 146, 148n.47, 212, 214, 227; Simon Magus, 17, 20, 21, 68-84, 88, 134n.9, 212-27; Basileides, 35, 36, 48, 50-1, 52-8, 62-3, 67; Marcion, 85, 97-108, 119, 128-9, 146; Valentinus, 69, 77, 111
  Monarchian, 134, 135, 141, 151n.56, 155n.74, 164; Noetus, 85, 134-9, 140-81 *passim*; Callistus, 14, 135, 138-9, 164, 172
hermeneutics, *see* interpretation
Hershbell, J.P., 94, 97, 100
Hesiod, 115, 117, 118, 164n.92, 165-6, 177-8, 181, 187
Hippolytus, 14
  interests, 13-15, 16-17, 185-6, 210
  strategy, 15-17, 58, 70, 97-8, 106n.92, 134, 189
  style, 148n.47
  handling of sources, 35-6, 68-84, 142, 171, 187-211, 214-25
  method of work, 53, 84, 96, 188-9, 206, 210, 213, 215-17, 225; muddleheaded?, 170
  use of 'he says', 17-19, 56n.44, 59-60, 68, 171n.109, 180n.134, 213, 217-20, 223
  knowledge of Aristotle, 20n.35, 40-51; of Plutarch, 92-4; of Scepticism, 36-40, 134, 209; of Sextus Empiricus, 21, 37n.3, 88, 89-92, 94, 96, 134n.8, 214
  Refutation of all heresies, 11, 13-17
  other works: *Syntagma*, 52, 135n.10, 189; *Contra Noetum*, 135
Hippon, 187, 189, 192, 194-5
Holy Spirit, 55, 56, 79
Homer, 152, 162-3, 181, 220, 221, 222, 353
homonymy, 50-1, 56-7
honour, 157, 160-9, 181
Hussey, E., 3

ignorance
  in Empedocles, 120, 121-2, 126, 128
  in Heraclitus, 132, 178-9; of men in general, 132-3, 154n.68, 156, 160, 178; of Homer, 162-3; of Hesiod, 165
immortality, 136, 158, 169

Marcovich, M., 142
marriage, *see* sex
mathematics, 21, 111, 112
matter, 38, 44, 48, 104
meat-eating, 99, 107, 121, 122-3, 126
methodology
  in theory, 1-13, 23-32, 58, 65-7, 85,
    97-8, 99-100, 108, 140-2, 183-6
  in practice, 13-23, 33-84, 87-182
misrepresentation
  by Hippolytus: suspected, 10; denied,
    60-1, 62-3, 179
  by Aristotle, 12-13
  by other doxographers, 1-2
  see also distortion
mode
  in theology, 151n.56; Monarchian,
    135, 149n.49, 151, 160n.82
  in music, 152
Monarchianism, modalist, 134, 135, 141,
  151n.56, 155n.74, 164
  Callistus, 14, 135, 138-9, 164, 172
  Noetus, 85, 134-81
  Praxeas, 135n.10
morality, 14, 135, 139, 167
mortality, 136n.13, 158, 169
murder (*phonos*), 115-16, 118, 120n.142
  of kin, 118n.136, 120, 121, 122, 123,
    124
  re-enacted, 120
  see also blood-guilt
mysteries, 92-3

names, 50, 57
  for God, 56, 76, 80, 137
  see also language
natural philosophy (physics), 25, 26, 30,
  108, 118
  prominent in doxography, 11, 14-15,
    184
  natural philosophers (*phusikoi*),
    187-211
Neoplatonic interpretation, 109-13
New Testament, 106-7, 213, 220
Noetus (heretic), 85, **134-9**, **140-81**,
  327-9, 335-7
  relation to Heraclitus, 134-42, 142-81
    passim
  identified Father and Son, 135, 136-7,
    141, 148, 157
  teachings: on creation, 155n.74;
    change, 151-2, 153, 159n.81;

mortality of God, 169, 176;
  resurrection of Christ, 137, 174-7
non-existence
  of God, 50, 53
  in reductio arguments, 37-9, 43-4, 47
  coming-to-be from what is not: attri-
    buted to Aristotle, 37, 44-5, 47,
    53-5, 58, 63; denied by
    Empedocles, 121, 124
nothing, *see* non-existence
numbers, 21, 111, 208

oath, 115, 117
O'Brien, D., 99, 109
Old Testament, 106-7, 136n.11, 220
Old Testament god, 107, 146
  responsible for evil things, 103, 105
  see also creator
opposites
  in Heraclitus, 133, 143-69, 181, 184;
    pairs of, 145; incompatibility of,
    166
  in Noetus, 136
Orphism, 93
Owen, G.E.L., 159n.80

palinode, 71, 75, 80
parallels
  between Empedocles and Hesiod, 115,
    117, 118; Heraclitus and Hesiod,
    177-8; Hippolytus and Irenaeus,
    73-84, 102n.64, 214-15; Hip-
    polytus and Sextus Empiricus,
    14n.24, 21, 37n.3, 88-9, 89-92, 94,
    96, 134n.8, 214; Simon Magus
    and Apsethos, 70-1
  in comparisons between philosophers
    and heretics, 52-8, 62-3, 98, 99,
    134-5, 139, 142, 145, 148n.46,
    151, 160, 164
paraphrase, 7, 17, 18, 61, 63, 65, 84, 212,
  213n.4
Parmenides, 7, 10-11, 192, 193, 194-5,
  209
passibility, 138, 159n.81
passion, of Christ, 136n.13, 138
Patripassianism, *see* Monarchianism
Pausanias (addressee of Empedocles),
  27, 28
Peratae, 19
perception, 88, 95, 171-2, 223-4
persons, of Trinity, 135, 145n.36, 150

world
  tripartite division of, 55-6
  'this world': in Marcion, 103-4, 107;
    in Empedocles, 110, 118, 119,
    125, 128, 129, 158n.78
  two worlds: in Empedocles, 109, 110,
    113, 119, 124, 127-8; properly one
    world, 110, 128
  in Heraclitus, 175n.117; identified

    with creator, 142, 158-9
  creation of, *see* creation
  world-seed, 53-5

Xenophanes, 7, 192, 194-5, 197, 209, *353*

Zeno of Elea, 209n.21
Zuntz, G., 123